CASS SERIES ON SOVIET MILIT.
Series Editor: David M.

THE SOVIET INVASION
OF FINLAND
1939–40

CASS SERIES ON SOVIET MILITARY EXPERIENCE
Series Editor: David M. Glantz

This series focuses on Soviet military experiences in specific campaigns or operations

1. David M. Glantz, *From the Don to the Dnepr, Soviet Offensive Operations, December 1942 to August 1943* (ISBN 0 7146 3401 8 cloth, 0 7146 4064 6 paper)

2. David M. Glantz, editor, *The Initial Period of War on the Eastern Front: 22 June–August 1941* (ISBN 0 7146 3375 5 cloth, 0 7146 4298 3 paper)

3. Carl Van Dyke, *The Soviet Invasion of Finland, 1939–40* (ISBN 0 7146 4653 5 cloth, 0 7146 4314 9 paper)

CASS SERIES ON THE SOVIET STUDY OF WAR
Series Editor: David M. Glantz

This series examines what Soviet military theorists and commanders have learned from the study of their own military operations.

1. Harold S. Orenstein, translator and editor, *Soviet Documents on the Use of War Experience*, Volume I, *The Initial Period of War 1941*, with an Introduction by David M. Glantz. (ISBN 0 7146 3392 5 cloth)

2. Harold S. Orenstein, translator and editor, *Soviet Documents on the Use of War Experience*, Volume II, *The Winter Campaign 1941–1942*, with an Introduction by David M. Glantz. (ISBN 0 7146 3393 3 cloth)

3. Joseph G. Welsh, translator, *Red Armor Combat Orders: Combat Regulations for Tank and Mechanized Forces 1944*, edited and with an Introduction by Richard N. Armstrong. (ISBN 0 7146 3401 8 cloth)

4. Harold S. Orenstein, translator and editor, *Soviet Documents on the Use of War Experience*, Volume III, *Military Operations 1941 and 1942*, with an Introduction by David M. Glantz. (ISBN 0 7146 3402 6 cloth)

5. William A. Burhans, translator, *The Nature of the Operations of Modern Armies* by V. K. Triandafillov, edited by Jacob W. Kipp, with an Introduction by James J. Schneider. (ISBN 0 7146 4501 X cloth, 0 7146 4118 9 paper)

6. Harold S. Orenstein, translator, *The Evolution of Soviet Operational Art, 1927–1991: The Documentary Basis*, Volume I, *Operational Art, 1927–1964*, with an Introduction by David M. Glantz. (ISBN 0 7146 4547 8 cloth, 0 7146 4228 2 paper)

7. Harold S. Orenstein, translator, *The Evolution of Soviet Operational Art, 1927–1991: The Documentary Basis*, Volume II, *Operational Art, 1965–1991*, with an Introduction by David M. Glantz. (ISBN 0 7146 4548 6 cloth, 0 7146 4229 0 paper)

8. Richard N. Armstrong and Joseph G. Welsh, *Winter Warfare: Red Army Orders and Experiences*. (ISBN 0 7146 4699 7 cloth, 0 7146 4237 1 paper)

THE SOVIET INVASION OF FINLAND
1939–40

CARL VAN DYKE

FRANK CASS
LONDON • PORTLAND, OR.

First Published in 1997 in Great Britain by
FRANK CASS PUBLISHERS
Newbury House, 900 Eastern Avenue
London IG2 7HH

and in the United States of America by
FRANK CASS PUBLISHERS
c/o ISBS, 5804 N.E. Hassalo Street
Portland, Oregon 97213-3644

Website http://www:frankcass.com

British Library Cataloguing in Publication Data:

Van Dyke, Carl
The Soviet invasion of Finland, 1939–40. – (Cass series on
Soviet military experience)
1. Russo-Finnish War, 1939–1940
I. Title
948.9'7'032

ISBN 0-7146-4753-5 (cloth)
ISBN 0-7146-4314-9 (paper)

Library of Congress Cataloging-in-Publication Data:

Van Dyke, Carl.
The Soviet invasion of Finland, 1939–40 / Carl Van Dyke.
p. cm. — (Cass series on Soviet military experience; 3)
Includes bibliographical references (p.) and index.
ISBN 0-7146-4753-5. — ISBN 0-7146-4314-9 (pbk.)
1. Russo-Finnish War, 1939–1940. 2. Soviet Union—History,
Military 3. Soviet Union—Politics and government—1936–1953.
I. Title. II. Series.
D756.3.V36 1997
948.9703'2–dc21   97-22032
                                                            CIP

Typeset by Vitaset, Paddock Wood, Kent
Printed in Great Britain by
Bookcraft (Bath) Ltd, Midsomer Norton, Avon

For Mary and Theo

CONTENTS

List of Figures   ix

Preface and Acknowledgements   xi

1. Diplomatic and Strategic Background to the Winter War   1

2. The Red Army Attacks Finland   35

3. The Red Army Reforms Its Military Doctrine   103

4. Timoshenko's Offensive   135

5. The Lessons of the War   189

    Epilogue   221

    Bibliography   225

    Index   259

LIST OF FIGURES

Figure 1.1   Map of the Baltic Fleet's Submarine Patrols,
30 November 1939 to 18 January 1940.   25

Figure 2.1   Distribution of Red Army forces along the
Soviet–Finnish border, 30 November 1939 to 13 March 1940.   36

Figure 2.2   Deployment of Finnish Army and Red Army
forces on the Karelian Isthmus, 30 November 1939.   37

Figure 2.3   Map of Lake Ladoga and the 8th Army's Invasion
of Ladoga-Karelia.   46

Figure 2.4   Map of Lake Ladoga.   48

Figure 2.5   The Red Army's artillery on the march, December
1939.   50

Figure 2.6   Situation Map of the 8th Army's 18th and 168th
Rifle Divisions on 7 January 1940.   70

Figure 2.7   A ski-patrol receives its orders, December 1939.   83

Figure 2.8   Situation Map of the 9th Army's 163rd, 44th and
54th Rifle Divisions in December 1939.   87

Figure 2.9a   Map of the Baltic Fleet Airforce's Bombing in
south Finland, 30 November 1939 to 13 March 1940.   92

Figure 2.9b   Table of the Baltic Fleet Airforce's Bombing in
south Finland, 30 November 1939 to 13 March 1940.   93

Figure 3.1   Distribution of Red Army forces in front of the
Mannerheim Line, January 1940.   106

Figure 3.2   'How Vasia Tërkin Helped the Tankists', *Na Strazhe Rodiny*, 13 February 1940.   122

Figure 3.3   'How Vasia Tërkin Unmasked a Gossip', *Na Strazhe Rodiny*, 19 January 1940.   123

Figure 3.4   'How Vasia Tërkin Dealt with a Sloven', *Na Strazhe Rodiny*, 29 January 1940.   124

Figure 3.5   'How Vasia Tërkin Appeared in Chamberlain's Dreams', *Na Strazhe Rodiny*, 20 March 1940.   125

Figure 4.1   Distribution of the 50th Rifle Corps' forces at Summa (Khotinen) and Hammer Grove, 10 February 1940.   140

Figure 4.2   Diagram of the 355th Rifle Regiment's Storming of DOT No.45, 1 February 1940.   141

Figure 4.3   Red Army sapper transporting explosives, February 1940.   143

Figure 4.4   Map of the Finnish Defensive System at Hammer Grove.   146

Figure 4.5   Red Army soldiers celebrating on the ruins of Finnish DOT No. 006, February 1940.   156

Figure 4.6   Map of the 50th Rifle Corps' advance towards Vyborg, 27 February 1940.   171

Figure 4.7   Map of the Winter Defence Detachment's Operations in early March, 1940.   173

PREFACE AND
ACKNOWLEDGEMENTS

Over the past several years historians have been re-evaluating Soviet security policy in the interwar period (1917–41) on the basis of newly accessible archival collections in Moscow and St Petersburg. Some historians have focused their attention on the relationship between Stalin, the *de facto* leader of the Soviet Union, and the commissars responsible for the formulation of foreign and military policy. Others have examined cultural politics within the Red Army, and a third group has analysed the ideational content of strategy and operational doctrine. Central to understanding all these facets of security policy is the Soviet invasion of Finland in the winter of 1939–40, as it represents the last major military operation conducted by the Red Army before the Nazi onslaught in 1941. The invasion, however, remains a significant lacuna in Soviet history. What motivated Stalin to launch an undeclared war against Finland? What lessons did the Soviet high command learn from the experience? The purpose of this book is to address these questions and others on the basis of archival research at the Central State Archive of the Soviet Army (TsGASA), the Russian Centre for the Preservation and Study of Documents of Recent History (RTsKhINDI) and the archives of the Russian Foreign Ministry (AVP Rossiia) as well as recently declassified studies from military academies in Moscow.

The Soviet–Finnish war was born out of dilemmas in Soviet security policy dating back to the October revolution of 1917. One of these dilemmas concerned diplomatic relations with governments that viewed the Bolsheviks' internationalist goals with suspicion and often with open hostility. Given this environment, the Soviet government's main priority was to prevent the formation of an anti-Soviet coalition. The first manifestation of this reactive policy came in the spring of 1922 when the Soviet government signed the Rapallo treaty with Weimar Germany to counter the post-World War I peace settlement embodied in the Versailles treaty. This policy culminated in 1934 when the Soviet Union joined the League of Nations to counter the rising

xi

militarism of Nazi Germany. A more active policy was to curry favour with neighbouring countries in order to create diplomatic buffer-zones between the Soviet Union and potential aggressors. The buffer-zone policy was promoted by means of 'contractual agreements' in the form of friendship, non-aggression and mutual-assistance pacts. The first such treaty was signed with Turkey in 1925, followed by agreements with Japan and Germany a year later and with the Baltic states, Finland and France in the early 1930s. So long as no threat of another world war existed, both policies could be pursued simultaneously without compromising each other. When the threat of war re-emerged in the early 1930s, Stalin's attempts to bolster the Soviet Union's interests at the expense of the League of Nations' policy of 'collective security' eventually compromised relations with the liberal democracies, obliging him to opt for a non-aggression treaty with Hitler in the autumn of 1939. Perhaps the most important factor influencing this *dénouement* in Soviet diplomacy was the concern for security in the Baltic region. Chapter One will examine the Baltic question from 1933 to the Stalin–Hitler treaty, and will then provide a detailed analysis of Soviet attempts to force the Baltic states and Finland to contribute to its buffer-zone policy up to the invasion of Finland in November 1939.

The dilemma facing Soviet military policy in the interwar period lay in predicting when the next world war would break out and how best to prepare for it. In 1916 Lenin set the rhetorical agenda for these questions in his work *Imperialism, the Highest Stage of Capitalism*. Subsequent interpretations were made in the mid-1920s, but it was the beginning of the Depression in 1929, the Japanese invasion of Chinese Manchuria in 1931, and the Nazi rise to power in 1933 that suggested to the Soviet high command that the countdown to war had begun. Partly in anticipation, partly in fear, and partly for his own political gain, Stalin initiated the rapid modernization of the Red Army. One component of this modernization programme was the reorganization of the Red Army from a mixed territorial-regular cadre army into a full cadre army, increasing its size. Another component was the institutionalization of 'Deep Battle and Deep Operations', a doctrine of combined arms warfare developed by Soviet military professionals on the basis of combat experience in the First World War and the Civil War. This military doctrine was perhaps the most theoretically sophisticated in Europe, promoting the principles of aggressive counter-attack, decentralized command, and organizational flexibility. However, the latter two principles contradicted Stalin's centralized political system.

Stalin responded by purging the Red Army's command corps in 1937. The resulting crisis in civil-military relations subsequently compromised the Red

Army's combat performance during the invasion of Finland and the first two years of the Great Patriotic War.

Chapter Two describes the organizational paralysis that immobilized the Red Army and Navy in the various theatres of military and naval operations from 30 November to 31 December 1939. Chapter Three analyses the strategic and operational implications of the Soviet high command's shift to the defensive in January 1940. Attention is devoted to the creation of the North-Western Front, the generalization of recent combat experience and its integration into the existing military doctrine as well as the military and political preparations for a new offensive. Chapter Four documents the successful offensive against the Finnish Army in conjunction with diplomatic efforts to negotiate a peace settlement with the Finnish government in Helsinki. The Soviet high command's evaluation of the lessons learned in Finland forms the subject of Chapter Five, with specific attention devoted to the re-professionalization of the Red Army command corps, the systematic reform of operational and tactical doctrine, and the debate over the content of Soviet 'military ideology'.

This book is the result of dissertation research that I conducted in Russia and the United Kingdom between 1991 and 1994. The narrative that follows would have taken a vastly different form, or would simply not have been completed at all, were it not for the guidance given by many people. My thanks go to Drs Jonathan Haslam and John Barber (Corpus Christi College and King's College, Cambridge) for setting the parameters of the research and guiding it to completion. Professors Georgii Kumanev and Leonid Nezhinskii (both at the Institute of Russian History, Russian Academy of Sciences) provided scholarly assistance while I was conducting research in Moscow in 1992. Research in the Russian archives would not have been possible without the institutional support of Emmanuel College, Cambridge and the Institute of Russian History, Moscow, with special thanks to Dr Susan Rankin, Professor Alexander Sakharov and Olga Sakharovna, and Dr Ludmila Kolodnikova. Dr Alexander Vatlin kindly invited me to give a paper to the Institute of Human Rights and Political Studies immediately after the heady weeks of the August 1991 coup. Igor Venkov (Chief of the Historical-Archival and Memorial Centre of the General Staff, Russian Army) and Mikhail Stegantsev (Director of TsGASA) graciously gave access to the Red Army's archives, and Ludmila Dvoinykh (Assistant Director, TsGASA) explained the intricacies of ordering document collections. Nikolai Sidorov at RTsKhINDI kindly directed my attention to documents used for the compilation of *Istoriia Velikoi Otechetstvennoi Voiny Sovetskogo Soiuza 1941–1945*, (Moscow, 1960), which had been copied from other archives and held at his Centre. Ray

Scrivens at the University of Cambridge Library and Alexander Kniazieff, the Head Librarian at the Russian Veterans of the First World War Society (San Francisco, USA), as well as Kent Lee and Karen Bronshteyn at East View Publications (Minneapolis, USA), provided me with priceless Soviet military publications from the inter-war period. Jonathan Dudley very kindly assisted me with the maps. I also wish to thank the following people for their comments and encouragement: Mr A. Beruchashvili, Professor G. Best, Dr G. Bordiugov, Dr T. Bruno, Professor J. Erickson, Admiral V. Eshchenko (former editor-in-chief of *Voenno-istoricheskii zhurnal*), Colonel D. Glantz (editor, *Journal of Slavic Military Studies*), Professor M. von Hagen, Dr M. Korobochkin (Institute of General History, Russian Academy of Sciences), Dr S. Koudriashov, Dr O. Manninen (Institute of History, University of Helsinki), Dr T. Ries (Institute for Defence Studies, Oslo), Professor C. Roberts, Professor O. Rzheshevskii (Department Director, Institute of General History, Russian Academy of Sciences), Dr V. Savin, Professor M. Semiryaga, Dr W.P.S Sidhu, Dr D. Spring, Mr R. Tarleton and Professor A. Upton. Thanks are due to the following people for their hospitality and friendship during my sojourn in Moscow: the Kim family, Johnny Crowfoot and Olga Nikitina, Alexander and Irina Kutuzov, Ruud Veltmeijer, Edwin and Deborah Bacon, Vladimir Pozniakov and Nikolai Semonov. Finally, I am deeply indebted to my wife Mary and our parents for their constant support and encouragement.

Carl Van Dyke, 1996

1
DIPLOMATIC AND STRATEGIC BACKGROUND TO THE WINTER WAR

One of the primary goals of Soviet foreign policy after Hitler's rise to power in Germany was to prevent German military and naval expansion in the Baltic region. In 1933 the Commissariat of Foreign Affairs tried to strengthen the Soviet Union's strategic position in the Baltic by seeking closer co-operation with the Polish government over the security of the Baltic Sea. When the Polish government broke off these negotiations in the spring of 1934 the People's Commissar of Foreign Affairs, M. Litvinov, reasserted the Soviet Union's interest in maintaining existing relations with Finland and the Baltic States by renewing its non-aggression pacts with them.[1]

A further blow to Soviet security in the Baltic region came in June 1935, when the Anglo-German Naval Agreement further tipped the balance of power in Germany's favour. These events provoked various circles within the Soviet government to call for a return to a more isolationist, non-conciliatory foreign policy. In the same month, the Soviet ambassador in Helsinki, E. Assmus, warned the Finnish Prime Minister, T. Kivimaki, that if a war should erupt between the Soviet Union and Germany the Red Army would enact the principle of 'forward defence' and occupy Finland within a week.[2] In January 1936, the Chief of the Red Army General Staff, M. Tukhachevskii, accused the Finnish government of building air bases in eastern Finland as an advanced base for a German aerial strike against the Soviet Union, while V. Molotov, the chairman of the Council of People's Commissars, made a speech to the Central Executive Committee calling for increased reliance on the Red Army to defend the Soviet Union's frontiers.[3] Later that year, the Leningrad party chairman, A. Zhdanov, issued a public warning to the Baltic States and Finland not to compromise their neutrality by engaging in security arrangements with Germany.[4]

After 1935, the Soviet government's main concern was not so much whether the Baltic States and Finland would maintain their neutrality under pressure from Germany, but that their neutrality could pose a major obstacle to the timely concentration of the Red Army and Baltic Fleet in response to a full-scale German invasion. According to the revelations of a former Red Army intelligence agent, E. Henri (Rostovskii), published in 1936, the Red Army high command assumed that a German invasion against the Soviet Union would be carried out by two armies advancing to the north and south around a neutral Poland, one of which would violate the neutrality of the Baltic States and march against Leningrad with the help of a navy in the Gulf of Finland, accompanied by pincer movements from Finland and Estonia.[5] These strategic assumptions changed as Soviet involvement in the Spanish Civil War further alienated the Entente powers and provoked Germany, Italy and Japan to sign an Anti-Comintern pact in November 1936.

When Tukhachevskii was arrested in June 1937 as part of Stalin's purge of the officer corps, he explained in a 'testament', written before his execution that the Red Army high command should expect a combined German–Polish offensive directed primarily toward the economically rich Ukraine rather than through the Baltic. If the Red Army high command was going to abide by the official military doctrine of 'forward defence' and defeat the German–Polish forces on Polish territory, the best way to accomplish this was to outflank them by counter-attacking through the Baltic States. Under this scenario the neutrality of the Baltic States was a severe disadvantage. Referring to the role Belgium's neutrality played in the unfolding of the First World War, Tukhachevskii explained the nature of the Red Army's security dilemma:

> For us, the neutrality of the Baltic States plays a dangerous role. Even if we suppose that it [the Baltic State's neutrality] lasts only two weeks it would already be harmful for us. By preserving this neutrality we will deny ourselves a more advantageous scenario, and if two weeks go by and the Baltic States' neutrality then is broken, it will be impossible to correct the situation as far as the process of strategic concentration is concerned.[6]

The military solution to this problem was to violate the Baltic States' neutrality in the event of war with Germany, but such a solution required permission from Stalin before it could be put into effect. Tukhachevskii declined to explain Finland's role in this scenario except to say that Finland had to be considered as a completely independent issue of great complexity. No diplomatic efforts were made to ameliorate this strategic dilemma until the spring of 1938, when events in Central Europe and the Baltic stimulated the Soviet government to seek a new *modus operandi* with the Finnish government. Major-General von der Goltz's arrival in Helsinki at the head of a German military mission to commemorate the twentieth anniversary of the German intervention against the Red Guard in the Finnish Civil War, coming only a few weeks after the German *Anschluss* with Austria and the opening of Swedish–Finnish negotiations over the rearmament of the Åland Islands, heightened suspicions in Moscow that the Finnish government was negotiating alternative security arrangements with its Baltic neighbours and that these threatened Soviet security. Two days after Goltz's departure, the second secretary at the Soviet mission in Helsinki, B. Yartsev (known by the Finnish government to be in charge of NKVD affairs in Finland), called on the Finnish Foreign Minister at that time, R. Holsti, to brief him on Stalin's security priorities and to initiate negotiations for a closer relationship between the Soviet Union and Finland. Yartsev's first conversation with Holsti was direct and to the point:

> That the Soviet government had reason to believe that a German attack on Russia was imminent, and that it was essential that they [the Soviets] should receive an unequivocal declaration that Finland would be neutral, otherwise they 'would not wait' but would be the first to invade Finland and Sweden as well.[7]

During the next five months of backdoor diplomacy between Moscow and Helsinki the Soviet government's diplomatic agenda became more clearly defined. On 18 August 1939 Yartsev presented a list of concrete proposals to the Finnish Minister of Trade, V. Tanner. Moscow's first priority was to strengthen Soviet–Finnish relations with a mutual-assistance pact whereby the Finns would defend themselves against German invasion with the aid of Soviet economic and military assistance. In addition, Moscow proposed that the Baltic Fleet be allowed to occupy and refortify the island of Suursaari (Hogland) in the Gulf of Finland in return for allowing the Finns to refortify the Åland Islands unilaterally.[8] Tanner informed Yartsev at the end of August that the Finnish government would not accept these proposals.

During the ensuing German–Czechoslovakian crisis in September 1938, the Soviet government partially mobilized the Red Army and sent the Baltic Fleet to protect the Åland Islands from attack by the German navy.[9] Subsequently excluded from the Munich consultations and increasingly fearful that the Entente's appeasement policy would permit further German expansion in Eastern Europe, Stalin ordered the military and naval defence community to prepare for war in the Baltic region. In December 1938, Defence Minister Voroshilov appointed K. Meretskov as the new commander of the Leningrad Military District and informed him that Stalin was worried about Finland's realignment with the imperialist powers and wanted Meretskov personally to conduct a detailed analysis of the theatre of military operations along the Soviet–Finnish border under all weather and seasonal conditions.[10]

3

At the People's Commissariat for the Navy the deputy commissars L. Galler and I. Isakov discovered that the Baltic Fleet was completely unprepared for naval operations in the Gulf of Finland and the Baltic Sea. The ambitious ship-building programme that Stalin had inaugurated the year before had not yet produced any of the additional surface ships required to extend offensive naval power in the Baltic, nor was it expected to do so in the near future.[11] Modernization of the existing fleet was proceeding slower than expected and the accident rate in the fleet was high. However, Galler and Isakov found that the largest problem bedevilling the Baltic Fleet was the low management standards of the commanders and their staffs: operational plans were compiled without proper reconnaissance, fire-support for land operations was disorganized, and no attention had been paid to mine-sweeping exercises.[12] Much time and preparation would be required before the Leningrad Military District and the Baltic Fleet command would be able to conduct large-scale operations. In the meantime, the Soviet government would have to rely on diplomacy to forestall further German expansion in the Baltic region.

In January 1939, the Finnish and Swedish governments signed a proposal to co-operate over the refortification of the Åland Islands and the German government expanded its ship-building programme in the Baltic.[13] The Soviet response to these events was to make a final attempt to strengthen its security relations with Finland by means of a concerted diplomatic campaign. On 3 March, Stalin's unofficial representative, B. Yartsev, once again contacted the Finnish Foreign Ministry in Helsinki to present the most generous set of Soviet proposals to date: the Soviet government would permit Finland to fortify the Åland Islands and Suursaari Island without Soviet interference if Finland agreed to explicitly guarantee to defend itself against German invasion and re-arm with Soviet military equipment for that purpose. Later that week, Litvinov regaled the Finnish minister in Moscow with promises to ignore the rearmament of the Åland Islands and agree to concessions over trade and territory in Ladoga-Karelia in exchange for a thirty-year lease of the islands in the eastern part of the Gulf of Finland. Unsatisfied with the Finnish minister's negative responses to these offers, Litvinov sent B. Shtein, a former Soviet ambassador to Finland, to present his offers directly to the Finnish Foreign Ministry in Helsinki. E. Erkko once again rejected these proposals despite conciliatory recommendations from the president of the Finnish Defence Council, Field-Marshal Baron von Mannerheim, and on 6 April Shtein returned to Moscow empty-handed.[14]

While Litvinov's diplomatic efforts were unravelling in Helsinki, Stalin was redefining the basis for the Soviet Union's relationship with the capitalist world. In a speech to delegates at the Eighteenth Party Congress in Moscow on 10 March, Stalin portrayed the contemporary world political situation in much the same terms he had used at the Seventeenth Party Congress five years before. Stalin was convinced more than ever that the final crisis of the capitalist world economic system was at hand. This time, however, the Entente's pernicious policy of non-intervention towards Germany during the 1930s had reduced the possible types of war from four down to two: a war between the Soviet Union and the Anti-Comintern powers which included Germany, Italy, and Japan (with the notable exception of Poland) or a coalitional war between the Fascist powers and the Entente.[15] The purpose of Soviet foreign policy was to avoid getting involved in either scenario and, if inter-imperialist war should break out, to 'observe caution and not let our country be drawn into conflicts by warmongers urging others to take the chestnuts out of the fire' and to join the coalition that did not 'undermine the foundations of Soviet power'.[16]

Events in Eastern Europe soon put Stalin's newly redefined foreign policy to the test. On the night of 14–15 March Hitler incorporated the rest of Czechoslovakia under the threat of armed force and a week later he seized the province of Memel from the Lithuanian government by the same means. The Soviet government's immediate reaction was to adopt a unilateral stance to prevent the possibility of further German expansion in the Baltic. On 29 March, Litvinov called in the Latvian and Estonian ministers in Moscow to warn them that any agreements their governments might make, 'whether concluded voluntarily or under external pressure, that would result in even the derogation or restriction of the independence and autonomy of their republics', would be regarded by the Soviet government as intolerable and would result in the termination of the non-aggression pacts they held with the Soviet Union with the implied threat of invasion by the Red Army and the Baltic Fleet.[17] Litvinov's declaration indicated that Stalin's hitherto ambiguous reference to the 'foundations of Soviet power' could now be more accurately defined to include Soviet political and, if necessary, military hegemony over the Baltic States.

Hitler attempted to repeat his recent diplomatic successes by threatening to seize control over Danzig from the Polish government in late March, provoking the British government to end its policy of appeasement towards German expansion. Britain unilaterally guaranteed the independence of Poland and Romania as sovereign states on 31 March. The Soviet government's immediate reaction to these events was to complain at once again being excluded from Entente decisions which involved the security of the Soviet Union's western border. However, the new strategic calculus in eastern Europe was now decidedly in Moscow's favour. On the one hand, Britain's

5

guarantee to Poland and Romania made it more dependent on the Soviet Union to reinforce its political commitment with military power. Likewise, Germany's dispute with Poland over Danzig signalled the effective end of the Anti-Comintern pact. As a consequence, the Soviet Union was now in a strong position to negotiate an advantageous agreement with either the Entente or with Germany.

On 17 April, the same day that the German State Secretary regaled the Soviet ambassador in Berlin with hints of a political and economic *rapprochement* in German–Soviet relations, Litvinov responded to a French proposal for an alliance by offering an alternative proposal which included a multilateral mutual assistance agreement between the Soviet Union, Britain and France and a security guarantee for all the countries on the Soviet Union's western border from the Baltic to the Black Sea.[18] During the first round of negotiations over this proposal two fundamental differences of opinion arose which were to remain unresolved in subsequent negotiations. The first of these disagreements lay in the definition of the terms of 'reciprocity' between the powers in the event that any one of them suffered a direct German attack. A more fundamental disagreement arose over the extension of automatic guarantees to the Baltic States and Finland. Whereas the Soviet government sought the freedom to come to the direct military aid of eastern European countries facing the threat of the German *Wehrmacht*, the British government was more interested in relegating the Soviet Union's role in the defence of eastern Europe to that of an arms arsenal. When Molotov took over Litvinov's portfolio at the Ministry of Foreign Affairs on 4 May, he continued to press for concessions on these two issues.

That month, Molotov also closely monitored the progress of the Finnish and Swedish governments in the revision of the international convention of 1921 and the implementation of the Stockholm plan to refortify the Åland Islands. The Stockholm plan had been delayed by Soviet opposition and German procrastination ever since its declaration in January. However, early in May, the German government finally gave its consent and the Stockholm plan was submitted to the League of Nations for approval. On 19 May, Molotov informed the Finnish minister in Moscow, Yrjö-Koskinen, that the Åland Islands had great strategic importance to the Soviet Union and demanded more detailed information about the Stockholm plan. When the Finnish government was unforthcoming, Molotov ordered I. Maiskii, the Soviet ambassador to Britain who was at that time also chairman of the League Council, to block discussion of the proposal in the League of Nation's Assembly.[19] Molotov did not prevent the Finnish parliament from ratifying the Stockholm plan on 6 June, but he did succeed in intimidating the Swedish government into delaying its ratification indefinitely, thus effectively isolating Finland from its Scandinavian neighbours.[20]

In the meantime, the Soviet Union's negotiations with the Entente were beginning to yield results. During a conversation with the British ambassador in Moscow at the end of May, Molotov had referred to the importance of Belgium's neutrality to the Entente's security in order to illustrate his argument for automatic guarantees to be extended to Finland and the Baltic States. The British government was slowly beginning to accept the legitimacy of the Soviet Union's security concerns in the Baltic region.[21] However, the British government felt obliged to consult with the Finnish government before adjusting its policy. The War Office sent a representative, General Sir Walter Kirke, to Helsinki for this purpose. Arriving in the Finnish capital on 18 June, General Kirke held extensive talks with Field Marshal Mannerheim before inspecting Finnish fortifications on the Karelian Isthmus and returning to Britain on 22 June. In his report to the War Office, Kirke stated that the Finnish government was steadfast in its refusal to accept protection from the Red Army and emphasized his opinion that 'They do not want anything to do with Germany but, rather than accept a Russian guarantee, they would join the Axis.'[22]

While circles in the British government speculated on the degree to which the Finnish government was serious about its threat to seek German protection, events in Helsinki were soon to force the issue to a dramatic conclusion. Denied an alliance with Sweden and increasingly fearful that the British government would renege on its promises, the Finnish government decided to foster closer contact with the German military. A week after the conclusion of General Kirke's visit, the Chief of the *Wehrmacht*'s General Staff, General Halder, arrived in Helsinki accompanied by five officers for an inspection tour of the Karelian Isthmus and military installations in Lapland.[23] News of this visit soon reached Moscow and London, provoking immediate responses from both capitals. On 29 June the newspaper *Pravda* published an article by Zhdanov entitled 'The English and French Governments do not Want Equal Negotiations with the Soviet Union', in which Zhdanov purposefully put pressure on the British government by accusing it of using the deadlock over the issue of guarantees to disrupt the negotiations and return to a policy of appeasement. The British government's response was to drop objections to the guarantee issue while simultaneously demanding a full explanation from Erkko, the Finnish Foreign Minister, about the purpose of Halder's visit. However, this reversal in policy came too late. In deliberations on 1 July Molotov told the British and French ministers in Moscow that Soviet policy had changed. Not only would the Entente powers have to agree to a guarantee against direct aggression by Germany in the Baltic, but this guarantee would have to be expanded to include protection against 'indirect aggression', by which Molotov meant an internal pro-German *coup d'état* or even 'a reversal of policy in the interest of the aggressor'.[24] The Soviet government's long-standing discomfort over the paradox that Baltic neutrality had posed for the security of the Soviet Union's north-western border had finally come out into the open. After Halder's visit to Helsinki the Soviet government would not settle for anything less than total political hegemony over the countries on its western border, especially Finland and the Baltic States. Unfortunately, these were terms that Britain and France were unwilling to accept.[25]

Indications of Finland's willingness to seek closer military ties with Germany, in conjunction with the growing threat of war with Japan, convinced Stalin that the time had come to prepare for the possibility of a two-front war. At the end of June, Stalin instructed B. Shaposhnikov, the Chief of the Red Army General Staff, to draw up a contingency plan for war with Finland. When Shaposhnikov submitted a plan for a major campaign which would last several months and require a majority of the Red Army's forces, Stalin turned it down and instructed Meretskov, the commander of the Leningrad Military District, to come to Moscow to discuss an alternative plan.[26] During this first meeting at the Kremlin, Stalin briefed Meretskov on Finland's potential role as a 'springboard' for the anti-soviet ambitions of Germany and/or Britain and France and ordered him to draw up a plan for a counter-offensive based on the military assets available to the Leningrad Military District.[27] In mid-July Meretskov returned to the Kremlin with an alternative plan and Stalin approved it in principle but insisted that the counter-strike be concluded within a few weeks. In response to Meretskov's protestations that this time-frame was too short for such an operation, Stalin and Voroshilov assured him that he could count on the entire resources of the Red Army. Based on this assumption, adjustments were made to Meretskov's plan and it was rubber-stamped by the Main Military Soviet at the end of July.[28]

While Meretskov was busy planning a land offensive against Finland, the People's Commissariat for the Navy was busy making preparations for operations in the Gulf of Finland and the Baltic Sea. Earlier in the year, Stalin had appointed the young commander of the Pacific Fleet, N. Kuznetsov, as the new People's Commissar for the Navy and had ordered him to begin preparing the Soviet Union's various fleets for war.[29] Kuznetsov's first priority had been to strengthen his centralized control over the various fleets and raise the general level of combat readiness. When Stalin's strategic priorities shifted to the Baltic in June, Kuznetsov travelled to Leningrad accompanied by his deputy commissar, Galler, and the Leningrad Party chairman, Zhdanov, to verify the combat readiness of the Baltic Fleet stationed at Kronstadt and Luga Bay.[30] In mid-July the Baltic Fleet command conducted a series of naval exercises along the entire length of the Gulf of Finland under the supervision of Kuznetsov and his colleagues on board the battleship *Oktiabr'skaia Revoliutsiia*. The primary exercise involved a review of the procedures by which to seize the islands in the eastern part of the Gulf, support the Leningrad Military District's counter-offensive on the Karelian Isthmus, and conduct amphibious landing assaults against Suursaari and Suur-Tiutärsaari islands.[31] The second in the series of exercises consisted in deflecting an enemy submarine attack at the mouth of the Gulf of Finland. Although these manoeuvres demonstrated to Kuznetsov and Zhdanov that the Baltic Fleet had made significant progress in preparations since the beginning of the year, they also reinforced the impression that the effective extension of naval power into the Baltic still depended entirely on the political goodwill of both Finland and Estonia.[32]

During the month of July and the first half of August, the Soviet government pursued its demand for political hegemony in eastern Europe and the Baltic States by continuing its courtship with the Entente powers while, at the same time, seeking a *rapprochement* with the German government.[33] Only on August 14, three days after the beginning of Anglo-French-Soviet military talks in Moscow, did the Soviet Ministry of Foreign Affairs receive confirmation from the German ambassador in Moscow that the German government was willing to agree to all the Soviet government's demands in return for freedom of action in its dispute with Poland.

The signature of the Soviet–German non-aggression pact and secret protocols at the Kremlin on 24 August 1939 signalled the end of the Soviet government's attempts to negotiate a multilateral agreement with the Entente powers over the security of eastern Europe and a return to the more isolationist buffer-zone system. According to the public terms of the pact, both signatories agreed to refrain from any 'act of violence, any aggressive action and any attack on each other either severally or jointly with other powers', and to maintain neutrality in any conflict between either signatory and a third party. As such, these terms greatly resembled the non-aggression treaties the Soviet Union had signed with the Baltic States, Finland and Italy in 1932–33 as part of Stalin's ploy articulated in the mid-1920s, to create 'islands of pacification' on the Soviet Union's periphery to mitigate the threat of capitalist encirclement.[34]

The secret protocols, on the other hand, assured Moscow's hegemony in eastern Europe from the Baltic States and Finland to Poland's eastern provinces and Romania in the event of a war between Germany and Poland. The origins of this more expansionist tendency in Soviet foreign policy dated back to the winter of 1917/18 when the newly established Soviet republic called on the peoples of the nations fighting in the world war and their governments to negotiate a 'democratic peace' on the basis of 'no annexations or indemnities' and the right of minority groups to national self-determination.[35] When this policy failed, the Soviet government then adopted a policy of establishing buffer zones by which socialist régimes in the territories of the former tsarist empire could, in the first instance, form a defensive alliance with the Russian Soviet republic. They could later be fully integrated, both politically and economically into the federation of Soviet republics.[36] The imminent threat of another inter-imperialist war suggested a return to the buffer-zone policy. However, the realization of that policy depended on the acquiescence of the governments on the Soviet Union's western border and the time to integrate them into the Soviet Union's 'forward defence' system. Neither of these requirements was guaranteed by the secret protocols.

I

Less than a fortnight after the signing of the pact, the balance of power in Europe began to shift eastward. On 1 September, Germany attacked Poland along the entire extent of the German–Polish border with the full might of the *Wehrmacht* quickly overwhelming the Polish army's strategic defences and driving its mechanized formations against Polish forces in East Prussia, Poznan, Lodz and Krakow.[37] Two days later the major powers of Europe were at war, except for the Soviet Union which adhered to its neutrality under the terms of the non-aggression pact with Germany. However, this situation soon changed. On the day when the British and French governments declared war on Germany, the German Ministry of Foreign Affairs telegraphed a message to Stalin requesting that the Red Army advance 'at the proper time against Polish forces in the Russian sphere of interest ...' as defined by the secret protocols, insinuating that if the Red Army did not, the *Wehrmacht* would occupy this area itself.[38] Hitler's request found Stalin and the Red Army high command unprepared militarily or diplomatically to enact the terms of the secret protocols. The Red Army was already preoccupied with a war against the Japanese *Kwantung* Army in the Soviet Far East. In late August the brilliant military commander, Corps Commander G. Zhukov, had launched an offensive across the banks of the Khalkhin-Gol River and had pushed the Japanese Army out of Soviet-Mongolian territory on 31 August, but no armistice had yet been signed. It seemed prudent to exercise caution in the west until the threat in the east was neutralized.[39]

Signs of a shift in Soviet policy soon began to emerge. On 5 September, the Soviet Ministry of Foreign Affairs reassured the German ambassador in Moscow that the Soviet government would soon respond to Hitler's request. Preparations were under way at the People's Commissariat for Defence to mobilize an additional 1.5 million men into the armed forces and Shaposhnikov, the Chief of the General Staff, ordered the Kiev and Belorussian Special Military District commanders S. Timoshenko and M. Kovalev to create Front-level commands and to organize mobile detachments for combat by 15 September. On 17 September, the day after the armistice was signed between the Soviet and Japanese governments, Timoshenko and Kovalev launched their 'liberation march' into Western Belorussia and Poland's eastern provinces and by 22 September they established full military control of the territory up to the Narev, Vistula and San rivers.[40]

During these five days of conquest Stalin was already making plans to reconfigure the Soviet Union's political and security arrangements in the Baltic region. Stalin's first step was to abandon all pretence at preserving the Polish nation as a buffer between the Soviet Union and Germany. On 25 September the German ambassador was called to the Kremlin to be informed that the Soviet government was interested in exchanging territory around Warsaw and Lublin for German recognition of Soviet hegemony over Lithuania.[41] The next step on Stalin's agenda was to assert limited Soviet military control over Estonia under the pretext that this country was unable to defend its sovereignty from foreign intervention. A suitable excuse presented itself on 17 September when the *Orzel*, a Polish submarine interned three days before by the Estonian government, managed to slip its moorings in Tallinn harbour and escape to Sweden. The Soviet government immediately took advantage of this excuse. On 18 September, *Pravda* published an article condemning the Estonian government for compromising its neutrality by harbouring submarines from Poland and other foreign powers. More clandestine measures were undertaken by the Naval Commissariat to mine the sea-lanes to Leningrad, place the Leningrad Military District's anti-aircraft defence system, the VNOS (Air Surveillance, Warning and Communications system) on combat alert, and to organize a detachment of surface ships under the command of the deputy commissar Isakov to search Estonian territorial waters for other submarines.[42] When Estonian Foreign Minister Selter arrived in Moscow on 22 September to discuss the terms of a new Soviet–Estonian trade agreement, Molotov confronted him with a radical revision of Soviet foreign policy for the Baltic region:

> The present situation in the Baltic constitutes a danger to the security of the Soviet Union, as is made particularly manifest by the escape of a Polish submarine from Tallinn harbour. It is indispensable to alter the status quo

11

in the Baltic area in such a way that the Soviet Baltic Fleet need not feel confined in a menaced position in the narrow end of the Gulf of Finland. The Soviet Union has become a powerful state with a highly developed industry, and in possession of a great military force. The *status quo* which was established twenty years ago when the Soviet Union was weakened by civil war can no longer be considered as adequate to the present situation and normal.[43]

Molotov's message was clear: the outbreak of war in Europe and the fall of Poland allowed the Soviet Union to abandon its conciliatory policy toward Estonia and the other Baltic secessionist states in favour of pressuring them into contributing directly to the Soviet Union's defence. Selter returned to Tallinn bearing Molotov's demands for an immediate ratification of a mutual assistance pact in Moscow at the end of the month.

During the temporary lull in Soviet–Estonian relations, Moscow took measures to back up its diplomatic stance with the threat of military force. The Baltic Fleet command at Kronstadt finalized plans for an offensive against the Estonian coast while Soviet military airplanes repeatedly violated Estonian airspace and the Leningrad Military District concentrated 160,000 troops opposite the Estonian fortified region at Narva on 26 September.[44] When negotiations resumed the next day Molotov took advantage of another incident, the staged submarine attack on the Soviet cargo ship *Metallist* in the Gulf of Narva, to demand additional concessions to the mutual assistance pact: the right to station 35,000 Red Army troops on Estonian territory.[45] Stalin eventually intervened and lent an air of conciliation to the negotiations by agreeing to reduce the number of troops by 10,000 and promising to remove them as soon as the war in Europe was over. However, by the time the pact was signed on 28 September, Estonia had suffered a severe blow to its sovereignty.

Similar pressure tactics brought equally advantageous results during negotiations with delegations from the Latvian and Lithuanian governments. Latvia signed a mutual assistance pact which granted the Soviet Union the use of naval and air bases at Liepaja on 5 October. Five days later, Lithuania signed a similar treaty and granted the use of a base at Memel in exchange for Stalin's magnanimous gift of the former Polish city Vilnius.[46]

Having successfully reconfigured Soviet security relations with the Baltic States, Stalin's next priority was to quickly relocate the Red Army and the Baltic Fleet to their new bases and ports. Stalin had already initiated these preparations during the diplomatic negotiations with Estonia by creating two war commissions to advise the Ministry of Foreign Affairs on strategic issues. The first of these commissions, the Army War Commission, headed by Meretskov, the commander of the Leningrad Military District, was responsible for facilitating the redeployment of 25,000 Red Army troops.[47] People's Commissar Kuznetsov and his two deputies, Galler and Isakov, comprised the Naval War Commission which was responsible for recommending the acquisition of coastal artillery batteries and air bases as well as negotiating the use of Tallinn harbour while larger port facilities at Paldiski were under construction.[48] During the first week of October the Naval War Commission sent Isakov on an inspection tour to Estonia. When he reported back to Stalin and the commission on 8 October, Stalin ordered the Baltic Fleet to begin redeploying its submarines, surface ships, aviation and support equipment. The first Soviet ships docked at Tallinn harbour three days later and throughout the rest of the month a total of four destroyers, nineteen submarines, three patrol boats and two floating repair docks sailed to anchorages at Tallinn and Paldiski. The battleship *Kirov* sailed to Liepaja accompanied by two mine-sweepers.[49]

The result of Stalin's diplomacy fulfilled a dream shared by many a Soviet military and naval planner since the inglorious retreat of the Baltic Fleet (the TsentroBalt forces) to Kronstadt and Petrograd in the spring of 1918: control over the southern coast of the Gulf of Finland and the enlargement of the fleet's operational zone to the Baltic Sea.[50] However, the realization of this dream brought attendant problems. The least of these was the need to recalculate, print and disseminate the Baltic Fleet's documentation concerning operations, organization and mobilization in the new zone of operations. Refurbishing the Estonian, Latvian and Lithuanian bases to full combat capability was far more problematic. Many bases did not have sea channels deep enough for the larger war ships, equipment for ship repair was scarce, storage for fuel and ammunition was inadequate and the Baltic Fleet command was unable to mobilize enough medical personnel in the Leningrad area to staff the new hospitals.[51] The most serious and ironic problem confronting the Baltic Fleet was that it did not have enough ships to effectively patrol the coast or even provide adequate security for the new bases. Two years earlier Stalin and Zhdanov had partially addressed this problem by consolidating the Soviet navy into the People's Commissariat for the Navy and inaugurating an ambitious ship-building programme for the Baltic Fleet, but construction was slow and attempts to buy capital ships from abroad were unsuccessful.[52] As a result, the Baltic Fleet was patently over-extended due to Molotov's diplomatic successes.

While the Baltic Fleet strove to resolve these problems the Naval War Commission conducted an historical and geographical analysis to compare the existing strategic situation with that extant before the First World War, when the tsarist navy exercised control over an elaborate defensive system on

13

both the north and south shores of the Gulf of Finland.⁵³ Restitution of the southern shore would protect the Red Army's flank and greatly strengthen the defence of Leningrad but the harbours themselves were shallow, exposed, and vulnerable to enemy mining. The north shore, by contrast, was characterized by deep water harbours, coastal batteries and a well-developed network of inland airfields which could easily close off navigation in the Gulf of Finland and the Gulf of Bothnia with long range artillery and aviation, especially in winter.⁵⁴

On the basis of this study, the Naval War Commission made the following conclusions. Assuming Finland was able to maintain its neutrality, the Soviet Union's minimum security objective on the north shore was to obtain bases and coastal artillery batteries on the Hangö and Porkkala–Udd Peninsulas west of Helsinki and gain control over the Suursaari (Hogland) and Suur-Tiutärsaari islands in the Gulf. If Finland's neutrality was compromised by either or both blocs of the belligerent Great Powers, then the entire territory of Finland could be used as a springboard for an invasion against the Soviet Union, especially on the Karelian Isthmus and along the Murmansk–Leningrad railroad where it skirted the Soviet–Finnish border at Ladoga-Karelia and Salla. Under these circumstances the commission was doubly anxious to protect sea communications in the Gulf of Finland from the threat of enemy minefields and coastal artillery. However, the Naval War Commission's principal concern was the threat of sudden attack from the air. In the autumn of 1939 Finland's airforce was no match for Soviet aviation but the Finnish Army did have a sophisticated anti-aircraft system and a large network of airfields built in the mid-1930s which could be used by a larger power to attack the Soviet Union. The majority of these airfields were located on the Karelian Isthmus, and during the previous year an additional 15 airfields had been constructed along the Finnish–Soviet border near Rovaniemi, Sodankiulia, Vuotso, Ivalo, Nautsi and Salmi-järvi. From these airfields the Finnish airforce, with the aid of a foreign power, could conduct surprise raids against both the Soviet Baltic and Northern Fleets.⁵⁵ Armed with these recommendations, the Ministry of Foreign Affairs prepared its brief for the resumption of diplomatic negotiations with Finland over the creation of a security zone in the Baltic.

II

Diplomatic contact between the Soviet Union and Finland after the outbreak of the war in Europe was resumed on 11 September 1939 when the Finnish ambassador in Moscow, Yrjö-Koskinen, visited V. Potemkin, Molotov's deputy commissar, to propose the re-opening of negotiations on trade and political relations on the basis of proposals discussed the previous spring. Yrjö-Koskinen's proposal met with a cool reception. Potemkin first demanded to know how large a trade agreement the Finnish government in Helsinki had in mind, then inquired whether opinion had changed over the re-fortification of the Åland Islands. Yrjö-Koskinen was unable to give satisfactory answers to both these queries but promised to obtain more information from his government. Before ending the interview Yrjö-Koskinen asked Potemkin the reason for the partial mobilization of the Red Army announced by the Soviet government a week before and whether these troops would be stationed on the Soviet–Finnish border.[56] Although Potemkin refused at this time to answer this question the Finnish government soon received an indirect answer. When the Red Army began its 'liberation' of western Belorussia and Poland on 17 September, Molotov handed Yrjö-Koskinen an official communiqué reassuring the Finnish government that the Soviet Union would continue to respect Finland's neutrality.[57]

This long hiatus in Soviet–Finnish relations and Molotov's laconic communiqué did not mean that Moscow had lost interest in Finland or that relations with Finland remained on the same footing. War between Germany and Poland, the two major Baltic powers, and the beginning of the war in Europe had considerably changed the strategic situation in the Baltic, and the Soviet leadership preferred to strengthen its situation *vis-à-vis* Poland and the Baltic States before making new demands of Finland. On 16 September Molotov received a report from the Soviet ambassador in Helsinki, Derevianskii, on the Finnish public's reaction to the Soviet–German Pact and subsequent events. On the basis of an analysis of the Finnish press, Derevianskii informed his superiors in Moscow that the economic dislocation brought about by the German–Polish war had split Finnish public opinion between those who called for stronger political and economic relations with the Soviet Union and the reactionary, fascist press which called for new defence expenditures to improve fortifications on the Karelian Isthmus and re-fortify the Åland Islands. Derevianskii concluded his report with the following observations:

> In general, the Soviet–German Pact and Molotov's subsequent speech has undoubtedly found the governing circles here, in the far corner of Europe, having to reconsider a change in their policies. It is more truthful to say that the pact has caused them confusion and disarray. In Finland it has become easier for them to recognise how incorrect their orientation has been all these years. For that reason Finland now stands at a distinctive cross-roads. Always inclined to side with the enemies of the Soviet Union

they now do not know exactly where to go or what to do. There is a deep process now going on in the depths of the ruling circles and which line wins will be seen in the near future.[58]

The Soviet government did not make a move to redefine its relations with Finland until the Red Army had completed its occupation of Poland and the People's Commissariat of Foreign Affairs had concluded mutual assistance pacts with Estonia and Latvia. Confirmation that the time had arrived to settle old accounts with Helsinki came on 5 October when Stalin and Voroshilov received information from L. Beria from intelligence sources in London that the Finnish government was now willing to accept Soviet demands made during the Anglo–French–Soviet military negotiations earlier that summer.[59] That same day Molotov informed Yrjö–Koskinen that the Soviet government wished to initiate negotiations with the Finns over 'concrete political questions' while, at the Naval Commissariat, Kuznetsov ordered his deputy, Galler, to gather information about the Hangö Peninsula and its past use by the tsarist fleet.[60]

Stalin had every reason to believe that the forthcoming negotiations would be as quickly and easily resolved as those with the Baltic States had been.[61] The Soviet Union had effectively asserted its hegemony over the former territories of the tsarist empire under the auspices of the Soviet–German non-aggression pact, and intelligence from several sources indicated that the threat of civil war in Finland would force the Finnish government to accept the Soviet Union's demands. However, Erkko, the Finnish Minister of Foreign Affairs, was aware that any concessions to Moscow would severely compromise the credibility of Finland's neutrality. On 6 October Erkko met with military leaders and members of the Finnish Cabinet to draft a set of instructions for the Finnish delegation's negotiations in Moscow.[62] This committee on foreign affairs ignored Moscow's impatience to begin the negotiations and finalized the draft instructions on 9 October. The first priority was to adhere strictly to the terms stipulated by the Tartu peace treaty of 1920 and the Soviet–Finnish non-aggression pact and to avoid discussing proposals which violated Finland's national constitution or which sought to alter its territorial sovereignty. Extrapolating from past Soviet proposals, Erkko specifically instructed members of the delegation not to discuss the concession of military bases on Finnish territory (i.e. the Åland Islands, the Hangö Peninsula and Suursaari Island), boundary changes on the Karelian Isthmus, or any proposals contributing to a mutual-assistance pact. The only compromise they were allowed to offer was the cession of several Finnish islands in the eastern part of the Gulf of Finland, and only in exchange for territorial concession

16

elsewhere along the Soviet–Finnish border.[63] Erkko entrusted the delegation to J. Paasikivi, the Finnish Minister to Sweden, preferring to co-ordinate political and diplomatic policy from Helsinki rather than conduct the negotiations himself. Measures were also taken to prepare the country for the threat of war. The Finnish Army's covering troops were sent to the frontier districts and reserve troops were partially mobilized. Erkko also consulted with the German minister in Helsinki, Blucher, over the possibility of German diplomatic support for Finland in the negotiations, but received a negative response.[64]

The discrepancy between the Soviet and Finnish positions became apparent to both parties when negotiations began in Moscow on 12 October. The Soviet delegation, which consisted of Stalin, Molotov, Potemkin and Derevianskii, initiated the proceedings with an oral statement of its priorities and proposals. True to the Naval Commissariat's military-geographic survey, the Soviet delegation's primary security interest in the Baltic region was to extend Soviet naval and military control to the entrance of the Gulf of Finland. Towards this end, the Soviet delegation suggested that Finland sign a mutual-assistance pact and agree to a series of territorial concessions which included the following: a Red Army base on the Hangö Peninsula, cession of all the islands in the Gulf of Finland including Suursaari and the coastal artillery batteries on the Björkö Archipelago, anchorage facilities at the port of Lappohja and territorial concessions on the Karelian Isthmus and up north on the Rybachii Peninsula in order to enlarge the defensive buffer around Leningrad and Murmansk.[65] After Paasikivi rejected the Soviet delegation's proposals on the second day of negotiations, Stalin himself explained the need for concessions at Hangö and the Björkö Archipelago. Stalin reminded the Finnish delegation that, in the past, the Soviet Union had been threatened by the British Navy operating in the Gulf and that, when the present war in Europe was over, nothing prevented the victor's navy from doing so again. Stalin considered the threat from Björkö to be even more transparent. Long range artillery stationed on that island severely restricted the Baltic Fleet's range of manoeuvre in the eastern part of the Gulf.[66] When Paasikivi remarked that these proposals compromised Finland's neutrality and the Finnish military attaché demanded to know how such proposals squared with the Soviet Union's defensive military doctrine, Stalin revealed the true nature of his foreign policy: 'In Poland we took no foreign territory. And now this is a case of exchange.'[67]

Clearly unable to reach a compromise on the basis of its very narrow directives, the Finnish delegation returned to Helsinki on 16 October to acquaint the Finnish government with the Soviet delegation's proposals and to receive further instructions. On 20–21 October a private session of the Finnish Council of State, composed of the Prime Minister and other civil and military leaders, met to hear Paasikivi's report and discuss the course of future negotiations. Paasikivi informed them that the Soviet delegation was primarily interested in concessions at Hangö, Suursaari Island and the Björkö Archipelago and a rectification of the border on the Karelian Isthmus. He warned those present that any counter-proposals should be considered as final.[68] In the ensuing discussion a debate erupted over whether the delegation's directives should be based on the inviolability of Finland's sovereignty, as defined by its constitution and international agreements, or on the recognition of the Soviet Union's security dilemma in the Baltic. The Defence and Foreign Ministers refused to consider further concessions at Hangö or the Karelian Isthmus on the assumption that the Finnish Diet would never approve them. On the other hand, Marshal Mannerheim, the chairman of the Defence Council, and Tanner, the Minister of Trade, argued that some of Moscow's security proposals were legitimate. They were willing to offer the Soviet Union the fortress of Ino on the south coast of the Karelian Isthmus as well as the islands in the Gulf and the southern half of Suursaari Island.[69] All agreed that Soviet proposals for lease of Hangö Peninsula and major border rectifications on the Karelian Isthmus were out of the question.[70] The crux of the issue remained whether Sweden would be willing to come to Finland's assistance in the case of a Soviet invasion, or whether it would remain neutral. During a meeting of the Scandinavian heads of state on 18–19 October, Erkko took the opportunity to explore the possibility of a Finnish–Swedish military alliance with the head of the Swedish Cabinet but only received an equivocal response.[71] When the Finnish delegation departed for Moscow on 21 October, its negotiating directives were only marginally more concessionary. Erkko gave permission to Paasikivi to offer the Soviet delegation the four islands in the Gulf, reconfigure the border on the Karelian Isthmus at the Kuokkala Bend and cede Suursaari Island under diplomatic pressure but not to discuss concessions at Hangö or Lappohja harbour, border revisions on the Rybachii Peninsula, or terms for a mutual assistance pact.[72]

During the second round of negotiations on 23 October, Stalin dropped recourse to overt threats and explained the Soviet delegation's proposals in relation to the war in Europe. In his opinion, the current war would become a world war of long duration and either or both of the imperialist powers might attack the Soviet Union from the south through Finland and the Gulf or from the north through Murmansk. When the Finnish delegation pointed out that the existing peace and non-aggression pacts had been sufficient to maintain security along the Soviet Union's north-western frontier, Stalin

18

refused to listen, arguing that changing circumstances had made these pacts obsolete. The Soviet delegation eventually offered a few concessions: the total number of Red Army troops on Hangö was reduced, all mention of a mutual assistance pact was dropped and the Ladoga-Karelian districts of Repola and Poräjarvi were offered in exchange for less territory on the Karelian Isthmus. However, even these proposals exceeded the Finnish delegation's directives and the negotiations adjourned on 24 October in order to allow the Finnish delegation to present Stalin's new proposals to its government in Helsinki.

Failure to reach an agreement during the second round of negotiations convinced Stalin to resort to more forceful means of persuasion. As soon as the Finnish delegation had departed for Helsinki, Stalin convened a meeting of the Main Military Soviet to update operational plans for the invasion of Finland and set military preparations in motion. Shaposhnikov took this opportunity to propose again the contingency plans that he had proposed that previous summer. Stalin, impressed by the rapidity of the Red Army's victories against Poland that autumn and convinced that the class antagonisms that had made those victories possible also existed in Finland,[73] rejected Shaposhnikov's proposals and re-approved Meretskov's contingency plan but with the following important amendment: 'The Leningrad front is commissioned to conduct the entire operation against Finland. The General Staff is not to have a hand in this; it is to concern itself with other matters.'[74] On 29 October, Voroshilov ordered Meretskov to develop an operational plan for the encirclement and full annihilation of the Finnish army by means of co-ordinated land, sea and air attacks. The Leningrad Military District's offensive was to consist of two main operational axes, one on the Karelian Isthmus (lasting no more than eight to 10 days) and the other in Ladoga-Karelia (lasting no more than 15 days). The remainder of his forces were to conduct simultaneous diversionary attacks along the Soviet–Finnish border from Petrozavodsk to Murmansk.[75]

Stalin combined these preparations for war with a corresponding shift towards a more 'demonstrative' foreign policy with Finland.[76] In a speech to the Supreme Soviet on 31 October, Molotov revealed the details of the negotiations with Finland to the press, repudiated rumours in the foreign press that the Soviet Union had demanded the cession of Vyborg and territory north of Lake Ladoga, and restated the Soviet Union's intent to sign a mutual assistance treaty with Finland on similar terms to those offered to Estonia and the other Baltic States. Molotov's speech was more than just a ploy to drag the Finnish delegation back to the negotiation table. Its principal intent was to aggravate class divisions in Finland and stimulate public pressure on the Finnish government to accept the Soviet Union's demands. Further confirmation of this new inflammatory policy emerged on 2 November, when *Pravda* published an anonymous article with the subtitle 'The Finnish Minister of Foreign Affairs calls for War with the Soviet Union'. Reproducing part of Erkko's impassioned response to Molotov's speech, the article made an ominous comparison between Erkko and the former Foreign Minister of Poland and concluded with a thinly veiled threat to use military force.[77]

Meanwhile, the Finnish Cabinet informed the leaders of the Diet on the course of the negotiations in Moscow. On the basis of their endorsement, Erkko drew up a third negotiating brief for Paasikivi and his delegation. Rather than adopt a more conciliatory policy towards Stalin's proposals, as Mannerheim, Paasikivi and Tanner had advised, Erkko instructed the delegation to hold firm against concessions on the Hangö Peninsula and to resist Soviet demands for border revisions on the Karelian Isthmus and the Rybachii Peninsula, confident that the Soviet government would not resort to war with Finland.[78] The source of Erkko's confidence was twofold. At this time a relative of Göring, Count Armfeld, had visited Erkko and Mannerheim, bearing a message from Berlin to 'hold firm' against the Soviet demands and a promise to aid Finland if her relations with the Soviet Union deteriorated, and the German navy had stationed battleships off the Gulf of Riga and at the mouth of the Gulf of Finland.[79] Additional cause for confidence came from a Defence Ministry intelligence report compiled on 28 October. The report stated that although the Red Army was well armed, troop morale was low and the Soviet high command was not flexible enough to conduct modern warfare. It ended with the conclusion that 'At this moment the Red Army is not ready for action. She can hardly go to battle even with the weakest opponents.'[80] When the Finnish delegation's journey back to Moscow was interrupted by news of Molotov's speech, Erkko reassured the delegation by telephone that Molotov's aggressive statements were only a 'tactical manoeuvre intended to intimidate us'.[81]

On 3 November, the Finnish delegation met with Molotov and Potemkin to begin the third round of negotiations. Paasikivi confirmed the Finnish government's willingness to cede the Gulf islands, including the southern half of Suursaari Island, and offer limited border revisions on the Karelian Isthmus and the Rybachii Peninsula, but repeated his government's objections to concessions at the Hangö Peninsula, Lappohja harbour and the destruction of the fortified region on the Karelian Isthmus. When no further progress could be made, Molotov concluded the session with a comment about referring the entire matter to the military, but his meaning was so ambiguous that the Finnish delegation disregarded it. The next day Stalin presided over the negotiations. Stalin emphasized the modesty of the Soviet government's proposals in comparison with the former tsarist government's harsh policies toward the Finnish nationalist movement and he surprised the Finnish delegation by offering to accept the islands of Hermansö, Koö, Hästö and Busö as alternatives to the Hangö Peninsula.[82] Paasikivi was unable to respond to this new development but promised to apply to Helsinki for more instructions. On that note the negotiations were adjourned until after the commemorative celebrations of the October Revolution.

On 9 November, Molotov attempted to jump-start Soviet–Finnish relations by sending the Soviet *chargé d'affaires* in Helsinki, Eliseev, to pay a personal call on Erkko. During their conversation Erkko repeatedly acknowledged the Soviet Union's growing military strength and emphasized Finland's willingness to continue the negotiations but only in so far as they did not conflict with Finland's own neutrality and defence. Eliseev replied to this by stating 'that the Soviet Union would undoubtedly fortify its security in spite of the wishes of our enemies to interfere with us'.[83] Eliseev tried to change the tone of the conversation by repeating Stalin's comparison between tsarist and Soviet policy towards Finland but Erkko countered this line of argument by stating that his own father had fought tsarist imperialism and had been imprisoned. The conversation ended without any resolution. When the Soviet–Finnish negotiations resumed in Moscow that evening Stalin asked Paasikivi whether the Finnish government would cede the island of Russarö and received a negative response. Although the negotiations had completely stalled over this issue Stalin tried one last manoeuvre. Late that evening Molotov sent a letter to the Finnish embassy clarifying the Soviet government's attitude towards the stalemate over Hangö. When the Finnish delegation returned to Helsinki on 13 November without making any positive reply Stalin's quest to improve the Soviet Union's security in the Gulf of Finland by diplomacy came to an end.

III

Stalin faced a difficult dilemma. His attempt to co-ordinate 'demonstrative' diplomacy with concessions had failed to strengthen the Soviet Union's new defences on the north coast of the Gulf of Finland before the onset of winter. The only remaining option was to seize control over the disputed territories by use of force, but even this option posed difficulties. On the one hand, the Soviet government was still obliged to respect Finland's sovereign rights according to the terms of the non-aggression pact of 1932. On the other hand, Lenin's teachings on the development of the 'world socialist revolution' did

21

not justify the conduct of limited wars for the purpose of territorial expansion.[84] Stalin's solution to these limitations was to orchestrate the denunciation of the non-aggression pact and to try to replace the existing Finnish government with a socialist government that, once in power, would automatically recognize the Soviet Union's security interests in the Baltic.[85] The first step of this new policy continued the propaganda campaign against the Finnish government launched by Zhdanov's article in *Pravda* on 3 November. Party activists contributed to this campaign by organizing political meetings and passing public resolutions urging the Soviet government to adopt stronger measures against Finland. The second step was to organize a surrogate socialist government from the few Finnish émigré communists who had survived the purges and place it at the nominal head of a revolutionary army. For this purpose the Karelian National 106th Rifle Division was created on 11 November under the dual command of A. Antilla and Political Commissar Egorov and unsuccessful efforts were made in mid-November to invite the general secretary of the Finnish Communist Party, A. Tuominen, living in Stockholm, to act as president of the new socialist government.[86]

Stalin's military preparations had progressed substantially since their initiation in late October. On 15 November, Stalin ordered the Leningrad Military District to hasten the concentration of troops and supplies along the Soviet–Finnish border and appointed the renowned artillery specialist, N. Voronov, as well as Meretskov and Zhdanov, to tour the front and report back to the Defence Commissariat for further instructions.[87] When Meretskov, Zhdanov, and Voronov met with Voroshilov in Moscow five days later they decided that the Red Army's main strike should be conducted by the 7th Army on the Karelian Isthmus while the 8th Army in Ladoga-Karelia attacked the Finnish railroad junction at Sortavala and the Soviet Baltic Fleet and Ladoga Flotilla suppressed Finnish coastal artillery batteries on both coasts of the Isthmus.[88] Meretskov was aware of the existence of a fortified region (UR, *Ukreplennyi Raion*) which stretched along a line from Suvanto-järvi Lake to the town of Humaljoki on the west coast of the Karelian Isthmus. Recent reconnaissance reports had also identified the construction of new defensive works between Metsäpirtti and Kivenapa on the eastern part of the Isthmus. Hoping to take advantage of the less-developed fortifications on the eastern side of the Isthmus, Meretskov ordered the commander of the 7th Army, V. Yakovlev, to concentrate his 150th and 19th Rifle Corps for a breakthrough operation at Taipale. The 7th Army was then expected to meet up with the 8th Army at Hintola, seize the Finnish army headquarters at Antrea and Vyborg, then march down the Simola–Lakhti Highway for the final offensive against Helsinki.[89]

The Naval Commissariat had already begun preparations for operations in the Gulf of Finland and the Baltic Sea. On 3 November, Kuznetsov ordered the commander of the Baltic Fleet, Flagman V. Tributs, to prepare a 'General Plan' for naval operations against Finland. In this General Plan the Baltic Fleet's first responsibility was to gain complete control over the Gulf of Finland by locating and destroying Finnish battleships before they could escape to Sweden, seizing all the islands in the eastern half of the Gulf and bombing Finnish airfields and *schutzkorps* bases at Kotka, Helsinki and on the Hangö Peninsula. In preparation for the assault on the Gulf islands Tributs created the 'Special Detachment' under the command of Captain Ramishvili on 10 November. Over the next 11 days Captain Ramishvili conducted three reconnaissance patrols to Lavansaari and Seiskari Islands without discovering any Finnish military activity.[90]

When Meretskov assumed unified operational control over the Baltic Fleet on 21 November he assigned the majority of the fleet's forces, including the Special Detachment and artillery support from the Northern and Southern Fortified Regions, to missions between Kronstadt and Suursaari Island (the 27th meridian). Captain Ramishvili's Special Detachment was instructed to assault the islands of Seiskari and Lavansaari, Narvi and Someri and establish bases there, then attack Suursaari and Suur-Tiutärsaari and begin concentrating an infantry regiment for an assault against the Finnish coast.[91] The main mission of the Northern and Southern Fortified Region commands and the Soviet battleship *Oktiabr'skaia Revoliutsiia* was to give artillery support to the 7th Army's 70th Rifle Division as it attacked along the western coast of the Karelian Isthmus from the Soviet–Finnish border to the former tsarist fortress at Ino and up to the Finnish coastal artillery batteries at Björkö.[92] Its second mission was to protect Leningrad, the naval bases at Kronstadt and Luga Bay and the eastern part of the Gulf of Finland from Finnish air attack. The Baltic Fleet and the two Fortified Region commands relied on the Leningrad Military District's VNOS system, three anti-air defence companies and 177 interceptor aircraft for this task.[93] The Baltic Fleet's third and final mission was to support the Red Army's offensive against the Finnish fortified region at Björkö (on the west coast of the Karelian Isthmus) with artillery and an amphibious landing operation.[94]

Although the Naval Commissariat did not regard the Finnish Navy alone as a serious threat to the Soviet Baltic Fleet, in combination with the Swedish Navy or the navy of another power, the Finnish Navy could take advantage of the Soviet Baltic Fleet's precarious situation on the south shore of the Gulf of Finland by sowing mine fields, attacking communications at sea by submarine and conducting joint aviation and surface-ship raids against Soviet

23

shipping and bases from skerries on the north shore. As early as 6 November Tributs sent out two submarines to monitor the deployment of the Swedish Navy off the coast of Stockholm and other naval activity in the Baltic Sea but ordered the submarine commanders not to fire on shipping in the Baltic Sea and Gulf of Bothnia until after the beginning of the war and the Soviet government's official declaration of a naval blockade against Finland. On 23 November, Meretskov assigned three more submarines, the *Shch-320*, *S-2* and *S-3*, to additional patrols off the coast of Stockholm, the waters north of Gotland Island and along the Latvian coast (see Figure 1.1). The Baltic Fleet's third and equally important mission was to locate and destroy the Finnish Navy and isolate Finland from the West by severing its sea communications in the Baltic and in the mouth of the Gulf of Finland. This mission was assigned to the submarines *S-1*, *L-1*, *Shch-309*, *Shch-310*, *Shch-318*, and *Shch-319* and five torpedo boats. The Baltic Fleet's fourth and fifth missions were to destroy Finnish coastal batteries and airfields along the coast from Russarö Island in the west to Kotka in the east and cover the eastern part of the Gulf of Finland from air attack. This was to be accomplished by the Soviet battleship *Kirov*, air reconnaissance from the 10th Aviation Brigade, and bombers from the 8th Aviation Brigade.[95]

IV

On the afternoon of 26 November, seven artillery shots were fired on the Karelian Isthmus near the border outpost of Mainila. Later that day Molotov called Yrjö-Koskinen to the People's Commissariat of Foreign Affairs to inform him that artillery had been fired from Finnish territory, killing and wounding a number of Red Army men, and to demand that the Finnish government withdraw its army from the border by 20 to 25 kilometres.[96] In a reply delivered the next day the Finnish government stated that a preliminary investigation had revealed that the shots had been fired on the Soviet side of the border. The Finnish government's note suggested that both governments withdraw their armies from the border and set up a commission to investigate the incident in accordance with the terms of the non-aggression pact. On 28 November Molotov announced that the Soviet Union was unilaterally abolishing the non-aggression pact on the basis of accusations that the Finnish government's actions and statements constituted hostility toward the Soviet Union and threatened the security of Leningrad. When Yrjö-Koskinen returned to the Soviet Ministry of Foreign Affairs the next day to deliver his government's response to this illegal abnegation of the pact and to offer to

FIGURE 1.1
MAP OF THE BALTIC FLEET'S SUBMARINE PATROLS,
30 NOVEMBER 1939 TO 18 JANUARY 1940

Adapted from *Sovetsko–finliandskaia voina 1939–1940 gg. na more*, Voenmorizdat, Moscow–
Leningrad, 1945–46.

withdraw Finnish troops from the border, he was received by Molotov's deputy, Potemkin, who informed him that the Soviet Union was severing diplomatic relations with Finland.[97]

Meanwhile, Meretskov at Leningrad Military District headquarters was busy completing the final concentration of Red Army formations and units on the border and issuing last minute instructions.[98] One of Meretskov's primary concerns was to monitor Scandinavian and foreign military response to the growing political crisis between the Soviet Union and Finland. Early on the morning of 28 November the Baltic Fleet command added two more submarines from Tallinn to patrol the entrance to Stockholm harbour. Later that day three more submarines set out to patrol the waters around Gotland Island and as far south as Karlskrona.[99] Up north in the Barents Sea a Soviet submarine, the *Shch-404*, had been patrolling the Norwegian coast as far west as the Makkaur Peninsula to monitor the Norwegian fleet and prevent foreign ships from approaching Varanger Fjord and the Rybachii Peninsula.[100] On 27 November the submarine reported sighting the Norwegian torpedo boats *Aegir* and *Sleilner* and the escort ship *Fritiof Nansen* sailing toward Varanger Fjord. Acting on this reconnaissance, Meretskov ordered the 14th Army to prepare for an offensive against the western coast of the Srednyi and Rybachii Peninsulas and the region of Petsamo while Kuznetsov ordered the Northern Fleet to provide the 14th Army with artillery support and to prevent enemy ships from entering the Gulf of Kola and the Gulf of Motov or allow enemy landings on the Murmansk coast.[101] Additional submarines were sent out on the afternoon of 28 November to patrol the approaches to Varanger Fjord and the Gulf of Kola, and the airforce conducted reconnaissance flights between Tarra Fjord and Kharlov Island and along the whole length of Varanger Fjord to the town of Petsamo. Commanders were instructed to expect hostilities with Norway but not to violate Swedish or Norwegian territory under any circumstances.[102]

At 00h15 on 30 November the Defence Commissariat finally ordered the Leningrad Military District to deploy its units for the invasion later that morning. As these last-minute preparations were underway Molotov delivered a speech over Radio Moscow explaining the reasons for terminating the Soviet Union's non-aggression pact with Finland.[103] Molotov's intention was to lay the blame for the deterioration of Soviet–Finnish relations at Finland's door and thus absolve the Soviet government from all responsibility for the more violent course of action it was about to follow. Repeating his accusations from the previous day, Molotov informed his audience that the Soviet government was recalling its political and economic representatives and had instructed the Defence and Naval Commissariats to 'be prepared for all manner of surprises'. Molotov then denied accusations in the foreign press that the Soviet government was merely intent on seizing Finnish territory, pointing out that territorial concessions had been offered and that the Soviet delegation would have even offered to cede the whole of Soviet Karelia to Finland if the Finnish government had been more co-operative. As for the accusation that the Soviet government was violating Finland's right to determine her own foreign and domestic policy, Molotov pointed out that the Soviet government had always respected the Finnish peoples' right to determine their foreign policy and he made an oblique reference to the friendship treaty with the Finnish Workers' Socialist Republic in March 1918 with the remark that

> Once before, the people of the Soviet Union did what they could to create an independent Finland. Today, the people of our country are prepared to give help to the Finnish people to guarantee their free and independent development.[104]

If there were any remaining doubts in the Red Army's ranks about the real intentions of their government these were soon dispelled by Meretskov's final communiqué to the Leningrad Military District. Repeating many of the points made in Molotov's speech, Meretskov called on his troops to cross the border and bring about the full destruction of the Finnish Army. Meretskov justified this strategy of annihilation with the following statement: 'We go into Finland not as combatants, but as friends and liberators, freeing the Finnish People from the clutches of the landowners and capitalists. We are not against the Finnish People but against the Kajander-Erkko government, clutching the Finnish People and provoking war with the Soviet Union.'[105] Meretskov's first order was not an appeal to the Red Army soldier to fulfil a grandiose internationalist duty nor was it a justification for a war of limited territorial expansion. The imminent war with Finland would be a 'preventive war' similar to the recent campaign in Poland, and had as its purpose the insulation of the Soviet Union from the threat of military intervention from Germany and the Entente.

NOTES

1 J. Degras, *Soviet Documents on Foreign Policy*, Vol. III (London: Oxford University Press, 1953) pp. 78–9.
2 D.W. Spring, 'The Soviet Decision for War Against Finland, 30 November, 1939', *Soviet Studies*, Vol. XXXVIII, No. 2, April 1986, p. 210.
3 M. Jakobson, *Finland Survived* (Cambridge: Harvard University Press, 1961) p. 18.
4 J. Haslam, *The Soviet Union and the Struggle for Collective Security in Europe, 1933–1939* (London: Macmillan, 1984) pp. 93, 209.

5 Ibid., p. 236.
6 M.N. Tukhachevskii, '1937. Pokazaniia marshala Tukhachevskogo' ('Plan porazheniia') *Voenno-istoricheskii zhurnal*, No. 8, 1991, p. 48.
7 PRO FO 371 23648, N3199, 'General Sir Walter Kirke's report to the War Office, 4 July 1939'.
8 V. Tanner, *The Winter War* (Palo Alto: Stanford University Press, 1957) pp. 8–10. See also Haslam, *The Soviet Union and the Struggle for Collective Security in Europe*, pp. 208, 238–9.
9 G. Jukes, 'The Red Army and the Munich Crisis', *Journal of Contemporary History*, Vol. 26, 1991, pp. 197–8, 207–9. See also C.G. Mannerheim, *The Memoirs of Marshal Mannerheim* (London: Cassel and Co., 1953) pp. 295–6. See also PRO FO 371 23648, N 1359, 'Finland. Annual Report 1938, 16 March 1939'.
10 K.A. Meretskov, *Na sluzhbe narodu* (Moscow: Politizdat, 1969) pp. 171, 173–4.
11 S.A. Zonin, *Admiral L.M. Galler* (Moscow: Voenizdat, 1991) p. 298. In December 1938 Isakov requested and obtained permission from Zhdanov to look into the possibility of buying the battleships *Washington* and *North Carolina* from the US Navy during his visit to the United States the following spring.
12 *Sovetsko-finliandskaia voina 1939–1940 gg. na more*, Chast' I, Kniga I (Moscow: Narodnyi Kommissariat Voenno-Morskogo Flota Soiuza SSR, Istoricheskii Otdel', 1945) p. 44.
13 B.A. Leach, *German Strategy against Russia, 1939–1941* (Oxford: Oxford University Press, 1973), pp. 17–18.
14 T. Ries, 'Manuscript for *Cold Will*', Chapter 3 (courtesy of the author), 1991, p. 6. See also Mannerheim, *The Memoirs of Marshal Mannerheim*, pp. 300–1, and *God Krizisa, 1938–1939* Vol. I (Moscow: Politizdat, 1990). See Document 181, 'Zapis' besedy polnomochnogo predstavitelia SSSR v Italii B.E. Shteina s ministrom finansov Finliandii V. Tanner, 13 March, 1939', pp. 270–1.
15 Although Stalin failed to mention the third option, i.e., an attack conducted by any one of the successor states with the support of Britain, France and/or Germany, his subsequent actions suggested that he still regarded this option as a possible threat.
16 I.A. Korotkov, *Istoriia sovetskoi voennoi mysli: kratkii ocherk 1917-iun' 1941* (Moscow: 'Nauka', 1980) pp. 118–19. See also Haslam, *The Soviet Union and the Struggle for Collective Security in Europe*, p. 205.
17 Haslam, *The Soviet Union and the Struggle for Collective Security in Europe*, p. 209.
18 S. Aster, *1939: The Making of the Second World War* (London: Deutsch, 1973), p. 163. See also G. Roberts, 'Infamous Encounter? The Merekalov-Weizsäcker Meeting of 17 April 1939', *The Historical Journal* 35, 4 (1992) pp. 921–6, for a recent reinterpretation of Soviet–German relations leading up to the August 1939 non-aggression pact.
19 *God Krizisa*, Vol. I, Document Nos. 356 and 361.
20 Jakobson, *Finland Survived*, pp. 76–7.
21 Ibid., p. 84.
22 PRO FO 371 23618, N3199, 'Notes by General Kirke on his visit to Finland, June 1939'.
23 On July 11 the head of the British Foreign Office's Northern Department, Collier, reported that on the basis of 'a source which is not altogether reliable' he had learnt that 'on the occasion of General Halder's visit conversations took place in regard to the protection of Finland by German air forces in the event of Russia's opening hostilities with Finland, and that it was agreed that air bases should be provided in the Karelian District, at Helsingfors [Helsinki] and at Petsamo in Finnish Lapland.' See PRO FO 371 23648, N3310.
24 Haslam, *The Soviet Union and the Struggle for Collective Security in Europe*, p. 223. See also Jakobson, *Finland Survived*, p. 86.
25 Haslam, *The Soviet Union and the Struggle for Collective Security in Europe*, p. 224.
26 A graduate of the Nicholas Imperial General Staff Academy before the First World War, Boris Mikhailovich Shaposhnikov embodied a tradition of staff work which was 'cold-blooded, systematic and thoroughly trained down to the tiniest technical detail in every speciality', a professional etiquette inspired by the famous Chief of the German General Staff, General Helmuth von Moltke (the Elder) and adopted by the Russian General Staff

during the final quarter of the nineteenth century. Shaposhnikov joined the Bolshevik cause in November 1917 and served as the chief of operations in the field staff of the Military Revolutionary Soviet alongside other ex-tsarist military specialists during the Civil War. From 1928 to 1931 he was head of the Red Army Staff and wrote many theoretical and operational studies including a three volume study on the management ethos of the General Staff entitled *Mozg Armii*, (Moscow: 1921–1929). Shaposhnikov survived a party purge in 1933 on the basis of a peer evaluation which portrayed him as 'versatile and knowledgeable, his only weak point being lack of character', traits which undoubtedly saved him from the executioner's bullet during the purges of the Red Army's command corps in the later half of the 1930s. He subsequently served as a commander of several military districts and as director of the Frunze Military Academy before taking over as the Chief of the General Staff in 1937. Shaposhnikov recognized the divinational nature of Stalin's leadership while Stalin valued Shaposhnikov's technical expertise and lack of personal charisma. As a result, relations between the two were conducted with formality and respect although Stalin would frequently ignore Shaposhnikov's advice. See Oleg Rzheshevsky's biographical sketch in *Stalin's Generals*, edited by H. Shukman (London: Weidenfeld and Nicolson, 1993) pp. 217–30, and Meretskov, *Na sluzhbe narodov*, p. 167.

Kirill Afanasievich Meretskov started his military career as a chief of staff to a Red Guard unit in the early days of the Revolution. He subsequently gained military experience and expertise by attending the first class of the Military Academy (later named after the War Minister, M.V. Frunze) and serving in various campaigns during the Civil War including the First Cavalry Army's advance on Lublin in the summer of 1920, a posting which undoubtedly promoted his subsequent career. During the inter-war years Meretskov served in a variety of staff positions before travelling abroad to Czechoslovakia to observe army manoeuvres and on to Spain to serve as a military advisor to the Republican Army. Meretskov was recalled to Moscow by Stalin at the height of the purges and appointed as Deputy Chief of the General Staff under Shaposhnikov for a year before being appointed to command first the Volga, then the Leningrad Military Districts. Not as technically proficient as Shaposhnikov nor particularly motivated by personal courage, Meretskov had a tendency to act as his own chief of staff at the expense of inspired battlefield command. However, Stalin appreciated his technical abilities and often assigned him responsibilities he was loath to assume. See Geoffrey Juke's biographical sketch in *Stalin's Generals*, pp. 127–34.

27 Meretskov, *Na sluzhbe narodu*, pp. 177–8.
28 K. Simonov, 'Glazami cheloveka moego pokoleniia: besedy s marshalom sovetskogo soiuza A.M. Vasilevskim', *Znamia*, No. 5, 1988, p. 70.
29 A graduate of the Naval Academy in the early 1930s, Nikolai Gerasimovich Kuznetsov made his career in the Black Sea Fleet before serving as naval advisor and attaché to the Republican government during the Spanish Civil War. Kuznetsov's career advanced rapidly after Stalin appointed him first deputy commander of the Pacific Fleet in August 1937. Stalin had made a good choice: Kuznetsov had a strong sense of professionalism which was manifested in his insistence on strict discipline, constant training and objective analysis of the combat preparedness in the various fleets. See G. Jukes, 'Nikolai Gerasimovich Kuznetsov', *Stalin's Generals*, pp. 109–15.
30 Zonin, *Admiral L.M. Galler*, pp. 304, 306. See also D.C. Watt, *How War Came* (London: Mandarin, 1990), p. 377.
31 *Sovetsko-finliandskaia voina 1939–1940 gg. na more*, Chast' I, Kniga I, p. 44.
32 Zonin, *Admiral L.M. Galler*, p. 307.
33 Haslam, *The Soviet Union and the Struggle for Collective Security in Europe*, p. 224.
34 Ibid., pp. 227–8. See also Ahmann, '"Localization of Conflicts" or "Indivisibility of Peace": the German and the Soviet Approaches towards Collective Security and East Central Europe, 1925–1939', p. 209.
35 G.F. Kennan, *Russia Leaves the War* (Princeton: Princeton University Press, 1989) pp. 74–5. See also C.J. Smith, Jr., *Finland and the Russian Revolution, 1917–1922* (Athens, GA: University of Georgia Press, 1958), pp. 27–33. For a discussion of Lenin's analysis of

militarism in the capitalist world-economic order see J. Kipp, 'Lenin and Clausewitz: The Militarization of Marxism, 1914–1921', *Military Affairs*, October, 1985, pp. 184–91. A. Gat, *The Development of Military Thought. The Nineteenth Century* (Oxford, Clarendon Press, 1992) pp. 226–46. V.R. Berghahn, *Militarism. The History of an International Debate, 1861–1979* (Leamington Spa: Berg Publishers, 1981) pp. 21–6.

36 Smith, *Finland and the Russian Revolution, 1917–1922*, pp. 57–9. E.H. Carr, *The Bolshevik Revolution, 1917–1923*, Vol. 1 (London: Macmillan, 1950), pp. 305–9, mentions that Stalin's involvement in the direct incorporation of Belorussia into the Russian Soviet Republic in November 1918 is discussed in a Soviet publication in January 1940.

This is the way some members of the British Foreign Office forecasted the future policies of the Soviet government in 1919:

> Whatever form of government eventually emerges from the present chaos in what was Russia, it can hardly be doubted that Russia will some day – and probably within a few years – be united again, whether in the shape of a unitary State or in a Confederation. The racial homogeneity (in spite of local differences) of far the greater part of its population, the lack of natural boundaries, the memories of past greatness, and the danger of disunion in the face of a resuscitated and united Germany, not to mention other factors, will inevitably tend to this direction. The probable effect of this on the border-States is obvious. ... the former Baltic provinces will scarcely be able to maintain their independence; and very severe pressure will be brought to bear upon Finland, which will be as necessary to a Russian Confederation in the future as it was to the Russian Empire in the past.

> - *The Åland Islands, Handbook* prepared under the direction of the Historical Section of the Foreign Office (GB), No. 58a (London: August 1919) pp. 38–9.

An illustration of this policy can be seen in a speech by A. Joffe to the Central Committee of the Belorussian Communist Party in 1918:

> In order not to repeat the mistakes of the past ... we, in the Central Committee of the VKP(b) have decided to separate Soviet Russia by buffers from Europe but in such a way that the buffer will not be seclusive. This buffer should inhibit the pressure from imperialists so that they will strike against an obstacle and lose their power.

> -F. Silnitskii, *Natsional'naia politika KPSS v period s 1917 do 1922 goda* (Munich: Sucasnist', 1981) p. 186.

37 D. Volkogonov, 'The Drama of the Decisions of 1939', *Soviet Studies in History*, Vol. 29, No. 3, Winter 1990–91, pp. 30–2.
38 J. Erickson, *The Soviet High Command* (New York: St. Martin's Press, 1962) p. 537.
39 J. Haslam, *The Soviet Union and the Threat from the East, 1933–1941. Moscow, Tokyo and the Prelude to the Pacific War* (Pittsburgh: University of Pittsburgh Press, 1992) pp. 132–7.
40 J. Erickson, 'The Red Army's March into Poland, September 1939', in *The Soviet Takeover of the Polish Eastern Provinces, 1939–1941*, ed. K. Sword (London: Macmillan, 1991) pp. 18–20.
41 Erickson, *The Soviet High Command*, p. 537.
42 *Sovetsko–finliandskaia voina 1939–1940 gg. na more*, Chast' I, Kniga I pp. 51–2.
43. A. Rei, *The Drama of the Baltic Peoples* (Stockholm: Kirjastus Valoa Eesti, 1970), pp. 259–60.
44 Dallin, *Soviet Russia's Foreign Policy* (New Haven: Yale University Press, 1942) p. 82. See also M.I. Semiryaga, *Tainy stalinskoi diplomatii, 1939–1940* (Moscow: Vysshaia shkola, 1992) p. 213, and *Sovetsko–finliandskaia voina 1939–1940 gg. na more*, Chast' I, Kniga I, pp. 49–50.
45 Rei, *The Drama of the Baltic Peoples*, pp. 264–5. Comment about testimony describing the events surrounding the staged sinking of the *Metallist* and other border provocations to the US Senate in 1954. A. Oras in *Baltic Eclipse* (London: Gollancz, 1948) p. 27, claims that the *Metallist* was seen safe in Paldiski harbour a few months after this incident. This conflicts with testimony collected by the *Wehrmacht* during the Great Patriotic War from

a crew member of the Soviet submarine *Shch-303* who recalled that his submarine received the combat order to sink the *Metallist* but that its torpedoes missed their target and the *Metallist* had to be sunk by a Soviet torpedo boat. See Semiryaga, *Tainy stalinskoi diplomatii*, p. 213.

46 Rei, *The Drama of the Baltic Peoples*, pp. 266–9, Mannerheim, *The Memoirs of Marshal Mannerheim*, p. 307, and Dallin, *Soviet Russia's Foreign Policy*, pp. 89–90. Dallin questions Stalin's motives for transfering Vilnius back to Lithuania and speculates that it may have been a result of negotiations with Ribbentrop a few days earlier. Rei attributes Stalin's actions to an egotistical impulse. There is also an historical precedent for this transfer; in the summer of 1920 the Red Army liberated Vilnius from the retreating Poles and gave it to Lithuania. See Fiddick, *Russia's Retreat from Poland, 1920*, p. 126.

47 New documentation concerning the Red Army's investiture of the Baltic States has been published in the collection entitled *Polpredi soobshchaiut Sbornik dokumentov ob otnosheniiakh SSSR s Latviei, Litvoi, i Estoniei, avgust 1939g.–avgust 1940g.* (Moscow: Mezhdunarodnye otnosheniia, 1990).

48 Zonin, *Admiral L.M. Galler*, p. 309. See also Rei, *The Drama of the Baltic Peoples*, p. 266.

49 *Sovetsko–finliandskaia voina 1939–1940 gg. na more*, Chast' I, Kniga I, p. 53, and Dallin, *Soviet Russia's Foreign Policy*, p. 85. Dallin states that eleven boats of the Baltic Fleet arrived in Tallinn harbour on October 15. The French military attaché in Helsinki interpreted the Baltic Fleet's arrival in Tallinn in a different way:

> The arrival of the Soviet squadron at Tallinn on October 15 was a demonstration directed against Finland in response to that country's mobilization. The squadron received the order to sail from Kronstadt on Saturday, October 14, after Mr. Paasikivi, the Finnish envoy, had left Moscow. At 0825 hours on October 15 it [the squadron] sailed south of Hogland Island (Suursaari) and then the cruiser Kirov and four C-type escorts sailed directly to Tallin[sic] while the OR-type battleship and the torpedo-boats Engels and Artem approached the Finnish coast, close to the light boat Kaladagrad, and three G-type torpedo boats sailed close to the Finnish light house at Söderskär. The Estonian authorities did not know of the Soviet squadron's imminent arrival until two hours after they had entered the roadstead.

> See S.H.A.T., 7N 2790 Dossier 2 'Rapports d'Attaché Militaire en Finlande'.

50 S.A. Zonin, *Admiral L.M. Galler: zhizn i flotovodcheskaia deiatelnost'* (Moscow: Voenizdat, 1991) p. 310. See also *Sovetsko–finliandskaia voina 1939–1940 gg. na more*, Chast' I, Kniga I, pp. 40, 54.

51 *Sovetsko–finliandskaia voina 1939–1940 gg. na more*, Chast' I, Kniga I, pp. 40–3.

52 Erickson, *The Soviet High Command*, p. 474. Zonin, *Admiral L.M. Galler*, pp. 291, 298. According to Galler's recently published memoirs, in December 1938 Isakov requested and obtained permission from Zhdanov to look into the possibility of buying the US Navy battleships *Washington* and *North Carolina* during a visit to the United States in the Spring of 1939.

53 *Sovetsko–finliandskaia voina 1939–1940 gg. na more*, Chast' I, Kniga I, pp. 7–17, and Zonin, *Admiral L.M. Galler*, p. 311.

54 This rationale is criticized by Jakobson as a cliché of Russian strategic thinking. See Jakobson, *Finland Survived*, pp. 14–17. The British Foreign Office held a different opinion: 'If Bormarsund [Mariehamn], Reval [Tallinn] and Libau [Leipaja] were in the hands of a single naval power or confederation of States, they would appear to constitute one of those triangles to which naval strategists attach such importance, and would dominate the whole of the Baltic.' See *The Åland Islands*, p. 38.

55 *Sovetsko–finliandskaia voina 1939–1940 gg. na more*, Chast' I, Kniga I, pp. 17, 26–7. See also *Voenno-vozdushnye sily Rumanii, Finliandii, Estonii, Latvii, Litvy, Shvetsii* (Moscow: Izdanie Razvedyvatel'nogo Upravleniia RKKA, 1938), p. 63. In a lecture to the faculty and students of the Frunze Military Academy on 26 June 1940, Meretskov claimed that Finland had built and equipped 150 airfields to receive airplanes from foreign airforces. See TsGASA, fond 34980, opis' 14, delo 6, l.1.

56 AVP Rossiia, Fond 0135, opis' 22, 1939, delo 4, ll. 13–15, 'Welcome to Emmissary from Finland, Mr. Ir'e Koskinen, 11 September, 1939'.
57 Tanner, *The Winter War*, p. 6. In fact, the Leningrad Military District began to reinforce Red Army units stationed on the Soviet–Finnish border on the evening of 16–17 September and was under Voroshilov's strict orders not to reveal their presence to the Finns.
58 AVP Rossiia, Fond 0135, opis' 22, 1939, delo 11, ll. 14–16, 'Finnish reactions to the Soviet–German Pact and Molotov's Speech, sent by Derevianskii and received at NKID, 16 September, 1939'. See also C. Roberts, 'Prelude to Catastrophe: Soviet Security Policy between the World Wars', PhD dissertation, Columbia University, 1992, p. 496.
59 D. Volkogonov, *Stalin. Triumph and Tragedy* (London: Weidenfeld & Nicolson, 1991), p. 364.
60 Tanner, *The Winter War*, p. 21. See also Zonin, *Admiral L.M. Galler*, p. 312.
61 During the Soviet–Finnish negotiations the Soviet Ministry of Foreign Affairs was also negotiating with Turkish government for a similar mutual-assistance pact. See Mannerheim, *The Memoirs of Marshal Mannerheim*, p. 316–17, and Dallin, *Soviet Russia's Foreign Policy, 1939–1942*, pp. 107–10, for a more detailed discussion of the Soviet–Turkish negotiations.
62 Jakobson, *Finland Survived*, p. 106.
63 Erkko's minimum concession greatly resembled Litvinov's maximum concession made the previous Spring. Erkko must have assumed that it still represented the Soviet government's bottom line for negotiations.
64 Jakobson, *Finland Survived*, p. 109, and Tanner, *The Winter War*, pp. 22–4.
65 Tanner, *The Winter War*, p. 25. See also Jakobson, *Finland Survived*, p. 116.
66 Tanner, *The Winter War*, p. 28.
67 Ibid., p. 30.
68 Ibid., p. 31.
69 Jakobson, *Finland Survived*, p. 123.
70 Tanner, *The Winter War*, p. 33.
71 Jakobson, *Finland Survived*, p. 121–2.
72 Tanner, *The Winter War*, pp. 33–4.
73 A.M. Noskov, *Krasnaia Zvezda*, 30 November 1989, cited in Roberts, 'Prelude to Catastrophe: Soviet Security Policy between the World Wars', p. 497. Stalin may have been equally influenced by a report from Voroshilov which stated that 'Most of the Finnish equipment consists of pre-war models of the old tsarist army ... The mood of their reservists is depressed ... The working masses of Finland ... are threatening to mete out justice on those who pursue a policy hostile to the Soviet Union'. See D. Volkogonov, 'Kliment Yefremovich Voroshilov', in *Stalin's Generals*, p. 316. For comments about Stalin's appreciation of the Red Army's reception in Poland during the 'liberation march' in September 1939, see Volkogonov, 'The Drama of the Decisions of 1939', *Soviet Studies in History*, Vol. 29, No. 3, Winter 1990–1991, p. 32.
74 K. Simonov, 'Glazami cheloveka moego pokoleniia: Besedy s marshalom sovetskogo soiuza A. M. Vasilevskim', *Znamia*, No. 5, 1988, p. 79.
75 G. A. Kumanev, 'Chto my znaem ob "zimnei voine"', *Sovetskaia Rossiia*, 10 March 1990. See also M. Semiryaga, 'Nenuzhnaia voina', *Arkhivy raskryvaiut tainy* (Moscow, 1991), p. 126.
76 Kennan, *Russia Leaves the War*, pp. 75–6. Kennan defines this as a 'diplomacy designed not to promote freely accepted and mutually profitable agreement as between governments, but rather to embarrass other governments and stir up opposition among their own people'. This policy found its first expression in Lenin's 'Decree on Peace' announced to the world on 8 November 1917. According to Semiryaga (*Tainy stalinskoi diplomatii*, p. 197) on 10 November the General Staff reported to Voroshilov that 'the working masses and poorest sector of the peasantry are showing latent dissatisfaction with the policies of the government and that they are demanding improved relations with the USSR and threaten violence against those who conduct policies harmful for the Soviet Union ...' During an interview with A. Kollontai, the Soviet ambassador to Sweden, Molotov admitted that the Soviet

government had begun planning for a war with Finland and instructed Kollontai to discourage Sweden and other Scandinavian countries from aiding Finland. See A. Kollontai, 'The Seven Shots in the Winter of 1939', *International Affairs*, January 1990, pp. 185–6.

77 Jakobson, *Finland Survived*, p. 135. See also M.I. Semiryaga, *Tainy stalinskoi diplomatii*, p. 152, and Mannerheim, *The Memoirs of Marshal Mannerheim*, p. 318.

78 Jakobson, *Finland Survived*, p. 131.

79 G.L. Rozanov, *Stalin/Gitler, 1939–1941* (Moscow: 1991) p. 134.

80 Lt. General Raimo Kheiskanen, 'Vliiannie informatsii finskoi voennoi razvedki i ee otsenok na priniatie finliandiei reshenii v khode vtoroi mirovoi voiny', paper given to the XIII International Colloquium on Military History, Helsinki, 1988, p. 8.

81 Jakobson, *Finland Survived*, p. 135.

82 Tanner, *The Winter War*, p. 68. Erkko's response to Stalin's concessions was to instruct his delegation to remain firm in its refusal of Soviet proposals. See Jakobson, *Finland Survived*, p. 136.

83 AVP Rossiia, fond 0135, opis' 22, papka 145, delo 1, ll. 22–23, 'To the Deputy Peoples' Commissar, comrade V.G. Dekanosov, from the Charge d'Affairs in Finland, Eliseev, November 12, 1939'.

84 T. Vihavainen, 'The Soviet Decision for War Against Finland, November 1939: A Comment', *Soviet Studies*, Vol. XXXIX, No. 2, April 1987, p. 315. For a more extended discussion on the ideological justification for war see C.D. Jones, 'Just Wars and Limited Wars: Restraints on the Use of the Soviet Armed Forces', *World Politics*, Vol. XXVIII, October 1975, No. 1, pp. 44–68.

85 A.G. Dongarev, 'Predliavliamcia li finliandii ul'timatum?' *Voenno–istoricheskii zhurnal*, No. 3, 1990, p. 45.

86 Spring, 'The Soviet Decision for War Against Finland, 30 November 1939', p. 217, and Kumanev, 'Chto my znaem of "Zimnei voine"'. See also Semiryaga, 'Nenuzhnaia voina', p. 120.

87 Dongarev, 'Predliavliamcia li finliandii ul'timatum?' p. 43, See also N.N. Voronov, *Na sluzhbe voennoi* (Moscow: Voenizdat, 1963) p. 134.

88 Kumanev, 'Chto my znaem of "zimnei voine"', and *Sovetsko–finliandskaia voina 1939–1940 gg. na more*, Chast' I, Kniga I, p. 59. See also *Konflikt. Komplekt dokumetov o Sovetsko–finliandskoi voine (1939–1940 gg.)* compiled by L.V. Dvoinykh and N.E. Eliseeva (Minneapolis: 1992), Doc. No. 4, 'Prikaz voiskam 7 armii o vydvizhenii chastei k granitse s Finliandiei, 22 noiabria 1939 g.'. In his speech to the students of the General Staff Academy in June 1940 Meretskov claimed that the main strike army was originally assigned to the 8th Army on the assumption that it would by-pass the Mannerheim Line on the north flank, and that for various reasons this mission was re-assigned to the 7th Army. See TsGASA, fond 34980, opis' 14, delo 6, 'General Meretskov's lecture to the students of the General Staff Academy on the lessons of the war with Finland, 26 June, 1940', l.17.

89 *Konflikt*, Document No. 4.

90 *Sovetsko–finliandskaia voina 1939–1940 gg. na more*, Chast' I, Kniga I, p. 59.

91 Ibid., pp. 59–62.

92 Ibid., p. 62.

93 Ibid., pp. 63–4. The Soviet Baltic Fleet had begun to build its own VNOS system in September 1939 but it was not completed by the time the Soviet–Finnish War broke out on 30 November.

94 Ibid., pp. 57–61.

95 Ibid., p. 60.

96 Tanner, *The Winter War*, p. 86

97 Ibid., p. 88. See also Dongarev, 'Predliavliamcia li finliandii ul'timatum?' p. 45.

98 Meretskov, *Na sluzhbe narodu*, pp. 181–2. For comments about Voronov's conversation with Kulik and Mekhlis at LMD HQ before the offensive, see Voronov, *Na sluzhbe voennoi*, p. 136. Dr Spring rightly emphasizes the existence of a disagreement between military specialists, such as Voronov, and the 'political generals', such as Kulik and Mekhlis, over

the Red Army's readiness for combat and the likely duration of the conflict. However it is difficult to believe that Stalin took advantage of this disagreement to keep negotiations open to the Finns even after the Mainila incident. See Spring, 'The Soviet Decision for War Against Finland, 30 November, 1939', p. 215.

99 *Sovetsko–finliandskaia voina 1939–1940 gg. na more*, Chast' I, Kniga I, p. 67. Tributs wanted to send a detachment of submarines to patrol the Gulf of Bothnia but Meretskov postponed the detachment's departure, citing the lack of accurate navigation maps for safe sailing, but probably motivated by the need to gauge the Swedish Navy's response.

100 Ibid., Chast' II, pp. 20–1.

101 Ibid., p. 19.

102 Ibid., p. 20.

103 *BBC Monitoring Service Reports. Daily Digest of Foreign Broadcasts*, Reports from 18 November 1939 to 7 December 1939. Moscow (Russia) LW: For Russia in Russian. 03.50 GMT 30.11.39.

104 The text of this speech was published in *Izvestiia*, 30 November 1939.

105 *Konflikt*, Doc. No. 16, 'Prikaz voiskam Leningradskogo voennogo okruga o perekhode sovetsko–finskoi granitsy v sviazi s nachalom voennykh deistvii, 30 noiabria 1939 g.'.

2

THE RED ARMY ATTACKS
FINLAND

Since the peace treaty of Tartu in 1920 the Finnish General Staff had regarded
the Soviet Union as the single greatest threat to Finland's security and
assumed that, in the event of war, the Red Army would concentrate the main
force of its offensive on the Karelian Isthmus while simultaneously conducting
an outflanking manoeuvre along the north shore of Lake Ladoga (see Figure
2.1).[1]

There were several factors which contributed to this assumption. The first
was that the Karelian Isthmus lay directly adjacent to Leningrad, and any
territory seized by the Red Army on the Isthmus would greatly contribute to
improving that city's defence. The second factor was that the Isthmus was
easily traversed by road and rail and provided the shortest route into the
heartland of Finland. The Finnish General Staff dismissed any serious threat
to the rest of the Finnish–Soviet border north from Lake Ladoga to the
Rybachii Peninsula because the terrain was densely forested and there were
few roads or population centres which could support a mechanized army.[2]

In accordance with this threat assessment the Finnish army had built a series
of permanent field fortifications, known informally as the 'Mannerheim Line',
across the width of the Karelian Isthmus.(see Figure 2.2) These fortifications
were not as extensive as those on the Maginot or Siegfried Lines due to a lack
of government funding for defence programmes in the years leading up to
1939 but the fortifications were, none the less, extremely resilient because
they were designed for use with the tactical doctrine of 'defence in depth'
developed by the German army.[3] The first component of the Mannerheim
Line was the 'obstacle zone'. Extending several kilometres deep from the
border, the obstacle zone was characterized by scattered mine fields and
machine gun nests manned by Finnish cover units. Its main purpose was to
delay the Red Army for as long as possible while the field army completed its
deployment on the isthmus.[4] Immediately behind the obstacle zone lay the
'main defensive zone', a discontinuous series of concrete fortifications

The Soviet Invasion of Finland, 1939–40

FIGURE 2.1
DISTRIBUTION OF RED ARMY FORCES ALONG THE
SOVIET–FINNISH BORDER, 30 NOVEMBER 1939 TO 13 MARCH 1940

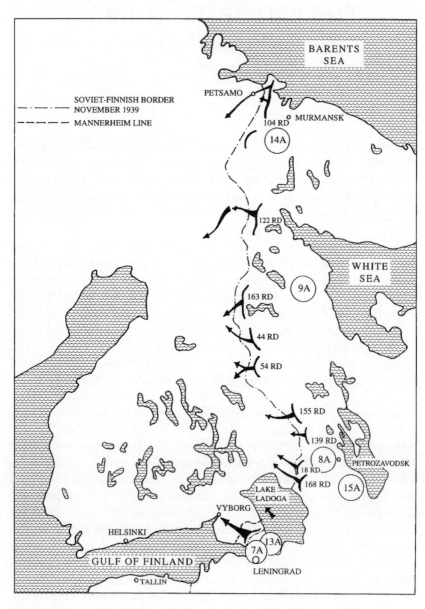

Adapted from *Istoriia Ordena Lenina Leningradskogo Voennogo Okruga*, Moscow, 1988.

36

FIGURE 2.2

DEPLOYMENT OF FINNISH ARMY AND RED ARMY FORCES ON THE KARELIAN ISTHMUS, 30 NOVEMBER 1939

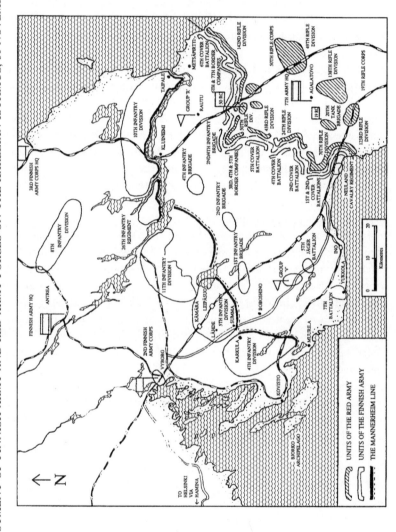

(otherwise known as DOTs, or *dolgovremennye ognevye tochki* – permanent fire points), machine gun nests, anti-tank traps and anti-personnel barriers of various types interconnected by a system of trenches located in defiles between lakes and swamps or on high ground overlooking major roads and railways.[5] This main defensive zone stretched 70 kilometres from the fortress at Taipale on the east coast of the Karelian Isthmus to the complex of fortresses at Muurila and Saarenpää on the west coast, with clusters of fortifications along the north shore of Vuoksi River and along the Vyborg Highway at Summa (Khotinen) and Karhula. Between the main defensive zone and Vyborg lay another two, but less well fortified zones: the 'second defensive zone' which was made up of approximately 40 DOTs scattered along a line from Vuoksi River to the town of Kaislakhti on Vyborg Bay and the 'rear defensive zone' on the outskirts of Vyborg which consisted of an additional 18 DOTs. These four layers of defensive fortifications were manned by six Finnish infantry divisions organized into the II and III Army Corps and trained according to the defensive tactics outlined by the German field manual *Basic Rules for Conducting Positional Warfare*, compiled in the 1920s on the basis of tactics developed during the First World War.[6]

In order to respond to additional threats from the Red Army along the north shore of Lake Ladoga the Finnish General Staff organized the remaining two infantry divisions into the IV Army Corps and stationed this new army in the vicinity of Sortavala. A few independent companies and battalions were assigned to cover the forest roads at Kuhmo, Salla and Petsamo on the chance that the Red Army might attempt to cut road and rail communications with Sweden and the West. These troops had been trained to use special *motti*, or guerrilla tactics for attacking the flanks and rear of road-bound mechanized columns.[7]

At the end of November 1939 the Finnish army could count on a few positive assets which enhanced its strategic position. Due to the call-up of forces in response to the opening of diplomatic negotiations in early October the field army and cover units were fully mobilized and concentrated on the border, thus denying the Red Army the advantage of strategic surprise. The approaching winter also played into the Finns' hands because the shorter days and increasingly inhospitable weather compromised the missions of the Soviet airforce and inhibited the mobility of mechanized units and the infantry. The least quantifiable, but perhaps the most important factor in Finland's favour was that its soldiers, regardless of their class background, were motivated by the conviction that they were protecting the nation from an age-old enemy. However, other factors greatly hindered the Finnish army's strategic position. Finland's population was very small in comparison with that of the Soviet

Union and for this reason its army lacked adequate reserves of manpower to hold off an invasion indefinitely. Tight budget constraints during the inter-war years had prevented the Finnish army from developing a strong arms industry or building up adequate stockpiles of ammunition and arming itself with anti-tank and anti-aircraft weapons and heavy artillery. Ultimately, the war in Europe meant that Finland's traditional allies were unable to aid Finland with arms supplies and troops which it desperately needed to fight against a Red Army that was free to concentrate the bulk of its forces on the Soviet–Finnish border.[8]

Meanwhile, on the other side of the border, the Red Army was hastily concluding preparations for its imminent offensive. During the previous month Meretskov had deployed four armies along a 1000 kilometre-long front stretching from the Karelian Isthmus to the Rybachii Peninsula: an invasion force which numbered 450,000 men and included 23 rifle divisions, 2000 tanks and 1000 aircraft. This represented approximately one quarter of the Red Army's entire active Order of Battle for 1939, significantly more than the figure of 12 divisions which the Finnish General Staff had used to form the basis for its threat evaluations throughout the 1930s.[9] On the Karelian Isthmus the 7th Army alone consisted of 12 rifle divisions, one mechanized corps, three tank brigades and 12 artillery regiments: approximately 200,000 men and 1,500 tanks representing 43 per cent of the Leningrad Military District's existing forces. However, Meretskov's strategic reserve had not yet been fully concentrated: only four out of nine first-echelon divisions were ready for combat on 30 November due to mobilization delays and the unexpectedly early date set for the invasion.[10]

Likewise, the Leningrad Military District's deployment of three armies north of Lake Ladoga greatly exceeded the Finns' operational calculations. Since the beginning of the year Meretskov had supervised the construction of supply depots and additional road and rail transport along the Leningrad–Murmansk railroad in order to facilitate the deployment of entire armies in this largely uninhabited region.[11] By the end of November, the 8th Army, under the command of Corps Commander I. Khabarov, had deployed six rifle divisions and two tank brigades in the vicinity of Petrozavodsk. Khabarov's army totalled 130,000 men and 400 tanks, or 26 per cent of the Leningrad Military District's forces. Further to the north, the 9th Army, under the command of Corps Commander M. Dukhanov, had deployed five rifle divisions in three separate columns between Reboly and Kandalaksha, and the 14th Army, under the command of Division Commander V. Frolov, had deployed three rifle divisions opposite the border from Petsamo. Between them the 9th and 14th Armies consisted of 140,000 men and 150 tanks, or 31 per cent of the Leningrad Military District's total.[12] All in all, the Leningrad Military District command enjoyed a material superiority over the Finnish army by 3 to 1 in manpower, 80 to 1 in tanks, 5 to 1 in artillery of all types and 5.5 to 1 in aircraft.[13] These were statistics which far exceeded the Finnish General Staff's most pessimistic assessments. However, there were less obvious socio-political factors at large in Soviet society which off-set the Red Army's numerical advantages over the Finns. The source of these factors originated in the organizational ideology of the Bolshevik Party.

During the Bolshevik Party's struggle against the tsarist autocracy and other revolutionary parties in Russia at the turn of the century, Lenin sought to manipulate consensus within the party leadership by appealing to the concept of 'democratic centralism', whereby the leadership would reach a unanimous decision on the basis of political objectives and detailed reports on the local political situation from party activists. The object of this organizational principle, best explained by the founder of the Italian Communist Party, A. Gramsci, was to institutionalize 'a continuous insertion of elements thrown up from the depths of the rank and file into the solid framework of the leadership apparatus which ensures continuity [of policy] and the regular accumulation of experience'.[14] Lenin referred to this vertical flow of strategic directives and initiative of party activists as *edinonachale*, a concept which had a corollary in military affairs in the person of the supreme commander responsible for quickly reaching strategic decisions on the basis of personal experience and formal abstract knowledge.[15] Once in power, the Bolshevik Party was transformed into a highly regimented organization which placed increasing value on 'revolutionary discipline' – the subjugation of the individual Party member's will to the unity of the Party. Stalin compounded this process by gradually appropriating the authority to form political decisions along the lines of military *edinonachale*. The effect of this shift from 'democratic centralism' to 'military centralism' on the internal functions of the party and the state was the vertical compartmentalization of communication, the discouragement of 'horizontal' communication between different organizations within the party and a reduction in the frequency of public inter-party debates (often referred to as the 'cult of secrecy').[16]

In 1934 Stalin began to increase the numerical size of the Red Army and introduced a series of organizational reforms to transform it from a mixed territorial-cadre army to a regular cadre army, ostensibly in response to Japanese military incursions in the Far East and German rearmament in the West, but also as a bid to consolidate his own political power.[17] The primary goal was to centralize the Red Army's command hierarchy. Stalin abolished the collegiate Military Revolutionary Soviet (*Revvoensovet*) in favour of a

People's Commissariat for Defence under the direction of Marshal K. Voroshilov, a zealous administrator and loyal colleague of Stalin since the Civil War when they had both served in the First Cavalry Army. A year later Stalin re-established the General Staff under Yegorov.

The next step was to homogenize the Red Army's command corps. Tension had always existed between those political and military personalities such as Stalin and his subordinates Voroshilov, Shchadenko, Budennyi, Kulik and Mekhlis who laid claim to the formulation of security policy on the basis of their revolutionary ardour and heroism during the Civil War, and the military professionals such as Tukhachevskii, Yakir, Uborevich, Kork, and Eideman among others, who sought to create a modern mechanized army manned by a highly educated and technically competent command corps. When the time was ripe Stalin responded to the potential challenge of this alternative authority by destroying it physically. In June 1937 the party newspaper *Pravda* announced that Tukhachevskii and a number of his colleagues had been tried and executed on charges of treason. This event inaugurated a wave of repression which only began to subside in September 1938 after 36,761 army commanders and some 3,000 naval commanders had been dismissed, shot or imprisoned.[18] In their places, younger, less experienced and consequently more politically pliant personnel were appointed. Stalin consolidated the homogenizing effect of the purges by reintroducing the so-called principle of 'collective' command. In January and March 1938 the Main Military and Naval Soviets were created under the chairmanship of Voroshilov and Zhdanov respectively, and military soviets consisting of the commander, a military commissar and representatives from the regional party and NKVD organizations were created in field formations down to divisional level. Far from being forums for debate and the pooling of professional expertise, these soviets served to further strengthen political *edinonachale* in the Red Army and compromised the field commander's authority. These policies destroyed many years of accumulated knowledge and experience which greatly hindered the Red Army's ability to wage war successfully.

Traditional concepts of military command had been in a state of flux since the second half of the nineteenth century and first quarter of the twentieth century when the tremendous growth in the physical and spatial dimensions of the modern European armies had introduced centrifugal tendencies over the commander's control of the battlefield. The Russian Imperial General Staff's responses to this dilemma, among other things, was to develop a 'unified military doctrine', or sociology of military knowledge.[19] This project was immediately revived and expanded by the Red Army's military specialists after the October Revolution and the termination of the Civil War. The first effort to define the parameters of Soviet military doctrine was made by Frunze, Tukhachevskii and others who sought to legitimize the Soviet Republic's use of armed force by concocting a military-political doctrine on the basis of dialectical materialism and the writings of Marx, Engels and Lenin.[20] An additional dimension in the Red Army's professionalization was the formulation of an organizational ideology. This ideology was most concisely defined in a treatise entitled *Tekhnika shtabnoi sluzhby. Operativnaia sluzhba voiskovykh shtabov (v voennoe vremia)*, published in 1924 by N. Varfolomeev, a lecturer in strategy and operational art at the Red Army Academy. Varfolomeev referred to the 'scientific' management theories of F.W. Taylor and H. Fayol to explain the principles of leadership, or 'troop control', in terms of a balance between the creative decision of the supreme commander (analogous to Lenin's political *edinonachale*, but in the form of the 'conceptual unity of command') and the translation of that decision into legally defined organizational procedures by the operational staff, itself organized according to the principle of the 'division of labour'.[21] By the end of the 1920s, Tukhachevskii and fellow military specialists at the Main Commission for Manuals had completely rewritten the Red Army's organizational legislation and field regulations to reflect the new military-political doctrine and organizational ideology.

The most immediate dimension of Soviet military doctrine was combined arms tactics. Tukhachevskii and fellow military specialists had experienced at hand the growing significance of increased firepower and logistics during the First World War and the civil wars. On the basis of this experience Tukhachevskii developed the theory of 'Deep Battle' which he presented to the Military Revolutionary Soviet in 1933 and which became recognized as official doctrine in the *Vremennyi Polevoi Ustav RKKA 1936* (PU–36).[22] Based on an organizational ideology which balanced the principle of *edinonachale* with *vzaimodeistvie*, or 'interaction' between units by means of horizontal communication links and field briefings, Deep Battle envisioned the combined use of infantry, aviation, tanks and artillery in simultaneous frontal and outflanking attacks against an opposing army's tactical depth.[23] The assault itself was conducted by infantry units in close co-ordination with tanks and independent tank formations while artillery suppressed the enemy's fire systems and aerial bombardment paralysed enemy command functions and logistic links, thus isolating the enemy's reserves for piecemeal destruction. In response to the Red Army's modernization programme in the early to mid-1930s Tukhachevskii updated the field regulations and expanded the spatial and organizational scale of Deep Battle to create the basis for what later became known as the 'theory of Deep Operations'.[24]

Even after Tukhachevskii's execution in 1937 the General Staff continued to subscribe to the theory of Deep Battle and responded to combat experience in the Spanish Civil War and clashes with the Japanese *Kwangtung* Army at Lake Khasan and Khalkhin-Gol River by revising the field regulations in the autumn of 1939 to reflect increases in the density of firepower, deep echeloning of formations, and the rotation of units between the front and the reserve.[25] But formal recognition of the existing doctrine was not sufficient to assure operational flexibility and co-ordination in the heat of battle. The Red Army needed a command corps which was both knowledgeable and proficient in the ways of modern warfare as well as an organizational ideology which fostered local *edinonachale* and *vzaimodeistvie*. Stalin's imposition of his political authority had wiped out all these qualities.

On the occasion of the Supreme Soviet's unanimous ratification of the Soviet–German non-aggression pact on 31 August 1939 Voroshilov sub-mitted a new 'Law on Universal Military Duty' and announced to the delegates assembled in the Supreme Soviet that the military reforms over the previous five years had succeeded in unifying the Soviet people into a strong workers' front, tripling the size of the armed forces while simultaneously transforming it into a regular cadre army armed with technologically advanced weapons. However, in Voroshilov's opinion these reforms were not enough:

> Today's army, if I may put it this way, represents a *kombinat* which is complex and densely packed with multifarious complex mechanisms and weaponry. Neither an illiterate nor even a well educated person can nowadays effectively exercise even the functions of a simple communications operator without having undergone basic training, let alone [fulfil the responsibilities of] the junior officer corps.[26]

Voroshilov announced that he was going to lengthen the training period for junior commanders to three years.

Although this legislation appeared to offer the Red Army a desperately needed opportunity to build up the combat competence of its command corps there was little time left in which to do so. The Red Army's invasion of Poland less than three weeks later demonstrated to the Soviet high command that troop control in the field armies was very slack. When the invasion was completed the General Staff's regulation commission reviewed the recent combat experience and adopted the following principle:

> The greater the density of battle order and the greater diversity and numbers of forces, the more exact must be the battle plans and the more centralized must be the control.[27]

Combined arms staffs were now instructed to strengthen troop control through the use of *nastavlenii*,[28] orienteering tables and maps, and artillery fire plans which all had to be verified by political commissars in higher staffs. Such a highly centralized hierarchy staffed by an inadequately trained and inexperienced officer corps in command of an enormous influx of raw recruits was, at best, only capable of the most rigid operational and tactical manoeuvres. At worst, it would disintegrate into *shaikazakidatel'stvo*, or 'mob tactics'.[29]

I

At 06h50 on the morning of 30 November, the Leningrad Military District under Meretskov's command began its systematic artillery and aerial bombardment of targets in Finland without issuing a formal declaration of war. When the artillery barrage lifted at 08h00 Meretskov's four armies, poised at key road-heads along the Soviet–Finnish border from the Karelian Isthmus to the Rybachii Peninsula, began their offensives into Finnish territory.

On the Karelian Isthmus the offensive of Yakovlev's 7th Army was divided between two corps, the 50th Rifle Corps under the command of Division Commander F. Gorolenko and located on the eastern side of the Isthmus, and the 19th Rifle Corps under the command of Division Commander F. Starikov located on the western side of the Isthmus. Gorolenko's corps launched its attack in the region between the town of Lipola and the shore of Lake Ladoga and immediately encountered resistance from Finnish cover groups, anti-tank obstacles and minefields which significantly slowed its progress.[30] On the western side of the Isthmus, Starikov's 70th Rifle Division, under the command of Division Commander M. Kirponos, launched its attack along the railroad tracks from Sestroretsk across the Sestra River to the first rail station at the border town of Terijoki while the 24th and 43rd Rifle Divisions, under the command of Brigade Commander P. Veshchev and V. Kirpichnikov, advanced up the forest roads toward the towns of Kivennapa, Jaarila and beyond. Although the crossing of the Sestra River presented no serious difficulties, the troops of the 70th Rifle Division soon encountered resistance from small groups of retreating Finnish forces which conducted ambushes along the forest roads and left behind minefields and burnt-out settlements. During the remainder of the day, and well into the evening, units of the 70th Rifle Division fought their way from the outskirts of Terijoki to the centre of town, encountering minefields and becoming involved in hand-to-hand combat with Finnish troops over barricades built in the streets. As the morning of 1 December dawned, the last detachment of Finnish defenders, firing on the Red Army troops from the church tower, was finally destroyed.[31] The 70th Rifle Division had fulfilled its first mission but was already well behind schedule.[32]

On the evening of the invasion's first day Yakovlev reviewed the situation reports from his corps commanders and came to the conclusion that their slow progress was due to poor troop control at all levels of command and that regimental commanders had deployed their men and *matériel* according to field regulations formulated for operations in open terrain. The problems posed by inappropriate tactics were the easiest to address. Yakovlev instructed his regimental commanders to limit deployment in extended order to reconnaissance units in the vanguard while the rest of the regiment was to follow in closed order along the roads. However, the situation reports indicated to Yakovlev that the absence of communication between the vanguard and the regimental staff was the real cause for the delay. On the basis of these reports Yakovlev blamed regimental and higher staffs for not organizing the maintenance of battlefield observation points and instructed these staffs to send representatives to the vanguard units and supplement telephone communications with radio. Yakovlev emphasized the importance of tighter troop control by explaining to his subordinates that better communications between battlefield and staffs would permit artillery batteries to fire at individual targets rather than conduct the more ineffective 'quadrant system' of fire, and it would also allow sapper units to clear Finnish minefields more quickly.[33]

Yakovlev's analysis of the situation at the front did not noticeably improve the 7th Army's slow rate of advance. As operations on the Karelian Isthmus continued in early December, the 7th Army's troop control problems were compounded by the discovery of increasing numbers of Finnish minefields. Yakovlev's corps commanders responded to this new problem by organizing more sapper reconnaissance patrols and the Leningrad Military District's newspaper, *Na Strazhe Rodiny*, published articles on how to detect and clear mines. The problem became so acute that Zhdanov, in his capacity as political commissar at the Leningrad Military District headquarters, ordered two engineers from Leningrad to invent and develop a mine detector. However, despite these efforts, the Finnish Army's minefields had already induced their desired demoralizing effect. The 7th Army's rank-and-file were now gripped by a 'phobia of mines' which would require improved reconnaissance tactics and weeks of sapper work to overcome.[34]

A similar lack of success characterized the offensives of Captain Kobyl'skii's Ladoga Flotilla and Division Commander Khabarov's 8th Army to the east and north of the Karelian Isthmus. According to the 'Operational plan' of the Ladoga Flotilla, drawn up by the Ladoga Flotilla staff at

Schlusselburg with the help of staff delegates from the 7th and 8th Armies, the Flotilla's primary mission was to support the flanks of both armies with artillery fire and diversionary landings at Kakisalmi and Sortavala while the 8th Army outflanked the Karelian Isthmus from the east by attacking Finnish defensive forces stationed between Yanis-järvi Lake and the north shore of Lake Ladoga (see Figure 2.3).[35] In order to honour these missions the Flotilla was assigned three battleships from the Baltic Fleet transported through the Stalin Canal to Schlusselburg. Due to the early onset of winter and sub-zero temperatures on 20 November only one of the three battleships, the *Orangenbaum*, was able to join the Flotilla on 29 November. Possessing substantially less naval forces than originally planned, Captain Kobyl'skii chose to restrict his combat missions to only one axis, the support of the 7th Army's flank

FIGURE 2.3

MAP OF LAKE LADOGA AND THE 8TH ARMY'S INVASION OF LADOGA-KARELIA

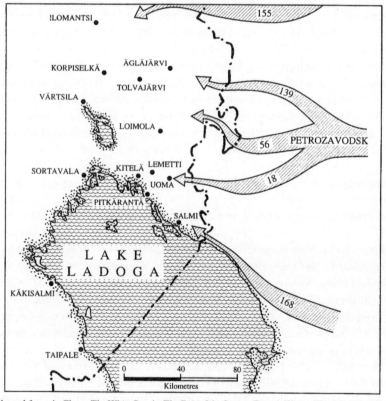

Adapted from A. Chew, *The White Death: The Epic of the Soviet–Finnish Winter War*, Michigan State University Press, 1971.

along the coast from Taipalen Bay to Sortanlakhti. Early on the morning of 30 November Kobyl'skii sent telegrammes to the Leningrad Military District headquarters, the Baltic Fleet headquarters at Kronstadt and the 7th and 8th Army commands, informing them of the change in plan. However, due to poor communications between Schlusselburg and the 8th Army command at Petrozavodsk, the 8th Army's 168th Rifle Division staff was unaware that it would not have naval artillery support until the fourth day of the war.[36]

By evening of 30 November the 1st Detachment of the Ladoga Flotilla, commanded by Captain Trainin and consisting of two cutters (nos. 413 and 414), two minesweepers (nos. 31 and 37) and the battleship *Orangenbaum*, set out for Nikuläsa Bay. When they arrived there early the next morning Trainin sent the two patrol boats further north along the coast to Saunaniemi to make contact with the 142nd Rifle Division headquarters. When these two patrol boats encountered Finnish machine-gun fire from the shore Trainin called in nine Soviet medium-range bombers to knock out the Finnish defenders, but the bombers never located the target area. At 15h05 Trainin ordered the two cutters to conduct a reconnaissance patrol of Taipalen Bay. When these two cutters encountered Finnish artillery fire from a Finnish coastal artillery battery at Jarisevänniemi Point they returned to Nikuläsa where they hit a rock and developed leaks below water-line. The next evening Trainin and his detachment set out to conduct a demonstration artillery barrage against the Finnish battery at Jarisevänniemi Point. During the fight Trainin failed to check the course of the *Orangenbaum* and beached his only battleship on a sandbar outside Taipalen Bay (see Figure 2.4). Although the *Orangenbaum* was not structurally damaged and was eventually re-floated, the rescue operation lasted until the middle of December. In the meantime the 1st Detachment was unable to conduct any more missions.[37]

The 8th Army, under the command of Division Commander I.N. Khabarov, had been stationed at Novgorod before being mobilized to the Petrozavodsk region in late October. By late November it was concentrated at several points along the Finnish border from Vidlitsk on the shores of Lake Ladoga to as far north as the road to Suojärvi.[38] The Leningrad Military District's assignment for the 8th Army's 56th Rifle Corps was to help the 7th Army break through the Mannerheim Line by conducting a strategic encirclement from the east against Finnish fortifications between Yanisjärvi Lake and the north shore of Lake Ladoga before turning to the southwest to threaten the Finnish Army on the Karelian Isthmus. Khabarov's timetable for completing this strategic encirclement was 12 to 15 days. This meant a daily advance of at least 10 kilometres a day by all four divisions under his command. The first day's quota, to be met by the 168th, 18th and 56th

FIGURE 2.4
MAP OF LAKE LADOGA

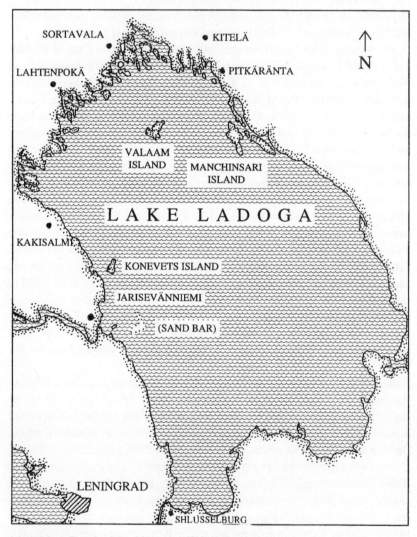

Adapted from *Sovetsko–finliandskaia voina 1939–1940 gg. na more.*

Rifle Divisions, was to take the towns of Salmi, Käsnäselkä and Suojärvi, respectively.[39]

On the morning of 30 November, after a 10 minute artillery barrage, the three divisions of the 56th Rifle Corps began their advance down forest roads into the depths of Finnish territory. Although they did not meet much active opposition, their progress was much slower than expected due to obstacles on the roads such as felled trees, mines, and bridges that had been destroyed by the retreating Finnish covering units (see Figure 2.5). When the 56th Rifle Division reached the Shvia River on the first evening, the division was only half way to its primary objective. The next day's river crossing was conducted with great difficulty and the division immediately encountered fierce resistance from a battalion of Finnish infantry outside Suvilakhti. The 168th Rifle Division met similar resistance outside Salmi while the 18th Rifle Division managed to take Käsnäselkä and proceed up the road to Uoma before it was stopped by a blown bridge at the Uksan-joki River and Finnish guerrilla attacks on its communications.[40]

To the north, the 1st Rifle Corps, consisting of the 139th and 155th Rifle Divisions with the 75th Rifle Division in reserve, was assigned to fill the gap between the 8th and 9th Armies. The 139th Rifle Division was expected to accomplish this and the mission by advancing along the road north of Suojärvi Lake to the town of Korpiselkä, then outflank the Finnish defences at Vartsila and join the 56th Rifle Division in the final offensive against Vyborg. Further north, the 155th Rifle Division was expected to seize the town of Ilomantsi and then turn north to join forces with the 54th Rifle Division of the 9th Army in its drive to reach the Gulf of Bothnia at Oulu. Such divergent missions presented a serious command problem for the commander of the 1st Rifle Corps, Brigade Commander R. Panin, and the missions were further complicated by poor roads and the lack of existing telephone communications. Panin was further hampered by the lack of adequate intelligence information gathered in peacetime. When his divisions crossed the border he was unable to provide them with information about the size of Finnish forces in the area, the nature of their defensive fortifications, or their location.[41]

Nevertheless, when the 139th Rifle Division, under the command of Brigade Commander N. Belaev, crossed the Finnish border on 30 November and proceeded up the forest road to Suojärvi, Finnish border troops were too few and too demoralized to stop them. Suojärvi fell on 2 December and Belaev's troops pursued the retreating Finns to the banks of the Aittojoki River. Here the Finns dug into defensive positions on the west shore and attempted an unsuccessful counter-attack. During the night of 3 December Belaev and his men tried to take the Finnish positions first with a frontal

FIGURE 2.5
THE RED ARMY'S ARTILLERY ON THE MARCH, DECEMBER 1939

Courtesy of TsGASA, fond 34980, opis' 14, delo 195

attack, then with a flanking manoeuvre from the south. On both occasions they were repelled by stubborn rifle and machine-gun fire and only successfully forced the Finns to continue their retreat the next morning. On the basis of this combat experience, Belaev concluded that even his superior numbers could not guarantee success in attacking Finnish defences frontally, and that his attempts to conduct outflanking manoeuvres indicated weaknesses in troop control and tactical training.[42] Even so, the Finnish high command was impressed by Belaev's daring tactics and considered him an able and energetic leader in comparison with his colleagues.[43]

The Leningrad Military District's strategic mission for the 9th and 14th Armies, commanded by Corps Commander M. Dukhanov and Division Commander V. Frolov, respectively, was to seal Finland off from foreign aid by taking the Finnish–Swedish rail junction at Kemi and the arctic port of Petsamo. Dukhanov decided to organize his attack against Kemi by splitting his four divisions, the 44th Motorized Rifle Division and the 54th, 122nd and 163rd Rifle Division, into three columns. The southernmost of these columns was the 54th Rifle Division, commanded by Brigade Commander N. Gusevskii. This was deployed at Revoly with orders to attack the Finnish rail junction at Kuhmo. Gusevskii's regiments encountered resistance from the Finnish 14th Independent Battalion, but managed to advance to within 20 kilometres of Kuhmo during the first few days of the war. Further north at Ukhta, Dukhanov deployed the 163rd Rifle Division under the command of Brigade Commander A. Zelentsev to attack the town of Suomussalmi via a secret road to the Soviet–Finnish border at Juntusvanta which had been built during the previous few months. Zelentsev's division achieved complete tactical surprise and managed to capture Suomussalmi on 3 December with little resistance from the Finns, while the 759th Rifle Regiment attacked up the road at Raate and joined the 163rd Rifle Division on 7 December. The northern most column, Brigade Commander P. Shevtshenko's 122rd Rifle Division, encountered stiff resistance from the Finnish 18th Independent Battalion on the Kandalaksha–Salla road and only managed to capture Salla on 10 December.[44]

At Murmansk the 14th Army and Northern Fleet headquarters received orders to conduct joint operations to seize the port at Petsamo while the Northern Fleet's air reconnaissance and submarines continued their patrols in Varanger Fjord and along the Norwegian coast. The first of the Northern Fleet's missions was to deploy the torpedo boat *Karl Libknekt* to Motka Bay at the western end of the Motov Gulf to provide artillery cover for the 14th Army's attack against the isthmus between the Srednyi and Rybachii Peninsulas. At 04h00 on the morning of 30 November, the commander of the

14th Army radioed the *Karl Libknekt* with orders to begin the artillery barrage at 06h00. However, the commander of the *Karl Libknekt* failed to receive this message and proper communications were re-established only ten minutes before the offensive was due to start. In the waters off the coast of Rybachii Peninsula the torpedo boats *Grosnyi* and *Kuibyshev* were ordered to fire on the Finnish villages of Vaitolakhti and Kervanto while a detachment of minesweepers was sent to patrol the mouth of Petsamo Bay to prevent any enemy boats from escaping. The Finnish Army only had the 10th Independent Covering Troop Company in the area and this unit was forced to abandon Petsamo to the 14th Army without much of a fight.[45] When this mission was completed, the 14th Army continued its offensive down the Arctic Highway towards Rovaniemi, the capital of Lapland. On 3 December the commander of the Northern Fleet, N. Kulakov, landed at Petsamo harbour to supervise the construction of defensive works and choose locations for coastal artillery batteries for protection against potential foreign naval intervention.[46] The Northern Fleet continued its submarine patrols along the Norwegian coast for the rest of the war.

II

At the other end of the Leningrad Military District's operational theatre, the Baltic Fleet command was responsible for monitoring the Swedish navy's response to the Soviet invasion of Finland. Thirty hours before the invasion commenced, two Soviet submarines set out from naval bases recently established at Tallinn to patrol the entrance to Stockholm harbour. A few hours later three more submarines set out to patrol the waters around Gotland Island and the Swedish coast as far south as Karlskrona (see Figure 1.1).[47] The commander of the Baltic Fleet, V. Tributs, had intended to supplement these patrols with a detachment of submarines stationed in the Gulf of Bothnia, but on the eve of the invasion the Leningrad Military District Command ordered him to postpone the detachment's departure.[48] In the early hours of 30 November Tributs received the coded signals '*taran*' and '*fakel*' from the Naval Commissariat in Moscow, ordering him to deploy his surface ships and permitting him to use weapons against Finnish warships and against the Swedish navy if it offered aggression.[49] During the first two days of the war these submarine patrols reported back to Kronstadt that the Swedish navy was not preparing offensive operations but was strengthening its defences outside Stockholm and redeploying in the South Kvarken Straits as well as escorting cargo convoys to Finnish ports.[50] This was good news for the

Soviet high command who had feared the existence of a military alliance between Sweden and Finland. For the time being the Soviet Union had achieved Finland's military isolation.

After patrolling the Swedish coast in the first few hours of the war, the Light Forces Detachment, made up of the cruiser *Kirov* and two torpedo boats, received new orders from Tributs to destroy the Finnish coastal battery on the island of Russarö south-west of Helsinki. During the transmission of orders over the radio, Tributs warned the *Kirov*'s commander about the danger of enemy artillery and submarines but did not warn him about a minefield discovered by a Soviet submarine patrolling the area, nor did he indicate the exact location of the Finnish coastal battery.[51] The *Kirov* and its escort steamed across the Baltic Sea during the early morning of 1 December, alert to the possible presence of enemy submarines and intent to fire on the Finnish coastal battery at sunrise. As the *Kirov* approached the Finnish coastline it sighted a submarine and was about to fire when the submarine identified itself as the *S-1*, a Soviet submarine. The *S-1* was not aware that the war had started, due to a misunderstanding over the meaning of the code-word '*fakel*' received over the radio from Kronstadt the day before, and thus was not as circumspect as it should have been toward engaging warships.[52] Neither the *Kirov* nor the *S-1* knew of each other's activities due to the failure in communications; a state of affairs which not only denied them the advantages of mutual support but which almost resulted in an accidental confrontation. Arriving at Russarö two hours late, the *Kirov* conducted a quadrant barrage against the Finnish coastal battery. The result was a desultory fire-fight between ship and shore with no hits gained on either side. However, during the engagement the *Kirov* unknowingly strayed into the minefield and inexplicably developed a problem with its paravane which forced its commander to call off the operation. Under the escort of the two torpedo boats, the *Kirov* steamed back to port at Liepaja, arriving there on the evening of 2 December.[53]

The Baltic Fleet's second mission was to capture the six Finnish islands in the eastern half of the Gulf of Finland (Seiskari and Lavansaari, Narvi and Someri, Suursaari (Hogland) and Suur-Tiutärsaari Islands) which had been the subject of intense discussion during the diplomatic negotiations in Moscow the previous month. The two islands closest to Kronstadt – Seiskari and Lavansaari Islands – were to be seized by the Special Detachment, based at Luga Bay and commanded by Captain Ramishvili, which consisted of a landing party on the transport ships *Leningrad Sovet* and *Buria* under the escort of the torpedo boats *Karl Marks*, *Engels* and *Volodarskii* with air support from Kronstadt.[54]

Aware that amphibious assaults required a high degree of protection from enemy interference, the Baltic Fleet command at Kronstadt was particularly anxious to secure adequate support for the Special Detachment and even postponed the mission until more reliable reconnaissance confirmed the absence of Finnish troops on the islands. Ironically, when the operation finally began on the morning of 30 November, three hours later than scheduled, the Special Detachment proved to be its own worst enemy. Over-cautiousness combined with a total lack of co-operation between the Detachment's various components led to a series of blunders and near disasters. The first error occurred when a Soviet medium-range bomber, assigned to bomb Seiskari Island, mistook the torpedo boat *Karl Marks* for a Finnish ship and attempted to bomb it. The bomber's mistaken identification was compounded by the crew of both the *Karl Marks* and the *Volodarskii*, who returned fire and reported to Kronstadt that they had been attacked by enemy aircraft. The commanders of the transport ships and the torpedo boats were also afraid of being attacked by Finnish submarines, despite the fact that the shallowness of the water was not conducive to submarine operations. For this reason depth charges were set off every 15 minutes or whenever an unconfirmed sighting of a periscope was made, resulting in a total of 400 depth charges being dropped by the end of the operation that day. When the Special Detachment finally reached the islands and conducted an amphibious assault, the islands were found to be deserted and devoid of mines. The next day's operations against Narvi and Someri met with a similar lack of resistance.[55]

Encouraged by the unexpected ease of these successes and the favourable reports from air reconnaissance, the Baltic Fleet command decided to launch the operation against Suur-Tiutärsaari Island on 1 December without taking time to make appropriate preparations. The result was a series of misunderstandings between the Baltic Fleet command and the Special Detachment which took most of the day to resolve. In the meantime, the Special Detachment's air support flew bombing missions over Suur-Tiutärsaari Island, encountered anti-aircraft fire from a Finnish garrison on the island, and lost one of its medium-range bombers. By the time the Special Detachment reached the island on 2 December, the Finnish garrison had already fled. The amphibious assault against Suursaari Island the next day would have been equally uneventful except that the Special Detachment's air support strafed its own troops on the beach, wounding six soldiers.[56]

The Baltic Fleet command was also responsible for supporting the 7th Army's left flank with artillery fire. At 08h03 on the morning of 30 November, the Northern Fortified Region opened fire against Finnish troop concentrations at Pukhtola Hills and the train station at Terijoki.[57] Thirty minutes later these guns were joined by the Southern Fortified Region's batteries and the artillery on the gunboats *Kronstadt, Krasnaia Gorka* and the *Sestroretsk* stationed off the coast of the Seivaste Peninsula. However, this fire-support was conducted according to the inaccurate 'quadrant' method because no arrangements had been made to provide aerial or naval fire-correction patrols. Artillery support from the Southern Fortified Region and the gunboats had to be lifted in order to avoid firing on the 7th Army's troops as they approached the fortress at Ino, allowing the Finnish Army to continue its opposition there until 6 December. The Baltic Fleet command recognized that this was a serious problem but could do nothing to address it until the second week of the war.[58]

Further out in the Gulf of Finland the Baltic Fleet set up submarine patrols to paralyse all sea communications in the area and attack the Finnish navy if it should appear. However, these patrols were soon brought to a halt by diplomatic complications: the Soviet Embassy was still stranded in Helsinki and had to be evacuated. The Soviet Ministry of Foreign Affairs made arrangements with the German Foreign Ministry for the German cargo ship *Donau* to go to Helsinki on 2 December to pick up the Soviet Embassy's *retinue* and return to Tallinn on 5 December. In the meantime, the submarines patrolling the coast around Helsinki were called back to Kronstadt to avoid complications. After the *Donau* arrived in Tallinn the Baltic Fleet command found that it could not re-establish a constant patrol without basing additional submarines in the newly acquired Estonian ports. A deputy command was established at Paldiski on 5 December and the 23rd Submarine Squadron was transferred there the same day, but continuous surveillance of the Finnish coast was not re-established until after the first week of the war.[59]

The Baltic Fleet's final mission was to use air detachments to bomb strategic and economic targets, such as Finnish battleships, coastal artillery batteries, railroad junctions and airfields along Finland's southern coast. At 10h00 on the first day of the invasion, two flight sections of long-range bombers set out from Kronstadt to search for and bomb any Finnish battleships found along the northern coast between Kotka and Turku. The first section, assigned to the region from Kotka to Helsinki, did not find any battleships and was subjected to heavy anti-aircraft fire immediately outside Helsinki which shot down two of the section's bombers, killing its commander, Captain Bel'skii. The other section, flying along the coast between Helsinki and the Hangö Peninsula, spotted two Finnish battleships anchored off the island of Russarö and attempted to bomb them but failed. The Baltic Fleet command, informed of these results, immediately sent out a squadron of eight long-range bombers commanded by Captain Tokarev to destroy the battleships. This squadron arrived at Russarö two hours later and found that the battleships had long since disappeared. On its way back to Kronstadt the squadron dropped its 600 bombs on Helsinki in contravention of orders.[60] Later that afternoon, the Baltic Fleet command sent out two squadrons of medium-range bombers, under the command of Major Rakov, to destroy naval airfields around Helsinki.[61] These two squadrons managed to destroy 12 airplanes and several hangars before returning home without suffering losses. Thirty-five sorties were flown by the end of the first day of the war but no Finnish battleships were destroyed and two medium-range bombers were lost to Finnish anti-aircraft fire. Unable to pursue the Finnish fleet any further, the Baltic Fleet command turned its attention to destroying Finnish coastal defences at Porvoo, Helsinki and Lovina with negligible results.[62]

III

The first day of the war found the Finnish Prime Minister, A. Kajander, the Foreign Minister Erkko and others in the Finnish government still clinging to the belief that the Soviet Union would not resort to a full-scale invasion. The Finnish Cabinet met that morning to declare a state of war and appoint Marshal Mannerheim as commander-in-chief of the Finnish armed forces but only after the Soviet airforce bombed the centre of Helsinki was action taken to adopt more substantial measures. That evening Kajander tendered his government's resignation at a meeting of the Council of State and on 1 December President Kallio appointed R. Ryti, the governor of the Bank of Finland, as the new prime minister. Ryti retained many of the ministers of the old government but appointed Tanner as Foreign Minister and J. Paasikivi as Minister without portfolio.[63] During the first meeting of the Finnish Cabinet on 2 December, Ryti and his ministers agreed that the primary responsibility of their new government was to seek an armistice with the Soviet Union while simultaneously co-ordinating the war effort. To this end they accepted the United States government's offer to mediate an armistice and also asked the Swedish government to intercede on their behalf, but to no avail. Ryti's Cabinet then asked the Swedish government whether it would be willing to participate in a joint Finnish–Swedish defence of the Åland Islands, hoping in this manner to gain a powerful ally in the war against the Soviet Union. The Swedish government, with the exception of the Foreign Ministry, refused to accept this offer officially but the Swedish navy did intensify its defensive measures in the South Kvarken Straits.[64]

The Finnish government's efforts to re-establish diplomatic contacts with the Soviet Union were in vain. The Soviet government was already making alternative political arrangements to further its strategic interests. As fighting raged on the Karelian Isthmus during the night of 1 December, Radio Moscow announced the creation of the Finnish People's Republic under O. Kuusinen, the exiled leader of the Finnish Communist Party and an executive secretary of the Comintern. Kuusinen appealed to the working class of Finland to support the new government and to join the ranks of the 1st Corps of the Finnish People's Army. Along with other announcements, his communiqué sought to allay fears that the Red Army's intent was to annex Finland to the Soviet Union and reassured his Finnish, international and Soviet audience that: 'The Soviet Union, in following its national policy, does not want to widen its borders at the expense of Finland, it only wants to ally itself to Finland with a mutual assistance treaty.'[65]

Kuusinen travelled from Terijoki to Moscow the next day to conclude a series of contractual agreements including a defence alliance, a trade agreement, and a promise to exchange Finnish territory on the Karelian Isthmus and islands in the Gulf of Finland for Soviet territory in eastern Karelia.[66] Later, the Finnish People's Republic's propaganda campaign emphasized the Soviet Union's desire to reunite the Karelian people with the rest of Finland. In a draft article written for publication in the Soviet press, Kuusinen argued that such a 'socialist nationalist' policy toward the Finnish People's Republic was antithetical to the foreign policy of the imperialist powers and that its manifestation in relations with the Finnish People's Republic was a first in diplomatic history.[67] In fact, the Soviet Union had often used such mechanisms for extending its influence over neighbouring countries. During the Soviet–Polish war of 1920 the Soviet government had tried to support its military offensive against Warsaw by concluding a similar contractual agreement with Julian Markhlevskii's Provisional Revolutionary Soviet of Poland.[68] Similar tactics had been used to overthrow the Menshevik government in Georgia in 1921, and a less extreme variant of the contractual agreement, the bilateral mutual assistance pact, had been forced on the Baltic States the previous autumn.[69]

Adopting the political lessons that had been learned during the Soviet–Polish war, Kuusinen sought to allay fears amongst the Finnish population that the newly created Finnish People's Republic would have a 'soviet' type of government.[70] The communiqué stressed that: 'Such an important question as the core restructuring of the entire social system cannot be decided by one party or even by the working class.'[71] The intended message was that Kuusinen's government would be a parliamentary form of government that would conduct domestic politics in much the same way as its predecessors.

Kuusinen's subsequent actions proved otherwise. After signing agreements in Moscow with Molotov, Kuusinen devoted his attention to the assumption of administrative control over the territories seized by the Red Army.[72] Kuusinen's first priority, as laid out in his 'Project Instructions: How to begin the political and organizational work of communists in the regions liberated from the White Finns', was to establish 'normality' in the occupied territories as quickly as possible to win the co-operation of the residual population:

> Do not forget that the huge majority of the working population will make up their minds about the new government powers, especially how much their representatives, and communists in general, from the very beginning are concerned about the affairs of most interest to the working people.[73]

Activists were to promote this state of 'normality' by distributing food handouts, transporting evacuees back to their homes, taking care of orphan children and the sick, collecting and compiling inventories of discarded property, and organizing a temporary militia force.[74]

As soon as communist activists had established these social welfare services they were to prepare for the first meetings of the Working People's Front in local communities.[75] Although Kuusinen wanted these meetings to be held as soon as possible, he also feared that they were susceptible to political manipulation by 'enemies of the people', such as 'Tannerite agents' and other 'unsuitable political elements,' who might persuade the local community to resist incorporation into the wider political agenda of the Working People's Front. In order to avoid subversion by such agents, activists were instructed to organize local committees of the Communist Party and to call upon the Left Social Democratic workers' societies, trade unions and party organizations of the petty peasantry and small landowners to purge Tannerite agents from their executive organs. When these preparations had been carried out, activists were to invite representatives of each interest group to the first meeting of the Working People's Front. The purpose of the first meeting was to issue a formal statement condemning the Helsinki government, pledge allegiance to the Terijoki government and then elect an executive committee that would delegate self-government obligations to different groups in the community. In the event that Kuusinen's government was eventually installed in Helsinki, these regional executive committees would select candidates for elections in a newly re-constituted Seim.[76]

Kuusinen's government also conducted an agitprop campaign in newly occupied territories by publishing a newspaper entitled *Kansan Varta, (Will of the People)* from the former offices of the newspaper *Karelia* in Terijoki.

The government also organized social events such as public lectures, community dances and films in local communities while simultaneously monitoring the political influence of these propaganda methods.[77] Kuusinen himself was closely linked to the Political Administration of the Leningrad Military District. He proofread many of the propaganda articles printed in the military press, wrote agitational leaflets to be dropped behind enemy lines and monitored interrogations of Finnish POWs to gauge political sentiments in Finland.[78]

The creation and activities of the 1st Corps of the Finnish People's Army also provided insight into the nature of Kuusinen's government. In its radio broadcast on the first day of the war, the Finnish Communist Party called upon communists in Finland and soldiers in Mannerheim's army to join the 1st Corps.[79] During the first days of the invasion, Kuusinen's Minister of Defence, A. Antilla, was present in the immediate rear of the 7th Army giving interviews to Soviet journalists. The Soviet military newspaper *Na Strazhe Rodiny* at this time printed articles about a combat socialist competition between sub-units of the 1st Finnish Corps to be the first to plant the flag of the Finnish People's Republic on the top of the Seim building in Helsinki.[80] Finns who joined the 1st Finnish Corps were either veterans of the Finnish revolution of 1918 who had subsequently emigrated to the Soviet Union or Soviet Karelians who were recruited into the Red Army and then transferred into the corps. Their military oath was similar to that of the Red Army.[81] Kuusinen's new army also incorporated the military institution of 'dual command' between commander and commissar, and the troops received tactical training in the spirit of combat socialist competition.[82]

Not only did the 1st Corps legitimize Kuusinen's government by associating itself with the Red Army's internationalist role but it was also instrumental in maintaining administrative control over the occupied territories. One of the Corps' first reported activities was to help hunt down any enemy troops remaining in Terijoki, then inspect and catalogue habitable houses, clean up mines left by the retreating Finnish Army, re-establish telephone lines to Leningrad and the area around Terijoki, provide militia, and help Narkomtorg representatives reopen food and clothing shops.[83] Later in the war, the military press conducted a propaganda campaign to emphasize that the 1st Finnish Corps was instrumental in preserving the property of the peaceful population in the occupied territories. This was explicitly for protection against Finnish guerrilla raids in the rear of the Red Army. However, the underlying purpose of this campaign may have been to help mitigate the unease among the population about the nationalization and redistribution of property by the popular front committees.[84]

IV

While Molotov was signing agreements with the representatives of the Finnish People's Republic, Voroshilov and Shaposhnikov at the People's Commissariat for Defence and the General Staff were beginning to show concern regarding the slowness of the Leningrad Military District's offensive.[85] On 3 December Meretskov responded to his superiors' admonitions by issuing a general order to the 7th, 8th and 9th Armies to speed up their offensives. Meretskov was particularly worried by the 8th Army's lack of progress, not only because it was failing to divert Finnish forces away from the Karelian Isthmus, but also because it had not fulfilled its mission to cut Finland's land communications with Sweden. Meretskov replaced Khabarov with a more senior and competent commander, Corps Commander V. Kurdiumov, in an attempt to reassure Moscow that the 8th Army's performance would improve.[86] However, this change in command did little to rectify the situation unfolding in Ladoga-Karelia. By 6 December the 56th Rifle Division, travelling down the Suvilakhti–Sortavala road, had stalled in front of Finnish defences at Loimola and the 18th Rifle Division on the Käsnäselkä–Sortavala road was increasingly harried by Finnish guerrilla attacks.[87]

At this time the 7th Army had succeeded in routing the Finnish covering units and was on the verge of expanding its offensive into a breakthrough. On the evening of 6 December, Grendal's 50th Rifle Corps reached the southern shore of the Vuoksen-virta and Suvanto-järvi waterways and one of his vanguard units had even pursued the retreating Finns across the Taipalenjoki River to establish a bridgehead at Koukunniemi (see Figure 2.2).[88] When this news reached 7th Army headquarters at Agalatovo Yakovlev immediately ordered Grendal to concentrate his forces and attack the northern shore. Unfortunately, Grendal and his staff were unable to begin the attack until the next day, and even then their preparations were too hasty to ensure a successful river crossing by so many with so much equipment. The main reason for the delay was that Yakovlev had not given Grendal and his staff sufficient time to organize artillery support; and assemble their troops and explain to them how best to conduct a river crossing. Another reason for Grendal's hesitation was that the river was wide and the opposite shore was controlled by an elaborate system of Finnish DOTs. Furthermore, a successful river crossing was virtually impossible because Grendal's corps possessed only 34 pontoons.[89] To the west, the 19th Rifle Corps' vanguard had stumbled upon six DOTs on the western shore of the Kosen-joki river and had been beaten back with severe losses.[90] The 7th Army had missed its one and only chance to bring its offensive to a rapid and victorious conclusion.

When news reached the General Staff in Moscow that the retreating Finnish Army had managed to escape encirclement and dig in behind their fortifications on the north shore of Taipalen-joki, the chief of the General Staff, Shaposhnikov, issued an order reprimanding Meretskov and Yakovlev for mismanaging the river crossing. Shaposhnikov was particularly annoyed with the behaviour of Yakovlev, who had inexplicably cut his communications with Moscow during the operation:

> You [Yakovlev] are a front commander and do not have the right to leave the command of your army for an entire twenty-four hour period. This is the last time I warn commander Yakovlev about the purposeful negligence of his staff concerning the actions of his own troops ...[91]

The Soviet high command ordered Yakovlev to send a detailed report of his actions for examination. This report generated dramatic reforms in the Red Army's senior command. On 9 December Stalin, Voroshilov, Shaposhnikov and Kuznetsov (with the nominal participation of Molotov) took over direct strategic leadership under the rubric of Stavka (Supreme Command) and demoted Yakovlev to a purely administrative command at the Leningrad Military District headquarters. Meretskov, in turn, took over Yakovlev's field command of the 7th Army.[92]

Meretskov's first responsibility as the new commander of the 7th Army was to reinforce the 19th Rifle Corps with divisions from his army reserve and deploy the 50th Rifle Corps to Perk-järvi in the centre of the Isthmus for a second offensive against Vyborg on 15 December.[93] In the meantime, Division Commander F. Aliabushev's 123rd Rifle Division resumed the attack from Boboshino up the Vyborg Highway towards the rail junction at Kämärä. On 12 December, one of this division's vanguard regiments reached the northern edge of 'Tooth' Grove under the foot of Hill No. 65.5 near the village of Summa. Aliabushev's 123rd Rifle Division had unwittingly come up against one of the strongest sections of the Mannerheim Line.[94]

On 12 December, Meretskov received a directive from Shaposhnikov at Stavka ordering him to improve the 7th Army's troop control before relaunching the offensive. Shaposhnikov's first priority was to ensure that field commanders maintained continuous battle reconnaissance patrols. His second priority was to improve close co-operation between infantry and artillery, and he insisted that infantry assaults be directly supported by their own tank and mortar fire as well as artillery fire from regimental batteries. As regards troop control, Shaposhnikov ordered front line commanders to demand more intensive preparatory work from their staffs, emphasizing the importance of this work with the threat that 'Only inertness, lack of will, or absolute inability can explain the non-fulfilment of orders',[95] and he warned commanders that transgressions against these organizational ethics would be severely punished. Shaposhnikov's first suggestion for improving combat preparedness was for staffs to draw up a detailed plan of the forthcoming battle for distribution to all unit and sub-unit commanders. Reconnaissance would be collected by corps staff and discussed on location with the commanders of the various services before the beginning of battle. Corps staffs were accused of being particularly slow in carrying out these duties and the threat to punish anyone found obstructing the timely transmission of orders was repeated.[96] Shaposhnikov also commented on the remaining confusion concerning the importance of destroying DOTs and how to accomplish this mission.[97]

None of these techniques represented a radical departure from established Soviet military doctrine. In the early 1930s, Red Army military theorists had identified the importance of reinforced concrete forts (DOTs) to the conduct of 'defence-in-depth' tactics but had not fully understood the implications of this new defensive technology for their offensive Deep Battle tactics. Subsequent combat experience in Spain and the Far East generated increased appreciation for the balance between offence and defence, but by the end of 1939 the General Staff had still not codified these changes into the new field regulations or put them into practice in training programmes.[98] The consequence of this major lapse in doctrinal development was that military theorists in the General Staff were forced to search for the most effective method to fight against modern concrete fortifications while battle raged on the Karelian Isthmus. Once an effective technique had been developed, the problem remained of how to disseminate it to the troops in such a way that it could be put to immediate use against the Finnish defences. Shaposhnikov's intensive training programme was a first serious step towards accomplishing this goal, but it was not enough. For the time being, this didactic responsibility was to be taken over by the journalists in the Department of Combat Training at the editorial board of *Na Strazhe Rodiny*.

The initial task of these doctrinal journalists was to clarify the junior commander's responsibilities when approaching the enemy's main fortified region. After much speculation these journalists reached the consensus that the commander should organize his *own* reconnaissance patrols in order to gain information about the location and characteristics of individual DOTs in his sector.[99] The question then facing the junior commander was how to attack these fortifications. At the beginning of the invasion, the Main Military Soviet in Moscow had issued instructions to its troops to avoid frontal clashes with the enemy in favour of encirclement and outflanking manoeuvres.

However, combat experience showed that the fortifications making up the Mannerheim Line could not be outflanked and that individual DOTs had to be isolated and assaulted directly. The doctrinal journalists suggested numerous ways of accomplishing this task and then settled on the following method: the junior commander was to rely on artillery cover and the use of special combined arms detachments called 'blockade groups' to approach the DOT, suppress its fire, then destroy the DOT with hand-placed explosive charges.[100] They suggested that a typical blockade group be composed of two or three sappers responsible for clearing anti-personnel obstacles on the approach to the DOT; three or four infantry soldiers armed with grenades to throw at the occupants inside the DOT; a section of infantry armed with sub-machine guns to suppress the DOT's fire; and a team of sappers carrying sand-bags, stones and small trees with which to stop up the DOT's embrasures. The DOT would then be blown up with one hundred kilogrammes of explosives.[101] During the assault, the junior commander was to support the blockade groups' actions by suppressing adjacent enemy fire with machine-gun fire, infantry escort artillery fire, and larger calibre fire from artillery divisions.[102]

While Stavka was busy reorganizing the command of the ground forces on the Karelian Isthmus, the Naval Commissariat received reports from the reconnaissance submarines stationed off Sweden's coast that the Swedish navy showed no signs of preparing for war with the Baltic Fleet. On 8 December Kuznetsov recalled these submarines and publicly announced in the name of the recently created Finnish People's Republic that the Baltic Fleet would henceforth blockade Finnish territorial waters from the estuary of the Torni River in the north of the Gulf of Bothnia to the 23' 51" meridian in the Gulf of Finland.[103] The Baltic Fleet's blockade consisted of five submarine patrols in the Gulf of Finland, four patrols in the Baltic and Åland Seas, and two patrols outside the ports of Rauma and Kristiina in the Gulf of Bothnia. The Baltic Fleet also had the use of three air squadrons based at Paldiski, Kukel'konn and Liepaja, a total of 28 airplanes, but they were slow and limited in payload capacity, poor weather severely restricted their operations, and eight to 10 of the airplanes were out of commission at any given time.[104]

The first week of the Baltic Fleet's blockade in the Gulf of Finland was not very effective. The only submarine to succeed in sinking any cargo ships in the blockade zone was the *Shch-322* stationed outside Helsinki harbour. On 10 December, the crew of the submarine sighted and hailed a large cargo ship sailing west but received no response. A chase ensued, and once the submarine came within torpedo range it fired and sank the cargo ship which later turned out to be of Swedish registry transporting Finnish wood cellulose. On the night of 12 December the *Shch-322* exchanged artillery fire with a German cargo ship but without result. In the South Kvarken Straits the submarine *Shch-318* discovered that the Swedish navy was laying mines in an attempt to prevent submarine activity in the Gulf of Bothnia. While patrolling the Åland Sea, submarines *Shch-319* and *L-1* sighted a large number of cargo ships sailing between Sweden and Finland under Swedish naval escort. Kuznetsov acted on this information by sending more submarines to the Åland Sea and in mid-December extended the blockade to the Abo-Åland Archipelago. In the Gulf of Bothnia the *Shch-319* and the *S-1* patrolled the entrances to the ports at Kristiina and Rauma but their attempts to disrupt shipping were foiled by faulty torpedoes. Both submarines were forced to return to base at Liepaja by 16 December.[105]

In the eastern half of the Gulf of Finland the Baltic Fleet was preparing for simultaneous amphibious assaults against the left flank of the Mannerheim Line and along the Finnish coast between Vyborg and Hamina.[106] On 4 December Kuznetsov ordered Tributs and his staff to destroy the Finnish coastal batteries at Torsaari, Pukkionsaari, Kikkomannsaari and Kilpisaari Islands as well as the 254 mm. gun emplacements on Saarenpää, followed by an amphibious assault by an entire rifle division against Saarenpää. However, this operation was continually beset by logistics problems at Kronstadt and bad weather conditions.[107]

By the evening of 9 December, the left flank of the 7th Army was unable to advance any further due to heavy artillery fire from the Finnish coastal batteries on the Björkö Archipelago, especially from the battery at Saarenpää. That evening, Meretskov ordered Tributs to conduct a combined arms operation using the gunboats of the Eastern Contingent Squadron and air detachments stationed at Kronstadt to attack the Finnish coastal batteries at Saarenpää, Torsaari and Seiveste. On 10 December the gunboats *Leningrad*, *Minsk* and *Steregushchii* sailed to positions off the shore of Saarenpää and fired at the island but were forced to cease fire due to poor visibility. Tributs repeated this order over the next several days but bad weather prevented the gunboats from venturing forth. Meanwhile, the left flank of the 123rd Rifle Division and a battalion from the Soviet Karelian Fortified Region command had fought their way along the west coast of the Isthmus until they were stopped by heavy artillery fire from the batteries at Saarenpää and Muurila. Unequipped with artillery heavy enough to suppress the Finnish fire, the 123rd Rifle Division petitioned the Baltic Fleet command for naval artillery support. On 12 December, Tributs repeated the order to the gunboats *Leningrad*, *Minsk* and *Steregushchii* to fire at Saarenpää while the *Karl Marks*,

Artem and *Sestroretsk* supported the left flank of the Soviet Karelian Fortified Region's battalion.[108]

The gunboat squadron was plagued from the very beginning of the operation by a series of problems with its communications and reconnaissance that severely compromised its combat effectiveness. The *Sestroretsk*'s radio was unable to receive the signal from the battalion's artillery observation point, forcing the *Sestroretsk* to reroute its communications with the battalion via Kronstadt and the headquarters of the Northern Fortified Region command. Aerial artillery correction was also not possible because all the airplanes under the Baltic Fleet's subordination were flying other missions. The gunboats were thus obliged to fire according to the quadrant system which was very indiscriminate. Poor reconnaissance information about the location and armament of the Finnish coastal batteries led the gunboats to sail within range of the Finnish guns.[109]

On 18 December, Tributs ordered the gunboats *Oktiabr'skaia Revoliutsiia*, *Minsk*, *Steregushchii*, *Karl Marks*, *Artem*, *Engels*, *Lenin* and several smaller vessels to repeat the mission while air squadrons bombed and strafed the islands and provided air cover and reconnaissance. The bombers scored a direct hit against one of the batteries at Saarenpää by pure chance. Otherwise, the combined operation did not significantly weaken the Finnish defences. Thirty-five bombers and 52 fighters conducted 33 sorties against the island, dropping a total of 32 tons of explosives, but their bombing was indiscriminate and had little more than a psychological effect.[110]

Further west along the Finnish coast, the 8th and 10th Aviation Brigades continued their search for warships of the Finnish navy. On 19 December, nine long-range bombers from the 8th Aviation Brigade flew along the coast towards Hangö-Turku in search of Finnish warships hiding in the coastal skerries. When they failed to find any warships they dropped their bombs on a shipyard and airfield at Turku and returned home after evading Finnish anti-aircraft fire and an attack by six Bristol Bulldogs. Concurrent with the 8th Aviation Brigade's mission, two medium-range bombers from the 10th Aviation Brigade discovered a Finnish battleship hiding in a skerry near Korpoo. Their attack failed and they were unable to call in the more heavily armed medium-range bombers still in the area because no means of communication existed between the 8th and 10th Aviation Brigades.[111]

Meanwhile, to the east of the Karelian Isthmus the Ladoga Flotilla's 1st Detachment remained inactive until 5 December, at which time Captain Kobyl'skii, the commander of the Ladoga Flotilla, joined the detachment at Saunaniemi Bay, bringing with him the torpedo boat *Dozornyi* accompanied by two mine-sweepers. In the presence of his superior commander, Captain

Trainin abandoned efforts to made radio contact with the right flank of the 7th Army and sent out a courier to link up with whatever Red Army authority could be found on the isthmus.

That evening the courier returned in the company of a staff representative from the 49th Rifle Division stationed at Metsäpirtti, the 142nd Rifle Division having transferred to assignments elsewhere on the isthmus. The staff officer brought Trainin news of an offensive planned by the 49th Rifle Division headquarters to force the Taipalen-joki River and break through the Finnish fortifications on the opposite shore of the river the next day. On the morning of 6 December Trainin and Kobyl'skii despatched the only remaining operational forces at their disposal, the torpedo boats *Razvedchik* and *Dozornyi* and all the mine-sweepers, to Taipalen Bay to threaten the Finnish fortifications from the sea. At 14h40 the two torpedo boats fired on the Finnish coast from the range of 75 cables in order to stay out of range of the Finnish artillery battery at Jarisevänniemi Point. The two torpedo boats ceased firing an hour later and returned to Saunaniemi Bay having expended all their ammunition, most of which had landed in the water of Taipalen Bay.

This was the extent of the 1st Detachment's participation in the 7th Army's almost successful attempt to overtake the retreating Finnish Army and prevent it from consolidating its positional defences. Although the Ladoga Flotilla had been particularly ineffective in executing its assignments, its commanders none the less managed to paint a more positive picture of their activities, reporting to their superiors that the torpedo boats had 'successfully avoided danger' during their raid against Taipale on 6 December.[112]

Harbour-bound by thick fog on 7 December, the 1st Detachment found itself caught in a Finnish artillery ambush at noon on 8 December. Disregarding the onset of a blizzard, Captain Trainin ordered all his ships out of the bay but, in the rough water, the torpedo boat *Razvedchik* collided with a rock, the *Moskva* developed problems with its propellers, and the commander of one of the minesweepers was forced to beach his boat after it sprung a leak in the engine-room. The gun crew of the torpedo boat *Vidlitsa* attempted to fire back at the Finns but, after the fifth shot, a shell exploded in the firing mechanism of their gun, killing five sailors and inflicting two concussions.[113] After spending the night anchored off the Orli Peninsula, Trainin and his detachment returned to Saunaniemi Bay. However, the advanced disrepair of his ships, problems with refuelling and the increasingly inclement weather terminated his operations. The *Orangenbaum* was refloated on 15 December and towed back to Politorno in the company of the *Moskva* and the *Vidlitsa*, which were also due for capital repairs. When Trainin took over responsibility of the Ladoga Flotilla from Kobyl'skii five days later, all naval operations on Lake Ladoga had effectively ceased.[114]

The naval operations of the Baltic Fleet and the Ladoga Flotilla during this period demonstrated a host of deficiencies in combat preparedness. Reconnaissance patrols assigned to monitor the Swedish navy and the flow of shipping between Sweden and Finland in the Gulf of Bothnia were compromised by a lack of navigational experience in these waters as well as difficulties in sustaining effective radio communication over such long distances. The *Kirov*'s lacklustre operations against the Hangö Peninsula were marked by similar intelligence and communications problems which contributed to an absence of co-ordinated interaction with other Soviet naval forces in the area. Limited base facilities in the western half of the Gulf of Finland, seasonal bad weather, and diplomatic inconveniences had disrupted submarine patrols along Finland's southern shore during the first week of the war, allowing the Finnish navy in the area to redeploy to safer waters. Finally, the beaching of the *Orangenbaum* and the poor performance of the Special Detachment's landing operations on the six islands in the Gulf of Finland illustrated to Stavka the real extent of the Ladoga Flotilla's and Baltic Fleet's inability to conduct co-ordinated naval operations even within the immediate vicinity of Kronstadt.

The high expenditure of ammunition in proportion to minimal Finnish opposition was the most obvious manifestation of poor combat preparedness. The Baltic Fleet's airforce conducted a total of 387 sorties against the six islands, dropping 2,110 bombs containing 64.5 tons of explosive and firing 95,465 machine-gun bullets on islands which, with the exception of Suur-Tiutärsaari Island, had been evacuated by the Finnish Army during the first hours of the war. Another manifestation of poor preparedness was the high incidence of air accidents. In addition to fraternal fire during the amphibious assault on Suursaari Island, there were accidents at the airfield at Kronstadt and mistaken identifications between airplanes during the bombing missions over the Finnish coast. On 1 December an inexperienced pilot flew his long-range bomber into a bomb depot during take-off. He destroyed the bomber and its crew while killing three people on the ground, injuring another 29 people, and damaging seven airplanes parked off the run way.[115] In another incident, a medium-range bomber shot another soviet fighter out of the air because it was improperly marked. The Baltic Fleet command's explanation for the high incidence of accidents placed the blame on inadequte organization, unnecessary haste, bad weather conditions and insufficient training of air personnel in combat conditions.[116]

A less obvious contribution to the poor combat performance of the Baltic

Fleet and the Ladoga Flotilla was disorder in the rear services, especially in supply. In the hours preceding the Red Army's invasion, the Baltic Fleet was placed on alert but no formal declaration of mobilization was made and the fleet was not permitted to consume existing stocks. The absence of a formal declaration of war also compromised the Baltic Fleet's timely supply because the regional rail network remained on the slower, peacetime schedule until two weeks after the beginning of the invasion and alternative modes of transport, such as the merchant fleet and trucking, were adversely affected by the worsening weather conditions.[117] This administrative oversight had a profound effect on the Baltic Fleet's operations. For example, the provisioning of the *Engels* for its mission against the Finnish coastal artillery battery at Björkö on 8 December was delayed, thereby compromising the entire mission. Assimilation of new naval air bases in the Baltic States also overstretched the logistics services. The re-basing of ships at Tallinn, Paldiski and Liepaja was conducted without a contingency plan, completely disorganizing the Baltic Fleet's supply schedules. More than the available two months was required to prepare these new bases for war, and further disruption occurred when the Baltic Fleet established additional bases on the recently conquered Suursaari and Suur-Tiutärsaari Islands.

The 8th Army was unable to maintain its projected tempo of advance on the north shore of Lake Ladoga. Meretskov issued a general order on 3 December to the 7th, 8th and 9th Armies to speed up their offensives and specifically directed his criticism to the 8th Army, stating: 'We can no longer bicker with Finland, going four to five kilometres a day.' The 8th Army's offensive had to be conducted more quickly, not only on the axis joining with the 7th Army, but also with the 9th Army, in order to cut Finland in two and prevent the unloading of Swedish military aid at Uleaborg (Oulu). Meretskov ordered the 8th and 9th Army commanders to use more aerial bombing to help accelerate their road-bound formations but strictly forbade the bombing of population centres, perhaps a belated recognition that the indiscriminate bombing doctrine used during the first hours of the invasion had done more political harm than military good.[118] To assure the Defence Commissariat in Moscow that the 8th Army's offensive would be speeded up, Meretskov replaced the 8th Army's commander, Division Commander Khabarov, with Corps Commander V. Kurdiumov on 4 December.[119]

Meretskov's threats and interference with the 8th Army's command did little to improve the situation on the forest roads of Ladoga-Karelia. By 6 December, the 56th Rifle Division had progressed only as far as the outskirts of Loimola before being halted by heavy Finnish machine-gun, rifle and artillery fire. The 18th Rifle Division continued to advance up the road to the junction at Kitelä, but it was having to secure its forward movement from Finnish guerrilla raids.[120] On 11 December, the 18th Rifle Division's vanguard units made contact with the 168th Rifle Division which had progressed as far as the coastal town of Pitkaranta. This tentative union of forces represented the fulfilment of the 56th Rifle Corps' second mission and the furthest advance of its forces to date. However, this success was illusory. In the push to establish communications with the 168th Rifle Division, the commander of the 18th Rifle Division, Brigade Commander G. Kondrashov, had over-extended his lines of communication and had exhausted his troops. By mid-December the Finnish high command had sufficiently reinforced its defensive forces in the area to halt Kondrashov's offensive. When Finnish guerrilla detachments attacked the 18th Rifle Division on the evening of 16 December and had separated the Division into isolated groups along the road to Lemetti, Kondrashov did not have enough reserves to counter-attack (see Figure 2.6). Finnish detachments also succeeded in splitting the 18th Rifle Division from the 168th Rifle Division, now dug in at positions north of Pitkaranta, and threatened the 168th Rifle Division's rear from the lake.[121]

Meanwhile, Belaev's 136th Rifle Division had advanced very quickly, seizing Raukhala on the evening of 4 December and routing the Finns at Ägläjärvi before pausing on the eastern shore of Ala Tolvajärvi Lake and despatching the 718th Rifle Regiment to outflank Finnish forces holding the town of Tolvajärvi from the north. On the evening of 7 December, Belaev's vanguard, the 3rd Battalion of the 364th Rifle Regiment, crossed the Ristisalmi straits and collided with Finnish defenders straddling the road to Tolvajärvi. During the early hours of 8 December, Belaev's division attacked these defences several times before falling back to the east shore of Ala Tolvajärvi Lake and digging in.[122] Having learned for a second time that outflanking manoeuvres were more effective against Finnish defences than frontal attacks, Belaev radioed his superior commander, Panin, for permission to place the weight of his force behind the 718th Rifle Regiment. Belaev's request could not have been made at a more inopportune time. Panin had received a Defence Commissariat directive the day before, reprimanding him for maintaining his corps headquarters in the safety of Soviet territory and not conducting the offensive quickly enough.[123] Panin's response was to order Belaev to conduct a frontal assault against Finnish defences while the 718th Rifle Regiment was to speed up its encirclement. With these categorical orders in hand, Belaev attacked with the combined forces of his division and advanced several kilometres up the road to within sight of Tolvajärvi. The 609th Rifle Regiment established their headquarters at a tourist hotel on the southern shore of Hirvas-järvi Lake while the 364th Rifle Regiment set up camp south

FIGURE 2.6

SITUATION MAP OF THE 8TH ARMY'S 18TH AND 168TH RIFLE DIVISIONS ON 7 JANUARY 1940

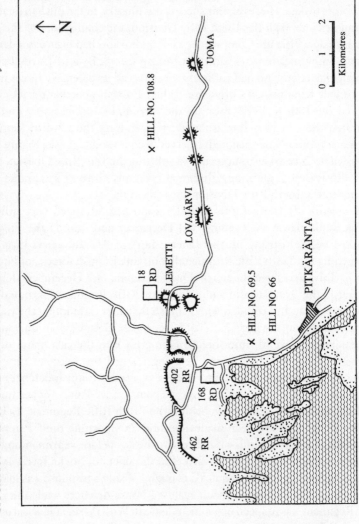

Adapted from *Konflikt. Komplekt dokumentov o Sovetsko–finliandskoi voine (1939–1940 gg.)*, East View Press, Minn., 1992.

of Kivisalmi Bridge and on Kotisjärvi Island.[124] Although Belaev's troops had managed to overwhelm the Finnish defences, they were still vulnerable to guerrilla attacks. During the night of 8 December a Finnish raiding party infiltrated the 364th Rifle Regiment's rear and opened fire with sub-machine guns on the sleeping Red Army troops. In the ensuing fight the Finns retreated across the ice of the lake, leaving units of the 364th Rifle Regiment to shoot at themselves until a battalion from the 609th Rifle Regiment arrived the next morning to help them.[125]

While Belaev's division approached Tolvajärvi from the east, the 718th Rifle Regiment struck out along the shore of Ala Tolvajärvi Lake to approach Tolvajärvi from the north east. On 8 December they reached the village of Honkavara at the top of the lake, having lost communication with divisional headquarters and in a state of complete exhaustion.[126] From Honkavara the 718th Rifle Regiment joined the road south to Tolvajärvi, arriving on the eastern shore of Hirvas-järvi Lake some time between 9 and 10 December. During the evening of 10 December, the 718th Rifle Regiment attacked the rear of the Finnish defences at Tolvajärvi and engaged in fierce hand-to-hand combat until Finnish reinforcements arrived at the scene to fight them off. Although this attack had not succeeded in promoting Belaev's advance towards Tolvajärvi, it had unwittingly disrupted Finnish preparations for a major counter-offensive against the 139th Rifle Division's positions the next day, delaying these plans until 12 December. During the rest of the evening, and into the next day, Belaev's regiments made several unsuccessful attempts to attack the Finns at Tolvajärvi with frontal and outflanking manoeuvres.[127] After an advance of nearly 50 kilometres and several days of continuous fighting, the 139th Rifle Division had reached a state of total exhaustion.

V

When Tanner realized that his attempts to re-establish diplomatic contact with the Soviet Union had failed, he instructed the Finnish representative in Geneva, Rudolph Holsti, to appeal to the Secretary General of the League of Nations for support in mediating an armistice with the Soviet government.[128] The Secretary General forwarded this appeal to the People's Commissariat of Foreign Affairs on 4 December and requested that the Soviet government send a representative to Geneva to settle the conflict. Moscow's response to the League's request was categorically negative.[129] In a reply printed in *Izvestiia* Molotov stated that the Soviet Union was not at war with Finland

71

or the Finnish people, that peaceful relations had just been concluded with the Finnish People's Republic and that together with the help of the Red Army and the Finnish People's Republic they were quickly removing the dangerous sources of violence left by the previous government.[130]

Despite this negative response the League continued to support Helsinki's appeal. On 11 December, the League's Assembly appointed a special committee to deal with the matter and the next day this committee formally called upon the Soviet Union and Finland to cease military activities and conduct peace negotiations under the League's auspices. Stavka chose to ignore the League's request with the result that the League's Assembly voted by a narrow margin to expel the Soviet Union from membership of the League on 14 December.[131]

Stavka's reaction to this news was to publicly deprecate the League in the strongest terms. An official TASS communiqué was published in *Izvestiia* the same day, reporting that the League's vote to expel the Soviet Union had elicited 'sarcastic smiles' in Soviet government circles, coming as the vote did from the intrigues of the ruling circles in England and France who had neither the moral nor the formal right to accuse the Soviet Union of any 'aggression'.[132] The communiqué went on to explain to the Soviet public that the expulsion was in fact a blessing because it released the Soviet Union from obligations to the League's Charter and 'left its hands free' to pursue other policies. The Soviet government was resolved to continue its war of 'national liberation' against Finland.

Aware that the League's declaration increased the likelihood of concerted foreign military aid to Finland, Stavka instructed Meretskov to prepare for a second offensive on 15 December. Stavka envisaged a breakthrough operation against the Mannerheim Line between Summa and Lake Muolan-järvi with secondary operations towards Kakisalmi in the east and an encirclement operation against Vyborg in the west. In response to these instructions Meretskov ordered the 19th Rifle Corps to conduct the breakthrough operation up the railroad tracks on the western shore of Lake Muolan-järvi towards Liepäsuo while the 138th and 123rd Rifle Divisions, seconded from Grendal's 50th Rifle Corps, were to attack Finnish defences at Hill No. 65.5 and cut off the Finnish Army's retreat to Kämärä. Meretskov ordered the 10th Tank Corps to enlarge the 19th Rifle Corps' breakthrough into a Deep Operation with the aid of 59 medium-range bombers and the 70th Rifle Division in reserve.[133]

Meretskov's order announcing the new offensive concluded with a short discussion about the Deep Battle tactics which would be required to overcome the Mannerheim Line. The first line of infantry was expected to penetrate the gaps between the fortified flanks and outflank these points with the direct support of battalion and regimental artillery fire.[134] Meretskov further elaborated these tactics in a doctrinal pamphlet entitled 'How to Capture Permanent Fire-Points', published as a supplement to the *Red Army Soldier's Combat Book*. The pamphlet briefly summarized the preparatory role of artillery in 'softening up' the Finnish DOTs and the combined efforts of tanks, artillery and blockading units to destroy them completely.[135] Doctrinal journalists at *Na Strazhe Rodiny* further supplemented Meretskov's pamphlet with a series of articles on the destruction of Finnish DOTs. It suggested that reconnaissance patrols should be given the additional responsibility to destroy enemy DOT observation points and comb the forest near DOTs for enemy snipers. These journalists also suggested that DOTs could also be destroyed by heavy artillery batteries firing over open sights from concealed positions.[136]

The blockade group was also reorganized, equipped with greater firepower, and given a more important role in the conduct of Deep Battle tactics. Blockade groups now consisted of two or three platoons of infantry, a machine-gun platoon, an artillery platoon armed with heavier calibre guns, and a sapper team equipped with larger amounts of explosives. Although doctrinal articles continued to mention the tanks' contributions to the tactics of blockade-groups they were no longer considered decisive and were not organic to the blockade group's organization. The blockade group's growing importance in Deep Battle tactics was acknowledged by V. Butylev in an article entitled 'Breakthrough of the Fortified Zone' (*Na Strazhe Rodiny*, 18 December, p.2), where the author declared that breakthrough operations against fortified zones were now regarded as the single most important aspect of modern warfare because they required very close interaction and well-organized mutual assistance between all types of troops involved in the combined arms team. 'Interaction' between junior commanders of infantry, tanks, and artillery had become a new priority in Soviet military doctrine.

The most fundamental problem Meretskov had to address before launching a second offensive was the growing demoralization of the rank-and-file and the ensuing lack of discipline. The only way to correct this problem in wartime was to intensify the 'combat socialist competitions' and hold more frequent political meetings in order to raise the men's combat spirit. On 18 December *Na Strazhe Rodiny* published an article describing a typical political meeting. The political commissar of the unit began the meeting by reading out a declaration printed in *Na Strazhe Rodiny* to enlarge the combat socialist competition and then rhetorically challenged the unit to accept the terms of the competition. Short declarations of hatred for the enemy were

73

then made by each soldier, commander, and political worker in the unit followed by an unanimous vote to accept the terms of the competition. The basic terms of the competition were as follows: inflict harm on the enemy, seize the enemy's defensive zone with lightning speed, avoid casualties, show mutual aid in battle, always hit one's target and preserve one's combat equipment. At the end of the political meeting a draft resolution was drawn up; each soldier in the unit was obliged to read the draft, and then the resolution was signed by all the unit and sub-unit commanders present.[137] In this way the mechanism of combat socialist competition became part of the Soldier's Oath. If the unit or sub-unit did not perform its duties according to the resolution it could be held legally accountable.

Meretskov's second offensive on the Karelian Isthmus began early on the morning of 15 December with an eight-hour artillery preparation and aerial bombardment against Finnish fortifications at Taipale. When the barrage lifted, the remaining rifle divisions in Grendal's 50th Rifle Corps launched their attack across the Taipalen-joki river.[138] Two days later the 19th Rifle Corps launched its breakthrough operation in the region between Summa and Lake Muolan-järvi. Both operations were ultimately compromised by organizational incompetence at every level of the 7th Army's command hierarchy. Captain Yanov, a tank battalion commander who was later captured by the Finnish Army, described the extent of confusion in the 138th Rifle Division during its operation against Hill No. 65.5.

> At 0600 hours 17.12 [17 December] the movements began to the jumping-off positions in the area of the village of Vosi. This presented incredible difficulties, since the roads were cluttered up with various units. I smashed my way through to Vosi ... On arrival at the jumping-off point I discovered a grim situation. Another battalion of tanks had crept into my area and a second battalion had also arrived there. All units were intermingled, and it was quite impossible to elucidate who, how, or in what order units were to carry out their duties. The regimental and light divisional artillery were at that moment also moving into the area, hours late, and the second line of infantry were also forcing their way into the crowd. In fact, there was incredible chaos. It was now about 1200 hours and [the] attack was timed for thirty minutes later, but so far nothing had been done for co-operation among arms. I decided to contact the commander of the 650th Rifle Regiment. He stated 'I do not know you. The 95th Tank Battalion is co-operating with me.' I explained that in accordance with instructions of corps I was also acting with him, but only with the second wave of attack. He tried to sort out the orders, but, giving no indication [explanation ?], sent

me to his chief of staff who also could make nothing out of the existing circumstances. He thrust at me the battle orders, which had apparently been written thoughtlessly and hurriedly. I offered to establish communication primarily with the artillery, but nothing came of this, as his chief of communications was inexperienced and even illiterate. All those subordinate to this regimental commander for the purpose of the action were piling up round the chief of staff for instructions, and everything was being rushed as the attack was due to take place in thirty minutes time. Since everything was done in a hurry, he got tangled up in the wave length to several different units. Meanwhile, the diapason of the waves was not suitable, since the radio stations were of different types, [and] no communications were established. I decided to give it all up, as I could make no sense of it, and to await events and, on instruction to enter the action, to take independent personal decisions depending on the course of the battle.[139]

The 138th Rifle Division made no headway against the well-constructed Finnish fortifications at Summa that day.[140] Further east in the vicinity of Hill No.65.5, battalions of the 123rd Rifle Division had no better luck. The 1st Battalion assaulted the hill to the west of Hill No.65.5 with a detachment of sappers to clear anti-tank and anti-personnel obstacles, followed by tanks and infantry. However, it was not until the 3rd Battalion approached the foot of Hill No 65.5 itself that the entire fire-system of the Finnish fortifications on the hill revealed its presence with an intense barrage of interlocking artillery, mortar and machine-gun fire. According to the political worker of the 1st Battalion, he and his men were caught in this crossfire for the next five days.[141]

On the evening of 17 December, Meretskov tried to downplay the failures of the offensive's first day by congratulating the 19th and 50th Rifle Corps on flushing out the full forces of the Finnish defences. Meretskov ordered a repeat offensive for the next day but suggested a few amendments in tactics. Infantry assaults were to be preceded by special sapper detachments to remove tank obstacles, and manoeuvre under the fire of forward artillery. Under no circumstances were Deep Operations to begin before the breakthrough was completed: 'The 10th Tank Corps is not in any case to consume itself in its own breakthrough, but is to fully preserve its strength for the development [of the breakthrough].'[142]

Despite Meretskov's instructions, the next day's offensive was conducted in some sectors without any artillery support or engineering removal of anti-personnel and anti-tank obstacles from the forward area.[143] Only on

75

19 December did the 138th Rifle Division sufficiently rectify its command problems to attempt to put Meretskov's tactical recommendations into practice. The previous night, under cover of darkness, tanks had been ordered to test the approaches to the Finnish defences in order to gain more information about them, and in the morning tanks protected sapper detachments from enemy fire as they demolished the anti-tank obstacles.[144] Although there was no preparatory artillery barrage, these co-ordinated efforts set the stage for what was to become the culmination of Meretskov's offensive: a limited breakthrough of Finnish defences at Summa. Captain Yanov, the captured Soviet tank commander, described what happened:

> I was again set the task at 1000 hours to support infantry without artillery preparation, and to break through northwards for four or five kilometres. On our left, another tank battalion supported by infantry was to co-operate. At 1030 hours the battalion moved to the attack and at 1130 hours I was ordered to retire, since there was to be ten minutes of intensive artillery fire. With great difficulty I withdrew the battalion and at 1200 hours received an order to attack again. I went through the second row of tank obstacles and came up to the concrete fire-points. The infantry did not follow up with the tanks, as it was separated from them by artillery fire and enfilade machine-gun fire from the wood. I was thus stationary about twenty minutes, but the infantry did not move forward. During this time a second battalion of tanks came up, and I informed the commander that in accordance with my task I was leaving the concrete points and moving further since, some four or five kilometres further north we were to converge with him, as his task was to go through on our left and emerge at the cross-roads north of the village of Hatonen [Khotinen, otherwise known as Summa]. Sending out a reconnaissance platoon (two machines), I moved forward about three kilometres when the leading tank was mined. The commander of the reconnaissance platoon reported that on his left front was infantry. I shut off motors and listened. The infantry were Finns obviously surrounding me through the woods. Becoming convinced that the other battalion had not come up level with me, I gave the order to retire. Having turned the column about, I became the last machine, since the other reconnaissance tank following me passed me and followed the battalion. On the way back, mines exploded under us twice and the gear box was injured. The tank in front of me caught fire and I was too close to pass and unable to use reverse gear. At that moment the motors died, the machine in front exploded, the crews of both jumped out and escaped into the wood; I remained.[145]

VI

By 20 December, Meretskov's second offensive began to recede. Meretskov blamed this failure on bad weather and the awesome resilience of the Finnish defenders while Gorolenko at 50th Rifle Corps headquarters reached the conclusion that the offensive failed because the Red Army was incapable of conducting combined arms operations and Deep Battle tactics.[146] Likewise, Voroshilov at the Defence Commissariat in Moscow interpreted the causes for the failure from a third point of view. In a letter written to Stalin and Molotov on 21 December he accused Meretskov of repeating the same mistakes made by Yakovlev before him. Voroshilov suggested to Stalin that Meretskov be threatened with court martial and that a purge be conducted at 7th Army command if the situation at the front did not improve: 'I consider it necessary to conduct a radical purge of corps, divisional and regimental commands. [We] need to replace these cowards and laggards (there are also swine) with loyal and efficient people ... [147]

Stalin did not heed Voroshilov's advice. Instead, he ordered Meretskov and G. Isserson, his chief of staff at 7th Army headquarters, to prepare for a third offensive against Vyborg code-named Plan *Ladoga*. On 22 December this plan was distributed to the 19th, 50th Rifle Corps and the 10th Tank Corps, ordering them to begin preparations for another offensive on 26 December.[148] Far more ambitious than its predecessor, drawn up ten days earlier, Plan *Lagoda* envisaged a vast concerted effort by Soviet airforces to bomb the Finnish Army's strategic reserves, the intensification of artillery fire to soften up the Finnish defensive fortifications, continuous reconnaissance patrols day and night, sapper units to clear minefields and tank obstacles up to the Mannerheim Line and the formation of blockade-groups in the forward areas in preparation for another general offensive.[149]

In order to prevent the fiasco that had occurred during the previous offensive, Meretskov and Isserson gave the commanders of these formations a detailed schedule to follow and three days to accomplish the preparations. Engineering units were to complete the construction of forward command and observation points by 23 December, and on the following day they were to complete the construction of jumping-off positions at 400 metres and battle security positions at 150–200 metres from the Finnish defences.[150] On December 24 and 25, one battalion in the front of each division was to conduct 'demonstration' attacks after a short period of artillery preparation fire. The purpose of these demonstration attacks was to capture partially softened-up enemy DOTs and establish a fingerhold in the enemy's fortified region for further development by successive echelons. During this time, division commanders were to convene orientation exercises between regimental and battalion commanders and their subordinate artillery and tank commanders while the corps commander was responsible for monitoring the organizational work of the divisional and regimental staffs. On the evening of 25 December the 138th Rifle Division was ordered to join the reserve 10th Rifle Corps, relinquishing its front sector to the incoming 100th Rifle Division. At the same time, infantry and tank units of the 19th and 50th Rifle Corps were to occupy their forward positions in preparation for the general offensive while units of the 10th Tank Corps were to follow a day later to develop the successes of the general offensive.[151]

Meretskov hoped to disrupt Finnish Army strategic reserves in the operational depths of the Mannerheim Line. Normally, such a mission would be carried out by aerial bombing but Finnish re-deployments occurred at night and winter weather conditions on the Karelian Isthmus prevented Soviet aviation from carrying out effective bombing schedules. The only other option was long-range artillery bombardment. The 7th Army lacked sufficiently large calibre artillery to reach the Finnish Army's operational rear. Meretskov had to ask Tributs' naval staff at Kronstadt for the transfer of several railroad artillery battalions from coastal defences south-west of Leningrad to his command. On 22 December, the railroad artillery battalion No. 17, consisting of four trains equipped with 180 mm. cannon, arrived at Perkjärvi and was ordered to conduct a methodical shelling of south Vyborg and the railroad junctions at Liimatta, Kämärä, Honkaniemi and Heinioki.[152] Unfortunately for Meretskov, the railroad artillery battalion arrived without its own air detachment for fire-correction, and airplanes attached to the 7th Army aviation park were unable to establish reliable two-way communications with the battalions, thus denying fire accuracy and reducing its value to purely psychological significance. The railroad artillery battalion achieved a certain modicum of success in this limited capacity. Two weeks after the battalion became operational the Defence Commissariat learned from TASS world press summaries that long-range artillery bombardment of Vyborg was having a greater psychological effect than Franco's aerial bombardment had had on Madrid during the Spanish Civil War. Not only was long-range artillery bombardment impervious to the vagaries of the weather but it could be conducted 24 hours a day and defied Finnish efforts to defend against it.[153]

As the details of Meretskov's Plan *Ladoga* were being consolidated and distributed to the formations and units of the 7th Army, the Leningrad Military District command published in the military and civilian press an *apologia* for the decreasing tempo of the Red Army's offensive against Finland. Written explicitly as a diatribe against Western military observers who had made comments in the international press about the Red Army's 'low combat capability' and inability to conduct a 'lightning strike' against the Finns, this article also served as an implicit warning to Red Army commanders, commissars and troops of a reversal in Stavka's strategic preconceptions of how the war should be conducted. The article declared that, contrary to Western (and domestic) rumours, the Soviet high command had always taken account of the Mannerheim Line and Finland's unsuitable terrain for modern offensive manoeuvres and had never counted on the success of a lightning strike. In a final justification of the new, more attritional strategic posture, the authors compared the Red Army's daily forward advance against the Mannerheim Line with that of the British and French forces against the Siegfried Line. According to them, the comparison indicated that the Red Army had achieved 'serious successes' against modern fortifications.[154]

While the 7th Army was preparing for a third offensive on the Karelian Isthmus the Finnish high command decided to seize the initiative and conduct a counter-offensive. One of the fundamental concepts the Finnish General Staff had borrowed from German tactical doctrine was the concept of *Schlagfertigkeit*, translated literally as 'quickness of repartee', which recommended the use of *gegenstoss* (immediate counter-strike) and *gegenangriff* (deliberate counter-attack) against an enemy's offensive in order to disrupt and stop it.[155] The commander of the II Army Corps, Lt. General Öhquist, had drawn up proposals for a deliberate counter-attack in the centre of the Karelian Isthmus as early as 11 December. However, at that time Mannerheim believed that the Finnish Army was not ready for such a counter-attack until it was armed with more anti-tank guns. When the 7th Army's second offensive began to lose steam on 19 December Lt. General Öhquist resubmitted his proposal and this time it was accepted.[156]

On the morning of 23 December the Finnish 6th Division, reinforced with infantry regiments from the coast defence, conducted an audacious encirclement offensive from Karhula against the west flank of the 50th Rifle Division while the Finnish 1st Division attacked along the shores of Lake Muolanjärvi against the eastern flank of Meretskov's 19th Rifle Corps. From the very beginning of the counter-offensive the Finnish divisions suffered the same problems of operational manoeuvre that had plagued the Red Army and were forced to retreat to their original positions later the same day.[157] However, the Finnish Army's counter-offensive had seriously disrupted Meretskov's carefully choreographed Plan *Ladoga*.

Stavka's response to the Finnish counter-offensive was to strike back with forces that had not been disrupted during the recent mêlée. One last attempt was made to break through the Mannerheim Line. On 25 December Stavka ordered Grendal to reorganize his corps command at Kaidalovo into a new army command, the 13th Army, and entrusted him with the execution of Plan *Ladoga*.[158] Grendal and his staff drew up a highly detailed plan describing the intended movements of each unit down to battalion level and the tactics which they were to use in their offensive across the ice of Suvanto-järvi River towards Finnish defences at Taipale, Sakkola, Kelia and Riiskan. After a two-hour artillery barrage, Grendal's four divisions launched their attack and managed to seize a bridgehead near the villages of Volossula and Kelia before being forced to retreat under heavy Finnish artillery, mortar and machine-gun fire. By 28 December, when the offensive was called off, approximately 2,000 Red Army soldiers lay dead on the river's ice.[159]

VII

North of Lake Ladoga the Finnish Army's counter-offensive inflicted even greater defeats on Stavka's armies. By mid-December Finnish forces opposite the 8th Army's 56th Rifle Corps had been reinforced to counter-attack the 18th and 168th Rifle Division, isolate them from each other and cut them off from the main body of the 8th Army (see Figure 2.6).[160] Kurdiumov at 8th Army headquarters in Petrozavodsk tried to reverse the situation by ordering these two divisions to break out of their encirclements and continue their offensive, but weeks of unfamiliar forest-swamp warfare and lack of reinforcement left them too exhausted to carry out these orders.[161] Additional attempts were made by Stavka to support the 8th Army's left flank with artillery fire from the Ladoga Flotilla but the Flotilla's only gunboat, the *Orangenbaum*, was still under repair and the lake was frozen solid.[162]

At Tolvajärvi, Finnish units launched a counter-attack against the 1st Rifle Corps' 139th Rifle Division on 12 December. The Finnish High Command's original plan was to encircle Belaev's division from the north and south, then assault the 609th Rifle Regiment headquarters in the centre. However, this counter-attack did not unfold as intended. The northern encirclement operation unexpectedly encountered two battalions of the 718th Rifle Regiment on the eastern shore of Hirvas-järvi Lake. The 718th Rifle Regiment managed to repel the Finns after a skirmish but the regiment's commander was wounded in the fray and his staff lost control, nullifying any further efforts to outflank the Finns. In the south, Finnish encirclement operations against the 364th Rifle Regiment were compromised by poor co-ordination.[163]

Although Belaev was able to fend off these initial threats to his flanks, the arrival of his superior commander, Panin, at divisional headquarters on the morning of 12 December made control over his troops more complicated. Panin, still agitated by the Defence Commissariat's rebuke a few days earlier, was determined to press the offensive against Tolvajärvi. Under his personal supervision Belaev conducted a half-hour artillery barrage against Finnish positions on the other side of the Hevos-salmi straits and then ordered the infantry to advance at 10h00. The troops were too exhausted to respond and disobeyed this order. Belaev was forced to send his own staff to the front line in a fruitless attempt to prod the groggy troops into the attack.[164] When this attack failed, Panin ordered the 139th Rifle Division to retreat back to the south shore of Ala-Tolvajärvi Lake, leaving Belaev to hold out against further Finnish counter-attacks as best he could. That afternoon, when the Finns overran the positions held by the 609th and 364th Rifle Regiments, Belaev ordered the remainder of his division to retreat eastward on the Tolvajärvi–Suojärvi road.[165]

By the evening of 12 December Belaev's division had fallen back to defensive positions they had held four days earlier: units of the 364th Rifle Regiment took up defences on the peninsula between Ala-Tolvajärvi and Kuojärvi Lakes and the remainder of the 609th Rifle Regiment straddled the road at the Ristisalmi straits while the 718th Rifle Regiment retreated back to the east shore of Ala Tolvajärvi Lake. Belaev's division had suffered heavy casualties. The 364th Rifle Regiment had suffered 400 killed and wounded and had left behind 40 medium calibre machine-guns, six 76 mm. cannon, and almost all its infantry weapons. The 609th Rifle Regiment was so disorganized that it did not know how many casualties it had suffered, but reported the loss of four 45 mm. cannon, 24 medium calibre machine-guns, and many infantry weapons. The 718th Rifle Regiment also did not provide figures for its losses but assured its superior commander that they were much less than those of the other two regiments. The command corps as a whole sustained the most significant losses. Most of the junior commanders of battalions, companies and platoons had been killed or wounded, greatly reducing the combat capability of the division.[166] Belaev's conclusion, drawn from the day's combat experience, was that he (and by implication, Panin) had committed a fundamental mistake in using exhausted troops to attack a reinforced enemy. The result was the first retreat by a Red Army division since the beginning of the invasion. Belaev's new priority was to establish a sustainable defence against an enemy invigorated by its first major victory.

The Finnish counter-offensive resumed on 14 December, attacking Belaev's defences at the Ristisalmi straits and slowly forcing his troops to retreat up the road to Ägläjärvi. During these road battles Belaev rotated his troops with fresh units from A. Stepanov's 75th Rifle Division, but even these

81

reinforcements were unable to stop the Finnish counter-offensive. Casualties were mounting in the 139th Rifle Division and the troops were completely demoralized. Even Stepanov's units were suffering heavy losses.[167] By 18 December, Belaev and Stepanov had retreated to Äglajärvi, where they established new defensive positions and attempted to stall the Finnish offensive with increased artillery and air support.

Over the next two days, Stepanov's and Belaev's divisions dug into defensive positions at Äglajärvi in an attempt to contain the Finnish onslaught which attacked with units up to a battalion in size.[168] Red Army defensive lines began to crumble on the evening of 21 December when the Finns had assembled enough forces to launch an encirclement operation across the ice of Äglajärvi Lake and down the road into Äglajärvi from the north. Fierce hand-to-hand combat for control of the town continued until midday on 22 December when Stepanov and his division began to retreat south along the road towards Pojasaara. The Finns were enheartened by their recent victories and continued to harass the retreating Red Army divisions from the forest and along the road. The final clash occurred outside Raukhala where a Finnish vanguard detachment isolated a machine-gun platoon attached to Stepanov's division and annihilated it in hand-to-hand combat.[169]

Stepanov's and Belaev's divisions finally came to a halt on the evening of 23 December when Panin gave them permission to dig into defences on the banks of the Aitto-joki River. Although these two divisions still had to fend off Finnish guerrilla raids they no longer had to contend with a serious threat. The Finnish high command had ordered its troops to transfer to the defensive in order to concentrate more troops on the Karelian Isthmus.[170] However, the Finnish counter-offensive had inflicted enormous losses on the 139th and 75th Rifle Divisions. According to Finnish sources, these two divisions left behind 4,000 dead, 580 prisoners, 59 destroyed tanks and 220 machine-guns without counting the dead and wounded evacuated by the divisions themselves. During the remainder of December, and for the rest of the war, these two divisions maintained their defences and took advantage of the relative calm to study forest combat in winter conditions and organize ski-units (see Figure 2.7).[171]

Further north at Ilomantsi the 155th Rifle Division had advanced as far as the approaches to Kallioniemi Ferry and Oinaansalmi before being stopped by Finnish defensive detachments on 9 December. During the following week both belligerents attempted to break the deadlock with renewed offensives and counter-offensives, but neither could develop a significant advantage over the other and both remained in their positions for the duration of the war. The 155th Rifle Division managed to avoid the fate of the 139th and 75th

FIGURE 2.7

A SKI-PATROL RECEIVES ITS ORDERS, DECEMBER 1939

Courtesy of TsGASA, fond 34980, opis' 14, delo 195.

Rifle Divisions further south but had failed to execute its mission to seize Ilomantsi and join forces with the 9th Army to the north due to chronic communication problems and the resulting lack of interaction between units.[172]

As reports of these failures reached Petrozavodsk, G. Kulik, the Main Military Soviet's[173] representative at 8th Army headquarters, reported the seriousness of the 8th Army's situation back to Moscow on 19 December. Describing the heavy casualties that the Finnish Army had inflicted on the 18th and 168th Rifle Divisions, Kulik warned the Main Military Soviet that the situation on the north shore of Lake Ladoga would become dire unless a contingent of at least 20,000 troops came at once to the aid of these beleaguered divisions by the end of the month. On receiving this alarming report the Main Military Soviet immediately sent a more competent representative, Colonel Raevskii, to the 8th Army to interview senior and junior commanders for their frank opinions about the situation. Raevskii reported back to Moscow that the 8th Army was trying desperately to follow the specific orders issued by the Main Military Soviet to annihilate the enemy with encirclement operations. In other circumstances these tactics would be commendable, but the forested terrain, deep snow, and the lack of ski–troops to maintain mobility in these conditions confined the 8th Army to a 'road strategy' whereas the Finns were in a perfect position to practice annihilation tactics on the road-bound Red Army troops. Given this situation, the 8th Army had found itself in the uncomfortable position of being unable to mount an effective offensive while, at the same time, compromising the international prestige of the Red Army. Raevskii suggested that there was only one way to overcome this dilemma: adopt an entirely new tactics totally alien to the Red Army, the tactics of 'thorough combing' (*sploshnyi prochesyvanie*) whereby a massive wall of troops on skis would advance through the forest, seeking and destroying all enemy resistance. Raevskii acknowledged that these tactics would require tremendous numbers of men and a great deal of time, but did not regard this as an insurmountable problem. After all, in his opinion, the demographic might of the Soviet Union was enormous compared with that of Finland.[174]

The Main Military Soviet responded to Colonel Raevskii's report by removing Kurdiumov as commander of the 8th Army and replacing him with Army Commander G. Shtern, a favourite of Stalin who had served under Marshal Bliukher during the fiasco at Lake Khasan in the summer of 1938 and was promoted to command the Far Eastern Front's 1st Independent Red Banner Army after Bliukher's execution.[175] Shtern's first decision was to re-establish contact with the encircled 18th and 168th Rifle Divisions. A detachment was formed on 6 January and set out on a relief mission the next day but was soon forced to return to base due to poor troop control and deep snow.[176]

As news of this latest failure came trickling into 8th Army headquarters on the evening of 7 January, Shtern received a telephone call from Stalin in Moscow who was worried about the over-use of trucks to transport reinforcements and the likelihood of traffic jams on the icy roads.[177] Shtern confirmed that there were serious transportation problems holding up supply but that these were caused by horse-drawn carts and tractors as well as a complete lack of spare parts for cars and a lack of petrol distribution facilities. However, there were more fundamental problems on Shtern's mind and he quickly changed the subject of the conversation:

> Comrade Stalin! Yesterday and today four divisions were taken away from us in exchange for only two and who knows when they will arrive. I must report frankly that I do not think this is correct. This completely changes the army's work perspective, significantly postpones the time of the beginning of our present activity, creates a real threat of exhaustion in our troops before large reinforcements can arrive and it forces us to use the reinforcements to fill these holes. I think that the 8th Army offensive is highly essential for overall success. For that success, the according forces and their quick transport is needed ... Of course, for such troops one needs rear support. I ask you to give me forces and the time which was indicated on comrade Shaposhnikov's ciphered telegram of 4 January.

Stalin's response was the following:

> The direction of the 8th Army is possibly essential to future success. This we all recognize. You are preserved with thirteen divisions ... To this we will add two more divisions in mid-January, making fifteen divisions. It was desired to perform the transfer more quickly but that did not work out. We are not rushing you into an offensive because there is no possibility of haste. Let us start another [offensive elsewhere]. That will draw away some of the enemy's forces which should make things easier for you, and then you can strike.[178]

From this telephone conversation Shtern surmised that Stavka would not be reinforcing the 8th Army. His hopes dashed, Shtern re-evaluated his operational plans. Neither of the 8th Army's two rifle corps were making progress towards their goals, so Shtern re-deployed the 97th Rifle Regiment from the 1st Rifle Corps, placed it under the command of Colonel Ievlev and assigned it the mission to rally the 18th and 168th Rifle Divisions for a new offensive against the Finnish forces defending Sortavala on 21 January.[179]

Colonel Ievlev began his attack up the Uoma road on 13 January and three days later had advanced as far as Lovajärvi, halfway between Uoma and the 18th Rifle Division's headquarters. Here his detachment met a ski-battalion which had managed to break out of the Finnish encirclement but was too exhausted and demoralized to contribute to Ievlev's offensive and had to be evacuated. Ievlev resumed his attack against the last segment of road separating his detachment from the 18th Rifle Division the next day. Fearful that he might also be encircled, Ievlev left one of his battalions behind at Lovajärvi as a reserve while his two other battalions continued the attack. Needless to say, Ievlev's fear was fulfilled and he was forced to abort his attack.[180] Shtern's attempt to restart the 8th Army's offensive had failed.

The Finnish Army's most spectacular victory during its counter-offensive in mid-December was against the 9th Army at Suomussalmi (see Figure 2.8). When the 163rd Rifle Division encountered Finnish resistance south of Suomussalmi, the 9th Army commander, M. Dukhanov, sent the 44th Motorized Rifle Division under the command of A. Vinogradov to his aid. Vinogradov's division de-trained at Kemi on 14 December and began its march to the Soviet–Finnish border at Vazhenvaara. At this point Vinogradov made a decision which severely compromised the subsequent combat effectiveness of his division. An insufficient number of troop transport vehicles at Kem' obliged him to divide his forces: heavily armed combined arms units were transported to Vazhenvaara by truck while the lighter-armed vanguard units marched by foot. When Vinogradov's division began its attack up the Raate road towards Suomussalmi on 20 December, these vanguard units took up the rear and were unable to carry out their reconnaissance and road-security missions.[181] Vinogradov's operations were further compromised a day later when the 9th Army's Communications Department relayed unciphered orders to him over the radio.[182] As a result of this indiscretion the Finns were fully informed of Vinogradov's intentions.[183] Using a combination of guerrilla raids and a road block, they stopped the 44th Motorized Rifle Division several kilometres outside Suomussalmi on 23 December.

After completing the destruction of the 163rd Rifle Division north of Suomussalmi the Finns turned their attention to destroying Vinogradov's division piecemeal. On 4 January, Vinogradov radioed to 9th Army headquarters asking for assistance. That evening the new commander of the 9th Army, Corps Commander V. Chuikov, reported to Stavka that the situation was very serious and that if it did not improve the next day Stavka should give Vinogradov permission to retreat.[184] Stavka did not give Vinogradov permission to act on his own initiative until the evening of 6 January. When Vinogradov and the remnants of his division struggled back to Vazhenvaara

FIGURE 2.8
SITUATION MAP OF THE 9TH ARMY'S 163RD, 44TH AND 54TH RIFLE
DIVISIONS IN DECEMBER 1939

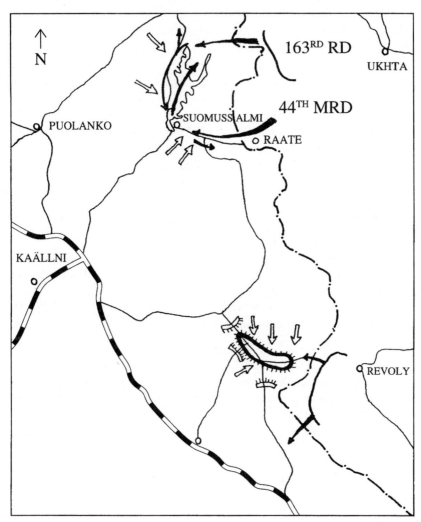

Adapted from *Konflikt*.

on the evening of 7 January the division had suffered 1,001 killed, 1,430 wounded, 82 frost-bitten and 2,243 missing in action.[185]

Stavka's reaction to this news was to send Mekhlis, the chief of the Red Army's Political Administration, to sort out the fiasco. Mekhlis was more interested in setting an example to instil greater discipline in the rest of the Red Army than he was in revealing the real causes of the defeat. Brushing aside the local military procurator's attempts to create a commission to study the full circumstances leading to the defeat, Mekhlis immediately placed Vinogradov and his staff under arrest and accused them of wilfully ignoring orders, abandoning war *matériel* on the battlefield, and neglecting to follow established doctrine in securing the Raate–Suomussalmi road. Vinogradov, and his commissar and chief of staff were executed in the presence of their staff.[186] However, not everyone at the 9th Army was willing to place the final blame on Vinogradov. In a report submitted to Voroshilov and Shaposhnikov in early January, Chuikov stated that the Red Army throughout the north was unable to free itself from 'road strategy' because its tactical doctrine was unsuited to the terrain of northern Finland. Chuikov's chief of staff, D. Nikishev, further elaborated this critique of Red Army tactics, reporting to Voroshilov that:

> Our units, saturated by technology (especially artillery and transport vehicles), are incapable of manoeuvre and combat in this theatre: they are burdened and chained down by technology which can only go by road ... Combat in special conditions is not studied – they [the troops] are frightened by the forest and cannot ski.[187]

On 19 January Stavka and the Main Military Soviet issued a circular to all the forces in the Leningrad Military District declaring that the inglorious defeat of the 44th Motorized Rifle Division was due to a lack of troop discipline, weak military training, and low political education which had led the troops to forget their duty to the nation and break their Soldier's Oath.[188] Five days later the People's Commissariat for Defence and the NKVD issued a joint order to create 'preventative detachments' (*kontrol'no-zagraditel'nye otriady*) for the explicit purpose of controlling desertion and cleaning up 'harmful elements' operating in the rear of the active armies. Directly subordinate to the Defence Commissariat and the NKVD, these preventative detachments were attached to army staffs but were not answerable to the army commander. The largest number of such detachments were assigned to the 8th Army operating in Ladoga-Karelia, and the second largest contingent was assigned to the 7th Army. There were 27 such preventative detachments in all, each made up of approximately 100 men.[189]

After the execution of Vinogradov and his staff, Mekhlis and his deputies remained in Kandalaksha to audit the 9th Army's staff work from the beginning of the crisis at Suomussalmi in early December up to current operations. In a report to Shaposhnikov at the Defence Commissariat on 12 January, Mekhlis described how the seeds which led to the eventual destruction of the 163rd Rifle Division were sown by the negligence of the 9th Army's Chief of the Operations Department, Ermolaev, and were compounded by the incompetence of the 163rd Rifle Division's commander, Zelentsov, and his superior commander, Dashichev, the commander of the 47th Rifle Corps.[190] At the end of January Mekhlis's audit revealed that Ermolaev had 'sabotaged' all the diary entries in the 9th Army's journal of military operations for December 1939 and early January 1940. What was more interesting, in light of Vinogradov's execution, was the revelation that not only had Ermolaev delayed the transmission of a Stavka order to Vinogradov on 22 December, instructing him to build entrenchments and to secure communications along the Raate road, but that he had falsified a report to the 9th Army's military soviet about the 44th Motorized Rifle Division's situation on 1 January and continued to delay the timely transmission of orders.[191] On 30 January Mekhlis placed Ermolaev under arrest, thereby implicitly acknowledging that an authority higher than Vinogradov's was responsible for the disaster at Suomussalmi.

Further to the north, the 122nd Rifle Division at Salla was joined by the 88th Rifle Division and the two divisions embarked on the next stage of their offensive towards the crossroads at Pelkosenniemi. The Finnish high command responded to this threat by sending seven reserve battalions to the region. A battle ensued in which the 122nd and 88th Rifle Divisions were stopped and were forced to retreat to Raatikka, a few kilometres north-west of Salla. To the south, a detachment of the 122nd Rifle Division had reached the town of Markajärvi where it was defeated on 20 December.[192] To the north, two vanguard regiments from the 14th Army had captured the nickel mines at Salmijärvi and were on the outskirts of Nautsi before the Finnish covering units, reinforced to battalion strength, managed to drive them back to Hoyhenjärvi on 21 December where they remained for the rest of the war.[193]

While the Red Army was encountering stiff opposition and, in some cases, defeat along the full length of the Soviet–Finnish border, the Baltic Fleet was desperately trying to isolate Finland from Scandinavia and the rest of Europe. Following the Naval Commissariat's extension of the naval blockade to the Abo-Åland Archipelago in the second week of December, Tributs sent two submarines, the *S-3* and the *Shch-324*, to patrol the Baltic Sea at the entrance to the South Kvarken Straits.[194] On 17 December the *S-3* encountered two cargo ships outside the blockade zone and fired warning shots at them. One of the cargo ships, which turned out to be German, responded by firing back 48 shells, none of which hit the Soviet submarine. The same day the *Shch-324* engaged two Finnish convoys but both attacks were compromised by malfunctioning torpedoes.[195] When Kuznetsov was informed of these confrontations he ordered Tributs to instruct the submarine commanders in the Baltic not to open fire on neutral shipping outside the blockade zone and to verify the combat readiness of their weapons.[196] Further south in the Baltic Sea, between the Eland and Gotland Islands, Soviet surface ships continued to monitor the flow of neutral shipping while the *S-4* continued to monitor the movements of the Swedish navy.[197]

At this time the Baltic Fleet decided to augment its submarine patrols in the Gulf of Bothnia with four additional submarines from bases at Tallinn and the Latvian port of Liepaja. These submarines were ready for long-range operations on 20 December and were sent to positions in the Baltic Sea to await orders to pass through the South Kvarken Straits.[198] The first submarine to attempt the passage was the *Shch-317* on 21 December. The submarine's commander chose to make the passage fully submerged and the submarine touched bottom several times before clearing the straits. The second submarine in the sequence was the *S-1*, but its passage through the straits was complicated by command and control problems between Tributs in Kronstadt, who was responsible for strategic command of the submarines in the Gulf of Bothnia, and his deputy in Tallinn, who was responsible for their initial deployment in the Baltic. After a delay of 24 hours the *S-1* finally ran the straits under periscope. During the passage, the *S-1* sailed across the course of a Finnish gun-boat and was spotted, but managed to clear the straits to take up its patrol outside the Swedish port of Gävle.[199] The third submarine, the *Shch-311*, hit a bad storm during its passage on 25 December but the submarine's commander managed to inspire the crew with 'Stalinist exercises' and the submarine survived the passage to take up patrol outside the port of Vaasa. The fourth submarine, the *Shch-318*, developed trouble with its electric motor and postponed its mission until 30 December, passing the straits on 2 January 1940.[200]

At the end of December, Stavka concluded that the submarine patrols in the Gulf of Bothnia were having little or no effect in stemming the flow of convoys between Sweden and Finland. Hoping to increase the effectiveness of the blockade, Kuznetsov ordered Tributs to widen the range of these patrols and assign two more submarines, the *S-2* and the *Shch-324*, to patrol additional navigation channels. During its passage through the straits, the *S-2* lost radio contact with Kronstadt and was presumed to have perished in a Swedish minefield.[201] The *Shch-324* had no difficulty making the passage and took up its patrol alongside the *S-1* outside Gävle on 10 January. Ice, increasingly rough seas, and dwindling fuel supplies brought all the submarines back to their bases in Latvia and Estonia by 19 January.[202] The Baltic Fleet command's submarines had sunk only five cargo ships during the four weeks that they had patrolled the Gulf of Bothnia.

After mid-January, responsibility for continuing the blockade fell to the Baltic Fleet's 10th Aviation Brigade, commanded by Major Kravchenko, which had been relocated to Paldiski on 19 December and since then had accumulated a force of three bombers, one fighter and two reconnaissance squadrons.[203] During the month of December, Kravchenko's brigade had flown bombing missions over Turku and Rauma when the weather permitted, but their raids did not affect the activity of these ports (see Figure 2.9). The brigade took over sole responsibility for the blockade on 20 January and began experimenting with a new military technology: the laying of naval minefields from the air. Specialists in this new form of warfare joined the brigade and performed their first mission in the channels outside Turku at the end of January. This innovative technique had a greater effect in harassing navigation, but the Finns soon strengthened their anti-aircraft defences and sent out British and German fighter aircraft to intercept the brigade's bombers, bringing down two long-range Soviet bombers on 3 February.[204] Sea communications between Finland and Sweden were ultimately halted by the severity of the winter storms, and even then communications were reopened between Vaasa and Umeå via an ice bridge across the Northern Kvarken Straits. This communication was conducted without the Baltic Fleet's knowledge until after the war had ended.[205]

FIGURE 2.9a

MAP OF THE BALTIC FLEET AIRFORCE'S BOMBING IN SOUTH FINLAND, 30 NOVEMBER 1939 TO 13 MARCH 1940

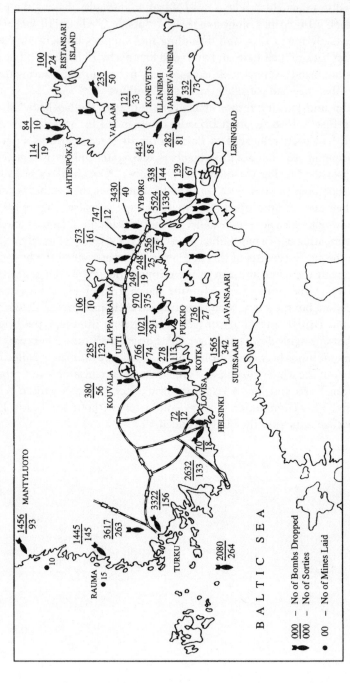

Adapted from *Sovetsko–finliandskaia voina 1939–1940 gg. na more.*

The Red Army Attacks Finland

FIGURE 2.9b
TABLE OF THE BALTIC FLEET AIRFORCE'S BOMBING IN SOUTH FINLAND, 30 NOVEMBER 1939 TO 13 MARCH 1940

No	Name of target	Number of sorties flown								Total no. bombs	Total weight Kg.
		DB	SB	I-16	I-15	I-153	MBR	R-5	Total sorties		
1	Seiskari Island	6	8					4	18	316	6170
2	Suusaari Island	6	65		270			1	342	1565	44958
3	Lavansaari Island		25					2	27	736	13508
4	Saarenpä Island	124	156						280	2277	166228
5	Fortresses on Saarenpä Is.		45						45	706	22284
6	Ronaniemi (old)	92	52						144	338	113270
7	Ronaniemi (new)	22	45						67	139	35260
8	Koivisto	198	42						240	432	204400
9	Ristniemi	115	197				63		375	970	192580
10	Pukkio	188	41	12			50		251	1021	204380
11	Tiurinsaari Island	9	20						29	297	15440
12	Sama Hamina (airfield)		12						12	72	7200
13	Helsinki	18							18	70	15750
14	Lovisa	28	23						51	169	29400
15	Kotka	43	13	53			2		113	278	34576
16	Koivisto	25	121	1157			18	15	1336	5524	132416
17	Koivisto (rail stn.)		20						20	120	12000
18	Lappenranta (rail stn.)	10							10	106	1000
19	Kurmi (rail stn.)	7	31		123				161	573	27690
20	Louko (rail stn.)	25							25	248	24800
21	Vainikkala (rail stn.)	19							19	240	17880
22	Hovinmaa (rail stn.)		12						12	742	8410
23	Kouvala (rail stn.)		9		47				56	380	4415
24	Inkerdinen (rail stn.)		31		43				74	756	17980
25	Vyborg	20	20						40	2925	18205
26	Utti (airfield)			123					123	235	2946
27	Konevets Island		14				19		33	121	15178
28	Taipale		18				55		73	332	23588
29	Illäniemi		47				38		85	443	37310
30	Punaniemi		23				50		73	382	23068
31	Battleships at Lahtenpökä		10						10	50	5000
32	Battleships at Valaam Is.		12				38		50	286	17416
33	Battery at Jarisevänniemi		26				35		61	282	24276
34	Ristinsari Island						24		24	100	5000
35	Monastery at Valaam		21				38		59	248	22580
	10th Air Brigade										
1	Hangö Port	8	58	11			56		133	2632	61904
2	Turku	32	176				55		263	3617	?172746
3	Rauma	24	121						145	1445	87534
4	Mäntylvoto	29	64						93	1456	63603
5	Cargo ships at sea	24	120		58		62		264	2080	95980
6	BBO	34	52		70				156	3322	73640
	Other targets									12211	264200

Adapted from *Sovetsko–finliandskaia voina 1939–1940 gg. na more.*

93

NOTES

1 J. Langdon-Davies, *Finland – The First Total War* (London: Routledge, 1940) p.5.
2 R. Heiskanen, 'The Effect of Finnish Military Intelligence Information and Evaluations on World War II Decision-Making in Finland', International Colloquium on Military History, Helsinki, 1988, p. 6.
3 G. Cox, *The Red Army Moves* (London: Gollancz, 1941) p. 62. See also Langdon-Davies, *Finland – The First Total War*, p. 101.
4 V. Stavskii, *Boi na karel'skom peresheike* (Moscow: Gospolitizdat, 1941) p. 15.
5 Soviet sources tend to refer to all permanent and semi-permanent fire-points as 'DOTs'. However, there were several classifications of 'fire points', ranging from the 'semi-kaponir' (a DZOT, or wood-and-earth structure with one flanking embrasure), the 'kaponir' (a DZOT with two flanking embrasures), the 'blockhouse' (a wood-and-stone structure with one or two frontal embrasures), to the 'DOT' (a reinforced concrete fortress with walls up to 2 metres thick and armed with one to three frontal or flanking embrasures protected by steel shields up to 10 centimetres thick).
6 Mannerheim, *The Memoirs of Marshal Mannerheim*, p. 325, and *Konflikt*, Document No. 76, 'Ukazaniia komandira 21 divisii finskoi armii ofitseram divizii o taktike pozitsionnoi voiny, 8 fevralia, 1940 g'. For a discussion of German defensive doctrine formulated during the First World War see M. Samuels, *Doctrine and Dogma. German and British Infantry Tactics in the First World War* (Westport, CT: Greenwood Press, 1992) pp. 72–82.
7 A.F. Upton, *Finland, 1939–1940* (London: Davis-Poynter, 1974) p. 55.
8 Mannerheim, *The Memoirs of Marshal Mannerheim*, p. 324.
9 Upton, *Finland, 1939–1940*, p. 60.
10 Meretskov, *Na sluzhbe narodu*, pp. 180–1. See also N.F. Kuz'min, *Na strazhe mirnogo truda, 1921–1940gg.* (Moscow: Voenizdat, 1959) p. 237.
11 A. Chew, *The White Death: The Epic of the Soviet–Finnish Winter War* (East Lansing, MI: Michigan State University Press, 1971) pp. 6, 8.
12 Upton, *Finland, 1939–1940*, p. 56. See also T. Reis, manuscript for *Cold Will*, p. 5.
13 Ries, 'Manuscript for *Cold Will*', p. 5.
14 M. Waller, *Democratic Centralism: An Historical Commentary* (Manchester: Manchester University Press, 1981), pp. 18–19.
15 Gareev, *M.V. Frunze – Military Theorist* (London: Brassey's, 1988) pp. 250–51.
16 Waller, *Democratic Centralism*, pp. 11, 138, and R. Tierskii, *Ordinary Stalinism. Democratic Centralism and the Question of Communist Political Development* (Boston: Allen & Unwin, 1985) pp. 69–70.
17 After 1934 Stalin increased the size of the Red Army to 940,000. By November 1939 the Red Army's total had grown to 2,300,000 troops. See Erickson, *The Soviet High Command*, pp. 366–73, and TsGASA fond 4, opis' 18, delo 49, l.15, 'Protocol No. 6. Main Military Soviet, November 21, 1939'.
18 R. Conquest, *The Great Terror* (London: Pimlico, 1990) p. 450.
19 C. Van Dyke, *Russian Imperial Military Doctrine and Education, 1832–1914* (Westport, CT: Greenwood Press, 1990), *passim*, and B.W. Menning, *Bayonets before Bullets. The Imperial Russian Army, 1861–1914* (Bloomington: Indiana University Press, 1992) *passim*.
20 J. Erickson and L. Hansen, *Soviet Combined Arms: Past and Present* (College Station Papers No. 1, The Center for Strategic Technology, Texas A and M University, 1981) p. 2. For a discussion of the debate over Unified Military Doctrine see M.V. Frunze, 'Edinaia voennaia doktrina i Krasnaia Armiia', *Izbrannye proizvedeniia*, Vol. 2 (Moscow: Voenizdat, 1957) pp. 4–22, and B. Semmel, *Marxism and the Science of War* (Oxford: Oxford University Press, 1981) pp. 17–24, and J.J. Schneider, 'The Origins of Soviet Military Science', *Journal of Soviet Military Studies*, Vol. 2, No. 4, December 1989, pp. 492–516, and A. Gat, *The Development of Military Thought*, pp. 239–42.
21 N. Varfolomeev, *Tekhnika shtabnoi sluzhy. Operativnaia sluzhba voiskovykh shtabov (v voennoe vremiia)* (Moscow: Vysshii Voennyi Redaktsionnyi Sovet, 1924) pp. 3–19.
22 M. Tukhachevskii, *Izbrannye proizvedeniia*, Tom I (Moscow: Voenizdat, 1964), p. 16 and

R. Simpkin, *Deep Battle. The Brainchild of Marshal Tukhachevskii* (London: Brassey's, 1987) p. 37.

23 Erickson, *The Soviet High Command*, pp. 208, 316–18. See also D.M. Glantz, *The Soviet Conduct of Tactical Maneuver. Spearhead of the Offensive*, pp. 76–80.

24 F.C. Turner, 'The Genesis of the Soviet "Deep Operations"': The Stalin Era. Doctrine for Large Scale Offensive Maneuver Warfare', Ph.D. dissertation, Duke University, 1988, pp. 198, 218.

25 Tarleton, 'What Really Happened to the Stalin Line? Part 1', *Journal of Soviet Military Studies*, Vol. 5, No. 2, June 1992, p. 204. See also Shilovskii, *Nastupatel'naia armeiskaia operatsiia. Vypusk. 5, Osnovy operativnogo proryva* (Moscow: AGSh RKKA, 1940) pp. 9–13. Shilovskii dismissed Zhukov's astounding victory against the Japanese *Kwangtung* Army at Khalkhin-Gol as a model for the initial period of war on the Soviet Union's western borders. In Shilovskii's opinion, neither the Japanese Army nor Zhukov's forces were able to create a saturated front, and for that reason deep flanking manoeuvres were possible. Even so, Zhukov had to conduct a frontal breakthrough of Japanese defences in addition to his wide, out-flanking manoeuvres. A description of the project Field Regulations for 1939 is given in Kuz'min, *Na strazhe mirnogo truda (1921–1940gg.)* pp. 226–8. See also Taylor, 'The Reorganization of the Soviet Command System for Total War: 1939–1941', p. 98–9, and Simpkin, *Deep Battle*, p. 49.

26 RTsKhINDI, fond 74 (Papers of K. Voroshilov), opis' 1, delo 163, ll. 40–51, 'Voroshilov's report to the IV Extraordinary Session of the Supreme Soviet USSR, 31 August 1939, on the new Law on Universal Military Duty'.

27 F.I. Trukhin, F.M. Isaev, and S.I Liubarskii, *Metodika i tekhnika raboty obshchevoiskovykh shtabov* (Moscow: Akademiia General'nogo Shtaba RKKA, 1939) p. 13.

28 A.A. Svechin in his seminal work, *Strategiia*, written in the mid-1920s, explained the connotations of this term in the following way: 'Sometimes instead of *direktiva* [directive] the Russian word *nastavlenie* [direction] is used, but it has a different meaning. A *nastavlenie* consists of relatively binding guidelines and advice, which often goes into detail.' Svechin went on to say that, 'A directive should not be confused with a *nastavlenie*. A directive's brief indications of a goal should never be semi[-]obligatory. The use of directives as a means of command is possible only when the commander to whom the directive is given has been indoctrinated not to abuse this freedom of action and will actually pursue the goal indicated in it ...' Cited from A.A. Svechin, *Strategy*, translated and published by East View Publications, Minneapolis, MN, 1992, p. 327.

29 Voronov, *Na sluzhbe voennoi*, p. 136. Voronov alerted Meretskov to this problem during an inspection tour of the Leningrad Military District shortly before the war.

30 *Konflikt*, Document No. 21, 'Iz otcheta o boevykh deistviiakh 50 str. korpusa v period s 30 noiabria po 19 dekabria 1939 g.' See also Document No. 20, 'Iz otcheta o boevykh deistviiakh 19 str. korpusa v period s 30 noiabria po 21 dekabria 1939 g'.

31 N. Virta, 'Terioki', *Na Strazhe Rodiny*, 6 December 1939, p. 3.

32 *Konflikt*, Document No. 20. See also TsGASA, fond 34980, opis' 14, delo 6, ll. 3–4.

33 *Konflikt*, Document No. 18, 'Prikaz voiskam 7 armii ob uluchshenii upravleniia voiskami, 30 noiabria 1939 g'. The English equivalent of the 'quadrant system' of artillery fire is 'predicted fire': the use of indirect fire solely on the basis of ballistics and map coordinates calculated in advance.

34 Voronov, *Na sluzhbe voennoi*, p. 138. See also Meretskov's lecture in June 1940 and *Konflikt*, Document No. 21. For a discussion on reconnaissance and sapper organization and methods see P. Egorov, 'Boi s razgrazhdeniem prepiatstvii', *Na Strazhe Rodiny*, 2 December 1939, p. 4.

35 *Sovetsko–finliandskaia voina 1939–1940 gg. na more*, Chast' I, Kniga III, p. 47. See also *Konflikt*, Document No. 23, 'Iz ocherka boevykh deistvii 56 str. korpusa v period s 30 noiabria 1939 g. po 1 ianvaria 1940 g'.

36 *Sovetsko–finliandskaia voina 1939–1940 gg. na more*, Chast' I, Kniga III, p. 47. The *Orangenbaum* was armed with two 130 mm. guns scavenged from the battleship *Aurora*.

37 Ibid., p. 50.

The Soviet Invasion of Finland, 1939–40

38 P.F. Vashchenko, 'Esli by Finliandiia i SSSR ...', *Voenno-istoricheskii zhurnal*, No. 1, 1990, p. 29.
39 *Konflikt*, Document No. 23.
40 Ibid.
41 *Konflikt*, Document No. 22.
42 Ibid.
43 Chew, *The White Death*, p. 33.
44 Ibid., pp. 8–10.
45 Chew, *The White Death*, p. 8.
46 *Sovetsko–finliandskaia voina 1939–1940 gg. na more*, Chast' II, pp. 21–8.
47 Ibid., Chast' I, Kniga I, p. 67.
48 Meretskov's explicit reason for deviating from the original plan was that no Soviet ships had sailed in these waters since the end of the First World War and that, for this reason, there were no accurate charts for guiding the submarines. However, Stalin may have decided to wait and gauge the Swedish government's reaction to the invasion before mobilizing the Soviet navy any further.
49 Ibid., Chast' I, Kniga I, p. 69.
50 Ibid., p. 91–2.
51 Ibid., p. 88.
52 Ibid., p. 69.
53 Ibid., p. 90.
54 Ibid., pp. 61–2.
55 Ibid., Chast' I, Kniga I, pp. 74–83.
56 Ibid., pp. 78–83.
57 Ibid., p. 71.
58 Ibid., p. 73.
59 Ibid., p. 88.
60 The Baltic Fleet's bombing of Helsinki on the first day of the invasion had a profound effect on the future course of the war. It galvanized Finnish public support and elicited foreign sympathy for Finland's war effort. Much speculation has been devoted to the Soviet leadership's motives for bombing Helsinki but, according to the official history of the Baltic Fleet, the sole purpose of the bomber crew was to dispose of their volatile cargo before landing back at Kronstadt. Perhaps the bombing was also a reprisal for Bel'skii's death. See *Sovetsko–finliandskaia voina 1939–1940 gg. na more*, Chast' I, Kniga I, pp. 83–4, and K-F. Geist, 'Bombi na stolitsu', *Rodina*, No. 12, Winter, 1995, p. 58. Meretskov subsequently ordered all air detachments operating in the Finnish theatre of war to avoid bombing population centres. See *Konflikt*, Document No. 26, 'Prikaz voiskam 7, 8, 9-i armii o forsirovanii tempov nastupleniia, 3 dekabria 1939 g'.
61 *Boevye deistviia VVS KBF v voine s belofinnami (s 30 noiabria 1939 g. po 13 marta 1940 g.)* (Moscow–Leningrad: Gosvoenmorizdat NKVMF SSSSR, 1941) pp. 97–8.
62 *Sovetsko–finliandskaia voina 1939–1940 gg. na more*, Chast' I, Kniga I, pp. 83–7.
63 Tanner, *The Winter War*, pp. 96–8.
64 Ibid., p. 100 and Upton, *Finland 1939–1940*, p. 72. For more about Sweden's military role in the war see M. Turtola, *Tornionjoelta Rajajoele: Suomen ja Ruotsin salainen yhteistoiminta Neuvostoliiton hyokkayksen varalle 1932–1940* [From the River Tornionjoki to the River Rajajoki: Secret collaboration between Finland and Sweden on the contingency of a Soviet attack, 1932–1940] (Helsinki: 1984).
65 A.G. Dongarov, 'Pravitel'stvo Kusinena: Epizod sovetsko–finliandskoi voiny 1939–1940', *Vestnik MID SSSR*, Vol. 22, (56) 1 December 1989, p. 75. In examining the drafts of this radio communiqué, Dongarov comments that this statement, as well as the statement about the political nature of the Finnish Democratic Republic, were not written in Kuusinen's original draft and were added in a subsequent draft by Molotov.
66 Ries, 'Manuscript draft for *Cold Will*', p. 21.
67 RTsKhINDI, fond 522, opis' 1, delo 42, ll. 1–14, 'Kuusinen, draft of article commemorating Stalin's sixtieth birthday, 21 December 1939'. Specific reference to the Soviet

Union's national foreign policy as 'socialist nationalism' was cut by Kuusinen and did not appear in the published article entitled 'Velikomu drugu finliandskogo naroda tovarishchu STALINU', *Na Strazhe Rodiny*, 29 December 1939, p. 1.

68 C.D. Jones, 'Just Wars and Limited Wars: Restraints on the Use of Soviet Armed Forces', *World Politics*, Vol. XXVIII, No. 1, October 1975, p. 63. See also Dallin, *Soviet Russia's Foreign Policy*, pp. 134–5.

69 In the case of Lithuania, Stalin had already demonstrated the territorial aspect of his national policy by giving the former Polish city of Vilnius to the Lithuanian government. See Rei, *The Drama of the Baltic Peoples*, p. 269.

70 In a book written by P.V. Suslov in 1930 entitled *Politicheskoe obespechenie sovetsko–pol'skoi kampanii 1920 goda* (Securing Political Support in the Soviet–Polish Campaign of 1920), the author indicated that, during the Soviet offensive against Warsaw, the Polish Communist Party and the Provisional Government underestimated the strength of Polish nationalism and the peasants' opposition to the transfer of large landed estates directly to government control. See Suslov as discussed in Jones, 'Just and Limited Wars ...', p. 64.

71 Dongarov, 'Pravitel'stvo Kuusinena', p. 75. G.A. Kumanev in an article entitled 'Chto my znaem o "zimnei voine"', *Sovetskaia Rossiia*, 10 March 1990 states that in a conversation between Molotov and Schulenburg on 30 November 1939, Molotov declared that 'This government will not be a soviet type, but a democratic republic type. No one will create councils, but we hope that it will be a government with which we can negotiate and secure the safety of Leningrad.'

72 J.J. Schneider, 'Introduction', in V.F. Triandafillov's *The Nature of the Operations of Modern Armies*, pp. xliii. Triandafillov explained the military operational significance of political agitation in the following manner: '... successful conduct of this political work among enemy troops can, along with other situational data, create conditions favourable for deep crushing blows. Major offensives with relatively small forces, with lower suppressive asset norms, also can be undertaken against morally unstable and politically vacillating enemy troops.' See Chapter 5 for the Red Army General Staff's comments on the relationship between 'lightning war' and the 'moral–political' stability of the enemy's armed forces.

73 RTsKhINDI, fond 522, opis' 1, delo 46, ll. 34–40, 'Project Instructions: How to Begin the Political and Organizational Work of Communists in the Regions Liberated from the White Finns, n.d.' In a recent article by M.I. Mel'tiukhov in *Otechestvennaia istoriia*, No. 3, 1993, entitled '"Narodnyi Front" dlia Finliandii? (K voprosu o tseliakh sovetskogo rukovodstva v voine s Finliandiei 1939–1940gg.)', Mel'tiukhov discusses identical documents found in A.A. Zhdanov's personal archive at RTsKhINDI which are dated 26 December 1939.

74 Another policy of Kuusinen's 'hearts-and-minds' campaign was to reopen food and clothing stores in population centres and establish credit for local residents. For this purpose, special trade representatives were sent from Narkomtorg. See N. Virta, 'Terioki', *Na Strazhe Rodiny*, 6 December 1939, p. 3, and RTsKhINDI, fond 522, opis' 1, delo 46, ll. 18–22, 'Summary Report from Work Brigade Brigadier Karpov to the President of the Finnish Peoples' Government, 28 January 1940'.

75 As Mel'tiukhov explains in his article about Kuusinen's government based on identical documents from A.A. Zhdanov's personal archives at RTsKhINDI, the concept of the 'People's Front' was defined by G. Dimitrov at the VII Congress of the Comintern in 1935. People's Fronts were organized by communist parties for the dual purpose of fighting fascism and promoting socialism. See Mel'tiukov, '"Narodnyi Front" dlia Finliandii?' p. 96.

76 Previous surrogate governments sponsored by the Red Army, for example Dzerzhinskii's Polish Revolutionary Committee during the war with Poland in 1920, followed a similar political agenda. See T.C. Fiddik, *Russia's Retreat from Poland, 1920. From Permanent Revolution to Peaceful Coexistence* (London: Macmillan, 1990), p. 186.

77 Virta, 'Terioki', *Na Strazhe Rodiny*, 6 December 1939, p. 3. See also RTsKhINDI, fond 522, opis' 1, delo 46, ll. 47–8.

78 RTsKhINDI, fond 522, opis' 1, delo 42, ll. 16–19. 'From the Political Administration of the Leningrad Military District, "Against Whom We Are Fighting", Leningrad, 1939'.

79 RTsKhINDI, fond 522, opis' 1, delo 42, ll. 1–14.
80 V. ˙Chernyshev, 'Vstrecha (between two old Finns in the 1st Corps of the Finnish People's Army)', *Na Strazhe Rodiny*, 10 December 1939, p. 4.
81 RTsKhINDI, fond 522, opis'1, delo 42, l.42.
82 Nesterov, 'Narodoarmeitsy Suomi', *Na Strazhe Rodiny*, 26 December 1939, p. 4.
83 Virta, 'Terioki', *Na Strazhe Rodiny*, 6 December 1939, p. 3.
84 Nesterov, 'Narodoarmeitsy Suomi', *Na Strazhe Rodiny*, 26 December 1939, p. 4. Kuusinen's nationalization programme is discussed in RTsKhINDI, fond 522, opis'1, delo 46, ll. 18–22.
85 RTsKhINDI, fond 71, opis'25, delo 46, 'Main Military Soviet to the Leningrad Military District on Deficiencies in Tactics, December 3, 1939'.
86 Otto Manninen, 'Neuvostoliiton operatliiviset suummitelmat 1939–1941 Suomen suunnalla', *Sotahistoriallinen Aikakauskirja*, No. 11 (Helsinki, 1992) p. 135
87 *Konflikt*, Document No. 23.
88 A. Chew, *The White Death*, pp. 18–19.
89 Ibid., and *Konflikt*, Document No. 21.
90 This vanguard, the 7th Rifle Regiment of the 24th Rifle Division, had tried to assault the Finnish DOTs and suffered 38 dead and 109 wounded. See *Konflikt*, Document No. 20.
91 Ibid., Document No. 29, 'Prikaz narkoma oborony K.E. Voroshilova komanduiushchemu Leningradskim voennym okrugom i komanduiushchemu 7 armiei o neobkhodimosti sovmestnykh deistvii pekhoty i artillerii, 7 dekabria 1939 g'.
92 RTsKhINDI, fond 71, opis' 25, delo 47, 'Main Military Soviet on the Formation of STAVKA, December 9, 1939'.
93 *Konflikt*, Document No. 21, 'Iz otcheta o boevykh deistviiakh 50 str. korpusa v period s 30 noiabria po 19 dekabria 1939 g'.
94 *Boi na karel'skom peresheike*, p. 113. See also Editorial, 'S nami ves' sovetskii narody', *Na Strazhe Rodiny*, 12 December 1939, p. 1.
95 *Konflikt*, Document No. 31, 'Direktiva Glavnokomandovaniia komanduiushchim 7, 8, 9, i 14-i armii o taktike boevykh deistvii i organizatsii upravleniia voiskami, 12 dekabria 1939 g'.
96 Ibid. STAVKA's directive was preceded a day earlier by an editorial article in *Na Strazhe Rodiny* entitled 'Vzaimodeistvie voisk reshaet uspekh boia' (11 December 1939, p. 1) emphasizing the role of staffs to maintain interaction between different services and to draw up well-conceived plans.
97 On 9 December the Finnish Army had captured a corps commanders' orders to his troops dismissing the threat posed by DOTs: 'On the whole there is too much talk about fixed firing points (DOTs)'. See PRO WO 208/582, Appendix G, 'Enemy Tactics in Attack'.
98 'Excerpts on Soviet 1938–1940 operations from *The History of Warfare, Military Art, and Military Science*, a 1977 textbook of the Military Academy of the General Staff of the USSR Armed Forces', *Journal of Slavic Military Studies*, Vol. 6, No. 1, (March 1993) p. 131. In this brief history of the Soviet–Finnish War, the authors admitted that the Red Army high command had launched the invasion without preparing beforehand for combat against fortified regions. In PU-36 only one article was devoted to the tactics of breakthrough. In PU-39 breakthrough tactics were discussed in nine articles but still had not received enough theoretical development to be of any use to the troops.
99 M. Iuvenskii, 'Kak unichtozhit' ognevuiu tochka vraga', *Na Strazhe Rodiny*, 4 December 1939, p. 3.
100 D. Piskunov, 'Unichtozhenie ognevykh tochek otdel'nymi orudiiami', *Na Strazhe Rodiny*, 6 December 1939, p. 3. See also A. Khadeev, 'Bor'ba za ovladenie ukreplenym raionom', *Na Strazhe Rodiny*, 3 December 1939, p. 4.
101 Khadeev, 'Bor'ba za ovladenie ukreplenym raionom', p. 4. See also the sequel to this article on 5 December p. 3.
102 D. Piskunov, 'Unichtozhenie ognevykh tochek otdel'nymi orudiiami', p. 3.
103 *Sovetsko-finliandskaia voina 1939–1940 gg. na more*, Chast' I, Kniga II, p. 4. Kuznetsov ordered the Baltic Fleet to sink all ships found in the blockade zone on 9 December.

104 Ibid., pp. 40–1.
105 Ibid., pp. 41–5.
106 Ibid., Chast' I, Kniga II, pp. 3–5
107 Ibid., Chast' I, Kniga III, p. 146, and Chast' I, Kniga II, p. 12.
108 Ibid., pp. 20–1.
109 Ibid., pp. 22–3.
110 Ibid., pp. 27, 35. When the war was over, Tributs set up a commission to study why the operations against the Finnish batteries at Bjorko and Muurila were so ineffective. The commission discovered that the Baltic Fleet command had failed to identify the existence of many Finnish batteries along the coast to Vyborg before the onset of the war, that during the war there was no established centre for collecting and redistributing reconnaissance information gathered in the course of operations, and that aerial reconnaissance remained ineffective until the end of December 1939 when airplanes were fitted with cameras. On the basis of these findings and a survey of the operations, the commission made the following generalizations: one needed to know the exact location of the target in order for artillery fire and aerial bombing to be effective, and that one needed to conduct an immediate amphibious assault against a coastal battery after it had been suppressed in order to destroy it. See Ibid., pp. 25–36.
111 Ibid., p. 37.
112 Ibid., p. 50.
113 Ibid., p. 52.
114 Ibid., p. 53.
115 Ibid., p. 84.
116 Ibid.
117 Ibid., Chast' I, Kniga III, pp. 130–1.
118 *Konflikt*, Document No. 26, 'Prikaz voiskam 7, 8, 9-i armii o forsirovanii tempov nastupleniia, 3 dekabria 1939 g.'
119 O. Manninen, 'Neuvostoliiton operatliiviset suummitelmat 1939–1941 Suomen suunnalla', *Sotahistoriallinen Aikakauskirja*, No. 11, Helsinki, 1992, p. 135.
120 *Konflikt*, Document No. 23.
121 Ibid.
122 *Konflikt*, Document No. 22.
123 *Konflikt*, Document No. 56. See also Document No. 22.
124 Chew, *The White Death*, p. 35. See also *Konflikt*, Document No. 22.
125 Chew, *The White Death*, pp. 36–7.
126 *Konflikt*, Document No. 22.
127 Chew, *The White Death*, pp. 40–1.
128 Nevakivi, *The Appeal that was Never Made: The Allies, Scandinavia and the Finnish Winter War, 1939–1940* (London: C. Hurst, 1976) p. 54.
129 Ibid.
130 *Rokovye gody, 1939–1940. Sobytiia v Pribaltiiskikh gosudarstvakh i Finliandii na osnove sovetskikh dokumentov i materialov* (Tallinn: 1990) p. 46.
131 Upton, *Finland 1939–1940*, p. 73.
132 Ibid., pp. 48–52.
133 Erickson, *The Soviet High Command*, p. 543. See also *Konflikt*, Document No. 33, 'Prikaz voiskam 7 armii o nachale nastupleniia na keksgol'mskom i vyborgskom napravleniiakh, 13 dekrabriia 1939 g'.
134 *Konflikt*, Document No. 33. Meretskov placed emphasis on this point by stating in a rather laconic way, '… this must become law'.
135 PRO, WO 208/582, 'Report on Russian Tactical Operations in Finland by Major R.O.A. Gatehouse and Captain C.H. Tamplin, December 1939–February 1940, Appendix E'.
136 V. Butylev, 'Kak razvedat' DOT'y', *Na Strazhe Rodiny*, 16 December 1939, p. 2.
137 Builov, 'Bit' vraga po-ugriumovski', *Na Strazhe Rodiny*, 18 December 1939, p. 2. In other newspaper reports about similar meetings in units of different services these terms were augmented to address the specific requirements of the unit. See D. Alekseev,

'Ukliuchaemsia v boevoe sorevnovanie', *Na Strazhe Rodiny*, 12 December 1939, p. 1, and Chernov, 'Predlozhenie boevykh tovarishchei voodushevliaet nas na novye podvigi', *Na Strazhe Rodiny*, 13 December 1939, p. 1.

138 Ries, 'Manuscript for *Cold Will*', p. 26. When this attack was lifted on 17 December Grendal's artillery and aviation barrage had expended 100,000 shells and 15,000 bombs. In S. Klavdiev's article entitled 'Proryv linii "Mazhino-Kirke"' (*Na Strazhe Rodiny*, 16 December 1939, p. 3), Grendal's offensive is portrayed not only as a successful break-through operation, but as the first offensive in the history of warfare to accomplish a breakthrough against a fortified region after forcing a river.

139 PRO WO 208/582, 'Report on Russian Tactical Operations in Finland by Major R.O.A. Gatehouse and Captain C.H. Tamplin, December 1939–February 1940, Appendix C: Report made by Prisoner of War Captain Yanov, late Tank Battalion Commander, on the Summa Operations (35-tonne tank)', pp. 19–20. The testimony of the Soviet tank commander was collected during an interview with two British military specialists sent to Finland in January 1940 to study the combat capabilities of the Red Army. This material is British Crown copyright and is reproduced with the permission of the Controller of Her Majesty's Stationery Office, London.

140 *Konflikt*, Document No. 21.

141 *Boi na karel'skom peresheike*, p. 114.

142 *Konflikt*, Document No. 40, 'Prikaz komanduiushchego 7 armiei voiskam armii o nastuplenii na khotinenskom napravlenii, 17 dekabria 1939 g'.

143 PRO WO 208/582, 'Appendix C', p. 21. The testimony of the captured Soviet tank commander indicated that he lost five or six tanks in the last two rows of granite obstacles in front of the Mannerheim Line.

144 Ibid. See also N.N. Korneev, *Boevye deistviia 50 SK po proryvu linii mannergeima* (Moscow: unpubl. ms., 1941) p. 44.

145 PRO WO 208/582, 'Appendix C', pp. 21–2. Captain Yanov was obviously not keen to follow his subordinates back to the Red Army lines. By abandoning his tanks he would have broken the terms of the combat socialist competition and, by implication, the military oath, and would have been punished accordingly.

146 TsGASA, fond 34980, opis 14, delo 6, l. 9. See also *Konflikt*, Document No. 21.

147 G.A Kumanev, 'Besslavnaia voina, ili pobeda, kotoroi ne gordilic", unpublished paper given to a seminar at the Institute of the History of Russia, Moscow, 29 January 1992, p. 6. See also M. Semiryaga, *The Winter War, Looking Back after Fifty Years* (Moscow: Novosti,1990) p. 26.

148 Korneev, *Boevye deistviia 50 SK po proryvu linii mannergeima*, p. 17. Korneev claimed that Plan *Ladoga* had been scheduled to begin on 25 December but that Stavka called it off.

149 *Konflikt*, Document No. 44, 'Direktiva komanduiushchego 7 armii komandiram 19, 50 str. korpusov, 10 tankovogo korpusa, nachal'nikam VVS i artillerii armii o podgotovke proryva na vyborgskom napravlenii, 22 dekabria 1939 g'.

150 Korneev, *Boevye deistviia 50 SK po proryvu linii mannergeima*, pp. 17–18. See also *Konflikt*, Document No. 44.

151 *Konflikt*, Document No. 44. See also Korneev, *Boevye deistviia 50 SK po proryvu linii mannergeima*, p. 18. Korneev claims that the 50th Rifle Corps command on 23 December ordered sapper units to clear pathways through the obstacle fields for infantry and tanks in preparation for the new offensive. This order was issued just as the Finnish counter-offensive was unfolding that morning.

152 *Sovetsko-finliandskaia voina 1939–1940 gg. na more*, Chast' I, Kniga II, p. 57.

153 TsGASA, fond 34980, opis' 14, delo 99, 'Secretariat of the NKO USSR: Press Summaries of Foreign Military Commentary on the Combat Capability of the Red Army', l.16.

154 'Trekhnedel'nyi itog boevykh deistvii v Finliandii (Communiqué from the staff of the Leningrad Military District)', *Na Strazhe Rodiny*, 23 December 1939, p. 1.

155 M. Samuels, *Doctrine and Dogma. German and British Infantry Tactics in the First World War* (Westport, CT: Greenwood Press, 1992) pp. 70–1.

156 Mannerheim, *The Memoirs of Marshal Mannerheim*, pp. 344–5.

157 Chew, *The White Death*, pp. 65–9.
158 TsGASA, fond 34980, opis' 6, delo 77, 'Operational Plan of the Right Group of the 7th Army', 24–5 December 1939, ll. 2–11.
159 Chew, *The White Death*, p. 70, and Ries, 'Manuscript for *Cold Will*', p. 28.
160 Chew, *The White Death*, pp. 73–4, and Ries, 'Manuscript for *Cold Will*', p. 29.
161 *Konflikt*, Document No. 23.
162 *Sovetsko–finliandskaia voina 1939–1940 gg. na more*, Chast' I, Kniga III, pp. 53–4.
163 *Konflikt*, Document No. 22, and Chew, *The White Death*, p. 44.
164 *Konflikt*, Document No. 22.
165 Chew, *The White Death*, pp. 35–48. and *Konflikt*, Document No. 22.
166 *Konflikt*, Document No. 22.
167 Ibid., Document No. 56.
168 Ibid., Document No. 22.
169 Ibid.
170 Chew, *The White Death*, p. 57. The Finnish counter-offensive had cost the Finnish Army 630 soldiers killed and 1,320 wounded which included 30 per cent of the officer corps. Proportionally, these were the heaviest losses suffered by the Finnish Army to date.
171 *Konflikt*, Document No. 22.
172 Ibid.
173 Stalin recognized that Stavka was too far removed from the theatre of war to exercise adequate control. At some time in mid-December he resuscitated the Main Military Soviet's executive functions and brought in competent military personnel. On 22 December the Main Military Soviet consisted of K.E. Voroshilov, S.M. Budennyi, G.I. Kulik, L.Z. Mekhlis, E.A. Shchadenko, B.M. Shaposhnikov, A.D. Loktionov, I.O. Proskurov, S.K. Timoshenko, Ya.V. Smushkevich, D.G. Pavlov and G.K. Savchenko.
174 *Konflikt*, Document No. 49, 'Iz dokladnoi zapiski polkovnika N.P. Raevskogo Narkomu oborony o boevykh deistviiakh na petrozavodskom napravlenii, 31 dekabria 1939 g.'.
175 TsGASA, fond 25888, opis' 15, delo 458, l.77, 'Order of the NKO No. 0040, September 4, 1938'. For a brief synopsis of Red Army operations at Lake Khasan see Haslam, *The Soviet Union and the Threat from the East*, pp. 116–18.
176 Ibid., Document No. 58, 'Iz ocherka boevykh deistvii 56 str. korpusa v ianvare 1940 g'.
177 Stalin's concern for road and traffic conditions in the 8th Army's theatre of war may have been inspired by the disaster facing the 44th Motorized Rifle Division at this time.
178 RTsKhINDI, fond 71, opis'25, delo 6861, ll. 411–414, 'Record of Direct Telephone Conversation between Stalin and Corps Commander Shtern, January 7, 1940'.
179 *Konflikt*, Document No. 56.
180 Ibid., Document No. 58.
181 O.A. Dudorovna, 'Stranitsy "Neizvestnoi Voiny". Iz istorii Sovetsko–finliandskoi voiny', p. 2. (Manuscript for article subsequently published in *Voenno-istoricheskii zhurnal*.)
182 TsGASA, fond 34980, opis' 5, delo 53, ll. 273–272, 'Mekhlis' Report to STAVKA on the incompetence of the Chief of Operations, 9th Army staff'.
183 Chew, *The White Death*, p. 103.
184 Dudorovna, 'Stranitsy "Neizvestnoi Voiny"', p. 8.
185 Ibid.
186 Ibid., p. 9.
187 Ibid., p. 12.
188 *Konflikt*, Document No. 60, 'Prikaz Glavnogo voennogo soveta RKKA ob izvlechenii opyta iz porazheniia 44 str. divizii, 19 ianvaria 1940 g'.
189 TsGASA, fond 34980, opis' 6, delo 77, ll. 117–119. The archives of the Red Army contain many collections of documents relating to the activities of these special NKVD units in the active Red Army. An example of two such collections concerning the 13th Army are: TsGASA, fond 34980, opis' 6, delo 15, 'Summaries and Reports of the Special Section of the NKVD in the army about the politico-morale situation and extraordinary occurrences in the units, 3 January–27 March', and delo 18, 'Materials on research into extraordinary occurrences'. Notes on summaries of the Special Section of the NKVD in the army,

5 January–26 March'. Neither of these two collections were available to the researcher in spring 1992. In his memoirs, Alexander Tvardovskii, a military journalist and poet assigned to the newspaper *Na Strazhe Rodiny*, recounts a conversation with a field doctor about the incidences of 'esesy' ('SS' – 'Samo-strel', or 'self-shootings'). See A. Tvardovskii, 'S karel'skogo peresheika', *Novyi Mir*, No. 2, 1969, p. 132. Only a detailed analysis of the Red Army's military archives will indicate the scale of spontaneous, unorganized mutiny in the 7th Army at this time.

190 TsGASA, fond 34980, opis' 5, delo 53, ll. 271–270, 'Mekhlis to Voroshilov on officer insubordination, 12 January, 1940'.
191 Ibid., ll. 273–272, 'Mekhlis to Stavka on the arrest of officers, 30 January, 1940'.
192 Chew, *The White Death*, pp. 70–3.
193 Ibid., p. 71.
194 *Sovetsko–finliandskaia voina 1939–1940 gg. na more*, Chast' I, Kniga II, p. 64.
195 Ibid., p. 65. When ice brought an end to these patrols in mid-January 1940 and the submarines returned to base at Tallinn, weapons repair teams carefully examined the torpedoes to determine why so many of them were faulty. They concluded that 30 per cent of all torpedoes stockpiled were out of order due to over-lubrication and dirt in the guiding mechanisms. See ibid., Kniga III, p. 135.
196 Ibid., Chast' I, Kniga II, p. 64.
197 Ibid., p. 79.
198 Ibid., p. 65.
199 Ibid., pp. 65–6.
200 Ibid., p. 67.
201 Ibid., p. 76.
202 Ibid., pp. 73, 76.
203 Ibid., pp. 50–62.
204 Ibid., pp. 82–4.
205 Ibid., Chast' I, Kniga III, p. 37.

3

THE RED ARMY REFORMS ITS MILITARY DOCTRINE

At the end of December, Stalin recalled Meretskov and his staff to the Kremlin to reprimand them and to discuss the future course of the war. Stalin was particularly furious with the situation on the Karelian Isthmus where the 7th Army's plans for a third offensive had been frustrated by the Finnish counter-offensive:

> The authority of the Red Army is a guarantee of the USSR's national security. If we struggle for a long time against such a weak opponent this will stimulate the anti-Soviet forces of the imperialists.[1]

Remedial action had to be taken. On 28 December the Defence Commissariat issued a directive ordering the Leningrad Military District's armies to adopt a temporary defensive posture.[2] This directive, couched in a style which was unmistakably Stalin's, warned the army commanders to beware of more Finnish encirclement operations and ordered them to secure their supply lines and stop their offensive operations. The directive explained that '... the war with Finland is a serious war, distinctly different from our autumn campaign in Poland', and for that reason the Red Army high command was reviewing the nature of offensive tactics and that offensive operations would continue only after the rank-and-file had been properly equipped and trained in the new techniques of combined arms warfare. Stalin had finally recognized that Meretskov's 'lightning' campaign had degenerated into a positional war. In order to avoid prolonging the war and the possibility of its escalation, Stalin was obliged to rely on military expertise to reassess the Red Army's strategic goals and to modify the tactics of Deep Battle.

Stalin initiated the rehabilitation of military professionalism that same day by calling an expanded session of the Main Military Soviet.[3] At this session, delegates from the Defence Commissariat and the western military districts listened to a report from the General Staff's Operations Administration which summarized the operations of the 7th Army during the first month of

103

the war.[4] The report concluded that the Leningrad Military District's strategy of conducting a 'wide-front' offensive had failed. The Leningrad Military District command had underestimated the strength of the Mannerheim Line and was subsequently unable to conduct a rapid offensive against this fortified region due to loose troop control and inadequate training in the combined arms tactics of breakthrough. The only strategic option available was to adopt the plan suggested by Shaposhnikov six months previously: concentrate an overwhelming superiority of force on the Karelian Isthmus for a 'narrow-front' offensive against the Mannerheim Line. Stalin accepted this plan and decided to create a Front-level command administration to orchestrate it.

At the next session Stalin asked who among the delegates would be willing to take command of the North-Western Front. The commander of the Kiev Special Military District, S. Timoshenko, volunteered his services on condition that he be given all the resources stipulated in Shaposhnikov's plan.[5] A machine-gunner during the First World War, Timoshenko had joined the Red Army upon its formation in 1918 and had served as a cavalry commander in the First Cavalry Army during the Civil War and the Soviet–Polish war of 1920. During the inter-war period Timoshenko furthered his military education at the Frunze and Lenin Military-Political Academies and later served as Yakir's deputy at the Kiev Special Military District. Upon the latter's arrest in May 1937, Stalin assigned Timoshenko to command a series of military districts until February 1938 when he returned to command the Kiev Special Military District. Timoshenko had a reputation for being a capable wartime leader well versed in tactical and operational concepts who insisted on strict discipline. A strong opponent of Tukhachevskii's 'war of manoeuvre', which he considered to be a degenerate form of warfare, Timoshenko was a dogmatic advocate of the frontal strike and the 'wall of fire' associated with the breakthrough component of Deep Battle.[6] Given the strength of the Mannerheim Line and the positional nature of the war on the Karelian Isthmus, Timoshenko was the most appropriate commander for the new front.

On 7 January, the Defence Commissariat officially informed the Leningrad Military District's army commanders that strategic command was being handed over to Timoshenko at the North-Western Front.[7] While the 7th, 13th and 8th armies kept up pressure against the Finnish Army by continuing their artillery barrages, aviation strikes and continuous battle reconnaissance, Timoshenko and his staff reinforced the 7th and 13th Armies for a new break-through operation against the Mannerheim Line and the eventual encircle-ment and annihilation of the Finnish Army on the Vyborg–Antrea–Kakisalmi salient.[8] Stalin facilitated Timoshenko's reinforcement programme by appointing E. Shchadenko, a member of the Politburo, to select quality troops from all the military districts and arrange their transportation to the active armies on the Isthmus.[9] These formations began to arrive by the middle of January and were subordinated to corps commands.[10] Stalin also appointed Zhdanov as Timoshenko's political commissar to centralize the improvement of road, rail, and telecommunications and to help mobilize production of armaments in Leningrad factories.[11]

By 18 January, the North-Western Front, the 7th Army and 13th Army staffs had conducted an inventory of the forces at their disposal and had drawn up a preliminary plan allocating these forces to operational targets, establishing the boundaries between them, and deciding the time allowed for them to accomplish their missions. The 7th Army planned to conduct the main strike against Vyborg with the intermediate goal of breakthrough somewhere along the Finnish fortified region between Karhula and Muolan-järvi towards the town of Kämärä and Pero.[12] Army Commander Pavlov was placed in command of Stavka's strategic reserve army and was expected to conduct secondary strikes across the frozen Bay of Vyborg while Army Commander Grendal, in command of the 13th Army, was expected to divert the Finnish Army with an offensive directed against Kakisalmi (see Figure 3.1).[13]

This organizational reform in the field command was highly significant. In contrast to an army command, responsible for combining the tactical activities of combined arms formations into a unified force along a single operational direction, the front command was responsible for organizing all land, air, naval and operational reserve forces into one predetermined strategic direction, requiring a qualitatively different style of management.[14] To this end, Timoshenko brought in competent staff officers from his previous command at the Kiev Special Military District, faculty and students from the General Staff Academy and the Frunze Academy, as well as personnel from the Leningrad Military District staff.[15]

I

The most important responsibility of Timoshenko's Front command was to study the lessons of recent battle experience, adjust tactical doctrine on the basis of these lessons, and then supervise the training of troops in this new doctrine.[16] The Defence Commissariat's directive on 28 December had specifically ordered that troops be trained not only how to overcome conventional field fortifications, but also how to break through fortified regions and their reinforced concrete 'permanent fire-points' (DOTs). For this purpose Timoshenko created, in the Operations Department of the North-Western

FIGURE 3.1
DISTRIBUTION OF RED ARMY FORCES IN FRONT OF THE
MANNERHEIM LINE, JANUARY 1940

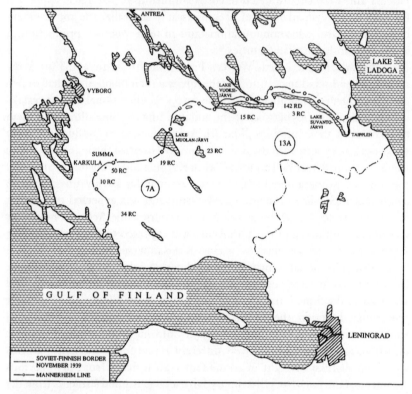

Adapted from *Istoriia Ordena Lenina Leningradskogo Voennogo Okruga.*

Front, the 'Section for the Study of Combat Experience and Troop Training' staffed by the military theorists V. Zlobin, N. Talenskii, N. Korneev and others.[17] These theorists referred extensively to established theories of combined arms warfare[18] and published a new tactical doctrine in a pamphlet entitled *Pri organizatsii i vypolnenii proryva ukreplennoi polosy* (On organizing and executing breakthrough of fortified regions) on 20 January 1940, which was distributed to the 7th and 13th Army for further elaboration and detailed training by the troops.[19]

The Section's first responsibility was to formulate a new Order of Battle which would reflect the most harmonious correlation of armed strength, means for manoeuvre and flexibility of command with which to overcome the enemy's positional defences most effectively. The special features of terrain on the Karelian Isthmus and the abnormally severe winter conditions also required consideration. The Isthmus was markedly different from the open steppes and comparatively moderate climate of the Central European plateau for which the Red Army's doctrine of combined arms warfare had been designed. Soviet commanders and staff officers after the war were notorious for over-emphasizing these topographical and climatic peculiarities as an excuse for the gross organizational incompetence which characterized the December offensives; none the less, these climatic factors had to be taken into account.[20] Deep snow conditions, for instance, made the concentration of armed force on the battlefield far more difficult than in summer conditions, the Red Army's favourite season for strategic manoeuvres and training exercises.[21] Red Army troops could be equipped with skis in order to regain tactical mobility and freedom of movement, but a majority of troops, and especially newly arriving reinforcements from other military districts, had not been trained how to ski and, of course, there was a deficit of equipment. Without this freedom of movement a rifle division would be forced to deploy its forces one regiment at a time along well-prepared roads while being harassed by Finnish artillery and sniper fire. During the final assault the troops would have difficulty maintaining their *élan* for battle, struggling in deep snow, and would suffer enormous losses in the final 150–100 metres to the Finnish DOTs. The very low temperatures (minus 35° C) recorded during the war also had a significant effect on the psychological and physical performance of the troops. Soldiers suffered from frostbite due to improper clothing, housing, and nourishment, jeopardising the efficiency of an entire military formation. Even when the troops were eventually supplied with warm clothes, the bulky clothing limited their mobility and complicated the use of weapons.[22]

The severe frost also took its toll on the machinery and weapons of the Red Army. Artillery guns had more difficulty gaining traction on icy roads and required increased support services to keep them rolling. The range of artillery dropped and grease in the guns' firing mechanisms froze solid. Communications, both by courier and by telephone, were unreliable and were often severed by snowstorms. Motors of automobiles, tanks, and aeroplanes systematically failed if they were not constantly kept warm by kerosene lamps, air compressors, or periodic start-ups which dramatically increased the rate of fuel consumption and the frequency of breakdowns. Tanks, in particular, could not operate in snow deeper than 30 cm. and therefore had a tendency to become stuck and were more susceptible to Finnish anti-tank weapons.[23] Deep snow and severe frost alone were enough to present a serious challenge to the operational and organizational integrity of the Red Army's military doctrine.

The Finnish fortified region on the Karelian Isthmus, popularly known in the Red Army and in the West as the Mannerheim Line,[24] was by no means as sophisticated as the Maginot or Siegfried Lines. However, in winter conditions, this complex network of permanent fire points in the form of reinforced concrete forts (DOTs) and more hastily constructed wood-and-earth gun-emplacements (DZOTs), interlaced with anti-tank weapons, anti-personnel obstacles and minefields, provided a surprisingly effective barrier against the Red Army. To overcome these defences the new Red Army Order of Battle set the following parameters (*normy*):

- A Rifle Corps formation was responsible for a total of 5–6 kilometres of front and was to be organized into two echelons. The first echelon was composed of two Rifle Divisions, whereas the second, or reserve echelon, was composed of one Rifle Division.

- A first-echelon Rifle Division was responsible for 2–2.5 kilometres and was composed of a single echelon of regiments lined up and in contact with the enemy's defences.

- The most forward combined arms formation, the Rifle Regiment, was responsible for a 700–800 metre segment of front.

These parameters provided the empirical basis for all subsequent Soviet combined arms tactics for Deep Battle during the offensive on the Mannerheim Line. As such, they were roughly equivalent to the concentration of force in depth used in the Brusilov Offensive of June 1916 but were far more dense than the norms specified in the *Proekt Polevogo Ustava RKKA (PU-39)*.[25]

The first section of the instructions concerned the preparatory measures for the successful breakthrough of the Mannerheim Line. The commanders, staffs and troops of the Red Army forces on the Karelian Isthmus were given 20 days for this period of preparation. During that time reconnaissance patrols were to gather detailed information about the Finnish armed forces and the fortified region, engineers would dig trenches as close as possible to the DOTs and prepare 'jumping-off' points for the infantry. Staffs would regroup and concentrate troops in the forward zone for the attack, while long-range artillery and aviation continually bombarded targets in the fortified zone and in the rear of the Finnish defences.[26]

When Meretskov and his staff at the Leningrad Military District HQ were originally planning the invasion of Finland in 1939, they relied predominantly on aviation reconnaissance. On the basis of this reconnaissance, they were aware of Finnish fortifications at Suvanto-järvi and in the south-eastern area of the Isthmus, but had little knowledge of additional fortifications making up the Mannerheim Line. Battle reconnaissance was particularly weak during the first few weeks of the 7th Army's invasion, although instructions on the conduct of battle reconnaissance had been compiled in a manual on combined arms co-ordination that had been issued to Red Army staffs on the eve of the invasion. According to these instructions, divisional staffs were responsible for organizing vanguard reconnaissance patrols to seek contact with the enemy and identify the presence of enemy defences which might obstruct a high-tempo combined arms offensive.[27] However, the 7th Army and all the other forces at the front were operating in an informational black-out due to poor staff control over these reconnaissance patrols, improper tactics to conduct battle reconnaissance, the poor mobility of these patrols (due to a lack of ski-troops) and snow-cover which provided natural camouflage to the Finnish DOTs. Meretskov implicitly admitted this when he told a gathering of students at the General Staff Academy after the war that on two occasions during the mid-December offensive he had personally visited the forward positions and had seen with his own eyes how well the Finnish DOTs had been camouflaged. On the first occasion he and Army Commander Pavlov had travelled to within 500 metres of Finnish defences at Kiviniemi and watched them for two hours without discovering the location of their fire. Later, Meretskov and his political commissar observed the main Finnish DOT at Hill No. 65.5 from an even closer range but still could not accurately locate it even as it was firing artillery salvos.[28]

The need to correct this ignorance of the Finnish Army and the configuration of the Mannerheim Line was the single most important operational mission of the Red Army during the January period. Various reconnaissance missions had to be conducted, depending on the requirements of the different services. The most fundamental reconnaissance mission to the efficient co-ordination of the army as a whole was command and surveillance reconnaissance organized by the army staff. On 5 January, Meretskov ordered that mid-level army staff officers be appointed to forward sub-units to report to army headquarters on a daily basis about operations at the front.[29]

Commanders of artillery, tank and engineering units also organized battle-reconnaissance patrols to keep them informed of changing circumstances at the front. Combat experience on the Karelian Isthmus and the study of Finnish guerrilla techniques had convinced Soviet tacticians that large reconnaissance units were too unwieldy in forest-swamp terrain and that the basic element of reconnaissance organization should be the infantry section operating in small groups of either a section or platoon in size.[30] Ideally, these battle-reconnaissance patrols would be conducted at night and were to accompany sapper detachments cutting passages through the anti-tank and anti-personnel obstacles in no-man's land or assist in the blockade group's destruction of a DOT.[31] Battle-reconnaissance was seen by the Red Army command to be of such importance to the development of the offensive that these reconnaissance patrols were to be covered by artillery support not only from battalion units but also by regimental, and even divisional artillery units.[32] During the month of January the 50th Rifle Corps of Meretskov's 7th Army continuously conducted reconnaissance patrols along its section of the Mannerheim Line and managed to gain a fairly detailed picture of Finnish forces manning the defences and reserve echelon. Even so, the organization and conduct of battle-reconnaissance was still far from perfect, testified by the fact that the 123rd Rifle Division of the 50th Rifle Corps was not able to identify all the Finnish DOTs in its sector until the last few days before Timoshenko's new offensive.[33]

The key to a solution involved giving more mobility to the reconnaissance patrols. Stalin ordered the creation of new ski-brigades for this purpose. Many ski-brigades were formed with the help of an active recruitment campaign for volunteers bolstered by articles in the Soviet press praising the heroic exploits of the ski reconnaissance patrols.[34] Adequate reconnaissance tactics also had to be developed. On the basis of battle experience gained during December, patrols were split into three groups. The first group was the 'holding group' responsible for going as far forward as possible to gather information. The 'diversion group' would use tanks in a feigned attack or some other means to divert the attention of the Finnish defenders away from the presence of the 'holding group' while the 'cover group' would support the first two groups with fire against the Finnish fortifications.[35] On the basis of this reformed battle reconnaissance the forward echelons of the 7th and 13th Armies were gradually able to develop an accurate understanding of the first belt of fortification on the Karelian Isthmus, but only with great difficulty and enormous losses.

Breaking through of positional defences also required significant engineering preparation. During the First World War sappers had come to play an important role in studying the enemy's defensive works, removing wire and other anti-personnel obstacles, and organizing the construction of 'jumping-off' points for the combined arms assault. This last responsibility had played a critical role in General Brusilov's preparation for his breakthrough operation in 1916 when sappers built trenches to within 150–200 metres of the enemy defences.[36] On the Karelian Isthmus sappers were ordered to build trenches to within 100–150 metres of the Finnish DOTs in frozen earth, as well as to construct dug-outs to protect combined arms units from enemy fire and the night frost. Sappers then transported the mortars, light artillery and machine-guns to these combined arms units at the 'jumping-off' points.[37] In mid-January these entrenchments were supplemented by a network of inter-connecting roads to allow the efficient approach, transfer and evacuation of forward artillery supporting the infantry advance.[38]

Anti-personnel and anti-tank obstacles had to be cleared away after these preliminary construction projects had been completed. This mission was accomplished by a detachment of sappers armed with wire cutters, entrench-ing tools and explosives, and supported by the rifle fire and artillery of the battle reconnaissance units. Even under the cover of darkness or fog this was an extremely dangerous mission fraught with a multitude of difficulties. The sappers were often threatened by Finnish ambushes and their work was continually frustrated by Finnish efforts to reassemble the obstacle fields. Eventually, divisional and regimental commanders responded to the situation by ordering their front line units to keep the passages open by covering them with continuous machine-gun and artillery fire.[39] Sappers had also been given the responsibility of constructing and camouflaging command and artillery posts, laying communications and transporting 2,500 portable barracks for accommodating the new reinforcements.[40] From 21 to 23 January, Meretskov issued a series of orders to the 50th Rifle Corps to study existing accommo-dation facilities in the immediate rear of the front line units and supervise the construction of dug-outs suitable for habitation using materials brought in from the rear.[41]

The engineering troops sometimes did not fulfil all their duties, given the extensive array of responsibilities and the severe climatic and organizational conditions under which they had to perform. A specific incidence of negligence became apparent to the 7th Army commander, Meretskov, when Soviet aerial photo-reconnaissance of the 7th Army's own positions revealed that its newly deployed artillery batteries were not being camouflaged. Meretskov attempted to rectify this major oversight by issuing an order to corps and division commanders to practice more stringent measures of camouflage and to improve the efficiency of the anti-aircraft gunners.[42] When a Finnish aviator eluded Soviet air-defences on 1 February and photographed the artillery batteries concentrated in the Summa region he discovered that Red Army engineers still had not attended to this problem.[43]

Stalin's directive also criticized the use of long-range artillery during the first few weeks of the war. Artillery preparation by map co-ordinates had not proven accurate enough to destroy Finnish fortifications, suppress enemy artillery fire, or seriously disrupt the enemy's logistical support.[44] During the month-long preparation period artillery commanders were ordered to systematically organize artillery observation points and reconnaissance, accurately identify Finnish DOTs, and then fire at these specific targets while also firing at targets in the rear of the Finnish fortified zone.[45] The main task was to improve artillery reconnaissance and fire-correction. Two direct hits on a Finnish DOT were not enough, even when an extensive reconnaissance and fire-correction network was established and the largest calibre artillery was used. Timoshenko's new tactical instructions warned artillery commanders that approximately four or five direct hits with 200 mm. shells were necessary, attainable by the average expenditure of 80–100 such shells.[46] Corps commanders would have to concentrate an average of 61 large calibre guns per kilometre of front in order to develop this degree of fire-power, promoting a significant increase in the rate of artillery expenditure which would further tax the supply system. Artillery commanders were also responsible for suppressing enemy reinforcements behind the fortifications. These fire-raids were to last two to three hours and were conducted both day and night.[47] Artillery was also employed to rake the tree-tops to clear the forest of 'cuckoos' (Finnish snipers) and to fire special 'agitational' shells, stuffed with propaganda leaflets, behind enemy lines.[48]

In the final countdown to the renewed offensive the artillery commanders were to provide cover for the assembly of combined arms units at the 'jumping-off' points.[49] The main objective of this preparatory artillery barrage was to prevent Finnish front line troops moving from their protective dug-outs to their forward positions. Easily manoeuvrable, high-trajectory mortar fire was the answer. In mid-January 1940 Timoshenko ordered the creation of mortar batteries and companies to assist in this new mission.[50]

One last doctrinal reform had to take place before the renewed offensive began: the abolition of the 'quadrant system' and its replacement by a responsive fire-control system. At the beginning of the invasion the Red Army high command had mistakenly assumed that unorganized artillery fire would be enough to destroy the morale of the Finnish Army. For this reason no provisions had been made for the organization of artillery observation points to correct artillery fire and verify the destruction of targets. Efforts to correct the situation began on 9 and 10 January, when V. Bolotnikov and A. Sazhin published doctrinal articles in the Leningrad Military District newspaper *Na Strazhe Rodiny* explaining the organization of observation-point networks. Bolotnikov recommended that battery commanders rely on company commanders in their sector to provide artillery reconnaissance. In order to increase the effectiveness of communications between infantry reconnaissance patrols and the battery commander, a special communications section led by a mid-ranking commander needed to be created. In addition to this mission, the reconnaissance patrols were expected to report to the battery commander about the movements of forward Red Army units, no doubt to mitigate the incidence of fratricidal fire.[51] Sazhin commented that the nature of the terrain might further complicate effective artillery reconnaissance, requiring the use of mobile observation points (a tank with radio communications) or balloons and airplanes.[52]

All these elements culminated in the final aspect of the preparatory stage: the drafting of battle plans by combined arms staffs in preparation for the breakthrough assault. Before the beginning of the war Red Army doctrine stipulated that combined arms staffs were to exercise strict centralized control over the evolution of battle. Timoshenko's new instructions tried to decentralize this control while, at the same time, preserving organizational unity of action by rationalizing the battle plan.

Ideally, the *army* command was responsible for indicating the main goal, determining the duration of the artillery preparation, setting the hour for the combined arms assault to start and locating the boundaries for the aviation bombardment. The *corps* command was to determine the region for the breakthrough assault to take place, specify the targets for long-range artillery to suppress, and then draw these factors up into a Table of Battle (otherwise known as a 'nomogram').[53] *Division* command used the Table of Battle to help define the places of jumping-off and manage the artillery preparation of the forward area. The division was also responsible for managing the horizontal flow of battle information between the various services (*orientirovaniia*), especially between the artillery commanders and the infantry commanders, by standardizing the use of signals (a series of coloured flares, radio, telephone, or courier) as well as drawing up a unified 'orientation' map to indicate what team should be doing in relation to each other in the combined arms formation conducting the assault. The *regimental* commander, as the final arbitrator of combined arms battle, defined the immediate goals for the battalions and managed the artillery support for the infantry and tank assault.[54]

Timoshenko and his aides quickly realized that the root of the Red Army's operational ineffectiveness lay in the poor organizational and communication skills of sub-unit staffs. Efficient staff work at battalion and company level was especially crucial because these were in immediate proximity to the battlefield and were ultimately responsible for executing orders and relaying reconnaissance reports to assist in the planning process of higher staffs.[55] In order to promote more initiative at battalion level, the battalion commander was instructed to conduct orientation meetings with his unit commanders to study terrain, set boundaries for artillery suppression, agree to signals between infantry and tanks and other details of combined arms combat against Finnish defences.[56] At company level the co-ordination of reconnaissance, choice of artillery targets and correction of artillery fire would be enhanced by the battery commander's continuous presence at the company command point. Extending *edinonachale* and *orientirovaniia* to the company level was hopefully the key to close, organized interaction of infantry and artillery in forest-swamp combat.[57]

Finally, sub-unit staffs were instructed to maintain continuous communications with their combined arms detachments, reconnaissance patrols and artillery platoons by equipping these detachments with telephones and radios. This improvement of communications between front and rear played a vital role in Timoshenko's programme to gain control over the battlefield. Colonel Kurochkin, one of Zlobin's tactical advisors on combined arms communications at North-Western Front headquarters, wrote an article entitled 'The Organization of Communications for the Offensive Against Enemy Fortifications' in the 4 February 1940 edition of *Na Strazhe Rodiny*, explaining the importance of this new policy to the rank-and-file and suggesting ways to preserve communications in low temperatures and combat conditions.[58] Other doctrinal articles suggested that battery commanders draw up firetables based on the orientation exercises, distribute them to each artillery platoon, and personally verify that each gunner had this fire-plan pinned to the inside of his gun-shield. This tighter control over infantry and artillery sub-units allowed closer interaction without a corresponding increase in fratricidal fire, thus significantly improving the morale of the troops. In the words of one doctrinal journalist, 'When infantry know they have real artillery support they push fearlessly ahead. This creates conditions for brave innovation and creativity.'[59]

II

The second section of the tactical instructions concerned the actual assault, or breakthrough, of the Mannerheim Line. Under the cover of the artillery preparation the combined-arms units were to assemble at the 'jumping-off' points 30 minutes before the attack. When the regimental commander received the order from divisional headquarters to begin the attack he was instructed to order the artillery commanders to switch from artillery preparation to creeping barrage in order to pave the way for the assault by combined arms units.[60] This was Timoshenko's legendary 'wall of fire'

114

adapted from artillery tactics of the First World War.[61] For this technique to be effective, the new tactical doctrine stipulated a concentration of 48 artillery pieces per kilometre of front in the area of the main assault, similar to norms used during the Brusilov Offensive.[62] Strict battle control was required because combined arms units were following in the immediate wake of the creeping barrage. Battle control fell to the regimental commander who was responsible for maintaining continuous communication with his artillery commanders via radio, telephone and courier.[63]

Advancing 200 metres behind the creeping barrage was the first echelon of infantry and tanks, clearing a way through the defensive obstacles up to the DOTs.[64] In a doctrinal article published in *Na Strazhe Rodiny* on 6 January 1940, Talenskii explained to the rank-and-file that, although the Finns had constructed a complex system of fortified fire-points, they did not have enough forces to fill all the gaps in the front. The first echelon's duty was to find these gaps and exploit them. Talenskii recommended that the first infantry echelon carry forward their own medium machine-guns, mortars and artillery, then verify communications with higher command staffs, dig in, and wait for the second echelon to destroy individual fire-points.[65] Enemy machine-gun and mortar fire could be lethal even on a relatively undefended sector of the enemy's front. In December, Red Army troops had responded to this problem by following in single file behind the infantry support tanks. When this proved equally disastrous the troops were ordered to ride in armoured sleds dragged behind the tanks.[66]

On the tail of the combined infantry and tank advance followed the mortars and 45 and 75 mm. guns, making up the close support artillery, for the purpose of suppressing enemy fire and destroying DOTs over open sights. This dual mission of close support artillery over open sights was apparently suggested by Voronov, an artillery expert and veteran of the Spanish Civil War. He, in turn, had borrowed the idea from the technique of 'successive fire concentration', a way of concentrating fire to compensate for shortages of ammunition, developed in preparation for the Brusilov Offensive.[67] When used against the Mannerheim Line the technique would help to make up for the occasional lack of a supportive 'creeping barrage' and the absence of heavily armed tanks as well as reliable aerial bombing.[68]

The most elementary component of combined arms organization and the fundamental key to resolving the deadlock between the offensive and defensive forms of warfare was the adaptation of storm troop tactics. In December this tactical formation was known as a 'blockade group', but by mid-January it had been renamed 'storm group' in an attempt to emphasize its offensive nature. Following immediately after the first echelon, the storm group's purpose was to blow up the remaining DOTs which had survived the artillery preparation and tank fire.[69] These storm groups were formed from one infantry platoon, one machine-gun platoon, a few mortars, two or three snipers, at least three tanks, one chemical tank, one or two 45 mm. (and 75 mm.) guns and one section of sappers with explosives.[70] Once the storm groups had managed to force their way through the obstacle fields under heavy enemy fire they were expected to block up the embrasures of the enemy DOTs with sand bags, or park the tanks in front of the embrasures, then dynamite the DOTs.[71] This combined arms unit and its tactical employment bore surprising resemblance to the German *Angriffsgruppe*, a elemental component of German offensive doctrine.[72]

III

The third section of Timoshenko's instructions concerned the development of this tactical breakthrough into operational success, the Deep Operation. Whereas in the early and mid-1930s, Deep Operations had received most of the attention of Soviet military theorists, this theory barely received a mention in the North-Western Front's instruction, and none whatsoever in the more detailed instruction worked out by the 13th Army. This suggested that by mid-January the 13th Army was merely to conduct diversionary attacks with no pretence of operational development.

The Deep Operations of the 7th Army on the Karelian Isthmus in January 1940 consisted of the following: after overcoming the enemy's first major zone of positional defences in a specific sector the first and second echelons were to continue advancing in extended order under the cover of air, forward artillery and tank support.[73] If they came to a significant obstacle that impeded their forward advance into the Finns' immediate rear while their neighbours were conducting successful breakthroughs, they were to join neighbouring forces and, with the continued support of the tanks, move along the flanks and the rear of the enemy's defences.[74] If there was continued success in this sector, then the division, corps, and army commanders would dedicate their reserve forces to develop this tactical success into operational success.[75] Although this tactical progression incorporated local superiority which rolled up the flanks of the enemy's defences (known as *schwerpunkt* and *aufrollen* in German tactical doctrine) it amounted to little more than tactics of pursuit. Only after the war did Rotmistrov, a Soviet theorist of tank warfare, develop these tactics into the final stage of Deep Operations. He suggested that once the breakthrough had been completed, mobile groups, formed on the basis

116

of a tank brigade (the elemental unit of the former moto-mechanized corps) should be inserted into the breach.[76] The lack of a heavily armoured tank with sufficiently powerful fire-power to survive enemy anti-tank artillery and destroy the embrasures of DOTs remained a serious impediment to the practice of both Deep Battle and Deep Operations theory.[77] For this reason, the decision was taken in December 1939 to deploy the recently designed heavy (47.5 ton) KV tank, as well as the lighter, but identically armed and powered T-34. The KV was introduced into tank brigades on the Karelian Isthmus in February 1940.

Although Timoshenko's new tactical doctrine was conceptually similar to the *Proekt Polevogo Ustava RKKA (PU-39)*, recent combat experience on the Isthmus had resulted in some important corrections and amendments. The most radical of these was the creation of the storm group: highly trained, heavily armed with an assortment of weapons and firmly linked into the Red Army's troop control system by telephone, signals and orientation meetings. Much more attention was devoted to the role of engineering troops in the preparation and conduct of the breakthrough, and artillery fire was more integrated into the army's reconnaissance system and battle plan. Order of Battle *normy* had also decreased, signifying an even greater tactical density at the front and the need for sophisticated troop control by regiment, battalion and company staffs.

This last component, troop control, was considered the 'sacred thread' of Soviet military doctrine and was the focus of Timoshenko's military theorists at North-Western Front headquarters during the tactical training exercises at the end of January and the offensive that followed.[78] Troop control consisted of battle planning as well as continuous vertical and horizontal communications with superior, subordinate and neighbouring staffs and services. Without troop control the Red Army would not be able to overcome the Mannerheim Line and hasten the end of the war.

IV

Timoshenko's review of Soviet tactical doctrine was complemented by a major reassessment of political indoctrination to strengthen military discipline in the ranks of the Red Army. This entailed a major reorganization of political work, this being carried out by Zhdanov, political commissar of Timoshenko's North-Western Front, and A. Zaporozhets and N. Vashugin, commissars of Grendal's 13th Army and Meretskov's 7th Army on the Karelian Isthmus.[79] Their first priority was to strengthen the political apparatus within formations and units. This was done by sending out representatives to give lectures on the proper conduct of political work and arrange meetings with local political commissars to discuss the change in the mission of political work brought about by the war.[80]

On 15 January 1940 the Political Administration of the 13th Army sent out a group of inspectors from the 'Organizational Instruction Department' to examine the situation in the formations and units at the front. Ten days later, these inspectors returned to army headquarters to report that, in many units, especially the regimental commands, military discipline was very low. Commissars and political workers were not properly promoting 'combat socialist competition', the morale of the troops had fallen into a 'devil-may-care' attitude, troops were not taking care of their weapons, and supply depots were badly mismanaged. Under Zhdanov's authority this inspection group demoted a division commander and a regimental commissar[81] and similar measures were being carried out in other Red Army formations. The inspection groups also conducted political-organizational meetings for political workers on such subjects as:

- generalizing the experience of party-political work in battle;

- organizing communists and komsomol activists from newly arrived formations;

- instructing these activists in their new responsibilities and methods of party political work.[82]

Military reverses and the excessive carnage of December's battles had taken their toll on the moral motivation of the Red Army troops. Motivation had to be resuscitated before the revised tactical doctrine and reinforced armies could be successfully employed in the new offensive.

Since the mid-1930s the Political Administration had conducted its indoctrination programme on the basis of 'socialist competition', using agitational techniques borrowed from the factory floor to animate soldiers to exceed norms in construction projects, set records in marksmanship competitions, and gain technical knowledge of other weapons.[83] In peacetime the programme promoted inter-service rivalry, pitted unit against unit, and encouraged competitive and spectacular performance between individual soldiers, rewarding the hero with increased access to membership in the Party and Komsomol, much like the Stakhanovite movement had done on the economic front. When the Red Army switched from a peacetime to a combat footing by invading Finland, this programme became known as 'combat socialist competition'. Initially, inter-unit competition was confused with combat against the enemy and was highly detrimental to the conduct of combined arms tactics against sophisticated enemy defences. As the war dragged on through December and early January, meetings of communists and 'non-Party Bolsheviks' began to emphasize new goals of combat socialist competition such as mutual assistance between soldiers and tactical interaction between units and services.[84]

On 22 January the Political Administration announced a new 'law' to regulate the relations between Party and non-Party Bolsheviks in the Red Army. In the heat of battle everyone in the vanguard was equal. If a member of the vanguard unit showed extraordinary offensive spirit in battle the rest of the unit was obliged to support him regardless of whether he was a party member or not.[85] In the early days of the war, thin ranks of party-members and political workers had goaded the troops from the rear.[86] Since then, sufficient numbers of party members had been mobilized to fight alongside the raw, uninitiated troops in order to set a good example of bravery and 'revolutionary' discipline. The principle of class warfare had percolated down to the smallest sub-unit and out to the cutting edge of the war between nations.[87]

In conjunction with these organizational attempts to improve the combat capabilities of the troops, the Political Administration launched a propaganda campaign on military discipline and the offensive traditions of the 'Russian' army. From the end of December onwards the military press began to print articles on the military genius and extraordinary victories of the eighteenth century Russian commander, A. Suvorov. One of these articles discussed the fundamental principle of Suvorov's *Science of Victory*, that success in battle was predominantly determined by discipline and the moral factor. Suvorov's close paternal relationship to his men was praised while Frederick the Great's 'discipline of the rod' and alienation of the officer corps from the rank-and-file was eschewed. Another fundamental principle in the Suvorovian legacy was that 'each soldier should know his manoeuvres' and study only those exercises useful in war. These two principles, obedience in a patriarchal family and knowledge of tactical doctrine, were the basis of conscious, 'revolutionary' discipline and the source of Russia's greatness.[88] The article ended with the recommendation that the Suvorovian legacy updated would 'enrich the operational-strategic art of the Red Army'. Later articles on military discipline discussed Clausewitz's doctrine on the moral factor in warfare and how Lenin, Stalin and Voroshilov had integrated the moral factor into the concept of *edinonachale* in Soviet military doctrine.[89]

According to the propagandists, 'revolutionary' discipline gave the Red Army a qualitative advantage over other armies which allowed the development of superior tactics and prevented excessive loss of life in combat. In a conception of tactics which resembled the nineteenth century Russian tactical theory of a dialectical relationship between fire and shock, political propagandists emphasized that fire would only carry the army so far before the infantry would have to seek decision in hand-to-hand combat with the bayonet.[90] In possession of revolutionary discipline, the Red Army soldier was able to practise tactics that were superior to those of his counterparts in other armies because he had the moral strength to conduct the final, decisive stage of hand-to-hand combat. Propagandists argued that this was certainly the case in the context of the war with the Finns because the Finns avoided hand-to-hand combat and only resorted to the bayonet when they were drunk.[91]

One of the methods to promote revolutionary discipline in the ranks was to publicly praise heroic exploits of individual soldiers and units. The celebration of heroes was the primary purpose of pamphlets known as *Boevye Listy* (Combat Pages), written and published by military journalists assigned to individual sub-units. These pamphlets were posted on a board in a unit's encampment area or distributed to other units via travelling artists attached to 'Agit-trains'.[92] In the words of one journalist, 'We must make sure that the heroism of individual soldiers is known throughout the unit so that everyone acts in battle as soldiers of a socialist country should.'[93] In the more widely circulated military newspapers, such as *Na Strazhe Rodiny*, this propaganda technique took the form of 'hero portraits' and tended to dominate the content of that newspaper.

Another mechanism to raise the level of revolutionary discipline involved awarding medals and distinctions to individual soldiers and units who had demonstrated exceptional performance in the combat socialist competitions and to publish their names in the military and civilian press. This publicity campaign began on 2 January 1940 with the announcement of the award of the 'Order of Lenin' to Shaposhnikov and Smorodinov and the 'Red Star' to Red Army commanders and commissars working in the Main Administration of the General Staff and the Defence Commissariat, and was followed by a mass award-giving ritual which lasted well after the end of the war.[94] In mid-January the Political Administration of the Leningrad Military District created a special fund of 'valuable gifts' in the form of watches, bicycles, gramophones, cameras and other items to be awarded to exceptionally brave commanders, commissars and men as a further incentive to revolutionary discipline and bravery.[95]

One of the many ways political workers disseminated the new tactical techniques and reinforced military discipline and the offensive spirit in the ranks was to organize collective reading of the press.[96] This consisted of appointing a literate political worker, Party member, or non-Party Bolshevik to read the newspaper to the troops in his unit. Normally, the reader would first read the day's operational report, major combat stories and doctrinal articles, then the main international stories and last, but by no means least, the comics section.[97] The reader would discuss the day's news with his comrades and then report to his senior political officer about the questions raised by the troops and his responses to them. In this manner the political officer was able to monitor the effectiveness of the propaganda and the morale of the unit, and promote combat socialist competitions with other units.

A fundamental obstruction to the political workers' discipline campaign was military humour. The absurdities and horrors of the first month of the war had given rise to jokes and humorous stories which ridiculed superior officers and commissars while indulging in self-deprecation. Eventually, a more benign expression of this humour found its way into the military press in the character of Pasha Brezhuntsov ('The Liar'), who was a creation of the editorial board of the newspaper *Boevaia krasnoarmeiskaia*. In early February the editors began printing the fictional letters of Pasha the Liar, depicting a gossiping, undisciplined soldier incapable of shooting or skiing and unfamiliar with regulations, whose exploits poked fun at Soviet weaponry, military food, the excessive formality of military bureaucracy, and traffic-jams on the roads. These stories came to the attention of the Political Administration of the Leningrad Military District which condemned such humour as politically subversive and a mockery of the Red Army soldier.[98]

A more politically sympathetic alternative was the cartoon character 'Vasia Tërkin' created by the military journalist A. Tvardovskii with the help of the artists V. Briskin and V. Fomichev at the newspaper *Na Strazhe Rodiny*. Tvardovskii based his cartoon character on a truck driver he had met during the invasion of western Belorussia a few months before, embellishing him with traits of a folk hero. Tvardovskii's intent was to portray the role model of a combat-ready soldier who combined cheerful, quick-witted but unpretentious humour with resourcefulness under fire 'without undermining the sacred principles of military discipline'.[99] 'Vasia Tërkin' was introduced to the reading public on 31 December 1939 (see Figures 3.2 to 3.5). Throughout the rest of the war the cartoon, depicting Vasia's fantastic exploits, appeared periodically in *Na Strazhe Rodiny*. By combining folk-tale characteristics, cheerfulness and native resourcefulness in graphic art and simple poems, the creators of 'Vasia Tërkin' sought to co-opt the potential subversiveness of military humour and transform the discipline campaign's slogans into social

FIGURE 3.2
'HOW VASIA TËRKIN HELPED THE TANKISTS', *NA STRAZHE RODINY*,
13 FEBRUARY 1940

memory. The magic formula of rhyme and humour would prove more memorable than the legalistic prose of field regulations.

More coercive techniques were used in parallel with these positive incentives for discipline and bravery. On 17 January 1939, almost a year before the war with Finland, the Council of Peoples' Commissars responded to rising levels of insubordination in the Red Army by passing a law to create 'comrades courts' and 'courts of honour for commanders'.[100] The courts consisted of a forum, not unlike the village courts of post-Emancipation Russian rural society but supervised by the political workers, to discuss cases of deviant behaviour by individual soldiers in the unit to induce peer pressure on the 'guilty' individual.[101] Although these forums held no formal legal power, they could issue warnings to the minor offender and inform his parents, family, and former employees of his behaviour. In the case of more serious offences, the courts could recommend courts martial.

FIGURE 3.3
'HOW VASIA TËRKIN UNMASKED A GOSSIP', *NA STRAZHE RODINY*,
19 JANUARY 1940

In mid-January 1940 the Political Administration ordered its political workers to intensify their control over the functions of the comrades courts and courts of honour for commanders.[102] By the end of the month these courts were in full operation and military newspapers began to report cases which had been referred by them to the Military Procuracy. The first few reported cases consisted of criminal charges brought against truck drivers and car chauffeurs for violating the laws of the Anti-Air Defence – specifically the rule forbidding the use of headlights at night.[103] During the same week in January the military procurator of the 3rd Rifle Corps in the 13th Army was also actively reinforcing military discipline by organizing speeches on the

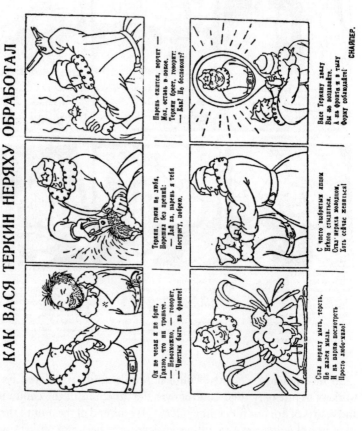

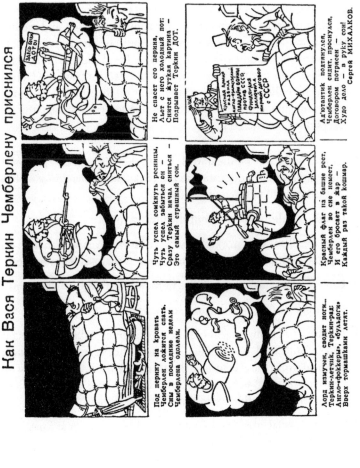

theme of punishments for betraying the Motherland and violating military discipline, as well as assuring the soldiers of the privileges enjoyed by the families of the rank-and-file and junior officers.[104]

Further coercive measures were used when individual soldiers were thought to have directly infringed the disciplinary code. The principle of *edinonachale* relied on a legal code of social privileges and criminal punishments. If a soldier fulfilled his combat duty and observed military regulations, he and his family were entitled on paper to a host of privileges consisting of preferential housing, government stipends, and exemption from certain taxes. However, these privileges could be revoked if the soldier *or his family* were found guilty of a crime as defined by Article 31 of the UK-RSFSR; either desertion from military duty or absenteeism from the factory.[105]

With the political situation at the front safely in hand, Zhdanov issued a directive on January 31 to all political organs on the Karelian Isthmus. Political workers were instructed to:

- Support all Party political work, strengthen the martial spirit of the officer corps and military discipline in the ranks while struggling with desertion, cowardice, and panic-mongering.

- Conduct a thorough study of the officer corps.

- Replace all political workers who were unable to cope with their duties with capable political workers who had proven themselves in battle.

- Collect accurate personnel files of members in the officer corps.

- Carefully study all battle goals, orders and instructions.

- Ensure a full complement of officer personnel and armaments for the first and second echelons and assault groups, the organization of conscientious political work, the execution of battle duties, the preservation of interaction (*vzaimodeistvie*)[106] between units and services, and the further development of the troops' confidence in themselves and their weapons.

- Devote special attention to political and organizational work in the reconnaissance groups and subdivisions.

- Help the NKVD establish 'control-preventative detachments' (*kontrol'-zagraditel'nye otriiady*)[107] for fighting against deserters and the activities of harmful elements in active units.

- Collect information about losses and weapons discarded on the field of battle.[108]

During the 20 days the North-Western Front had set aside to reverse the Red Army's morale and technical crisis these measures, in conjunction with a relaxation of postal censorship and mobilization of the home front to send patriotic letters and gifts to the troops on the Isthmus, helped to improve the troops' morale and determination to continue the offensive. The Red Army's psychological revitalization owed more to a collective sense of humiliation than coercive measures. Mikhail Solov'ev, a political worker under the command of Mekhlis, offered the following explanation in his memoirs written in exile:

> Mekhlis wrote reports about the psychological transformation in the army, exaggerating both his own role and the significance of the political commissars. In reality, however, the profound psychological transformation had issued from below. The Finns had to be beaten. All of us understood that. But there was no feeling of hatred for the Finns. Only a sense of shame and degradation. They had forced us to doubt that we were indeed a great nation. ... The Finnish War aroused something very deep and very important in the soul of the people – but something that shows itself seldom. Perhaps it should be called the historical memory of the people.[109]

Solov'ev missed the point: Mekhlis' appeal to Great Russian nationalism and a patriotic war had been very effective. The political experience gained on the Karelian Isthmus would well serve the Red Army in coming years.

NOTES

1 Meretskov, *Ha sluzhbe narodu*, p. 185.
2 Kuz'min, *Na strazhe mirnogo truda (1921–1940 gg.)*, p. 238. Stalin's reference to the war between the Russian and Swedish empires over Finland, presaged by the Treaty of Tilsit (1807), suggests that he referred to Russia's imperial past in forming his security policy for the Baltic region. The Naval Commission's military-geographic review of the region before the Soviet–Finnish War was well aware of the historical significance of Finland and the Baltic States in defending the sea lanes to Leningrad (St Petersburg). See *Sovetsko–finliandskaia voina 1939–1940 na more*, Chast' I, Kniga I, p. 5. Voroshilov's report to the joint commission of the Central Committee and the Main Military Soviet in April 1940 (see Chapter 5) included an 'Historical Summary of Conflicts for the Gulf of Finland and Finland' which emphasized the importance of the 'Window on Europe' in the history of the Russian Empire. See K.E. Voroshilov, *Doklad (Voroshilova) o sovetsko–finliandskoi voine 1939–1940 gg. s prilozheniem istoricheskoi spravki o bor'be za Finskii zaliv i Finliandiiu* (Minneapolis, MN: East View Publications, 1993), pp. 104–10.
3 Semiryaga, *Tainy stalinskoi diplomatii*, pp. 163–4.
4 *Konflikt*, Document No. 55, 'Iz ocherka "Voina Sovetskogo Soiuza s belofinnami v 1939–1940 gg. Deistviia 7 armii"'.
5 Meretskov, *Na sluzhbe narodu*, p. 187. See also Simonov, 'Glazami cheloveka moego pokoleniia ...' p. 79.
6 V. Anfilov, 'Semen Konstantinovich Timoshenko', in *Stalin's Generals*, pp. 239–50. In the

The Soviet Invasion of Finland, 1939–40

memoirs of M. Solov'ev, a military correspondent for *Izvestiia* during the 1930s and a one-time lecturer in history at the Frunze Academy, Timoshenko is reported to have made the following statements about the nature of modern warfare:

> As things are at present [mid-1930s] it is doubtful whether we could surpass our enemies in technical respects in a short period. We shall advance in technical matters, but we cannot hope to surpass potential foes at all quickly. So it is sound policy to set ourselves the task of raising the precision of action of our forces to the point at which we can undertake a war of maneuver? [sic] I think it is, but we should also recognize that we shall not have time to complete the task, even if war shouldn't come for the next ten or fifteen years. So it's dangerous for us to regard the war of maneuver as the best for our situation. In any war of maneuver we shall always be weaker than the enemy, who is provided with better technique, and whose men and officers are on a higher technical level.
>
> But while it cannot be gainsaid that in a war of maneuver we shall be the weaker party, the position is different in regard to a frontal attack. In frontal attack no enemy, or any combination of enemies, can hope to compare with us. By making a succession of direct attacks we shall compel him to lose blood, in other words, to lose something he has less of than we have. Of course we shall have enormous losses, too, but in war one has to count not one's own losses but those of the enemy. Even if we lose more men than the enemy, we must view it dispassionately. In the course of incurring such losses we shall counterbalance our technical inequality, and the losses themselves will not be dangerous for us. I know of no army in Europe that could hold up our mass advance. And despite everything, that advance will deny the enemy any possibility of maneuver on a strategic scale, and will force him into a frontal war, advantageous to us and disadvantageous to him.
>
> ... Having the advantage in manpower, we concentrate our army into an enormous fist. The very fact that such a fist exists will prevent the enemy from dispersing his forces for a war of maneuver, he will not be given any opportunity to loosen the close 'interlinking' of his army; on the contrary, he will be forced to concentrate, to go over to the defense on as restricted an area as possible. In other words, we get conditions for a frontal war, we force the enemy to accept our view of the character of the war; he had prepared himself for a war of maneuver, but he is forced by us into a positional war, in which all the advantages are on our side. Having forced the enemy into this position, our object being his wholesale destruction, we strike a pulverizing blow not through a combination of sectional maneuvers in the hope that the sum of those sectional maneuvers will develop into a general success, but by frontal action, doing all we can to smash the enemy's front. Of course we strike simultaneously at his flanks. For us that frontal battle together with pressure on the flanks will constitute a single engagement; for the enemy it constitutes three different tasks. My plan allows plenty of scope for tactical maneuver, but such maneuver is to unfold in accord with the situation and is intended to be of a subsidiary nature. The base of all our operations would remain the frontal advance supported by the massed fire of artillery and aviation.
> (M. Solov'ev, *My Nine Lives in the Red Army* (London: Thames & Hudson, 1955) pp. 27, 28–9.)

7 RTsKhINDI, fond 71, opis'25, delo 59, 'NKO on the formation of the North-Western Front, 7 January, 1940'.
8 *IVOVSS*, Vol. 1, p. 266, and RTsKhINDI, fond 71, opis' 25, delo 59. Soviet geographical designations for some Finnish place names occasionally used the Swedish colonial variant rather than the original Finnish name. In this case 'Keksholm' refers to the town of Kexholm, or Kakisalmi on the eastern littoral of Lake Ladoga.
9 Semiryaga, *Tainy stalinskoi diplomatii*, p. 163
10 Korneev, *Boevye deistviia 50 SK po proryvu linii mannergeima*, p. 3. When the 7th Rifle Division arrived in the Leningrad Military District in late January 1940, it was subordinated to the 50th Rifle Corps command on 29 January. According to testimony during

the March 1940 joint commission between the Central Committee and the Main Military Soviet, Shchadenko was unable to organize the transport of the reinforcements to the Karelian Isthmus quickly enough and held up the launching of the new offensive. See Voroshilov, *Doklad (Voroshilova) o sovetsko–finliandskoi voine 1939–1940 gg.*, p. 16.

11 TsGASA, fond 34980, opis' 14, delo 50, l.30, 'Official History of the Soviet–Finnish War, January 1941'.

12 Ibid.

13 Ibid.

14 N.N. Shvarts, *Rabota komandovaniia fronta i armii i ukh shtabov po upravleniiu operatsiiami* (Moscow: AGSh RKKA, 1938) p. 4

15 TsGASA, fond 34980, opis' 14, delo 50, l.34. During the post-purge, pre-Second World War period the Main Military Soviet concentrated the Red Army's competent staff officers in the Kiev Military District which became the focal point of Soviet strategic planning and wartime staff expertise. See J. Erickson, *Organizing for War: The Soviet Military Establishment viewed through the Prism of the Military District* (College Station Papers, No. 2, The Center for Strategic Technology, Texas A and M University, 1983) p. 53. When Timoshenko greeted L.M. Sandalov at the North-Western Front Headquarters in early January he exclaimed 'Apparently, everybody from the Belorussian Military District is here at the Front,' referring to generals Chuikov and Kovalev who had volunteered for service in the Finnish campaign. See L.M. Sandalov, *Perezhitoe* (Moscow: Voenizdat, 1961), p. 49.

16 Shvarts, *Rabota komandovaniia fronta ...* p. 4. During Timoshenko's conversation with Sandalov in early January 1940, he acquainted Sandalov with the situation at the front and then observed the following:

> The tempo by which we customarily made the attack in academic games you will not see here. To chew through the fortified region in winter during a severe frost is more than difficult. Success in a given day is measured not in kilometres but in metres. History has not yet known such a war, and not one army, except our own, is capable of conducting an offensive in such conditions. However, I must admit that we poorly trained our troops for such a type of war. Go finish off their schooling at the front. You have arrived here in the company of a division. Are they participating in the exercises on breakthrough of fortified regions? A few commanders assumed that in winter, in a severe frost, one should not conduct exercises in the field in order not to freeze their soldiers. I agree with Ivan Vasil'evich [Smorodinov]. You must go teach the experience of war to the troops. (See Sandalov, ibid., p. 50.)

17 TsGASA, fond 34980, opis' 14, delo 50, l.46. See also *Voennaia Akademiia imeni M.V. Frunze* (Moscow: Voenizdat, 1988) p. 109. Colonel Talenskii was chief of the Faculty of the History of the First World War at the Frunze Military Academy. When L.M. Sandalov met with Zlobin, an acquaintance from his days at the General Staff Academy, to discuss a posting with the North-Western Front, Zlobin explained to him that the Front Operational Department's focus was not on operational questions but training the forward tactical units how to conduct the tactics of breakthrough. See Sandalov, *Perezhitoe*, p. 50. Timoshenko's institutionalization of continual assessment over combined arms doctrine later provided the model for the creation of the 'Department for the Utilization of War Experience' in the General Staff in July 1941 which, in turn, became the 'Administration for the Utilization of War Experience' in 1944. See N.M. Vasil'ev, 'Rabota General'nogo shtaba po oboshcheniiu opyta voiny v 1941–1945 godakh', *Voennaia Mysl'*, No. 5, May 1994, p. 69. This organization has only recently come to the attention of historians in the West. See D.M. Glantz, ed., *Soviet Documents on the Use of War Experience*, 3 vols (London: Frank Cass, 1991).

18 Voronov, *Na sluzhbe voennoi*, p. 144.

19 RTsKhINDI, fond 71, opis' 25, delo 6862, 'On organizing and executing breakthrough of fortified regions'. M.V. Zakharov, in an unpublished manuscript of his memoirs about the General Staff in the inter-war years, noted the significance of these instructions in the

history of Soviet military art but claimed that after the end of hostilities they were burnt. Cited in G.A.Kumanev, 'Vuosien 1939–40 neuvostoliitolais – suomalaisen sodan ("talvi-sodan") tapahtumat uusien lahetymistaponjen ja dokumenttien nakokulmasta' ('1939–1940, the event of the Soviet–Finnish War from the point of view of new documents'), p. 270. See also Korneev, *Boevye deistviia 50 SK proryvu linii mannergeima*, p. 19.

20 TsGASA, fond 34980, opis'14, delo 6, 1.23, 'General Meretskov's lecture to the students of the General Staff Academy on the lessons of the war with Finland, 26 June, 1940'. In this lecture Meretskov placed final blame for the fiasco of the December operations on the severe frost.

21 F. Kuz'min, 'Nastuplenie SD v zimnikh usloviiakh', *Voennaia mysl'*, January 1940, p. 34.

22 Ibid., p. 28.

23 S.N. Kuz'min, S.A. Kozak, 'Deistviia tankov v zimnikh usloviiakh', *Voennaia mysl'*, February 1940, p. 52.

24 There is an interesting dichotomy in Soviet terminology concerning Finnish permanent field fortifications on the Karelian Isthmus. Soviet literature of a purely military-doctrinal nature refers to them as Fortified Regions (UR, or *Ukreplennyi Raion*) made up of Long-Term Fire-Points (DOT, or *Dolgovremennaia Ognevaia Tochka*). Literature of a more political nature refers to them as the Mannerheim Line.

25 B.V. Panov *et al.*, *Istoriia voennogo iskusstva* (Moscow: Voenizdat 1984) (JPRS Translation UMA-85-009-L, 21 March 1985) p. 42. The Russian historian Pavel Aleksandrov has independently confirmed this relationship between Timoshenko's 1940 offensive and Brusilov's 1916 offensive. See P. Aleksandrov, 'Raskolotyi shchit', *Rodina*, No. 12, Winter 1995, p. 79. For a discussion about the projected Field Regulations (1939) see Kuz'min, *Na strazhe mirnogo truda (1921–1940 gg.)*, pp. 226–9, and Korotkov, *Istoriia sovetskoi voennoi mysli*, p. 159.

26 RTsKhINDI, fond 71, opis'25, delo 6862.

27 F.I.Trukhin, *et al.*, *Metodika i tekhnika raboty obshchevoiskovykh shtabov* (Moscow: AGSh RKKA, 1939) pp. 65–6.

28 TsGASA, fond 34980, opis'14, delo 6, ll. 19–20. Meretskov explicitly admits having weak aerial photo-reconnaissance and weak organization of battle reconnaissance on l.21.

29 Korneev, *Boevye deistviia 50 SK po proryvu linii mannergeima*, p. 31

30 I. Kubatko, 'Razvedka v lesu', *Na Strazhe Rodiny*, 10 January 1940, p. 2. See also V. Bobrinskii, 'Otdelenie v razvedke', *Na Strazhe Rodiny*, 3 February 1940, p. 2

31 Korneev, *Boevye deistviia 50 SK po proryvu linii mannergeima*, p. 28.

32 I. Kubatko, 'Razvedka v lesu', p. 2.

33 Korneev, *Boevye deistviia 50 SK po proryvu linii mannergeima*, p. 35.

34 J.V. Anzulovic, 'The Russian Record of the Winter War, 1939–1940: An analytical study of Soviet records of the war with Finland from 30 November 1939 to 12 March 1940', Ph.D. Dissertation, University of Maryland, 1969, p. 213. See also Iu.Ia. Kirshin, *Dukhovnaia gotovnost' sovetskogo naroda k voine* (Minneapolis, MN: East View Publications, 1991) p. 62

35 Anzulovic, 'The Russian Record of the Winter War', p. 214.

36 Panov, *Istoriia voennogo iskusstva*, p. 44

37 TsGASA, fond 34980, opis' 6, delo 77, 'Directive from the North-Western Front: Timoshenko's instructions after an inspection of the front, 9 February 1940'.

38 Korneev, *Boevye deistviia 50 SK po proryvu linii mannergeima*, p. 44.

39 Ibid., p. 29.

40 P.P. Chevela, 'Itogi i uroki sovetsko–finliandskoi voiny', *Voennaia Mysl'*, No. 4, 1990, p. 52.

41 Korneev, *Boevye deistviia 50 SK po proryvu linii mannergeima*, pp. 47–8. According to Korneev, sappers were not allowed to cut down trees in the area for this purpose, perhaps because the army command wished to preserve the forest as cover. The proper construction of dug-outs was actually a big problem. Dug-outs were normally built by the first troops stationed in the area and thus were not always well built. Improper ventilation and construction of the stove often resulted in the partial, and sometimes fatal asphyxiation of the troops living in it. For more information on the day-to-day life and hazards of a Red

The Red Army Reforms its Military Doctrine

Army soldier see the unpublished combat diary of A.I. Matveev edited by V.A. Savin from documents held at TsGASA, fond 34980, opis' 14, delo 84, ll. 130–205.

42 *Konflikt*, Document No. 63, 'Prikaz voiskam 7 armii ob uluchshenii organizatsii voisk PVO, 20 ianvaria 1940 g'.
43 Chew, *The White Death*, p. 142.
44 *Konflikt*, Document No. 55.
45 Sandalov stayed on at the 13th Army during the month of January to study how army and formation staffs conducted reconnaissance of enemy fortified regions and how the offensive strike was to be carried out. The commander and staff of the 13th Army were all artillerymen convinced that the key to breakthrough was artillery. See Sandalov, ibid., p. 51.
46 TsGASA, fond 34980, opis' 6, delo 187, l.5. Korneev states that some Finnish DOTs required the expenditure of 650 shells for their destruction. See Korneev, *Boevye deistviia 50 SK po proryvu linii mannergeima*, p. 38.
47 TsGASA, fond 34980, opis' 6, delo 187, l.6. See also fond 34980, opis 14, delo 50, l.29.
48 Korneev, *Boevye deistviia 50 SK po proryvu linii mannergeima*, p. 40.
49 RTsKhINDI, fond 71, opis' 25, delo 6862, ll. 3–4, 9.
50 TsGASA, fond 34980, opis' 6, delo 187, ll. 6–7.
51 V. Bolotnikov, 'Artilleriiskaia razvedka v usloviiakh lestisto-bolotistoi mestnosti', *Na Strazhe Rodiny*, 9 January 1940, p. 2.
52 A. Sazhin, 'Opyt raboty artillerii', *Na Strazhe Rodiny*, 10 January 1940, p. 2
53 These nomograms, or tables of battle, were a primitive attempt to synthesize information from the battlefield into standardized operating prodecures. Nomograms later became fundamental to automated troop control systems. For the historical development of the Soviet theory of troop control and the use of nomograms see J. Erickson, 'Soviet Command Technology: Problems, Programmes, Perspectives', *Jane's Defense Review*, No. 1, 1980, pp. 9–11, and Erickson *et al.*, *Soviet Ground Forces: An Operational Assessment* (London: Croom Helm, 1986) pp. 141–76.
54 RTsKhINDI, fond 71, opis' 25, delo 6862, ll. 6–7.
55 Vorob'ev, 'Shtab batal'ona v nastupatel'nom boiu', *Na Strazhe Rodiny*, 28 January 1940, p. 2.
56 Talenskii, 'Kak pravil'no organizovat' vzaimodeistvie voisk', *Na Strazhe Rodiny*, 6 January 1940 p. 2. See also Korneev, *Boevye deistviia 50 SK po proryvu linii mannergeima*, p. 35. Throughout the preparatory period *Na Strazhe Rodiny* published many articles extolling the leadership virtues of sub-unit commanders, exemplified in the exploits of Ugriumov and his battalion staff. See editorial article entitled 'Boevye zadachi shtaba', *Na Strazhe Rodiny*, 1 February 1940, p. 1.
57 S. Sapigo, 'Vzaimodeistvie artillerii i pekhoty v lesnom boiu', *Na Strazhe Rodiny*, 7 January 1940, p. 2, and N Shvankov, 'Sovmestnyi udar pekhoty i artillerii', *Na Strazhe Rodiny*, 13 January 1940, p. 2.
58 Colonel Kurochkin, 'Organizatsiia sviazi pri nastuplenii na ukrepivshegocia protivnika', *Na Strazhe Rodiny*, 4 February 1940, p. 2.
59 N. Shvankov, ibid., and S. Sapigo, ibid.
60 TsGASA, fond 34980, opis'14, delo 50, l.29.
61 Solov'ev, *My Nine Lives in the Red Army*, p. 119.
62 TsGASA, fond 34980, opis' 14, delo 12, l.23, 'Supplement to Instructions, 4 February 1940'.
63 Ibid. These tactics must have been responsible for a significant percentage of Red Army dead and wounded.
64 RTsKhINDI, fond 71, opis'25, delo 6862.
65 Talinskii, 'Kak pravil'no organizovat' vzaimodeistvie voisk', p. 2
66 PRO WO 208/582, 'Report on Russian Tactical Operations in Finland by Major R.O.A. Gatehouse and Captain C.H. Tamplin', p. 7
67 Voronov, *Na sluzhbe voennoi*, p. 144, and Panov, *Istoriia voennogo iskusstva*, p. 44. For a discussion of this method of artillery fire see Chris Bellamy, *The Red God of Fire. Soviet Artillery and Rocket Forces* (London: Brassey's, 1986), pp. 183–4.

131

68 TsGASA, fond 34980, opis' 14, delo 12, 'North-Western Front: Supplement to Instructions on how to overcome fortified gun-emplacements (artillery/tank), 4 February, 1940'.
69 RTsKhINDI, fond 71, opis' 25, delo 6862.
70 TsGASA, fond 34980, opis' 14, delo 50, 1.29.
71 TsGASA, fond 34980, opis' 14, delo 12, 1.24. See also M. Potapov, 'Blokirovanie i razrushenie dolgovremennykh ognevykh tochek', *Na Strazhe Rodiny*, 24 January 1940, p. 2. Potapov recommended using even larger calibre artillery, i.e., 76 mm. or 122 mm. guns.
72 F.O. Miksche, *Blitzkrieg* (London: Faber & Faber, 1941), p. 54.
73 RTsKhINDI, fond 71, opis' 25, delo 6862, 1.15.
74 TsGASA, fond 34980, opis' 14, delo 12, 1.24.
75 RTsKhINDI, fond 71, opis' 25, delo 6862, 1.15.
76 *Voprosi taktiki v sovetskikh voennykh trudakh (1917–1940)* (Moscow: Voenizdat, 1970) p. 297. This is an excerpt from P.A. Rotmistrov's work, 'Proryv sil'no ukreplennykh polos i ukreplennykh raionov strelkovym korposom', (Moscow, 1940).
77 P.A. Rotmistrov, *Stal'naia gvardiia* (Moscow: Voenizdat, 1984) p. 45
78 M. Gerasimov (Chief of the Combat Training Administration in the General Staff), 'Proekt Boevogo Ustava Pekhoty, Chast' Vtoraia', *Na Strazhe Rodiny*, 18 February 1940, pp. 2–3.
79 TsGASA, fond 34980, opis' 6, delo 31, 'Plan for the Political Security of the Operation to Destroy the Fortified Region by the 3rd Rifle Corps, 15–25 January 1940'. and TsGASA, fond 34980, opis' 14, delo 50, l. 31.
80 TsGASA, fond 34980, opis' 6, delo 35, ll. 10–11, 'Summary report of the 13th Army Instructional Section of the Political Department, 28 December–13 March 1940'.
81 Ibid.
82 TsGASA, fond 34980, opis' 6, delo 31.
83 T. Colton, *Commissars, Commanders and Civilian Authority. The Structure of Soviet Military Politics* (Cambridge: Harvard University Press, 1979) p. 80.
84 N. Zamiatin, 'Vzaimaia vyruchka i vzaimopomosh' v boiu', *Na Strazhe Rodiny*, 31 December 1939, p. 3.
85 Editorial article, 'Nastupatel'nyi poryv voinov Krasnoi Armii', *Na Strazhe Rodiny*, 22 January 1940, p. 1.
86 Colton, *Commissars, Commanders and Civilian Authority*, p. 75.
87 In the economic sphere this institutionalization of the class struggle between party and non-party member, manager and worker, during the Stakhanovite movement ultimately proved to be counter-productive because it disrupted purely bureaucratic processes. However, it had originally been born out of the Civil War and the Bolshevik Party's policy of War Communism and may have proven more effective in its original context. See Moshe Levine's discussion of the Stakhanovite movement in M. Levine, *The Making of the Soviet System* (London: Methuen, 1985), p. 38.
88 N. Sergeev, 'Polkovodcheskoe iskusstvo Suvorova', *Na Strazhe Rodiny*, 11 January 1940, p. 3. This concept of 'revolutionary discipline' was the basis of Tukhachevskii's proletarian military doctrine and played a key role in his theories of combined arms warfare. See Y. Kirshin, *The Soviet Military Doctrine in the Pre-War Period* (Moscow: Novosti,1990) pp. 72–3, for a discussion of the relationship between 'coercive' and 'conscious' control. See also the discussion in Chapter 5.
89 V. Krupatkin, 'Revoliutsionnaia distsiplina voinov Krasnoi Armii', *Na Strazhe Rodiny*, 6 February 1940, p. 3.
90 Editorial, 'Nastupatel'nyi poryv voinov Krasnoi Armii', *Na Strazhe Rodiny*, 22 January p. 1.
91 N. Tikhonov, 'O molodetskom russkom shtyke', *Na Strazhe Rodiny*, 3 February 1940, p. 3. Tikhonov also discusses the correlation of drunkenness with Finnish bravery within the context of bourgeois theories of military art and the British military theorist J.F.C. Fuller's 'fear' of the bayonet in the hands of the people.
92 I. Zakharov, 'Agitpoezd PU LVO v deistvuiushchei armii', *Na Strazhe Rodiny*, 7 January 1940, p. 4.
93 N. Nikolaev, 'Shire peredavat' boevoi opyt', *Na Strazhe Rodiny*, 7 January 1940, p. 3.

94 Announcement in *Na Strazhe Rodiny*, 2 January, p. 1, for awards made on 31 December 1939.
95 RTsKhINDI, fond 71, opis' 25, delo 6982, 'Communication between the Chief of the Political Administration of the Leningrad Military District and the Military Council of the North-Western Front about Gifts for Troops at the Front, January 15, 1940'.
96 See N.I. Baryshnikov *et al.*, *Istoriia Ordena Lenina Leningradskogo Voennogo Okruga* (Moscow: 1988) p. 133, for the political supervision of the press.
97 V. Ivanov, 'Sila bol'shevistskogo slova', *Na Strazhe Rodiny*, 7 February 1940, p. 3. Towards the end of December 1939 the editorial policy of the newspaper *Na Strazhe Rodiny* underwent a radical change in an attempt to reform its agitational message and make it more interesting to the tastes of the rank-and-file. Two of the changes were to occasionally feature a comics section on the fourth page and emphasize the day's political slogan in the headline.
98 Anon., 'Vrednye pis'ma Pashi Brezhuntsova', *Na Strazhe Rodiny*, 18 February 1940, p. 4.
99 A. Tvardovskii, 'S Karel'skogo peresheika: Zapiski 1939–1940 gg.', *Novyi Mir*, No. 2, 1969, p. 135. Vasia Tërkin is the archetypal 'Soviet Soldier', what General Yuri Kirshin refers to as a 'routine personality', devoid of political, spiritual and intellectual development. See Kirshin, *Dukhovnaia gotovnost' sovetskogo naroda k voine*, p. 28.
100 L.G. Ivashov, 'Oborona strany i zakon. (Pravovye osnovy podgotovke Vooruzhennykh Sil SSSR k otrazheniiu agressii)', *Voenno-istoricheskii zhurnal*, No. 10, 1992, p. 14.
101 See Levine, *The Making of the Soviet System*, pp. 74–81 for a discussion on village courts and customary law in rural Russia.
102 TsGASA, fond 34980, opis'6, delo 31, l.11, 'Plan for the Preservation of Political Security during the offensive against the Mannerheim Line (The Political Administration of the 3rd Rifle Corps, 13th Army), 15–25 January 1940'.
103 D. Fuks, 'V prokurature LVO. Shofery-Prestupniki', *Na Strazhe Rodiny*, 7 February 1940, p. 4, and TsGASA, fond 34980, opis'6, delo 35, ll. 238–239.
104 TsGASA, fond 34980, opis' 6, delo 18, ll. 1–23, 'Procuracy of the USSR. Military Procuracy of the 13th Army. Massive Political Work in the Units, January 26, 1940'. According to the procurator's report these speeches reached nine hundred soldiers. The archives of the Red Army are littered with collections of documents relating to soldiers' 'extraordinary' behaviour of all sorts ranging from drunkenness to the assassination of officers. Two collections relating to such phenomena in the 13th Army are: TsGASA, fond 34980, opis' 6, delo 16, 'Summaries, Reports from commanders and military commissars of army units about extraordinary occurences. Testimonies of military tribunals in the army, 1 January–8 April 1940', and delo 17, 'Reports from commanders and military commissars about extraordinary occurences in army units, 23 January–28 March'. The more serious offences were normally investigated by the Special Section of the NKVD. See footnote No. 176 for more discussion of the Special Section of the NKVD.
105 Vostrikov (Procurator), 'O l'gotakh dlia voennosluzhashchikh i ikh semei', *Na Strazhe Rodiny*, 14 February 1940, p. 4. In *The Making of the Soviet System* (p. 253), Lewin comments on the 1932 decree on labour discipline which embodied this aspect of *edinonachale*, the intervention of the criminal code into the civil code. Lewis Sieglebaum, in his article on Soviet labour discipline during War Communism, comments on this legal tradition of subordinating individual's personal and family well-being to larger collectives. See L.H. Sieglebaum, 'Defining and Ignoring Labor Discipline in the Early Soviet Period: The Comrades-Disciplinary Courts, 1918–1922', *Slavic Review*, Vol. 51, No. 4, Winter 1992, p. 709. Kirshin claims that during the war there were a total of 2,159 courts martial and 128 executions in the 7th and 13th Armies. See Kirshin, *Dukhovnaia gotovnost' sovetskogo naroda k voine*, p. 310.
106 Erickson in *Soviet Combined Arms: Past and Present*, p. 2, points out that Tukhachevskii was the first to coin this term in his early work on the tactics of combined infantry–artillery attack. Defined as 'interaction', 'co-operation', or 'co-ordination' it is a fundamental concept in Soviet theory of combined arms warfare which remains in use to the present day.

107 On 24 January 1940, the NKO and the NKVD issued a joint order to establish 'preventative detachments' for the explicit purpose of controlling desertion and cleaning up 'harmful elements' operating in the rear of the active armies. Directly subordinate to the NKO and the NKVD, these detachments were attached to army staffs but were not answerable to the army commander. The largest number of such detachments was assigned to the 8th Army operating in Karelia-Ladoga, and the second largest contingent was assigned to the 7th Army. There were 27 preventative detachments in all, each made up of a hundred men. See TsGASA, fond 34980, opis' 6, delo 77, ll. 117–19, 'NKO and NKVD order to set up control–defensive units, 24 January, 1940'.

108 TsGASA, fond 34980, opis'6, delo 35, l.225, 'Summary report of the 13th Army Instructional Section of the Political Department, 28 December–13 March 1940'.

109 Solov'ev, *My Nine Lives in the Red Army*, pp. 196–7.

4

TIMOSHENKO'S OFFENSIVE

Stalin's outburst to Meretskov in late December 1939, that a prolonged war with Finland would provoke foreign intervention, was not unfounded. The British and French governments had convened a meeting of the Supreme War Council a few days after the Soviet Union's expulsion from the League of Nations to discuss the strategic situation in Scandinavia and the Baltic region and, in the first instance, to ask Sweden and Norway to give direct military assistance to Finland.[1] The Swedish and Norwegian governments were anxious to maintain their neutrality and declined the Supreme War Council's proposal, but the significance of this proposal was not lost on the Soviet high command. Stalin and the Main Military Soviet decided that the war with Finland had to be brought to an acceptable conclusion as quickly as possible. Molotov began making arrangements at the People's Commissariat of Foreign Affairs to establish diplomatic contact with the Finnish government in Helsinki via Stockholm while Timoshenko re-armed and re-trained the troops of the North-Western Front for a new offensive on the Karelian Isthmus.

The first step towards peace negotiations was made by the Finnish government. On New Year's Day 1940, Hella Wuolijoki, a Finnish playwright who had often facilitated relations between the Finnish government and the Soviet embassy in Helsinki in the past, wrote to the Finnish Foreign Minister, Tanner, to suggest that she travel to Stockholm to visit her old acquaintance, Alexandra Kollontai, the Soviet ambassador to Sweden, to discuss Soviet war aims and the possibility of opening peace negotiations. Tanner accepted Wuolijoki's proposition and she departed for Stockholm for a meeting with Kollontai on 12 January.

Molotov responded quickly to Wuolijoki's meeting with Kollontai. On 20 January *Pravda* published a condemnation of the Entente's efforts to extend the European war to Scandinavia, the Balkans and the Middle East. This was intended as a message to the Swedish government to shun future Supreme War Council proposals and assist Moscow in secret peace negotiations. A day later, Yartsev and another representative from Moscow named Graver arrived in Stockholm to meet the Finnish *chargé d'affaires*, Erkko, to ascertain the seriousness of Wuolijoki's peace offers.[2] Upon receiving the Swedish government's official proposal to act as mediator in peace negotiations, Molotov sent a cable to Stockholm on 29 January acknowledging his agreement in principle to begin peace negotiations with the Finnish government in Helsinki.[3] The two-month-long hiatus in Soviet–Finnish diplomatic relations was over.

I

Meanwhile, Timoshenko's Operations Department at the North-Western Front headquarters in Leningrad had drawn up operational plans for the new offensive on the Karelian Isthmus. The first task had been to decide in which direction to launch this offensive; towards Kakisalmi via Taipale and Kiviniemi, towards Antrea via Vuoksi Lake, or towards Vyborg via Summa. Each route entailed overcoming significant artificial and natural barriers that had already demonstrated their effectiveness against Red Army offensive tactics. On the basis of reports from General Staff field trips to the isthmus, Stalin decided in favour of breakthrough and encirclement operations against Vyborg via Summa.[4]

On 18 January, a draft plan based on Shaposhnikov's original 'narrow-front' proposal was completed and given final approval by the Main Military Soviet on 3 February.[5] According to the approved plan, the 7th and 13th Armies were expected to attack simultaneously along the entire length of the Mannerheim Line while individual breakthrough strikes were focused against Finnish defences at Summa and Vuoksi Lake. Within four to five days from the start of the new offensive, the 7th Army should seize Kämärä Station, Huumola and Il'vec with nine divisions while the 13th Army seized Lohioki and Purpua with five divisions. As soon as the 7th Army broke through the Mannerheim Line and destroyed Finnish garrisons at Saarenpää and Taipale, D. Pavlov's Reserve Army, under the discretion of Stavka would conduct a second encirclement operation across the frozen Bay of Vyborg while Grendal's 13th Army would attack towards Kakisalmi. Timoshenko did not elaborate on pursuit operations to Vyborg except to state that 'the missions of the armies are to develop the offensive with the goal to encircle and destroy the main enemy group acting on the Karelian Isthmus'.[6] This plan indicated that the North-Western Front's strategic goals had been limited, in the first instance, to territorial annexations on the Karelian Isthmus and the north coast of Lake Ladoga.

During the month of January, Timoshenko's North-Western Front had also orchestrated the deployment of 23 new divisions along the border with Finland, bringing the total number of active divisions up to 45.[7] On the Karelian Isthmus, the main theatre of war, Meretskov's and Grendal's armies comprised 25 divisions, eight armoured brigades and 17 artillery regiments totalling approximately 600,000 men, 3,137 guns (1,033 of which were heavy calibre) and approximately 2,000 tanks.[8] According to Finnish calculations, these reinforcements gave the Red Army a four-to-one superiority in infantry, a 20- or 30-to-one superiority in artillery, and an absolute advantage in tanks and aviation.[9]

Timoshenko estimated that a successful offensive against the Finnish defences would require sequential military operations over a period of seven to 12 days supported by continuous material supply and rotation of troops. Due to the deployment of additional formations and units to the Karelian Isthmus during January 1940, Timoshenko was able to structure the North-Western Front's forces into four echelons. In the first echelon were 14 rifle divisions with sub-units occupying forward 'jumping-off' positions.[10] The second echelon consisted of three rifle divisions in the reserve of the 7th Army's strike group, the 50th Rifle Corps. Each army, in turn, had one rifle division composed of tank and machine gun brigades. The fourth echelon consisted of two rifle divisions and two divisions of the 1st Finnish People's Corps in the North-Western Front's reserve.[11] This echeloning system allowed Timoshenko and his subordinate field commanders the resources to rotate the forward divisions with fresh troops from nine divisions in the rear, and to take advantage of unforeseen opportunities and successful breakthrough assaults.[12]

Division commanders on the Karelian Isthmus paid special attention to training the storm groups during the final week of January. Formed within infantry battalions, these storm groups were armed with 45 mm. anti-tank weapons and were linked to battalion headquarters by dedicated telephone lines, as had been suggested by tacticians in the military press two weeks before.[13] Storm group exercises were conducted on mock fortifications in the immediate rear of forward regiments and divisions, as close as two to four kilometres from the front line, and were sometimes conducted at night in order to acquaint troops with night operations.[14] Additional exercises were organized for first echelon infantry battalions to train with artillery in order to shorten the gap between the artillery barrage and the infantry assault.[15] Division commanders also held joint exercises for mortarists, machine-gunners and snipers to instruct them in the use of new weapons in sub-zero temperatures, as well as to teach them how to ski. The 123rd Rifle Division had managed to put 3,000 troops, 160 stationary machine-guns, eight 45 mm.

137

guns, and 12 infantry support guns on skis by 28 January. The 100th Rifle Division had put 3,230 troops on skis. Gorolenko's 50th Rifle Corps also received from Leningrad factories more than a thousand armoured shields on skis and a few armoured sleds to be dragged behind tanks for the protection of sappers and infantry.

Another feature of Timoshenko's preparations for the new offensive was the re-deployment of strategic, long-range artillery on the Karelian Isthmus. The main mission of the heavy artillery was to disorganize the enemy's rear support facilities and demoralize the population of Vyborg.[16] In late January, Timoshenko ordered the Baltic Fleet command to transfer its coastal artillery battery No.9 to the railroad siding at Perki-järvi in preparation for the shelling of Vyborg on 11 February. He and Voroshilov had hoped to rely on aviation reconnaissance to correct the fire of this large calibre gun, but the pilots were unable to spot the shells' impact. During the new offensive, when the guns were ordered only to fire at night, other methods had to be developed to monitor the shells' accuracy. Inspired by the German's use of enemy news-papers to guide their shelling of Paris during the First World War, the North-Western Front relied on Finnish radio broadcasts and the interrogation of POWs to solve this problem. The North-Western Front also relied on other coastal artillery batteries to shell specific targets on the Mannerheim Line. Battery No. 17 moved to the railroad siding at Nauris-järvi in order to fire against the Finnish coastal battery at Saarenpää and Finnish strategic reinforcements moving along the Vyborg–Makslahti–Kallolatsi road. Battery No. 11, consisting of two trains armed with 356 mm. guns, joined Grendal's 13th Army on 6 February and was ordered to fire at Finnish divisional headquarters and ammunition depots at Piuhä-järvi as well as a group of six Finnish DOTs near Kiviniemi Lake.[17]

II

At the end of January, Stavka ordered Timoshenko to conduct five inde-pendent 'demonstration' operations on separate sectors of the Karelian Isthmus in preparation for the main offensive on 11 February.[18] The purpose of these demonstration operations was to experiment with a new type of decentralized troop control inspired by the German *Wehrmacht*'s directive-control system. Timoshenko instructed each rifle division commander who was assigned to conduct a demonstration operation to select his own inter-mediate goals and train his own troops as well as evaluate the effectiveness of the new combined arms tactics in combat.[19]

138

Although these organizational reforms represented a fundamental decentralization of command to facilitate operational flexibility, Timoshenko warned commanders against conducting their demonstration operations without the knowledge and authorization of his Front military soviet or without an adequately prepared battle plan. The purported reason was that military failures resulting from these oversights would undermine the initiative of local commanders and the combat discipline of the troops.[20] However, Timoshenko was aware that an army normally required years of strenuous training and combat experience before its command corps was proficient in directive control and its troops capable of combined arms tactics. He was not confident that the Red Army's tactical deficiencies would be ironed out by one week of training with untested techniques.

On the morning of 1 February 1940 the new tactical doctrine was inaugurated with a two-hour long artillery preparation and aerial bombardment against the Mannerheim Line and railroad junctions, depots, and other communication links in the rear. When the artillery preparation lifted, the 7th Army conducted three demonstration operations; the 100th Rifle Division at Summa, the 113th Rifle Division on Hill No. 38 south of Karhula, and the 42nd Rifle Division on Muurila. The 13th Army conducted two demonstration operations, one by the 150th Rifle Division on Piiskan and the other by the 50th Rifle Division between the Vuoksi and Puunus Lakes.[21] Each demonstration operation had a formal goal, but overall they were given the flexibility to choose the most important targets, train their own troops, and verify the effectiveness of the new tactical doctrine in battle.[22]

Two forward regiments in the 100th Rifle Division, the 355th and 331st (2nd Company) Rifle Regiments, were instructed to conduct battle reconnaissance and experiment with the new storming techniques against Finnish defensive positions at Summa, specifically 'Jackboot' Grove and 'Finger' Grove, respectively (see Figures 4.1 and 4.2).[23] The most important of these forays was against Summa, conducted by the 1st Battalion and its 4th Company. Before the artillery preparation began, the regimental commander held an orientation exercise with the battalion and company commanders to explain the battle plan. While the 1st Battalion was instructed to lead a demonstration assault directly against Summa, the 4th Company, under the command of junior lieutenant Grishin, was to make its way towards Jackboot Grove with a storm group consisting of a platoon of field artillery, a platoon of T-28 tanks, and a platoon of sappers from the 45th Engineering Battalion, and then to storm DOT No. 45 with the support of additional artillery cover from the neighbouring 2nd Battalion (see Figure 4.2).[24] Grishin was given a direct telephone line to the staff of the 2nd Battalion so that he could call on

139

FIGURE 4.1
DISTRIBUTION OF THE 50TH RIFLE CORPS' FORCES AT
SUMMA (KHOTINEN) AND HAMMER GROVE, 10 FEBRUARY 1940

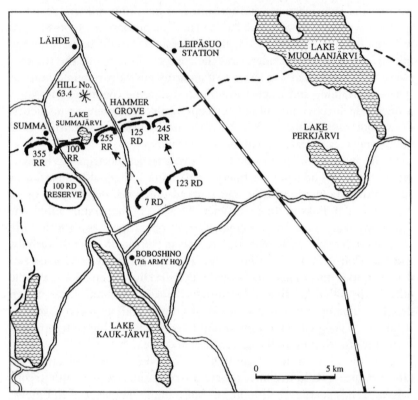

support from its artillery and correct its fire directly.[25] When the corps and divisional commanders began their artillery preparation, Grishin and his company moved forward to their jumping-off positions 400 metres away from DOT No. 45 and launched their assault at 12h45.[26]

Initially, the demonstration attack by the 1st Battalion and the forward movement of Grishin's company went according to plan. However, while the storm group was traversing the obstacle field their sled, filled with explosives, was hit by Finnish fire and blew up. The storm group suffered several losses and was forced to retreat to its jumping-off positions.[27] Meanwhile, the remainder of Grishin's company continued to advance toward DOT No. 45 under a hail of bullets and mortar fire. When they reached the DOT they threw a small pack of explosives through the embrasure, but the charge was too weak and did not silence opposition from within the DOT. After the

FIGURE 4.2

DIAGRAM OF THE 355TH RIFLE REGIMENT'S STORMING OF DOT NO.45,
1 FEBRUARY 1940

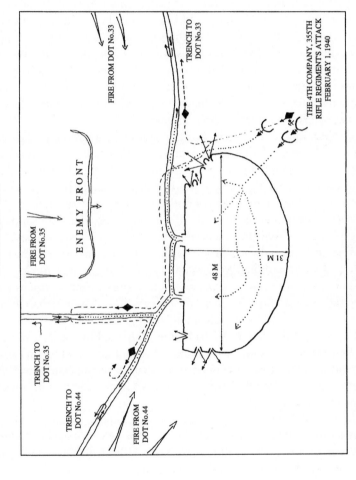

Adapted from Korneev, *Boevye deistviia 50 SK po proryvu linii mannergeima.*

explosion, Finnish troops from inside the DOT and from the trenches around DOT Nos. 44, 33, and 35 attempted to counter-attack, but were beaten off by the Red Army storm troops armed with hand-grenades.[28] During this mêlée, the 4th Company was supported by the tanks and artillery fire made possible by direct telephone lines with regimental artillery.[29]

Although Grishin's men had effectively isolated DOT No. 45 from the rest of the Finnish defence network, and had temporarily held the DOT against Finnish counter-attack, they could not fulfil their mission without more explosives and the expertise of the sappers. Waiting for the sappers to reorganize and transport the explosives out to the DOT under the cover of darkness, Grishin's men bided their time in the snow at the relatively exposed entrance to the DOT. During the delay the Finns counter-attacked a second time, and attempted to cajole the storm group into relaxing its defences with a ruse, before reverting back to a stalemate.[30]

Behind Red Army lines, Captain Korovin, a military engineer and commander of the 90th Independent Sapper Battalion, took command of the 4th Company's sapper platoon and led them out to the DOT when dusk fell. This time, the sappers brought forward 600 kg of explosives but were able to destroy only three embrasures and a further eight remained.[31] Captain Korovin ordered his sappers to retrieve another 1,600 kg. This third delivery of explosives arrived late that evening (see Figure 4.3). Korovin and his men had carefully packed the explosives against the eastern corner of the DOT by 04h15 the next morning. As Grishin's company took cover, leaving Korovin and his assistant Tsvetkov to detonate the charges, Finnish troops counter-attacked in an attempt to remove the charges. Tsvetkov shot three Finns and the rest retreated, but some of Korovin's preparations had been spoiled during the attack and the detonation had to be postponed for another two hours.[32] At 06h40 Korovin, once again alone at the DOT, his clothes and gas-mask riddled with bullet holes, detonated the charges and an enormous explosion destroyed the rest of DOT No. 45. Korovin, Grishin and his men then seized the ruined DOT.[33]

As the 4th Company was gripped in the struggle against DOT No. 45, advance news of the success was relayed to 7th Army commander Meretskov who was present at the headquarters of the 100th Rifle Division. Meretskov ordered the 100th Rifle Division commander, A. Yermakov, to destroy DOT 44 as well as to strengthen battle reconnaissance missions along other sectors of the front.[34] On the basis of these commands, Yermakov, on 2 February, ordered the 331st Rifle Regiment to send two infantry battalions and tanks against Finnish positions at Tongue Grove while the 355th Rifle Regiment was told to continue its attacks against Jackboot Grove and DOT No. 45. The

FIGURE 4.3
RED ARMY SAPPER TRANSPORTING EXPLOSIVES, FEBRUARY 1940

Courtesy of TsGASA, fond 34980, opis' 14, delo 221.

3rd Battalion was expected to conduct an offensive on Summa while the 2nd Battalion, 5th Company, was to storm DOT No. 44 according to the methods verified by its neighbour. The 5th Company, equipped with two T-26 tanks carrying a total of 1,000 kg of explosives in sleds, was escorted to DOT No. 44 by a platoon of T-28 tanks and artillery cover from two artillery divisions.[35] During the evening of 2 February, and into the next day, the 2nd and 3rd Battalions of the 355th Rifle Regiment, especially the sub-units holding the DOT Nos. 44 and 45, withstood a Finnish counter-attack.[36]

At this point, Korneev and his colleagues at the North-Western Front's Section for the Study of Combat Experience concluded that the independent 'demonstration' operations had been a success. The key to this success was the responsive and accurate artillery support for the storm group assaults facilitated by direct telephone communications between the storm group commander and the regimental artillery commander. Tanks also played an important role by transporting the storm groups and their explosives to the targets, giving cover to the storm groups as the demolition of the DOT was organized and holding off Finnish counter-attacks with their gun fire. The biggest surprise to the Red Army theorists was the enormous amount of explosives required to destroy a DOT. Even the extensive study of Finnish DOT construction carried out the previous month had underestimated the strength of these reinforced concrete forts. The theorists now recognized that a large amount of explosives had to be delivered to the target and that the infantry company assigned to escort the storm group (in conjunction with tanks) could help carry this burden in addition to its other responsibilities. Ultimately, Red Army tacticians recognized that detailed planning and overall preparations made by the division commander and his staff were important in assuring effective interaction between all the services at the front.[37]

On 3 February, Timoshenko, who had been closely informed about the 100th Rifle Division's success and encouraged by the favourable reports from the Section for the Study of Combat Experience, ordered Meretskov to continue the demonstration operations until 5 February. Meretskov was then told to expand the demonstration operations in order to gradually introduce more Red Army troops to the heat of battle and confuse the enemy about the time and direction of the new offensive.[38] Upon receiving this order, on 4 February Meretskov ordered the 50th Rifle Corps to concentrate on breakthrough operations with the forces of the 100th Rifle Division against the Finnish DOTs and field defences along the forest edge of northern Summa. Once accomplished, the next goal was to conduct battle reconnaissance of the Finnish second defensive zone and disrupt enemy activity in the rear of the first defensive zone opposite the forces of the 19th Rifle Corps. In order to support the breakthrough operations of the 100th Rifle Division, the 10th Rifle Corps was ordered to concentrate forces on the sector of the 138th Rifle Division to perform battle reconnaissance against the Finnish DOTs at Karhula. Both these operations were to verify and familiarize the units involved with the new storming techniques.[39] Meanwhile, Timoshenko, Zhdanov, Meretskov and Grendal, and the military theorists of the Section for the Study of Combat Experience, personally reviewed the battle-readiness of the forward units, studied the layout of the enemy defences, and supervised the staff work of each corps and division.[40]

Ironically, the focus of attention and fire-power on the operations of the 100th Rifle Division was reciprocated by the defensive efforts of the Finns. The 100th Rifle Division was unable to develop more than an artillery preparation against the Finnish fortifications on 4 February. On 5 February, the 355th and 85th Rifle Regiments tried to assault DOT Nos. 33, 34, 36, and 40, but soon were stopped at the anti-tank and personnel obstacle fields by heavy Finnish cross-fire. Although the 100th Rifle Division had neutralized DOT Nos. 44 and 45, there were still ten active DOTs in the Finnish defensive network at Summa and Red Army artillery was still incapable of suppressing their artillery fire.[41] During the night of 5 February the 100th Rifle Division rotated its front-line units and in the morning of 6 February, after a thirty-minute artillery preparation, the division attacked again but without significant results. The Finnish defenders were obviously strengthening artillery coverage and the Red Army command would have to seek a successful break-through operation elsewhere.[42] Although Yermakov's division had not executed their primary mission, they did succeed in convincing the Finns that the Red Army's general offensive had been thwarted while, at the same time, inflicting enormous casualties on the Finnish Army.[43]

On 9 February, Timoshenko confirmed that the new general offensive would commence at 12h00 on 11 February. The weight of the offensive would fall on the shoulders of Meretskov's strike group, the 50th Rifle Corps commanded by Gorolenko, which was to attack the Finnish defensive network between Summa, Summa-järvi Lake and Hammer Grove with its first echelon, the 100th and 123rd Rifle Divisions (see Figures 4.1 and 4.4).[44] Timoshenko designated the 100th Rifle Division as the main spearhead of the offensive on the basis of its successful 'demonstration' operations.[45] The 100th Rifle Division was ordered to seize the Finnish DOTs at Summa and advance up the Vyborg Highway to the town of Autio, while its neighbour on the eastern shore of Summa-järvi Lake, the 123rd Rifle Division, was expected to attack Finnish DOTs at Hammer Grove and Hill No. 65.5 and cut through the forest to the town of Lähde.[46] When these first echelon divisions had

145

FIGURE 4.4
MAP OF THE FINNISH DEFENSIVE SYSTEM AT HAMMER GROVE

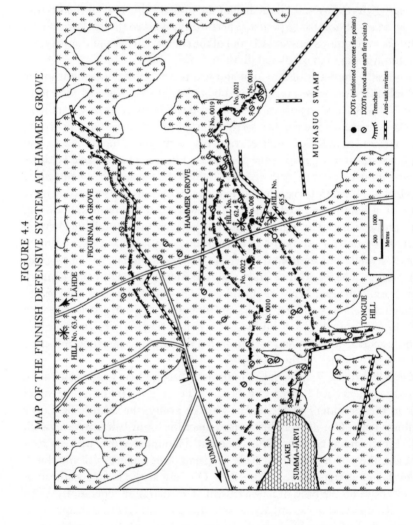

Adapted from Korneev, *Boevye deistviia 50 SK po proryvu linii mannergeima.*

146

broken through the Finnish defensive system, Gorolenko was to introduce the second echelon, the 7th Rifle Division and the 20th Tank Brigade, into the breach.[47] At this time Timoshenko also addressed the troops on the Karelian Isthmus, calling upon them to achieve the breakthrough of the Mannerheim Line and pursue the retreating Finnish Army to a decisive defeat and full destruction.[48] On the morning of 10 February, Meretskov relayed Timoshenko's battle order to the 50th Rifle Corps headquarters at Boboshino. In conjunction with the breakthrough operations of the 10th and 19th Rifle Corps to the west and east, the 50th Rifle Corps, as the strike group of Meretskov's 7th Army, was expected to concentrate divisions against specific Finnish DOTs and then develop its tactical breakthrough into operational advances towards Autio (mission of the 100th Rifle Division) and Lähde (mission of the 123rd Rifle Division).[49]

On the eve of Timoshenko's offensive the 50th Rifle Corps enjoyed a superior correlation of forces with its Finnish counterpart. Along the six-kilometre wide sector of the front, the 50th Rifle Corps had accumulated 4.5 battalions per kilometre of front compared to the Finnish Army's 3 battalions (a 1.5-fold advantage); 76.6 artillery guns per kilometre of front compared to the Finns' 25 guns (a three-fold advantage) and its original norm of 48 guns; 36 tanks per kilometre compared to the Finns' 12 anti-tank guns (a three-fold advantage), as well as total air superiority.[50]

Timoshenko's inspection tour of the front on 9 February had, however, indicated that serious problems remained in troop control. While announcing the imminent offensive, Timoshenko also issued an instruction to the 7th and 13th Armies criticizing their co-ordination of combined arms battle at the regimental-battalion-company level.[51] There was little that Meretskov and Grendal could do about this deficiency in the short term because their formations still lacked a full complement of trained officers. For example, on 10 February the 50th Rifle Corps still lacked 613 middle officers, 1,505 junior officers, and 6,588 rank-and-file.[52] Timoshenko's criticisms also included the following: the organization of battle and conduct of training was not thorough or systematic, senior commanders exercised poor control over junior commanders during combat, and army staff representatives sent to aid subordinate staffs were not helping to organize the battle or uncovering deficiencies in the formulation of battle plans.[53]

In order to overcome these deficiencies Timoshenko recommended that the field commanders be reissued with the new tactical doctrine.[54] Specific criticisms were directed toward the 13th Army, citing an incident during the demonstration operations when tanks had fired on their own infantry and had prematurely abandoned their storm groups before the completion of the assault, thus promoting the troops' distrust of the effectiveness of combined arms co-ordination and lowering discipline in the ranks. Timoshenko emphasized the need for personal orientation exercises between tank and infantry commanders in order to discuss the proper sequence of goals and agree to special signals for communication during battle, all of which compensated for the lack of radio communication.[55]

While last minute fine-tuning of combined arms tactics for the breakthrough was being completed, the political commissar for the 13th Army, A. Zaporozhets, reviewed German military-doctrinal documents on assault tactics given to him by the Chief of the Reconnaissance Department of the 13th Army. In the introduction accompanying the documents, the Intelligence Department reviewed German experimentation with storm troop tactics from the First World War up to the invasion of Czechoslovakia and their use in the invasion of Poland. Zaporozhets' specific interest in the documents was focused on how to prepare a storm group for another assault on DOTs after having already suffered a rebuff.[56] Ultimately, the success of the entire operation against the Mannerheim Line rested with this small group of soldiers at the outermost periphery of the Red Army's organizational hierarchy.

On the evening before the new offensive, Grendal's staff issued a final instruction to its corps, division and regiment commanders on the methods of maintaining operational unity in combined arms warfare. The most important principle was the maintenance of continuous battle reconnaissance so that the commander could base his decisions on a timely and detailed analysis of circumstances. Continuous reconnaissance allowed the commander to identify successful operations and reinforce success with reserves. Regimental commanders, in particular, were instructed to enhance their battlefield control by commanding from mobile observation posts (i.e. tanks) during the assault, and all commanders were instructed to widen their communications to monitor the activities of neighbouring units. In the event that neighbouring units were more successful in conducting the breakthrough, commanders were encouraged to lend their own reserves to develop a neighbour's success. Such mutual aid should help develop success in the commander's own area. This inter-communication and mutual aid between commanders embodied the principle of *vzaimodeistviie*, one of the organizational principles of Soviet combined arms warfare.[57] To illustrate the importance of *vzaimodeistviie* in conducting successful breakthrough operations, the 13th Army staff warned commanders that they should be prepared for the possibility of using an entire division's artillery fire to support the success of one regiment.[58] On the main axis of the imminent offensive, *vzaimodeistviie* was enhanced by equipping the staffs of the 100th and 123rd Rifle Divisions with two Morse cable-telegraph lines, a telephone, a radio, and automobile/ horse couriers for communications with the headquarters of the 50th Rifle Corps in addition to telephone, courier and radio communications with their subordinate tank brigades, and telephone lines to neighbouring divisional staffs.[59]

The fundamental purpose of the North-Western Front's emphasis on local troop control, *vzaimodeistviie* between commanders, and inter-service awareness of other services' roles in the combined arms formation, was to shift the Red Army away from an organizational ethic of political reliability to a professionalism based on a common operational knowledge and experience. The next day's offensive would reveal whether the officers and troops were able to translate this new professionalism into success on the battlefield.

Timoshenko's tactical doctrine, developed during January 1940, was far removed from the paralysing thrust of independent moto-mechanized formations deep into the enemy's strategic defences envisaged by Tukhachevskii and his colleagues in the early 1930s or demonstrated by the *Wehrmacht* during the German–Polish War the previous autumn. However, Timoshenko's doctrine was not a repudiation of Deep Operations theory, as several Soviet military commentators would claim after the war.[60] Timoshenko and his staff had recognized the need to commence with the fundamental principles of combined arms warfare and for that reason had resuscitated the theories of Deep Battle by drawing on the experience of the Brusilov Offensive during the First World War. In this learning process they borrowed the principle of directive-control and storm troop tactics from the *Wehrmacht* but the debt was, at most, selective and carefully integrated into the pre-existing doctrine. Whatever criticism could be made of Stalin's and Voroshilov's pre-war propensity to stifle the professional abilities of their officer corps, in late December and in January Stavka demonstrated a remarkable ability to learn from past mistakes and modify doctrine accordingly, the results of which soon became apparent to the Finnish high command.[61] Most foreign military commentators continued to dismiss the Red Army's ability to conduct modern warfare. Others, who had the patience to follow the development of Red Army operations on the Karelian Isthmus carefully, later acknowledged the Red Army's surprising degree of organizational adaptability.[62]

III

A few hours before the attack was to begin, Timoshenko, Voronov (in his capacity as Stalin's personal military expert at the North-Western Front), Meretskov and his political commissar, Vashugin, arrived at the headquarters of the 100th Rifle Division in order to supervise personally the preparation of the battle plans and observe the unfolding of the new offensive. Timoshenko was particularly anxious to oversee the preparations made by the regimental commanders and to satisfy his curiosity regarding their co-operation with tank and artillery commanders, commenting to the hapless staff officer assigned to him that if battle control at platoon level was improperly organized the entire operation would end in fiasco.[63]

At last, the appointed hour (12h00) for the beginning of the artillery preparation arrived and with it the moment of truth: would the 20 days of re-training, reorganization and reinforcement produce positive results? After the two-hour artillery preparation and the beginning of the assault, Timoshenko visited the artillery positions to supervise the work of the artillery and watch the progress of the battle. Timoshenko was impressed with the speed and accuracy of the gunners working the guns so furiously that their half-nude bodies glistened with sweat despite the sub-zero temperatures. He likened their work to the clockwork production line of a well-run factory.[64] This industry was the utopian ideal of Soviet military doctrine.[65] The carefully tuned division of labour would use fire and movement to resolve the perennial paradox between the offensive and defensive forms of warfare.

Although the previous night had been cold and crystal clear, a pea-soup fog descended on the Karelian Isthmus on the morning of 11 February which voided plans for an air-strike against the Finnish forward defence zone and reserves. Therefore, Gorolenko ordered the artillery preparation to begin at 09h40, an hour earlier than scheduled. At noon he called his division commanders, Yermakov and Aliabushev, on the telephone and ordered them to begin their combined arms assaults. They, in turn, relayed this order to their regiment commanders by telephone and fired yellow flares as redundant signals to ensure that all divisional sub-units were aware of the beginning of the offensive.[66]

Under the intent gaze of his superior commanders and Stalin's personal representative, Yermakov ordered his regimental commanders to conduct a frontal assault against Finnish fortifications at Jackboot Grove and Summa while simultaneously outflanking Finnish fortifications on the western shore of Summa-järvi Lake.[67] The frontal assault was caught immediately in deadly cross-fire between two DOTs. Subsequent reinforcements failed to gain any ground, and late that evening Yermakov ordered his regiments back to their jumping-off positions. The flank assault along the shore of Summa-järvi Lake was even less successful. Two hours late, the troops had reached their jumping-off positions and launched their assault only to be caught in enemy wire obstacles and flanking machine gun fire. Later that evening the troops

150

were forced to return to their jumping-off positions. Conclusions drawn from the 100th Rifle Division's combat activity that day were straightforward and embarrassing for a commander responsible for the spearhead of the new offensive: the 100th Rifle Division's assault had not been sufficiently sudden. Theorists at the Section for the Study of Combat Experience also noted that the Finns had built up their defences at Summa during the previous ten days of demonstration operations and the Finnish fire-system was still very much intact.[68] Without full artillery suppression of the Finnish fire-system, a joint artillery barrage and combined arms assault was pointless.

Contrary to the expectations of Timoshenko and his subordinates, Alia-bushev and his 123rd Rifle Division were achieving better results on the other side of Summa-järvi Lake. Aliabushev had planned a simultaneous three-pronged attack against the Finnish fortifications stretching from Tongue Hill on the left, Hills Nos. 65.5 and 62.4 in the centre, and a series of DOTs on the southern edge of Hammer Grove to the right. The 245th Rifle Regiment, under the command of Major Roslyi, was to attack Hill No. 65.5 and Hammer Grove while the 272nd Rifle Regiment was to attack Hill No. 62.4 from the left and the 255th Rifle Regiment was to attack Tongue Hill from the right (see Figure 4.4).[69] Instead of the normal artillery preparation, Aliabushev ordered his artillery divisions to conduct 10–15 minute intensive fire-raids against specific targets followed by false transfer of fire to targets in the enemy rear in order to confuse the Finns and catch them exposed in their trenches by the next raid.[70] Aliabushev had also devoted much attention to the establishment of communications between his forward battalions, artillery units, their observation points and his divisional headquarters for improved control of the assault.[71] On the evening before the offensive, regimental commanders took great care to promote combined arms co-operation by conducting orientation briefings between the sub-unit commanders of the various arms.[72]

At noon, Aliabushev's artillery switched to barrage fire and his regiments immediately began their assault. In Major Roslyi's assault against DOT No. 006 on Hill No. 65.5, a heavy tank company led the way, followed by lighter tanks pulling 'Sokolov' sleds filled with storm troops. As the tanks fired into the embrasures of the DOT and destroyed enemy anti-tank guns on the crest of the hill the storm groups quickly piled rocks against the main embrasure, laid the explosives, and blew up the DOT 28 minutes after the start of the assault. By 14h00 that afternoon Roslyi's battalion commanders had consolidated their hold on Hill No. 65.5 and destroyed DOTs Nos. 0021 and 0018 on the southern edge of Hammer Grove.[73] Combat for Hill No. 62.4 was more stubborn but battalion commanders were able to request regimental

The Soviet Invasion of Finland, 1939–40

artillery support directly by field telephone. By late evening the Finns were forced to retreat from Hill No. 62.4, leaving behind 700 dead.[74] Meanwhile, the 255th Rifle Regiment's assault on Tongue Hill got off to a slower start and ran into organized enemy fire. However, with the help of a reserve storm group and the initiative of a sapper battalion commander, the regiment managed to blockade the DOT and blow it up before digging in against the crossfire from Finnish DOTs and DZOTs (*derevo-zemlianaia ognevaia tochka*, or a wood-and-earthen fire point) to the north.[75]

By the end of 11 February, Aliabushev's 123rd Rifle Division had advanced 1,200 m. into the Finnish defensive system and his storm groups had destroyed eight DOTs and 24 DZOTs while his infantry and tanks had overcome a multitude of anti-tank and personnel obstacles and trenches.[76] The most impressive feat of arms was the destruction of DOT No. 006 which was attributed to the speed of the combined arms assault against enemy troops still dazed by the artillery barrage. Observers were not so impressed by the assault on Tongue Hill, but they praised the effectiveness of the reserve storm group.[77] This combat experience was immediately analysed by Timoshenko's military theorists at the Section on the Study of Combat Experience and their doctrinal recommendations were distributed to army and corps commanders the next evening.[78]

Timoshenko's theorists instructed the commanders of formations and units on the Karelian Isthmus to emulate the example set by the 123rd Rifle Division. Combined arms assaults, guided by detailed battle plans outlined by higher staffs and tables of co-operation between arms in combat, allowed for the continuous control of battle from division to company commander, and vice-versa.[79] Improved communications between artillery and infantry, and between artillery, its forward observers and higher staffs allowed combined arms units to follow the artillery barrage as closely as 75–100 m., and infantry sub-unit commanders to directly request artillery support against specific targets. The 123rd Rifle Division's experience even justified equipping infantry units with infantry-support artillery, anti-tank artillery and heavy calibre artillery to suppress enemy fire and field fortifications, and verified the effectiveness of roving artillery preparation.[80] The construction of jumping-off positions to within 200–300 m. of the enemy's forward defence zone had also demonstrated its effectiveness by reducing the time and effort needed by the combined arms units to engage the enemy. The armoured shields for protecting individual soldiers from enemy machine gun and rifle fire were of more limited value. The shields were too clumsy and were often discarded by the troops during the assault.[81] Not all praise for the 123rd Rifle Division's exploits was so prosaic. Later in the week *Na Strazhe Rodiny* published a poem by the poet and journalist, A. Tvardovskii, eulogizing the heroism of Aliabushev's men:

> At Dawn when wafts of smoke rose
> From the dug-out.
> The victorious regiments of the 123rd
> Began to move out.
>
> They moved out closer to the enemy
> And took up their jumping-off positions.
> The air was dry, squeezed by the frost
> In the night snow fell pure and fresh.
>
> Out from the colonnade's park,
> Snow like milling-dust,
> The tanks reared up from acceleration
> And moved out almost unheard.
> The infantry,
> Following step by step the barrage
> To the heights where the enemy is hiding,
> Moved out, Moved out, Moved out,
> Moved out Our Dearest. And how!
>
> The silence was such,
> As if everything round the whole world
> From end to end were listening.
>
> And suddenly –
>
> The earth roared and the fir trees
> Swayed forward and hoar-frost smoke
> Fell off the branches.
> Deadly fire flew from our hidden Batteries.
>
> The sky bent everything and everyone
> Closer to the earth like a low ceiling
> In the dug-outs sand started streaming
>
> From this joyful work,
> From the hammering of artillery
> Perhaps in the remote DOTs
> The foreheads of the Whites
> Were beaded with cold sweat

Running, jumping, crawling where necessary
To reach the enemy as soon as possible,
And tailing their artillery shells
To penetrate him, 'Give him the stick!'

Our cannons, paved they the road in vain?
Not the snow, but a plowed field opened up.

Forward, Samoilovskaia Company!
The overwhelmed enemy runs
And on the concrete DOT
The Red Flag is already unfurled.

The wind takes it up and outwards
Like a flame.

Forward, fighters of the 123rd!
Forward! Rifles! Forward!

Thus the Division rolled
Like lava on the enemy.
Yesterday's flicker is today's flame.

That evening Timoshenko reviewed the day's results on the Karelian Isthmus. The 34th Rifle Corps' efforts to outflank the Finnish fortifications at Muurila by attacking across the ice had been beaten off with heavy artillery from Koivisto Island. Timoshenko ordered the Baltic Fleet command to transfer its Coastal Detachment to the 34th Rifle Corps command and prepare for another assault across the ice the next day.[82] Elsewhere along the Mannerheim Line, the 10th Rifle Corps' 138th Rifle Division had managed to gain some ground west of Summa and the 15th Rifle Corps gained a foothold in the Finns' forward defence zone at the Punnus-joki River. However, the only significant success had been accomplished by the 123rd Rifle Division. Timoshenko decided to transfer the focus of his offensive to the 123rd Rifle Division's sector of the front.

In the early hours of 12 February Meretskov ordered Gorolenko to strengthen this new '*schwerpunkt*' with the 27th Rifle Regiment from his corps' reserve.[83] The mission of this new regiment, reinforced with units from the 95th Tank Brigade and the 23rd Artillery Regiment, was to fill the gap between the 123rd and 100th Rifle Divisions and attack along the eastern shores of Summa-järvi Lake in order to threaten the rear of Finnish defences at Summa.[84] Otherwise, the 123rd Rifle Division's mission remained as before:

to continue advancing northward against Finnish defences at Figurnaia Grove and Hill No. 63.4 towards the town of Lähde.[85]

In contrast to their dramatic conquests the day before, Aliabushev's regimental commanders encountered well-organized and reinforced enemy fire from Figurnaia Grove. Only by the combination of forward artillery support and outflanking manoeuvres were they able to advance 600 m. before the end of the day.[86] The 27th Rifle Regiment was more successful on the left flank. Having replaced the 255th Rifle Regiment at Tongue Hill, the 27th Rifle Regiment faced equally stiff Finnish resistance and was impeded by deep snow, but managed to destroy two DOTs and five DZOTs before halting the assault a kilometre north-east of Summa-järvi Lake.[87] After a day of fierce fighting, Aliabushev's division had destroyed a total of three DOTs and five DZOTs, and had overcome several anti-tank ravines, trenches and other obstacles before digging in against Finnish defences at Figurnaia Grove.[88]

Yermakov's 100th Rifle Division was as unsuccessful as the previous day although it gained experience in the use of direct-fire with heavy calibre artillery. When the 123rd Rifle Division's 27th Rifle Regiment showed positive results in the assault along the north-east shore of Summa-järvi Lake, Gorolenko ordered Yermakov to transfer some of his artillery and two tank battalions to support this effort. That evening, while Meretskov and Gorolenko were finalizing preparations for Aliabushev's breakthrough the next day, Yermakov was ordered to divert Finnish attention from these preparations by running the engines of all his tanks and tractors.[89]

On the morning of 13 February, Aliabushev's division continued the offensive against Finnish positions on the southern edge of Figurnaia Grove. Supported by additional tanks from Meretskov's reserve and relying on the tactical techniques tested and proven over the previous two days, his regiments quickly overran the remaining Finnish defences and by mid-day were in pursuit of the Finnish army's *arrière-garde*.[90] That night, when Aliabushev ordered his regiments to dig in, they had forced a four-kilometre wide opening in the first line of the Finnish defensive system through which other, more mobile reinforcements could develop into an operational encirclement of the Finnish army.[91] The North-Western Front's month-long preparations were at last producing results (see Figure 4.5).

Ecstatic with the news of Aliabushev's breakthrough, Timoshenko issued an order to Meretskov and Grendal supplementing his praise of the night before with comments about the effectiveness of Aliabushev's use of his second echelon, thrown into battle at the psychologically decisive moment.[92] This order was immediately followed by the announcement over the radio and in the morning press that the Supreme Soviet of the USSR had awarded

FIGURE 4.5
RED ARMY SOLDIERS CELEBRATING ON THE RUINS OF FINNISH
DOT NO. 006, FEBRUARY 1940

Courtesy of RGAKFD.

the 123rd Rifle Division with the Order of Lenin, a major stimulus to the Political Administration's hero campaign.[93]

However, the rest of Gorolenko's strike corps was still encountering stubborn resistance. Meretskov had ordered Gorolenko to reinforce the 123rd Rifle Division's left flank with the 7th Rifle Division while the 27th Rifle Regiment was instructed to continue the offensive against Finnish defensive positions on the hills north-west of Summa–järvi lake. That morning, the 27th Rifle Regiment launched its assault and was about to storm these hills when a Finnish detachment counter-attacked on the right flank.[94] In the ensuing fight the regiment commander organized his infantry-support artillery and machine guns and called on the support of neighbouring regiments and heavy artillery support from the 100th Rifle Division to eventually rout the Finnish attackers and force them to retreat.[95] At Timoshenko's headquarters, the military theorists of the Section for the Study of Combat Experience reviewed the reports about this counter-attack. Explicitly, they praised the 27th Rifle Regiment commander's quick and appropriate response. Implicitly, all the theorists at North-Western Front headquarters had recognized that the Finnish counter-attack had stalled the 7th Rifle Division's flanking manoeuvre and had disrupted Yermakov's frontal attack.[96] Stavka's expectations of a major breakthrough that day at Hammer Grove and Summa were dashed.

After reviewing Meretskov's and Grendal's situation reports on the evening of 13 February, Timoshenko decided that the 123rd Rifle Division's breakthrough was wide enough to begin the operational pursuit. Timoshenko telephoned Meretskov at Boboshino and ordered him to deploy the 84th Motorized Rifle Division on the left flank of the 19th Rifle Corps to attack across trackless terrain to the rail station at Leipäsuo, while the 123rd Rifle Division continued its advance north through Lähde and the 7th Rifle Division threatened the rear of Finnish defences at Summa.[97] Meretskov had already begun moving the 84th Motorized Rifle Division forward from his army reserve that morning, and when he received Timoshenko's orders he passed them on to the division's commander with the instructions that the division should begin the attack at 10h00 the next morning.[98] Simultaneously, the Finnish II Corps command was planning a major counter-attack on the opposite side of the front line. However, the Finnish counter-attack was cancelled due to a critical shortage of artillery ammunition.[99]

Early on the morning of 14 February, the 84th Motorized Rifle Division broke camp and set out on the Boboshino–Lähde road towards its jumping-off positions at Valosuo Swamp.[100] Opposite Hill No. 65.5 the division encountered an enormous traffic-jam.[101] Tanks, destroyed during the previous three days' battle, and trucks forming the logistics train for the 123rd Rifle

Division littered the road, unable to move in the deep snow. The only way to circumvent these obstacles was to drive the division's motor vehicles along the verge while the troops marched through the snow at a rate of 100 m. per hour under constant threat of machine gun fire from Finnish cover units in the woods. Late in the day, when the division reached Hill No. 62.4, wheeled vehicles were unable to progress any further and the 84th Motorized Rifle Division had to continue advancing forward without any artillery or logistics support.[102] Needless to say, the 84th Motorized Rifle Division did not reach its jumping-off positions or fulfil any combat missions that day. The only division in Gorolenko's corps to make any progress was the 7th Rifle Division which managed to seize another three DOTs and reach the banks of the Maä-joki River before digging in. The 123rd Rifle Division, held up by the tardy 84th Motorized Rifle Division and unable to bring forward its own artillery on the Boboshino-Lähde road, limited activity to skirmishes with Finnish cover units while the 100th Rifle Division continued to bombard Summa.[103]

On the morning of 15 February, as the 84th Motorized Rifle Division launched its attack towards the railroad station at Leipäsuo, 23 hours late, two other mobile formations under Meretskov's direct subordination, Colonel V. Baranov's mobile group and Major B. Vershinin's mobile detachment, were deployed in front of Aliabushev's division to pursue the enemy to Lähde. Both the commanders had been instructed to conduct independent operations against Lähde, but as their staffs studied the terrain in front of them Aliabushev visited their headquarters and convinced them to co-ordinate their attack with his infantry.[104]

The battle for the crossroads at Lähde began early that afternoon.[105] Finnish defensive forces on the outskirts of town consisted of a few undermanned, exhausted and inexperienced units, but despite these handicaps the Finns managed to hold off Aliabushev's combined forces with artillery, mortar and machine gun fire until their ammunition ran out.[106] When Finnish fire slackened, Major Roslyi's 245th Rifle Regiment and Colonel Baranov's tanks pushed forward, burning the Finnish defenders out of their DZOTs with flame-thrower tanks. That evening, the town centre was captured and the two mobile units continued their independent operations towards Kämärä and Leipäsuo Stations while the 123rd Rifle Division consolidated its position around Lähde.[107]

Back at Timoshenko's headquarters in Leningrad, the military theorists at the Section for the Study of Combat Experience examined Aliabushev's, Baranov's and Vershinin's combined operations intently. This battle was the first example of Deep Operations since the beginning of the war and the theorists were amazed to find that three commanders, unbeholden to each other hierarchically, could co-operate with each other at the planning table and in the battlefield. They concluded that, if troop control was nominally assumed by one of the commanders, combined arms combat did not have to be so centrally controlled.[108] However, Aliabushev's inability to destroy the Finns' lightly defended positions quickly for lack of forward-based artillery and insufficient fire-control did not escape the attention of Timoshenko's military theorists. This convinced the Section for the Study of Combat Experience to reimpose more centralized control over the conduct of future operations. In a combat instruction issued the next day, the Section ordered corps commanders on the Karelian Isthmus to plan and co-ordinate the forward movement of artillery more carefully so that first echelon battalions and regiments were not left without artillery support. Longer range artillery units were to centralize their command and improve communications between forward observation points and infantry units before moving their firing positions forward by echelons. All plans to transfer artillery firing positions had to be verified by Army headquarters.[109] Because Aliabushev had incorporated Baranov's and Vershinin's mobile units into an infantry-support role Timoshenko's theorists were not able to draw any conclusions about the use of independent mobile units in the pursuit.[110] The experiment in directive-control was over. The Section began work to summarize its own analysis of the offensive.[111]

February 15 was also a day of reckoning for the 100th Rifle Division, which had been impeded by Finnish fortifications at Summa. Under new orders from corps commander Gorolenko, Yermakov shifted his divisional head-quarters and the bulk of his forces to the north-western shore of Summa-järvi Lake under the cover of darkness and the din of tractor engines parked in the division's centre to mislead the Finns about the direction of the impending assault.[112] After the now habitual artillery preparation, Yermakov's 331st Rifle Regiment and the 1st Battalion of the 85th Rifle Regiment launched their assault along the shore of the lake and were immediately halted by heavy enemy fire.[113] However, Finnish guns were no longer adequately manned or supplied to hold off Yermakov's assault indefinitely, and at 13h30 the remaining Finnish forces began to retreat to Turta, then to Huumola and Suokanta under the cover of units armed with submachine guns and artillery support from Huumola and Karhula.[114] At 18h40 units of the 100th Rifle Division seized the town of Summa. When they dug in that evening they had advanced 1,500 m. north of Turta and Jackboot Grove and had captured 19 DOTs and up to 20 DZOTs.[115]

Late that evening, Gorolenko transmitted Stavka's congratulations to the 100th Rifle Division while military theorists at North-Western Front headquarters summed up its combat experience. As usual, the Section for the

Study of Combat Experience biased the critique to the positive side, pointing out that the fortified region around Summa had been the strongest part of the Mannerheim Line, that the division had practised direct fire with 152 mm. and 203 mm. artillery against Finnish fortified points to great effect, and that the concentration of the assault on the right flank in co-ordination with the 7th Rifle Division's movements had led to a successful breakthrough. The theorists' only negative comment was to admonish Gorolenko and Yermakov for not trying this flank manoeuvre earlier.[116] They did not mention the 100th Rifle Division's relative ineffectiveness against lightly manned defences, perhaps unaware of the Finns' withdrawal that had begun the previous day, nor did they point out that the division had not encircled and destroyed the enemy's army after the breakthrough, as originally instructed in Timoshenko's plan for the offensive issue on 3 February.

Timoshenko's review of the situation on the Karelian Isthmus indicated that although the 13th Army's 15th Rifle Corps was able to gain limited successes at Punnus-joki, the staff had not been able to correct the severe deficiencies in command and control which had plagued operations since Timoshenko's reprimand on 10 February.[117] The North-Western Front would have to rely on the 50th Rifle Corps' pursuit operations towards Kämärä Station and the town of Huumola.

On 16 February, Colonel Baranov's mobile group continued the attack up the road from Lähde to Kämärä Station. The mobile group was permitted to transport infantry and sapper troops on the tanks while on the march for the first time.[118] The 84th Motorized Rifle Division, under orders from Gorolenko to redirect the attack away from Leipäsuo towards Kämärä Station, fought its way north against Finnish guerrilla attacks and pockets of mortar, rifle and machine-gun fire to arrive on the outskirts of Kämärä Station late that evening.[119] Gorolenko also ordered Aliabushev's division to follow the right bank of the Maä-joki River to arrive at Näükki Lake by nightfall. However, due to enemy guerrilla activity, deep snow, and trackless terrain, the division's forward movement was slower than expected and was only able to reach a wood more than a kilometre south of Urpola village. On its left flank, the 7th Rifle Division, advancing towards Huumola, experienced similar problems and was temporarily stalled by guerrilla units outside of Autio village.[120] The only division in Gorolenko's corps to fulfil its missions was Yermakov's 100th Rifle Division. With the help of the neighbouring 138th Rifle Division (10th Rifle Corps) Yermakov's division was able to force aside enemy guerrilla units and reach the village of Suokanta where the road terminated. The next day this division was transferred to Gorolenko's second echelon for a brief rest and additional reinforcement.[121]

IV

Molotov's cable to Stockholm on 29 January had opened up the possibility of peace negotiations with the Finnish government in Helsinki but did not give any indication of Soviet demands.[122] The onus was now on the Finnish government to keep diplomatic relations open. On 30 January, Ryti, Tanner and Paasikivi responded by drafting a proposal based on the terms discussed before the war. They reiterated the requirement that all Finnish concessions be matched by Soviet compensations but made no mention of the Hangö Peninsula. This proposal was delivered to Stockholm by Ryti and given to the Swedish mediator, Foreign Minister Gunther, for transmission to Moscow. Meantime, Kollontai had received instructions from Molotov to state that Hangö remained a prerequisite for the continuation of the negotiations. Kollontai forwarded the Finnish proposal to Moscow as a semi-official document 'for information only' and suggested that Tanner return to Stockholm to resolve the stalemate over Hangö.[123]

Tanner arrived in Stockholm and met Kollontai in secret on 5 February. During this interview Kollontai revealed that Moscow was conducting its diplomacy according to the 'logic of war' and that if Finland did not settle with Moscow's present terms, the terms would become more harsh as the war progressed. Kollontai asked whether the Finnish government could make any concessions over the Hangö Peninsula and Tanner replied that in a personal capacity he could suggest an island in the vicinity. Kollontai forwarded Tanner's suggestion to Moscow and received a negative response the following day.

The Finnish government's diplomatic position was enhanced by political events in Europe while these conversations were taking place. On 5 February, the Entente powers had convened a meeting of the Supreme War Council at which a decision was reached to send troops to Finland, contingent on gaining transit rights through Norway and Sweden.[124] The Finnish government was now able to pursue three options simultaneously: continue the peace negotiations with Moscow, apply pressure on the Swedish government for more military assistance, and encourage assistance from the Entente. In order to strike an appropriate balance between these three options, Tanner and Ryti consulted Mannerheim at Finnish Army headquarters on 10 February. Mannerheim advised them to place priority on the peace talks with Moscow despite the static situation on the Karelian Isthmus.[125] Consultations with the Foreign Affairs Committee on 12 February contradicted Mannerheim's advice in favour of closer relations with Sweden but Tanner, Ryti, Paasikivi and President Kallio met privately and agreed to continue negotiations with Moscow, this time offering the island of Russarö as an alternative to Hangö.[126]

By the time Tanner returned to Stockholm on 13 February to deliver his new proposal the diplomatic situation had changed dramatically. The Red Army's offensive on the Karelian Isthmus had recommenced and had broken through Finnish defences on the main road leading to Vyborg. In conjunction with these victories Molotov had cabled Stockholm to inform the Finnish government that Soviet demands no longer only insisted on Hangö, but now included the entire Karelian Isthmus and northern shore of Lake Ladoga as well. Tanner responded to Molotov's 'logic of war' by turning to the Swedish government for more military aid, but his requests were denied. To add insult to injury, news of this denial was leaked to the Swedish press a few days later, further undermining Tanner's bargaining position.[127]

On the evening of 16 February, Meretskov's 7th Army was pursuing the retreating Finnish Army up the centre of the Karelian Isthmus and along the coast towards the Björkö Archipelago and Johannes while the left flank of Grendal's 13th Army advanced towards Kangas-pelto.[128] Convinced that the final annihilation of the Finnish Army was close at hand, the North-Western Front command ordered Meretskov to reinforce the 50th Rifle Corps at Kämärä with an additional mobile group from his army reserve and continue his offensive up the Kämärä–Vyborg rail line.[129] The next afternoon the formations of the 50th Rifle Corps resumed their attacks towards Honkaniemi Station and the road to Pien-pero.[130] These formations encountered resistance from road mines, anti-tank obstacles and raids by Finnish cover-units and were eventually stalled by organized anti-tank artillery and mortar fire. Once again, the 50th Rifle Corps had advanced too fast without conducting reconnaissance patrols or bringing forward its heavy artillery and was forced to take refuge in Kämärä.[131]

Due to a rupture in communication between the Karelian Isthmus and Moscow, Stavka remained unaware of these developments and ordered the North-Western Front command to concentrate all the 50th Rifle Corps' forces on the Kämärä–Vyborg rail line and increase the rate of long-range artillery fire against Vyborg in preparation for the final offensive. When Timoshenko received these extraordinary orders he did not bother to integrate them into his operational plan. Instead, he passed them directly to Gorolenko at 50th Rifle Corps headquarters. Gorolenko, in turn, disregarded all situation reports and ordered the 84th Motorized Rifle Division and its mobile detachment to miraculously appear at Pien-pero the next morning and advance along the eastern shore of Kämärä-järvi Lake to seize the Pilppula-Pero rail line by evening. The 123rd Rifle Division and its mobile group were ordered to seize Säine Station (this goal had already been accomplished according to Stavka's information) while the 7th Rifle Division and the recently rotated 100th Rifle

Division were ordered to attack across trackless, forested terrain to seize Sommee Station.[132] In the rush to fulfil Stavka's unrealistic commands Gorolenko neglected to give his division commanders any information about the enemy's forces in the area.[133]

Stavka's delusions were shattered the next morning. The 50th Rifle Corps' two first-echelon divisions and their mobile groups once again set out on the roads leading north from Kämärä and collided with the Finnish Army's second line of DZOTs, trenches, wire and organized artillery, mortar and machine-gun fire two kilometres out of town.[134] During the fight that ensued, Gorolenko tried to organize a joint infantry-tank command between the 123rd Rifle Division and its mobile group, similar to the one organized before the battle for Lähde. However, Gorolenko's efforts failed due to the lack of escort artillery, which was still struggling to get to the front along jammed roads, and the lack of adequate reconnaissance information about the Finns' new defences.[135] The 7th Army was obliged to interrupt the pursuit and reorganize its forces for another breakthrough operation.

Despite failures to rupture Finnish defences at Kämärä, the North-Western Front's offensive was able to make headway on other parts of the Karelian Isthmus. On the western side of the Isthmus, Meretskov's 10th and 34th Rifle Corps were able to break through the Mannerheim Line at Karhula and Muurila and pursued the retreating Finnish army until they were stopped by Finnish defences at Koivisto-Björkö and Samola Bay.[136] In the centre of the isthmus, Grendal's 23rd and 15th Rifle Corps converged on Finnish defences between Muolan-järvi Lake and the Vuoksi-järvi lake system, while on the western shores of Lake Ladoga his 3rd Rifle Corps continued to bombard Finnish fortifications at Taipale.[137]

Meanwhile, Stavka mobilized its strategic reserve, the 28th Rifle Corps, under the command of Corps Commander Pavlov, to prepare for the double-encirclement of Vyborg. Stavka's strategic plan, inspired by Peter the Great's campaign against Vyborg in 1710, envisaged an encirclement operation from the north-west across the ice and islands of Vyborg Bay.[138] There were several complications in realizing this plan, the first being that the Finns still clung to their defences on Saarenpää and at Koivisto, and the second that the road and rail network on the Isthmus was too overburdened to accommodate yet another motorized corps. The only solution would be to bypass the Isthmus by transporting the corps across the Gulf of Finland over the ice. For this purpose, Pavlov's corps was deployed on the south shore of the Gulf of Finland near the railroad station at Orangenbaum in early February. The success of Stavka's entire strategic plan thus relied on the strength of the ice in the Gulf of Finland, despite the fact that the Red Army had never before transported so many tanks and trucks, nor fired howitzers, on such an expanse of ice.[139] On 16 February, Pavlov ordered the Baltic Fleet's Winter Defence Detachment to construct a road across the ice from the rail siding at New Krasnaia Gorka to the coastal village of Alipuumala on the other side of the Gulf of Finland. When the ice-road was completed on 19 February, Pavlov and his staff tested its strength by personally driving their T-26 tanks over it. Pavlov's test was successful and the go-ahead was given to send the rest of the corps. By the next morning traffic across the ice-road was so heavy that cracks had formed and three tanks had fallen through the ice. The convoys were forced to stop until 22 February when two more roads were completed and ice-monitoring patrols were established.[140]

As a counterpart to the 28th Rifle Corps' encirclement of Vyborg from the north-west, Stavka had created a new army, the 15th Army under the command of Army Commander M. Kovalev, from reinforcements and the 8th Army's 56th Rifle Corps for the purpose of continuing the offensive against Sortavala and eventually threatening Vyborg from the north-east. Earlier in the month, Kovalev had tried to rescue the 18th and 168th Rifle Divisions but his rescue detachments were ambushed on the road north of Pitkaranta and the remaining units of the 18th Rifle Division were annihilated by the Finns at Lovajärvi.[141] On 18 February, Kovalev reviewed the situation and concluded that his army lacked the necessary forces to prevent the Finns from infiltrating the gap between him and the 8th Army and threatening his rear communications.[142] Kovalev requested another two divisions as reinforcement and prepared for another, more organized offensive up the Pitkaranta–Lemetti road on 23 February. In the meantime, the 15th Army's offensive had to be postponed.[143]

V

On 21 February, the Finnish government in Helsinki appealed to the Swedish Foreign Minister, Gunther, to enquire in Moscow whether there had been any change in the Soviet terms for peace. Despite the temporary set-back on the Karelian Isthmus and the looming threat of foreign military intervention, Molotov responded by demanding even more exacting terms than before: in addition to the Soviet government's existing terms, Finland was expected to give up Kakisalmi and Sortavala, two towns which had not yet fallen to Red Army forces, and sign a mutual assistance pact with the Soviet Union and Estonia.[144] However, Molotov did not insist on territorial annexations in the Petsamo region or in the Åland Islands Archipelago, conscious that these

164

concessions might prevent Sweden and Norway from granting transit rights to British and French troops. The Finnish government was unwilling to resume peace negotiations on these terms. Soviet–Finnish diplomatic relations lapsed for a second time.

During this time, Meretskov and Grendal were reorganizing their forces for a breakthrough against the Finnish Army's second line of fortifications stretching from Samola Bay to Il'vec and Taipale.[145] On the 50th Rifle Corps' salient, the heavy artillery units finally arrived at their front-line fire positions on 19 February and, the next morning, supported the combined infantry and tank assault. Aliabushev's 123rd Rifle Division managed to advance a kilometre up the rail line toward Honkaniemi Station before being halted by Finnish artillery fire from fortifications on Hill No. 48. On Aliabushev's right flank, the 84th Motorized Rifle Division was more successful. Its mobile group, under the command of Baranov, had managed to seize Finnish fortifications on Hill No. 45.[146]

When the 50th Rifle Corps' two first-echelon divisions resumed their attacks on 21 February they met with some unpleasant surprises. The 123rd Rifle Division was unable to outflank and seize Finnish defences on Hill No. 48. To the east, Gorolenko had ordered Baranov and his mobile group to advance up the road towards the junction at Pien-pero without first gathering any reconnaissance about the Finnish Army's dispositions. That evening, under the cover of a snowstorm, the Finns suddenly counter-attacked Hill No. 45 and encircled it, thereby cutting off Baranov's mobile group from the 84th Motorized Rifle Division.[147] Faced with these set-backs, Timoshenko and his army commanders realized that the situation on the Karelian Isthmus was threatening to revert to a stalemate similar to that which existed before the breakthrough of the Mannerheim Line. This time, however, there was no question of relying on material superiority to tip the balance of forces: the chaos caused by traffic jams along every road on the isthmus had demonstrated the limitation of this option. The stalemate would have to be broken by improved troop control from corps level down to company level. Responsibility for this quality control fell to Timoshenko's Operations Department and the Section for the Study of Combat Experience.

While Finnish counter-attacks against the 84th Motorized Rifle Division and its mobile group continued on 22 February, the North-Western Front issued a directive to the 7th and 13th Armies criticizing the sluggishness of their offensive.[148] The directive blamed loose troop control as the main cause of the stasis, and specifically referred to the neglect of battlefield reports at corps and division level which slowed those formations' responsiveness to momentary opportunities and promoted conservative tactics.[149]

Gorolenko and his division commanders reacted to these comments by tightening up their troop control. The results were immediate. Aliabushev's division experimented with its first night operation on the evening of 23 February and managed to seize Hill No. 48 with little loss of life. The next evening, the 84th Motorized Rifle Division conducted its own night operation, recaptured Hill No. 45, and rescued its mobile group from Finnish encirclement.[150] The 7th Army was now free to recommence pursuit operations.

VI

At the end of February, peace negotiations between the Soviet Union and Finland remained at an impasse, despite the shift in the 'logic of war' once again to the Soviet government's advantage. As the Finnish Army began an organized retreat from the second to the third and final line of fortifications on the outskirts of Vyborg, Tanner travelled to Stockholm for the third time to gauge the commitment of Finland's potential allies and to choose which diplomatic option to follow. Tanner's interview with the Swedish Prime Minister, Hansson, on 27 February, convinced him that, although a post-war defensive alliance between Finland and Sweden might be possible, there was no hope of immediate military assistance from either Sweden or the Entente. The only remaining option was to conclude peace with the Soviet government, but an interview with Kollontai the same day indicated that Molotov still insisted on terms which the Finnish Cabinet was not willing to consider.[151]

The next attempt to break the deadlock in Soviet–Finnish relations came from Molotov who was intent to keep up diplomatic pressure against the Finns, short of provoking them to accept military assistance from the Entente. On 28 February, Molotov issued an ultimatum to Helsinki informing the Finnish government that they had 48 hours to draft a reply.[152] During the next two days the Finnish Cabinet consulted the Diet's foreign affairs committee and drafted a reply accepting Molotov's terms in principle, but on the night of 29 February fresh news from abroad persuaded them to postpone the delivery of their response. The French and British governments had decided to send 50,000 troops to Finland by the end of March.[153] Faced with the choice between capitulation to Soviet demands and continuing the war with the Entente's military assistance, the Finnish Cabinet decided to play for time. On 1 March, Tanner sent a message to Moscow via Stockholm asking Molotov to further clarify the boundaries of the territorial annexations. This message never reached Moscow. Gunther and Kollontai jointly decided to withhold

Tanner's message, hoping in this way to prevent Finland from widening the scale of the war. Molotov's ultimatum came and went without a Finnish response.[154]

By 27 February, Timoshenko's North-Western Front had destroyed key fortified positions at Il'vec, Pien-pero and Saarenpää and was once again in a good position to continue the offensive. Stavka's new instructions to Timoshenko were simple but ruthless: destroy the Finnish Army in a double encirclement of Vyborg, then concentrate force on the Helsinki–Sortavala highway for a strategic strike against Helsinki. To accomplish these instructions, Timoshenko subordinated the Baltic Fleet command to his North-Western Front headquarters and ordered it to organize diversionary strikes against the Finnish coast from Kotka to Ristniemi Peninsula while Pavlov's 28th Rifle Corps attacked the north-west shore of Vyborg Bay. Timoshenko entrusted the other pincer of the double encirclement to Gorolenko's 50th Rifle Corps which was to converge on the Saimaa Canal from the east, while the 10th and 34th Rifle Corps hammered at the Finnish defences on the southern approaches to Vyborg, and Grendal's 13th Army tied down Finnish forces along the Vuoksi lake system and at Taipale.[155]

This was a daring plan that could easily fail for a host of reasons, not least of which were a determined enemy, a change in the weather, and problems in the Red Army's chain-of-command. Timoshenko knew from personal inspections at the front and reports from his Operations Department that corps and division staffs were still not in touch with the pulse of battle at regimental level. In a directive issued concurrently with his orders for the new offensive, Timoshenko reminded his subordinates about the need for strict *edinonachale*. Poor control and communications between staff and battlefield not only meant that orders were often unfulfilled, but that co-ordination of massed artillery fire between batteries against specific targets was not possible, and timely rotation of troops from the front lines was compromised. Timoshenko ordered corps and division staffs to resolve this problem before the resumption of the offensive the next day.[156]

Reports on the prevailing military situation north of Lake Ladoga indicated to Timoshenko and his superiors at Stavka that they could not count on these armies to divert additional Finnish reserves away from the new offensive on the Karelian Isthmus. The 18th Rifle Division, encircled by Finnish units on the Uomaa–Lemetti road since mid-December, was in its final hours of existence. The next day, when the 15th Army commander finally gave permission to retreat, the 18th Rifle Division's commander, Brigade Commander G. Kondrashov, attempted to break out of the Finnish encirclement by dividing his forces into two groups. One of the groups managed to reach high ground with the loss of only 309 dead and wounded, out of a total of 1,237 men. The other group, consisting of 1,500 men, including the command staff of the 18th Rifle Division and the 34th Light Tank Brigade, was encircled and completely destroyed.[157] These inglorious defeats reminded Stavka of the gravity of the military situation north of Lake Ladoga. A quick victory or a peace settlement were necessary if further defeats were to be avoided.

Meretskov's 7th Army assaulted what remained of the Finnish Army's V-Line on the morning of 28 February after a 30 minute artillery preparation by the largest concentration of artillery in the history of the Red Army to date (133–135 guns/kilometre front).[158] By 16h00 that afternoon, Finnish resistance along the 50th Rifle Corps' sector was finally broken and the 123rd, 84th and 51st Rifle Divisions pursued Finnish cover-units as far as Vääräkoski village before digging in for the night.[159] The 51st Rifle Division conducted the most successful pursuit: by using well co-ordinated infantry-support artillery the division was quickly able to suppress any Finnish machine gun and mortar fire found in its path. However, the 51st Rifle Division was unable to encircle the retreating enemy as ordered because it was delayed in its pursuit by five hours due to a poorly co-ordinated battle plan, serious traffic jams, and a sabotaged bridge at the Pien-pero river-crossing.[160]

On 29 February, Gorolenko ordered his divisions to continue their pursuit operations as rapidly as possible. In particular, the 51st Rifle Division commander was ordered to create a mobile detachment to drive as far ahead as Repola village on the outskirts of Vyborg, where the detachment was instructed to wait until relieved by the main forces of the division. After a delay caused by petrol shortages at the front and late arrival of tanks from the corps' reserve, the 51st Rifle Division's mobile detachment sprinted ahead and captured a nail factory at Pero before halting there, far short of its goal. Unlike the previous day, the 51st Rifle Division lost control of its infantry-artillery co-ordination by trying to keep up with the mobile detachment. The mobile detachment had wreaked havoc on the division's rear support and the division was forced to remain at Pero for a day to replenish its provisions and ammunition stocks and to rest the troops.[161]

On the 51st Rifle Division's left flank, the 123rd Rifle Division conducted a night attack on Finnish positions at Säinie Station. When these positions fell the next morning the 123rd Rifle Division was rotated to Meretskov's army reserve for four days of rest in preparation for the final assault on Vyborg.[162] Meanwhile, in the 13th Army, the 136th Rifle Division (23rd Rifle Corps) was ordered to support the 7th Army's encirclement of Vyborg by attacking up the road to Ristseppälä and Heinioki. Responsibility for this mission fell to Colonel D. Leliushenko and his mobile detachment.[163]

However, there was only one road for the entire corps and deep snow prevented Leliushenko's detachment from travelling until the evening of 1 March.[164] During the first two days of March the North-Western Front was busy preparing plans and issuing orders for the final siege of Vyborg while the 7th Army pursued the retreating Finnish Army to the last defensive zone outside Vyborg. Meretskov temporarily turned his attention from the actions of the 50th Rifle Corps to concentrate on the 34th and 10th Rifle Corps, the two formations which were responsible for the direct assault on Vyborg's southern approaches. Meretskov intended to blockade Vyborg and attack with a small number of storm groups as if the city was merely an enormous DOT, rather than rely exclusively on quantitative superiority and a strategy of attrition.[165] In the 13th Army, plans were being drawn up for the final offensive against Antrea. Grendal, who was relinquishing his army command to his chief of staff, F. Parushinov, for a post as Chief of Artillery at Timoshenko's North-Western Front headquarters, instructed his 15th Rifle Corps to co-ordinate a breakthrough operation against Vuosalmi with the use of tactical aerial bombardment.[166]

However, the North-Western Front had not taken into account a new factor which threatened the success of the entire offensive. Four days before, when the Finnish Army had retreated to the T-Line, the Finnish high command had ordered the opening of the sluices of the Saimaa Canal dam at Juustila. Water from the dam was now beginning to submerge the area around Repola and Tali Stations.[167] Rumours of an impending flood quickly spread through the 7th Army. Timoshenko issued a directive reassuring his troops that the waters would not rise high enough to significantly threaten the 7th Army's operations, but planners at North-Western Front headquarters were fully aware of the implications this new twist of fate posed for the seizure of Vyborg.

Meanwhile, Pavlov's 28th Rifle Corps was busy preparing to encircle Vyborg from the west. On the evening of 3 March, Timoshenko issued a directive ordering Pavlov to attack across the ice of the Gulf of Finland towards Vilajoki and Mukhulakhti, to establish a beachhead there, and then to develop his offensive toward the Saimaa Canal and Simola Station with the help of Cherednichenko's 3rd Cavalry Corps.[168] The first and most dangerous stage of this offensive would be to seize and hold the islands of Tuppuransaari and Teikaransaari. The 86th Motorized Rifle Division set out from the north end of Koivisto Island and proceeded across the ice of the Gulf under the threat of enemy fire and without guidance from the Baltic Fleet's Hydrographic Service. During the division's march, cracks opened up in the ice and four T-26 tanks slipped through. Later in the evening, another road across the ice was established, but bad weather conditions brought the 86th Motorized Rifle Division to a temporary halt.[169]

To the west of the 28th Rifle Corps, the Baltic Fleet command was organizing diversionary strikes against Finnish coastal defences from Ristniemi Peninsula to the Finnish port at Kotka (see Figure 4.6).[170] Units from the Baltic Fleet's Winter Defence group, whose headquarters were established at Someri Island, were responsible for this mission. After some initial confusion over supply and communications, the Winter Defence group launched their diversionary operations on the night of 3 March.

The commander of the Winter Defence group had been instructed to send diversionary detachments against three different targets. The first of the these detachments was assigned to cover the left flank of the 86th Motorized Rifle Division by attacking the Ristniemi Peninsula. During the night of 3 March the first detachment set out from Tiurinsaari across the ice of the Gulf of Finland, but made slow headway. On the morning of 4 March they collided with a Finnish patrol and were forced to retreat. The second detachment, assigned to test the Finnish coastal defences at Kotka, had even less success: it lost its way in the middle of the night and had to return to base at Suursaari Island. The only successful diversion was conducted by the third detachment, which attacked Finnish coastal batteries at Kiuskeri and Kuovar Islands. The Finns were taken unawares by this attack and, thinking that it presaged a full-scale offensive, sent in airplanes to strafe the detachment exposed on the ice.[171] The Winter Defence group's diversionary attacks did not enjoy the support of artillery or tanks, and poor weather denied them air cover. However, their implicit threat to Helsinki forced the Finnish high command to divert reserves that were badly needed at Vyborg to strengthen coastal defences.[172]

The 86th and 70th Rifle Divisions continued their attacks against the Vilajoki Peninsula when heavy fog in the Gulf of Finland cleared on the morning of 4 March. Both divisions were now under Finnish artillery and aviation fire and were having difficulty co-ordinating their artillery support for infantry assaults. The next day, Pavlov's divisions managed to seize a small piece of territory on the mainland. However, due to heavy casualties in the stubborn combat which ensued, and the arrival of Finnish reinforcements, these divisions were not able to consolidate their bridgehead until 6 March.[173]

VII

The breakdown in diplomatic relations between Moscow and Helsinki was not redressed until 4 March when Molotov informed the Swedish minister in Moscow that the Soviet government was willing to repeat its ultimatum, but this time it increased its demands to include the annexation of Vyborg

FIGURE 4.6

MAP OF THE 50TH RIFLE CORPS' ADVANCE TOWARDS VYBORG,
27 FEBRUARY 1940

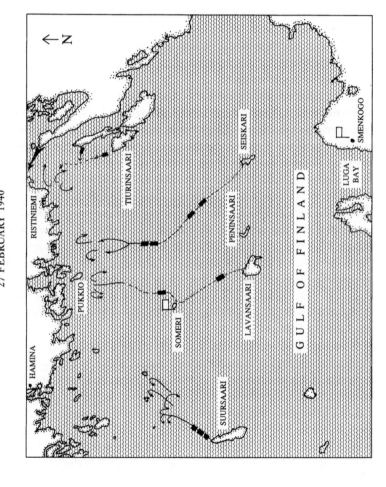

171

and Sortavala. Molotov warned the Swedish mediators that if the Finnish government did not respond within the next several days the Soviet government would unleash the Red Army and resume negotiations with the Kuusinen government. When the Finnish Cabinet received this message the next day, it had already decided to accept Molotov's terms in principle and asked the Swedish mediator to relay an acceptance to Moscow and arrange for an immediate armistice.[174] Molotov responded on 6 March by inviting the Finnish government to send a delegation to Moscow for negotiations, but warned that the 'logic of war' would continue until a peace treaty had been signed. The Finnish Cabinet agreed to send a delegation that same day despite the stringent Soviet terms.[175]

Encouraged by this diplomatic success, Stalin ordered the North-Western Front to begin its final offensive, not only against Vyborg but also along the entire length of the Soviet–Finnish border from Lake Ladoga to Revoly, Salla and Petsamo. On 5 March Timoshenko ordered his army commanders on the Karelian Isthmus and in Ladoga-Karelia to continue their attacks. On the west shore of the Gulf of Finland, the 28th and 10th Rifle Corps were ordered to fortify their beachheads and then to attack towards the Saimaa Canal. At Vyborg the 34th and 50th Rifle Corps were instructed to begin breakthrough operations at Tammisuo and Repola Stations while on the south shore of Vuoksi Lake the 13th Army's 23rd Rifle Corps continued its attack against Finnish fortifications at Vuosalmi.[176] The new factor in Timoshenko's operational plans was the 15th Army which had completed its concentration and was ready to attack up the Pitkaranta road, liberate the 168th Rifle Division from its two-month long siege, then continue towards Sortavala and the Karelian Isthmus.[177]

Timoshenko's intention was to seize Vyborg on 7 March. Towards this end he ordered Meretskov to increase the tempo of the offensive. Meretskov gave more detailed instructions to his 34th Rifle Corps commander on the evening of 6 March: the corps' main strike would be directed toward the village of Lavola on the eastern edge of Vyborg while a secondary strike, reinforced with units from the neighbouring 123rd Rifle Division, was instructed to attack toward Tammisuo Station. Gorolenko was instructed to divide his 50th Rifle Corps and send the right flank to attack Karisalmi while the left flank attacked along the railroad toward Tali Station and supported the 34th Rifle Corps with artillery (see Figure 4.7).[178] The 28th and 10th Rifle Corps were still struggling to maintain their beachhead on the west shore of the Gulf. To help them hold this ground, Timoshenko ordered the 1st Corps of the Finnish People's Army to secure the 28th Rifle Corps' west flank at Santa-joki Island and Ristniemi Peninsula from Finnish attack.[179]

Timoshenko's Offensive

FIGURE 4.7
MAP OF THE WINTER DEFENCE DETACHMENT'S OPERATIONS IN
EARLY MARCH, 1940

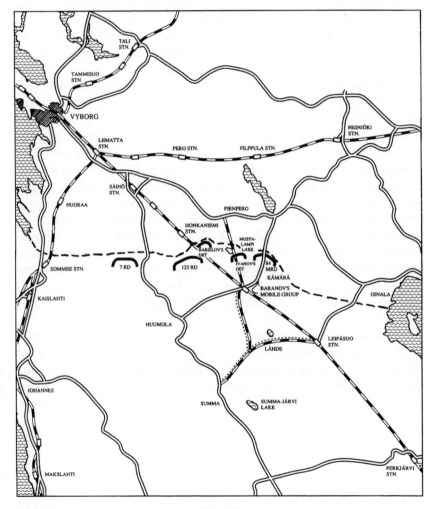

Adapted from *Sovetsko–finliandskaia voina 1939–1940 gg. na more.*

173

The largest impediment confronting the 50th Rifle Corps' attack against Vyborg was the flood water from the Saimaa Canal which had inundated the region around Repola and Tali Station with water over a half metre deep. The corps' 51st Rifle Division tried to outflank this barrier by attacking towards Lüükülä in the east, but was repelled by Finnish defensive fire.[180] The situation was much worse on the 123rd Rifle Division's sector. The Peronjoki River had steadily swelled with water from the dam while the 123rd Rifle Division was recuperating in the 7th Army's reserve. When the division returned to the front on 6 March they faced a major water barrier, 200 to 300 metres wide, with two Finnish strongpoints on the opposite shore. In order to continue the attack against Repola the 123rd Rifle Division would have to ford the water barrier in −10 to −15° C. The division's engineers devoted their energy to constructing wooden assault bridges for this purpose on the evening before the manoeuvre.[181]

When Gorolenko's divisions attempted to fulfil these orders the next day they were met with fierce enemy fire from the Finnish Army's third line of fortifications. Vigorous fighting had brought the 123rd Rifle Division up to the flooded area in front of the Finnish high ground protecting the eastern approach to Tali Station. The second water barrier did not pose any great difficulties because wooden bridges had already been built for the fording of the Peronjoki River the previous day. However, the 123rd Rifle Division's bridging operation was ambushed by two Finnish DZOTs hidden on the high ground. Only after an *ad hoc* storm group destroyed the DZOTs with the help of divisional artillery was the 123rd Rifle Division able to continue the offensive.[182] Elsewhere on the isthmus the 13th Army's 23rd Rifle Corps crossed Vuoksi Lake and established a two-kilometre-wide bridgehead on the north shore. On the west shore of Vyborg Bay, Pavlov's 28th Rifle Corps deployed the 173rd Motorized Rifle Division into the breach at Vilajoki and cut off Finnish communications out of Vyborg along the Helsinki–Vyborg highway.[183] The North-Western Front had not fulfilled Stavka's objectives, but its forces were now in position to begin their assault against Vyborg in earnest.

VIII

Stavka's diplomatic offensive had also entered its final phase. Concomitant with the Finnish delegation's arrival on 7 March, the Swedish minister in Moscow, Assarson, once again asked Molotov to agree to an armistice while the peace negotiations were in process. Any remaining hope for Soviet clemency the Swedish and Finnish governments may have held was extinguished by Molotov's response: 'Why stop the fighting if one cannot rule out the possibility of having to resume it over a difference?' Assarson tried to persuade Molotov to change his mind by suggesting that the Red Army had already regained its martial prestige by breaking through the Mannerheim Line, a feat of arms unsurpassed by the Germans and the French armies fighting in Western Europe, and argued that an armistice would be seen as a magnanimous gesture, rather than a sign of weakness. Molotov only promised to cease hostilities when the peace accord was signed.[184]

When the Finnish and Soviet delegations met the next day, Ryti's opening appeal for a lenient and durable peace was countered by Molotov's accusation that the Finnish Cabinet deserved no mercy because they had offered their country to third parties as a bridgehead for an attack against the Soviet Union. Molotov's subsequent exposition of Soviet terms for peace also came as an unpleasant shock to the Finnish delegation. In addition to the pre-war terms and the annexation of Vyborg and Sortavala, the Soviet delegation insisted that Finland give up the entire Rybachii Peninsula and the region around Salla and construct a rail line between Kemi-järvi and Kandalaksha for easier communications with Sweden. The only terms the Soviet delegation conceded to Finland was the repatriation of Petsamo, ostensibly to assuage Sweden, and the demand for a defence alliance. The Finnish delegation was dismayed to find that the goal posts for negotiation had once again been moved without their consent, but this was what Molotov understood as the 'logic of war'. Alarming reports from Helsinki on the combat situation at Vyborg convinced the Finnish delegation to continue their negotiations.[185]

In fact, by 9 March Timoshenko's double encirclement of Vyborg was far behind schedule. In the region south-east of Vyborg, the 7th Army's main problem was overcoming the ever-rising flood waters from the Saimaa Canal: troops who waded across inundated areas had to be immediately pulled from combat in order to dry their uniforms while Red Army artillery had to repel Finnish counter-attacks and suppress enemy fire.[186] Loose troop control and a severe crisis in morale in the 13th Army's ranks combined to create an 'extraordinary occurrence' so shocking that the new commander of the 13th Army, Parushinov, was obliged to report the incident in detail to North-Western Front headquarters.[187]

According to Parushinov's report, a regiment in the 4th Rifle Division of the 15th Rifle Corps had been given orders to assault the north shore of the Vuoksi River on the afternoon of 7 March. The regimental commander, Colonel Romanov, launched this assault without artillery preparation or co-ordination with neighbouring regiments – not an uncommon occurrence. More unusual was the Finns' willingness to retreat and the Red Army regiment's subsequent activities. That evening, Colonel Romanov's regiment did not dig in to the newly won positions, nor did they make contact with their neighbours. Suddenly, without cause, the regiment retreated back to an island in the river without reporting to army staff for permission to do so. When the regiment tried to retake the north shore of the river the next day the Finns offered greater resistance and, due to a complete lack of command and control, the regiment suffered heavy casualties. The following evening total panic set in. During the night patrol someone in the regiment shouted 'Help me, comrades', and in the resulting hysteria units began to shoot at each other and the regiment retreated illegally a second time, leaving behind most of their weapons. Parushinov's explanation for this behaviour was frank and to the point: divisional command had conducted a poor job training its regiments, representatives from corps and divisional staffs had not verified the regiment's combat readiness before the attack, divisional political workers had grossly neglected their duties, and there was a complete lack of discipline in the regiment. Parushinov accused Romanov and his troops of carrying in themselves 'germs of selfishness and cowardice'. In order to set an example he placed Romanov and others under court martial and ordered his chief of staff to distribute the report to every level of command down to platoon commanders.[188]

Despite these disciplinary problems the North-Western Front's forces continued to press forward toward Vyborg. By 10 March, Pavlov's 28th Rifle Corps had secured a five-kilometre-wide bridgehead at Vilajoki and had prepared jumping-off positions there. In the meantime, Cherednichenko's corps had left its base at Orangenbaum and had crossed the ice of the Gulf of Finland with the help of the Baltic Fleet's Hydrographic Service. It was now concentrated on Piisaari Island, ready to complete the encirclement of Vyborg.[189] Reconnaissance patrols on the 15th Army's front north of Pitkaranta discovered that the Finns were abandoning their positions and falling back. This raised hopes in the 15th Army command that the road was open for an attack against Sortavala. Both the 15th and 8th Armies announced a general offensive and Stavka sent Voronov to verify their combat readiness but Finnish resistance once again brought these armies to a standstill.[190]

IX

The Finnish high command's reaction to the Red Army's offensive across the ice of Vyborg Bay and south of that city was to send a report to the Finnish government in Helsinki warning them that the Finnish Army's defences would not last much longer and that measures to secure foreign military assistance or a peace accord with the Soviet Union had to be concluded soon before his front collapsed completely.[191] In Moscow, Ryti's intransigence over Soviet control of navigation in Vyborg Bay and the annexation of Kuola-järvi and the Hangö Peninsula provoked Molotov to remind the Finnish delegation that he could still revitalize relations with the Finnish People's Republic and continue the war.[192] Molotov's threat did not deter Ryti from holding out for the best terms possible. Over the next two days the Finnish and Soviet delegations continued to debate the details of the peace treaty.

At North-Western Front headquarters, Timoshenko repeated his order to storm Vyborg. Combined arms attacks from divisions in the 34th Rifle Corps located directly south of Vyborg and from the 50th Rifle Corps to the east destroyed the Finnish Army's final line of fortifications. As a result, the Red Army was 300 m. closer to its goal.[193] Supply problems and blizzard conditions in Vyborg Bay prevented the 10th and 28th Rifle Corps from making any further progress, although the 10th Rifle Corps' 43rd Rifle Division managed to seize Kouru-saari Island and the south shore of Karppila.[194] Further out in the Gulf of Finland, the Winter Defence group suffered a counter-attack by a battalion of Finnish women soldiers at Kiuskeri Island and was forced to retreat.[195] Early on the morning of 11 March a detachment of Finns attacked the Winter Defence group at Someri and attempted to blow up the ice-locked gunboat *Kazakhstan*, but failed. Both these Finnish counter-attacks suggested to Timoshenko that the Finnish high command was particularly worried about a major Red Army offensive in this area and that the Winter Defence group had succeeded in diverting Finnish forces away from Vyborg.[196]

Up north in the forests near Kuhmo, the 9th Army under Chuikov's nominal command was continuing its attempts to rescue the 54th Rifle Division which had been besieged and divided up into 'mottis' by the Finns during combat in late January.[197] Chuikov's main problem was not so much the armed resistance from the Finns as dissension in his own army headquarters at Kandalaksha where Mekhlis and a representative from the NKVD's Special Department were still auditing his staff work.[198] Mekhlis had reported to Stavka in late February that the Finns had used chemical weapons against several of the 54th Rifle Division's encircled sub-divisions, especially that of the 5th NKVD regiment, and had asked Stavka for permission to use chemical weapons in return.[199] Shaposhnikov emphatically rejected this request but Mekhlis continued to ply Stavka with special requests, and on 10 March forwarded to Moscow a particularly heart-wrenching plea from the 54th Rifle Division's political commissar, Sevastianov, in support for a request for more troops to relieve the plight of the encircled sub-divisions. This request also went unheeded.[200]

On the Karelian Isthmus, the 7th and 13th Armies' divisions continued their assault against the Finnish defences at Vyborg and along the Vuoksi River to Taipale. For the first time during the war the Finnish Army was able to challenge Soviet air superiority and bomb targets in the 7th Army's rear with military aircraft that had been received from abroad. Meretskov's response to this new threat was to order all his formation commanders to improve their communications with the VNOS network (the Air Surveillance, Warning and Communications system) and threatened to court martial every anti-aircraft battery officer who failed to respond to Finnish air-raids.[201] Flooding, supply problems, and incessant Finnish counter-assaults prevented the divisions from advancing any further.[202] By 12 March both the attackers and the defenders had reached a state of complete exhaustion.

The 'logic of war' finally drew to a close on the evening of 12 March. Ryti's delegation finally accepted Molotov's peace terms and cease-fire procedures were set to come into effect at noon the next day. As soon as the draft treaty was signed, Stavka sent a directive to Timoshenko summarizing the treaty's content and instructing the troops of the North-Western Front to continue fighting until the cease-fire hour, and if the enemy continued to resist, to 'beat the hell out of him' (*bit' ego po nastoiashchemu*).[203] During the following nine and a half hours Pavlov's 28th Rifle Corps, in conjunction with the 10th Rifle Corps and a ski battalion from the Finnish People's Army, deployed their forces on Porkansaari Island in Vyborg Bay in preparation for the double-encirclement of the entire Finnish Army.[204] Fierce fighting continued on the northern shore of Lake Ladoga and further north at Kuhmo, where the Finns made a final attempt to destroy the besieged 54th Rifle Division.[205] Fifteen minutes before noon Meretskov and Parusinov conducted a tremendous artillery barrage against the Finnish defenders with all the artillery at their disposal. When the guns stopped at noon an eerie silence reigned, soon broken by the music of the Red Army's marching bands.[206]

NOTES

1 Jakobson, *Finland Survived*, pp. 203–4.
2 Tanner, *The Winter War*, pp. 123–4. See also Jakobson, *Finland Survived*, p. 217.
3 Carlgren, *Swedish Foreign Policy during the Second World War*, pp. 35–6, and Jakobson, *Finland Survived*, p. 210, as well as Tanner, *The Winter War*, p. 125.
4 TsGASA, fond 34980, opis' 14, delo 50, l.34. See also *Konflikt*, Document No. 55, and Zakharov, *General'nyi shtab v predvoennye gody*, pp. 183–4. A possible explanation for choosing such a predictable direction for the offensive was that it was 'the most suitable part of the Karelian Isthmus for mechanized formations and orthodox Central European tactics'. See Langdon-Davies, *Finland – The First Total War*, p. 95.
5 *IVOVSS*, Vol. 1, pp. 267–8. See also Meretskov, *Na strazhe narodov*, p. 187, and K.

Simonov, 'Glazami cheloveka moego pokoleniia', p. 79.
6   TsGASA, fond 34980, opis' 14, delo 50, l.43 See also *IVOVSS*, pp. 267–8.
7   Erickson, *The Soviet High Command*, p. 549.
8   RTsKhINDI, fond 71, opis' 25, delo 6859, 'Preliminary Basic Conclusions on the Lessons of Battle on the Karelian Isthmus, n.d.', p. 22. This report cites six tank brigades and twelve tank battalions. Aleksandrov gives higher figures based on Russian archival sources: 700,000 men, 5,700 artillery guns and mortars, 1,800 airplanes, and 2,300 tanks. He also points out that the Finnish Army only had 100,000 men, 460 artillery guns, 200 airplanes and 25 tanks on the Karelian Isthmus. See P. Aleksandrov, 'Raskolotyi shchit', *Rodina*, No. 12, Winter 1995, p. 78.
9   Ries, 'Manuscript for *Cold Will*', p. 49.
10 TsGASA, fond 34980, opis' 14, delo 50, ll. 41–42.
11 Ibid., ll. 43–4.
12 Ibid.
13 Korneev, *Boevye deistviia 50 SK po proryvu linii mannergeima*, p. 23. See also A. Chaika, 'Protivotankovaia artilleriia v boiu', *Na Strazhe Rodiny*, 14 January 1940, p. 2
14 Korneev, *Boevye deistviia 50 SK po proryvu linii mannergeima*, p. 23.
15 Ibid., pp. 26–7. Korneev blocked out the paragraph which described what these additional exercises were.
16 Voronov, *Na sluzhbe voennoi*, p. 146.
17 *Sovetsko–finliandskaia voina 1939–1940 gg. na more*, Chast' 2, p. 58.
18 TsGASA, fond 34980, opis' 77, delo 6, ll. 1–15.
19 TsGASA, fond 34980, opis' 14, delo 50, l. 32.
20 Ibid.
21 Ibid.
22 Ibid.
23 Unnamed hills were referred to by their map co-ordinates, but groves of trees were referred to by the image their map outline evoked.
24 Korneev, *Boevye deistviia 50 SK po proryvu linii mannergeima*, pp. 54–60.
25 Ibid., p. 60. Equipping sub-units of the first assault echelon with telephones was the idea of Kurochkin who explained it in his article 'Organizatsia sviazi pri nastuplenii na ukrepiushegocia protivnika', *Na Strazhe Rodiny*, 4 February 1940, p. 2.
26 Korneev, *Boevye deistviia 50 SK po proryvu linii mannergeima*, p. 60.
27 Ibid. In Yu. Korol'kov's article entitled 'Geroicheskie podvigi saperov' (*Na Strazhe Rodiny*, 9 February 1940, p. 1) this detail was omitted.
28 Korneev, *Boevye deistviia 50 SK po proryvu linii mannergeima*, p. 61. Lychalov, in his article entitled 'V upor po ambrazuram', (*Na Strazhe Rodiny*, 6 February 1940, p. 1) describes this event and the heroism of politruk Fomichev who threw the grenades, shouting 'Coming to the rescue, are you? No chance!' Lychalov's story is confirmed in part by Korneev.
29 Korneev, *Boevye deistviia 50 SK po proryvu linii mannergeima*, p. 62.
30 Korol'kov, 'Geroicheskie podvigi saperov', p. 1.
31 Ibid.
32 Korneev, *Boevye deistviia 50 SK po proryvu linii mannergeima*, p. 62.
33 Ibid. A more general description of these events can be found in the article written by M. Sipovich entitled, 'Padenie pervykh dotov Khotinen', in *Boi na karel'skom peresheike*, pp. 132–4.
34 Korneev, *Boevye deistviia 50 SK po proryvu linii mannergeima*, p. 55.
35 Ibid., p. 64.
36 Ibid., p. 57.
37 Ibid., pp. 65–6. During the first ten days of February 1940 the 7th Army's airforce intensified its tactical bombing of the Mannerheim Line from one kilometre behind the Finnish forward line to a depth of 6–8 kilometres. Soviet aviation was not able to bomb closer to the forward line due to poor interaction with its ground forces; 132 medium-range bombers flew sorties on the north and north-east shore of Summa-järvi Lake while 174 medium-range bombers were assigned to bomb Khotinen. This six-kilometre-long

front received 653 sorties during the 10 day period, not counting fighter sorties. The 7th Army's airforces did not attempt to conduct any dive-bombing. Operational bombing was conducted against military and tranportation targets in the Finnish Army's deep rear. By 24 February the North-Western Front's and 7th Army's airforces consisted of 1,250 airplanes. See Korneev, *Boevye deistviia 50 SK po proryvu linii mannergeima*, pp. 41–4 and RTsKhINDI, fond 71, opis' 25, delo 6859, l.23.

38 Ibid., p. 67. Timoshenko's sole specific amendment to the conduct of these independent demonstration operations was that sappers should improve jumping-off positions before attack.

39 *Konflikt*, Document No. 73, 'Prikaz voiskam 7 armii ob ovladenii khotinenskim opornym punktom, 4 fevraliia 1940 g'.

40 TsGASA, fond 34980, opis' 14, delo 50, l.33

41 Korneev, *Boevye deistviia 50 SK po proryvu linii mannergeima*, pp. 70–2.

42 Ibid., pp. 72–3. Between 1 February and 9 February the 100th Rifle Division succeeded in advancing a total of 700–800 m.

43 Ibid., pp. 74–5. Reconnaissance and the interrogation of Finnish POWs convinced the Red Army high command that their demonstration operations had inflicted 80 per cent losses on the 1/7 Finnish Infantry Regiment on 7 February. Chew, *The White Death*, pp. 148–9, and the 'Official History of the Soviet–Finnish War', prepared by Korneev in January 1941, comment on the complacency of the Finnish high command and the premature conclusions by the international press after the lull in Red Army assaults on 7 February 1940.

44 Korneev, *Boevye deistviia 50 SK po proryvu linii mannergeima*, pp. 4–5. See also *Konflikt*, Document No. 87, 'Iz otcheta o boevykh deistviiakh 50 str. korpusa v period s 11 fevralia po 13 marta 1940 g'.

45 Subsequent military operational accounts assume that the 123rd Rifle Division was originally assigned as the spearhead of Timoshenko's offensive.

46 Korneev, *Boevye deistviia 50 SK po proryvu linii mannergeima*, p. 105.

47 *Konflikt*, Document No. 87, and Korneev, *Boevye deistviia 50 SK po proryvu linii mannergeima*, pp. 4–5.

48 *Konflikt*, Document No. 80, 'Prikaz voiskam Severo–Zapadnogo fronta o shturme linii Mannergeima, 9 fevralia 1940 g'.

49 Korneev, *Boevye deistviia 50 SK po proryvu linii mannergeima*, p. 105.

50 Ibid., p. 102. Reis agrees with figure of 4.5 battalions/km front. RTsKhINDI, fond 71, opis 25, delo 6859, l.2, 'Preliminary basic conclusions on the lessons of battle on the Karelian Ithsmus, n.d.', cites statistics of 61–64 guns/km front in the 100th/123rd Rifle Division's sector and concluded that for a successful breakthrough an average of 75–80 guns/km front was needed. During the demonstration operations from 1 to 10 February the 123rd Rifle Division's artillery used 4,419 203 mm. and 280 mm. shells to destroy five Finnish DOTs. See 'Excerpts on Soviet 1938–40 operations from *The History of Warfare, Military Art, and Military Science*', p. 135.

51 RTsKhINDI, fond 71, opis' 25, delo 6876, ll. 1–5, 'North-Western Front, Timoshenko's instructions after inspection, 9 February, 1940'.

52 Ibid., p. 27. To emphasize this point, Korneev claimed that the 100th Rifle Division, the spearhead of Meretskov's demonstration operations in early February 1940, lacked 222 middle-ranking officers and 2,599 rank-and-file despite January's reinforcements. During the Central Committee's and Main Military Soviet's joint commission to study the lessons of the war in mid-April 1940, K.E. Voroshilov revealed that this was due to chaos in the rear services. See Voroshilov, *Doklad (Voroshilova) o sovetsko–finliandskoi voine 1939–1940gg.*, p. 16.

53 RTsKhINDI, fond 71, opis' 25, delo 6876, l.1.

54 Ibid.

55 TsGASA, fond 34980, opis' 6, delo 77.

56 TsGASA, fond 34980, opis' 6, delo 186, l.50, 'German manual on how to attack fortified gun-emplacements, 9 February, 1940'. The full extent to which this organizational

restructuring and tactical review was influenced by German military doctrine will probably never be revealed. However, this single document is evidence that the Red Army command was aware of German tactical techniques and was willing to consult them to solve its own immediate problems.

57 *Edinonachale*, the vertical flow of responsibility and information between senior and junior commanders, and *Orientirovaniia*, the horizontal exchange of information between neighbouring commanders and other services, are the two fundamental concepts underpinning the Soviet unified theory of combined arms warfare. Both of these concepts were introduced in the 1890s and received elaborate theoretical and administrative development in the Russian Imperial General Staff after the Russo–Japanese War of 1904–05. For the history of these two concepts see C. Van Dyke, *Russian Imperial Military Doctrine and Education, 1832–1914* (Westport, CT: Greenwood Press, 1990), Chapters 4 and 5. These concepts have only recently come to the attention of military historians. See K.A. Larson, 'The Debl'tsevo Raid, February 1943: A Case Study in the Role of Initiative in Soviet Operational Art', *Journal of Soviet Military Studies*, Vol. 5, No. 3 (September 1992), pp. 426–32.

58 TsGASA, fond 34980, opis' 6, delo 85, 'From 13th Army to commanders of corps and independent units on the organization and conduct of battle actions, 10 February 1940'.

59 Korneev, *Boevye deistviia 50 SK po proryvu linii mannergeima*, pp. 108–9.

60 TsGASA, fond 34980, opis' 14, delo 50, l.28. See G.S. Isserson, *Novye formy bor'by. Opyt issledovaniia sovremennykh voin*, Vypusk pervyi (Moscow: Voenizdat, 1940) pp. 21–2, 24, for a particularly acerbic criticism of these tactics.

61 Mannerheim told the British military attaché General Lewin, in a conversation after the war, that German advisors must have directed the attack from 1 February onwards because after 1 February the Red Army's tactics resembled the German drill book. See PRO FO 24808, File N 4817, 22 April 1940.

62 B. Liddell-Hart, *This Expanding War* (London: Faber & Faber, 1942) p. 72.

63 *Boi na karel'skom peresheike*, p. 118

64 Ibid., p. 119.

65 During the 1920s many Soviet military theorists were inspired by Taylorism and equated the Red Army's functions with those of the factory. For overt examples see P. Sergeev and A. Toporkov, *NOT i voennoe delo* (Moscow: Gosvoenizdat, 1925) and N. Varfolomeev, *Tekhnika shtabnoi sluzhbe. Operativnaia sluzhba voiskovykh shtabov (v voennoe vremiia)* (Moscow: Vysshii Voennyi Redaktsionnyi Sovet, 1924).

66 Korneev, *Boevye deistviia 50 SK po proryvu linii mannergeima*, p. 110.

67 Ibid., p. 196.

68 Ibid., p. 194. See also *Konflikt*, Document No. 87.

69 Korneev, *Boevye deistviia 50 SK po proryvu linii mannergeima*, pp. 136–7.

70 Ibid., p. 144. At this time the chief of the 123rd Rifle Division's artillery, Colonel M.P. Kuteinikov, had 108 artillery guns at his disposal, some of which were 280 mm. mortars. See I.S. Prochko, *Artilleriia v boiakh za rodinu*, (Moscow: 1957) p. 158.

71 Kolosov, 'Sviazisty v boiu', and Stepanov, 'Proryv', in *Boi na karel'skom peresheike*, pp. 175–6, 204–6. Telephone cables were strung up on poles 4 to 5 metres high, rather than laid in the snow, to prevent them from being cut by tank tracks. Even so, they constantly had to be monitored by communications troops because the lines were frequently cut by Finnish artillery, sabotage ,and snow-storms. Radio was also used but was not as reliable or as secure as the telephone.

72 A description of the orientation meeting at Roslyi's 245th Rifle Regiment headquarters is provided in the memoirs of Stepanov and Kharaborkin, *Boi na karel'skom peresheike*, pp. 196–9. Kharaborkin, an experienced tank commander, found that his subordinate officers had only a vague idea how their tanks were supposed to attack fortified positions due to a lack of study and practical exercises. In an oblique reference to the effect of the purges on the tank officer corps, he attributed this inexperience to their youth.

73 Korneev, *Boevye deistviia 50 SK po proryvu linii mannergeima*, pp. 145–6, 151–2. See also Stepanov, 'Proryv', in *Boi na karel'skom peresheike*, p. 177.

The Soviet Invasion of Finland, 1939–40

74 *Boi na karel'skom peresheike*, p. 180, and Korneev, *Boevye deistviia 50 SK po proryvu linii mannergeima*, p. 147.
75 A very detailed description of this co-operative effort is given in Korneev, *Boevye deistviia 50 SK po proryvu linii mannergeima*, pp. 148, 153–4, and Lekanov, *Boi na karel'skom peresheike*, pp. 202–3. Praise and photographs of the heroes involved in these assaults can be found in *Na Strazhe Rodiny*, 15 February 1940, p. 2.
76 Korneev, *Boevye deistviia 50 SK po proryvu linii mannergeima*, p. 149.
77 N.F. Kuz'min claims that Roslyi's rifle regiment suffered 65.5 per cent losses in personnel, but does not specify the time frame. See Kuz'min, *Na strazhe mirnogo truda (1921–1940gg.)*, p. 250.
78 *Konflikt*, Document No. 88, 'Iz prikaza voiskam Severo–Zapadnogo fronta s razvitii nastupleniia pri vziamodeistvii pekhoty i artillerii, 12 fevralia 1940 g'. See also Korneev, *Boevye deistviia 50 SK po proryvu linii mannergeima*, p. 159.
79 Ibid.
80 *Konflikt*, Document No. 88.
81 Korneev, *Boevye deistviia 50 SK po proryvu linii mannergeima*, p. 160.
82 *Sovetsko–finliandskaia voina 1939–1940 gg. na more*, Chast' 3. pp. 6–8. See also Chew, *The White Death*, p. 154.
83 *Konflikt*, Document No. 89, 'Prikaz voiskam 7 armii o razvitii nastupleniia na khotinenskom napravlenii, 12 fevralia 1940 g'. See also Korneev, *Boevye deistviia 50 SK po proryvu linii mannergeima*, p. 157. The 27th Rifle Regiment was originally subordinated to the 7th Rifle Division which at this time was in Gorolenko's corps reserve.
84 'Excerpts on Soviet 1938–40 operations from *The History of Warfare, Military Art, and Military Science*, a 1977 textbook of the Military Academy of the General Staff of the USSR Armed Forces', *Journal of Slavic Military Studies*, Vol. 6, No. 1 (March 1993), p. 135. This was a mirror-image of Timoshenko's original plan.
85 Korneev, *Boevye deistviia 50 SK po proryvu linii mannergeima*, p. 157.
86 Ibid., pp. 161–4.
87 Ibid., pp. 165, 186.
88 Ibid., p. 166.
89 *Konflikt*, Document No. 90, 'Prikaz voiskam 7 armii o razvitii nastupleniia, 12 fevralia 1940 g'. See also Korneev, *Boevye deistviia 50 SK po proryvu linii mannergeima*, p. 199.
90 Chew, *The White Death*, p. 158, describes Aliabushev's assault as it was experienced from the Finnish side.
91 Korneev, *Boevye deistviia 50 SK po proryvu linii mannergeima*, pp. 121, 175.
92 Ibid., p. 177.
93 From 11 to 13 February Meretskov's and Grendal's armies expended a total of 2,642,215 artillery shells (4921.9 train wagons), 39,307,909 rifle cartridges (78.1 train wagons), and 303,888 hand-grenades (20.2 wagons). Not only was this a tremendous amount of fire-power, but it also was a significant load on the supply and transportation system which was already overburdened. Cited from the 'Preliminary basic conclusions on the lessons of battle on the Karelian Ithsmus', RTsKhINDI, fond 71, opis' 25, delo 6859, l. 20.
94 Chew, *The White Death*, p. 157.
95 *Konflikt*, Document No. 87.
96 Korneev, *Boevye deistviia 50 SK po proryvu linii mannergeima*, pp. 200–1.
97 Ibid., p. 122.
98 Ibid., p. 212.
99 Chew, *The White Death*, p. 160.
100 Korneev, *Boevye deistviia 50 SK po proryvu linii mannergeima*, pp. 123, 213.
101 Chew, *The White Death*, p. 159, reports the Finnish commanders' amazement that the Red Army did not immediately exploit its breakthrough and destroy the Finnish II Corps. Chew attributes this lost opportunity on the part of the Red Army to tardy planning and a newly instilled respect for the Finn's defensive strength. Indeed, operational planning from Timoshenko's Front down to Gorolenko's Corps was slow to respond to Aliabushev's successes, illustrated by their fixation on the development of the pursuit not towards Lähde,

but towards Leipäsuo. Complete chaos in Aliabushev's rear also played a significant role in compromising the North-Western Front's exploitation of the breakthrough. Division commanders were also not sufficiently confident in their troop's combat capabilities to continue offensive assaults at night. Only later in the offensive would they attempt night operations.

102 Korneev, *Boevye deistviia 50 SK po proryvu linii mannergeima*, p. 214.

103 Ibid., pp. 191, 202. The Finnish High Command met at the Finnish II Corps headquarters to discuss the threat of the Red Army breakthrough south of Lähde while the 50th Rifle Corps was trying to sort out the chaos in the rear of the 123rd Rifle Division. All three Finnish field commanders felt that the time had come to abandon their main defence line and organize an orderly retreat. The question remained whether to retreat to the intermediate V-Line stretching from Samola Bay on the Gulf of Vyborg to Kämärä Station and Vuosalmi, or all the way back to the T-Line in the suburbs around Vyborg. Eventually, Mannerheim chose to retreat to the V-Line and the II Corps headquarters began to pull its troops out of the fortifications at Khotinen on the evening of 14 February. See Chew, *The White Death*, p. 164.

104 Two days previously Meretskov created from his army reserve a 'mobile group' consisting of the 12th Tank Brigade and a majority of the 15th Rifle-Machine Gun Brigade under the command of Colonel Baranov and a 'mobile detachment' consisting of the 6th Tank Battalion and the 163rd Rifle-Machine Gun Battalion from the remainder of the 15th Rifle-Machine Gun Brigade under the command of Major Vershinin. See 'Excerpts from *The History of Warfare, Military Art, and Military Science*', p. 136.

105 In Aliabushev's mobile headquarters tank near Hill No. 63.4 these three commanders negotiated a general plan of attack consisting of assaults by Aliabushev's forward detachments (composed of one rifle battalion, a tank company from the 50th Rifle Corps' reserve 112th Tank Brigade, a battery of infantry-support artillery and a platoon of anti-tank guns) flanked by elements of Baranov's and Vershinin's mobile units. This combined assault was launched at 13.00 hours after a 20 minute artillery preparation. See Korneev, *Boevye deistviia 50 SK po proryvu linii mannergeima*, pp. 179–80.

106 Chew, *The White Death*, p. 165.

107 Korneev, *Boevye deistviia 50 SK po proryvu linii mannergeima*, pp. 126–7, 182.

108 Ibid., p. 185.

109 RTsKhINDI, fond 71, opis' 25, delo 6874, l.1., 'North-Western Front, Instructions on the Use of Artillery, February 16, 1940'.

110 All three commanders' artillery support was still held up by traffic-jams on the Boboshino-Lähde road. In the official account of the Battle for Lähde only Colonel Baranov's mobile group is mentioned, implying that this battle was accomplished according to the tactics of manoeuvre warfare. See *IVOVSS*, p. 269. On the other side of the front, Finnish commanders noted that the Red Army was reverting to its old habits of a month before, i.e., assaulting in close formation without artillery preparation. See Chew, *The White Death*, p. 167.

111 TsGASA, fond 34980, opis' 14, delo 12, ll. 12–21, 'List of fundamental questions used in the descriptions and analysis of the "Section for the Study of Combat Experience"'. The main issues identified in this list are the use of artillery, tanks and communications in the breakthrough of fortified regions as well as their troop control and supply.

112 Korneev, *Boevye deistviia 50 SK po proryvu linii mannergeima*, pp. 203–6.

113 Although the Finnish II Corps command had already ordered the evacuation of Summa (Khotinen), it had left a regiment and battalion as a cover force to delay the Red Army onslaught for as long as possible.

114 Ibid., p. 208.

115 Ibid., p. 208. *Konflikt*, Document No. 87, claims that the 100th Rifle Division only seized 14 DOTs. See also Voronov, *Na sluzhbe voennoi*, pp. 152–3. Voronov had to report this news to Voroshilov personally and swear that he saw it with his own eyes before Voroshilov would believe the good news.

116 Korneev, *Boevye deistviia 50 SK po proryvu linii mannergeima*, pp. 130, 209–10.

117 *Konflikt*, Document No. 97, 'Prikaz Voennogo sovets Severo–Zapadnogo fronta komandiram 15 i 23 str. korpusov ob uluchshenii upravleniia chatiami i aktivizatsii boevykh deistvii, 15 fevralia 1940 g'.
118 *IVOVSS*, p. 269.
119 Korneev, *Boevye deistviia 50 SK po proryvu linii mannergeima*, pp. 216–17.
120 Ibid., p. 192.
121 Ibid., p. 210. Korneev reports that the 100th Rifle Division's 331st Rifle Regiment remained at Summa (Khotinen) to bury its dead. Korneev cites 1,370 wounded and 161 killed during the previous day's assault. This seems low, but is possible if the Finns had actually pulled out the day before and had not shown as much resistance as Red Army sources claim.
122 Tanner, *The Winter War*, pp. 125–6.
123 Ibid., p. 128, and Jakobson, *Finland Survived*, pp. 210–13.
124 Tanner, *The Winter War*, p. 149
125 Ibid., p. 152.
126 Ibid., p. 157.
127 Ibid., p. 161, and Jakobson, *Finland Survived*, pp. 232–3.
128 *Konflikt*, Document No. 98, 'Prikaz voiskam 7 armii o presledovanii otkhodiashchero protivnika na vyborgskom napravlenii, 17 fevralia 1940 g'.
129 Korneev, *Boevye deistviia 50 SK po proryvu linii mannergeima*, p. 220.
130 *Konflikt*, Document No. 98. Ivanov's mobile detachment consisted of the 15th Rifle Regiment and the 1st Tank Brigade.
131 Korneev, *Boevye deistviia 50 SK po proryvu linii mannergeima*, pp. 221–30, Pospelov, in *IVOVSS*, p. 269, comments that the 7th Army maintained a tempo of 6–10 km. per day until it was stopped. He fails to mention that this tempo was only sustained for a day.
132 RTsKhINDI, fond 71, opis' 25, delo 51, 'Stavka to North-Western Front on 17 February, 1940'. See also Korneev, *Boevye deistviia 50 SK po proryvu linii mannergeima*, pp. 221, 227. The source of Stavka's erroneous information may have been Kulik, who was heading the political direction of the war from the Smolnyi Institute in Leningrad.
133 Korneev, *Boevye deistviia 50 SK po proryvu linii mannergeima*, p. 226.
134 Chew, *The White Death*, discusses the decision to form this line. Pospelov, *IVOVSS*, discusses where the 2nd Mannerheim Line was located. See also *Konflikt*, Document No. 87, Ries, 'Manuscript for *Cold Will*', p. 52, and Korneev, *Boevye deistviia 50 SK po proryvu linii mannergeima*, pp. 222–3.
135 Korneev, *Boevye deistviia 50 SK po proryvu linii mannergeima*, pp. 230–2.
136 *Konflikt*, Document Nos. 95 and 102, 'Prikaz voiskam 7 armii o zakreplenii na poberezh'e finskogo zaliva, 19 fevralia 1940 g'.
137 Chew, *The White Death*, p. 167, and Pospelov, *IVOVSS*, p. 269.
138 Chew, *The White Death*, pp. 179–80. See also *Sovetsko–finliandskaia voina 1939–1940 gg. na more*, Chast' I, Kniga III, p. 17.
139 Voronov, *Na sluzhbe voennoi*, p. 145. When Voronov visited Pavlov's headquarters to review the plans for the 28th Motorized Rifle Corps' offensive he was surprised to find that Pavlov had also assumed that such manoeuvres were possible and had not conducted any tests to prove their viability.
140 At this time two telegraph lines were also laid across the ice to facilitate communications with the corps on the Isthmus. *Sovetsko–finliandskaia voina 1939–1940 gg. na more*, Chast' I, Kniga III, p. 18.
141 *Konflikt*, Document No. 86. Red Army losses at Lovajärvi were: 1,000 dead and 250 POWs. The four regiments north of Pitkäranta were completely wiped out except for four men who reached the 168th Rifle Division's enclave. In other words, a total of 1,700 dead.
142 *Konflikt*, Document No. 99, 'Doklad komandira 8 str. korpusa kmodiva RUBINA v Voennyi sovet 15 armii o tselescöobraznosti vremennogo priostanovleniia nastupleniia, 18 fevralia 1940 g.'.
143 *Konflikt*, Documents No. 99 and 105, 'Prikaz voiskam 15 armii o perekhode v nastuplenie na pitkiarantskom napravlenii, 21 fevralia 1940 g.'.

144 Jakobson, *Finland Survived*, pp. 233–5. At this time the Soviet high command was closely monitoring the Entente's efforts to aid Finland militarily. One of its sources of information was the Estonian military attaché in Helsinki who, on 18 February, reported that foreign military aid was still relatively meagre. See *Konflikt*, Document No. 100, 'Iz doklada estonskogo voennogo attashe v Finliandii, 18 fevralia 1940'.
145 Chew, *The White Death*, pp. 167–8.
146 *Konflikt*, Document No. 87.
147 Korneev, *Boevye deistviia 50 SK po proryvu linii mannergeima*, pp. 237–40.
148 *Konflikt*, Document No. 87, Korneev, *Boevye deistviia 50 SK po proryvu linii mannergeima*, pp. 240, 253.
149 *Konflikt*, Document No. 108, 'Directiva komanduiushchego Severo-Zapadnym frontom voiskam 7 i 13 armii ob uskorenii tempov nastupleniia, 22 fevralia 1940 g'.
150 *Konflikt*, Document No. 87. However, four days of continuous fighting had taken their toll. From 11 to 23 February Aliabushev's 123rd Rifle Division had suffered 2,000 casualties. In its subsequent battles against the Finnish counter-attacks it suffered another 913 casualties. See Korneev, *Boevye deistviia 50 SK po proryvu linii mannergeima*, pp. 257, 265.
151 Tanner, *The Winter War*, pp. 178–85. See also Jakobson, *Finland Survived*, pp. 236–7 and Kollontai, p. 198.
152 Jakobson, *Finland Survived*, p. 238.
153 Tanner, *The Winter War*, pp. 195–6.
154 Jakobson, *Finland Survived*, pp. 241–2.
155 RTsKhINDI, fond 71, opis' 25, delo 41, 'North-West Front Directive for the capture of Vyborg, 27 February, 1940'. Pavlov's 28th Rifle Corps at this point consisted of the 86th Motorized Rifle Division, the 173rd and 91st Rifle Division, the 29th Independent Tank Brigade and 10 ski battalions borrowed from the Baltic Fleet's Coastal Escort Detachment. Cherednichenko's Cavalry Corps would join the 28th Rifle Corps later in the offensive.
156 *Konflikt*, Document No. 110, 'Directiva komanduiushchego Severo-Zapadnym frontom o likvidatsii nedochetov v upravlenii voiskami, 27 fevralia 1940 g.'.
157 *Konflikt*, Document No. 86.
158 'Excerpts on Soviet 1938–40 operations from *The History of Warfare, Military Art, and Military Science*', p. 136, and *Konflikt*, Document No. 87.
159 *Konflikt*, Document No. 87, and Korneev, *Boevye deistviia 50 SK po proryvu linii mannergeima*, p. 289.
160 Korneev, *Boevye deistviia 50 SK po proryvu linii mannergeima*, pp. 293–6.
161 Ibid., pp. 310–19.
162 Ibid., pp. 305–6.
163 *Istoriia Ordena Lenina Leningradskogo Voennogo Okruga*, p. 139. The composition of Leliushenko's mobile detachment is given in *Konflikt*, Document No. 101, 'Iz opisaniia boevykh deistvii 23 str. korpusa v period s 18 fevralia po 13 marta 1940 g.'.
164 *Konflikt*, Document No. 101.
165 Ibid., Document No. 116, 'Boevoe praporiazhenie komanduiushchego 7 armei komandiru 34 str. korpusa ob obladenii g. Vyborg, 1 marta 1940 g.', and Document No. 95.
166 Ibid., Document No. 117, 'Boevoe pasporiazhenie komanduiushchego 13 armii o razvitii nastupleniia na st. Antrea, 1 marta 1940 g.', and 'Excerpts on Soviet 1938–40 operations from *The History of Warfare, Military Art, and Military Science*', p. 136.
167 Korneev, *Boevye deistviia 50 SK po proryvu linii mannergeima*, p. 323.
168 *Konflikt*, Document No. 115, 'Iz otcheta o boevykh deistviiakh 28 str. korpusa v period s 28 fevralia po 13 marta 1940 g.'.
169 Ibid.
170 *Sovetsko–finliandskaia voina 1939–1940 gg. na more*, Chast' 3, p. 24.
171 Ibid., pp. 27–30.
172 Chew, *The White Death*, p. 181.
173 *Konflikt*, Document No. 115.
174 Tanner, *The Winter War*, p. 213, and 'The Winter War', *International Affairs*, January 1990, pp. 205–6.

175 Tanner, *The White Death*, p. 215, and 'The Winter War', *International Affairs*, 1990, pp. 213–14, and Jakobson, *Finland Survived*, p. 249.
176 Korneev, *Boevye deistviia 50 SK po proryvu linii mannergeima*, p. 323. See also *Konflikt*, Documents No. 101, and No. 128, 'Prikaz voiskam 7 armii o proryve ukreplennoi pozitsii v raione Vyborga i zakhvate ukreplennoi pozitsii v raione Vyborga i zakhvate platsdarma na zapadnom poberezh'e Finskogo zaliva, 6 marta 1940 g.'.
177 *Konflikt*, Document No. 154, 'Iz ocherka "Voina Sovetskogo Soiuza s belofinnami v 1939–1941 gg."', and Chew, *The White Death*, p. 173.
178 *Konflikt*, Document No. 127, 'Prikaz komanduiushchego Severo–Zapadnym frontom komanduiushchemu 7 armei, komanduiushchemu VVS fronta o shturme g. Vyborg, 6 marta, 1940 g.', and No. 128.
179 *Konflikt*, Document No. 129, 'Prikaz komandiushchego Severo–Zapadnym frontom komandiru korpusa FNA Antilla, 6 marta 1940 g.'.
180 Korneev, *Boevye deistviia 50 SK po proryvu linii mannergeima*, p. 313.
181 Ibid., p. 331.
182 Ibid., pp. 334–7. Lieutenant Yachnik's storm group was supported by 27 T-28s and artillery from Major Roslyi's regiment firing from the opposite shore of the flood. A more biographical description of this event can be found in Regiment Commissar S. Kovtushenko's 'Geroi Sovetskogo Soiuza lietenant S. Yachnik', *Boi na karel'skom peresheike*, pp. 350–2.
183 'Excerpts on Soviet 1938–40 operations from *The History of Warfare, Military Art, and Military Science*', p. 137, and *Konflikt*, Document No. 115.
184 'The Winter War', p. 207.
185 Tanner, *The Winter War*, p. 219, Kollontai, '"Seven Shots" in the Winter of 1939', *International Affairs*, January 1990, p. 200, and 'The Winter War', p. 208.
186 Korneev, *Boevye deistviia 50 SK po proryvu linii mannergeima*, pp. 339–50.
187 TsGASA, fond 34980, opis' 6, delo 85, l.207, 'Instructions from 13th Army to corps commanders criticizing their poor troop control, 7 March, 1940'. See also *Konflikt*, Document No. 132, 'Prikaz voiskam 13 armii ob uckorenii tempov nastupleniia i likvidatsii nedoctatkov vo vzaimodeistvii chastei, 7 marta, 1940 g.'.
188 TsGASA, fond 34980, opis' 6, delo 85, ll. 202–204, 'Report from the 13th Army to the North-Western Front on irregular behaviour of troops and officers, 7 March, 1940'.
189 *Sovetsko–finliandskaia voina 1939–1940 gg. na more*, Chast' 3, p. 22. See also *Konflikt*, Document No. 115.
190 *Konflikt*, Document No. 86. See also Voronov, *Na sluzhbe voennoi*, p. 155, and *Konflikt*, Document No. 135, 'Iz ocherka boevykh deistvii 8 str. korpusa v period s 8 po 13 marta 1940 g.'.
191 Tanner, *The Winter War*, p. 227, and Chew, *The White Death*, pp. 187, 202–3.
192 'The Winter War', p. 211.
193 'Excerpts on Soviet 1938–40 operations from *The History of Warfare, Military Art, and Military Science*', p. 138 and *Konflikt*, Document No. 87.
194 *Konflikt*, Document No. 101. The 13th Army's 23rd Rifle Corps attacked at Vuosalmi without breaking through the Finn's defences, but did inflict enormous losses. See Chew, *The White Death*, p. 184.
195 *Sovetsko–finliandskaia voina 1939–1940 gg. na more*, Chast' I, Kniga III, p. 33.
196 Ibid.
197 Chew, *The White Death*, pp. 173, 175.
198 The NKVD had collected testimony from the discredited former chief of the 9th Army's Operations Department to the effect that the chief of staff, Nikishev, was guilty of staff 'unculturedness', a capital offence. See TsGASA, fond 34980, opis' 5, delo 53, ll. 276–274, 'Boikov, Chief of the Special Department of the GUGB NKVD, to Voroshilov concerning allegations against 9th Army Chief of Staff, Division Commander Nikishev, 15 February, 1940'.
199 TsGASA, fond 34980, opis' 5, delo 53, ll. 293–292, 'Mekhlis to Shaposhnikov on the non-use of chemical weapons, 28 February, 1940'.

200 TsGASA, fond 34980, opis' 5, delo 53, ll. 331–329, 'Mekhlis to Voroshilov, transmitting plea from commissar Sevastianov of the 54th Rifle Division for speedy liberation, March 10'. Commissar Sevastianov radioed the following plea:

The political-morale situation in the units of the division is basically healthy, with up to 60 applications to the Party. Everyone has an enormous hope that they will be rescued without doubt. However, along with this is a lack of faith and a few are beginning to lose confidence in aid during 30 days of undernourishment. On some days we give out 100 grammes. On other days there is no horse-flesh. The enemy doesn't allow us to prepare food on a fire. Every day we are shelled by artillery and mortar fire. Every day the enemy conducts fire raids. There is the danger of typhus. Wounded are in bad condition. Few defenders, many die from wounds. These are the reasons why I as commissar am asking for quick aid. Liberate these thousand heroes and Soviet patriots. History doesn't know a 40-day-long encirclement. With the liberation of the 54th RD we will write the heroic pages of people in the Red Army.

Chew, *The White Death*, p. 175, records that the 54th Rifle Division withstood another strong Finnish attack on the last day of the war, and that the Finnish commander responsible for this attack, General Tuompo, later paid the 54th Rifle Division a public tribute for fighting so stubbornly.

201 *Konflikt*, Document No. 143, 'Prikaz voiskam 7 armii ob uluchshenii protivovozdushnoi oborony, 12 marta 1940 g.'. According to an Ukaz passed by the Supreme Council on 10 December 1939 any PVO personnel who did not fulfill all their orders would be sent to prison for ten years. TsGANKh, NKO Secretariat, l. 98.

202 *Konflikt*, Document No. 87, Korneev, *Boevye deistviia 50 SK po proryvu linii mannergeima*, pp. 356–7.

203 RTsKhINDI, fond 71, opis' 25, delo 52, l.2, and Semiryaga, *Tainy stalinskoi diplomatii*, p. 169. Semiryaga suggests that this final barrage against Vyborg was stimulated by Stalin's desire to raise the Red Army's international prestige as a ruthless and mighty military force. See also Kumanev, 'Beslavnaia voina, ili pobeda, kotoroi ne gordilis', p. 9.

204 *Konflikt*, Document No. 95.

205 Kumanev, 'Beslavnaia voina, ili pobeda, kotoroi ne gordilis', Seminar paper presented at the Institute of Russian History, 29 January 1992, pp. 7–9. See also Chew, *The White Death*, p. 175, and Voronov, *Na sluzhbe voennoi*, p. 156.

206 *Boi na karel'skom peresheike*, p. 380.

5

THE LESSONS OF THE WAR

On 20 March 1940, representatives from the Soviet and Finnish governments convened at the Kremlin for a final time to formally conclude a war which had never been formally declared. A few days later the Kremlin played host to another official occasion, the plenum of the Central Committee VKP (b), held to confirm the creation of the Karelian-Finnish Union Republic under the presidency of Otto Kuusinen and to take stock of the Soviet Union's security policy in the wake of the recent war.[1]

The 'logic of war' policy against the Finns allowed Molotov to drive a hard bargain and achieve the Soviet government's minimum security requirements on its north-western border which the Red Army was unable to acquire solely by force of arms. Molotov's first priority had been to close off the Gulf of Finland to invasion from the Baltic Sea. The peace treaty with Finland fulfilled this priority by gaining a 30-year lease to maintain a base on the Hangö Peninsula and patrol its surrounding waters. The six islands in the eastern part of the Gulf of Finland, seized by the Baltic Fleet in the early days of the war, were permanently annexed by the Soviet Union for the maintenance of naval bases and coastal artillery batteries to complement the bases acquired from the Baltic States the previous autumn.

Molotov's second priority had been to gain a buffer-zone on the Karelian Isthmus and along the north shore of Lake Ladoga for the protection of Leningrad from an invasion by land and air. Although Timoshenko's armies had stopped short of capturing Vyborg and had made very little progress elsewhere, the peace treaty annexed Finnish territory up to the boundary established by Peter the Great in 1721, a region that included the cities of Vyborg, Kakisalmi and Sortavala and territory as far north as Suojärvi. The third priority was the defence of Murmansk, the Soviet Union's only ice-free ocean port, and its communications with Leningrad via the Kirov railroad line. Territory on the Rybachii and Srednyi Peninsulas and in the area around Salla had been seized early in the war by the forces of the 14th and 9th Armies.

The peace treaty augmented these military conquests by stipulating the construction of a railroad line from Kandalaksha to the Finnish town of Kemi, ostensibly for the purpose of improving Soviet trade with Sweden but also as a means to project military power into northern Finland and the Swedish iron-ore mines at Gallivare and Kiruna if the need ever arose. All these concessions had been made possible by the Red Army, which was lauded by its commanders for successfully taking the war to the enemy's territory (the first principle of Soviet military doctrine) and waging war against an opposing army which enjoyed the material, financial, and political support of the major European powers.[2]

However, Molotov's hard bargaining with the Finnish delegation did not obtain all the desired results. The Soviet Commissar for Foreign Affairs had been forced to make two concessions: the evacuation of the 14th Army from Petsamo and the renewal of the non-aggression pact rather than the conclusion of a mutual-assistance pact similar to the pacts signed with the Baltic States the previous autumn. These concessions represented a fundamental failure in Soviet foreign policy and Molotov did his best to understate the significance of the second concession in his report to the Central Committee. The Soviet high command would have preferred an autonomous but pro-Soviet government in Helsinki which would defer to Moscow on foreign policy and security issues. Instead, the war convinced the Finnish government of the need to seek protection against the threat of another Soviet invasion by courting allies either in Scandinavia or Germany. During the peace negotiations the Finnish Foreign Minister, Tanner, had discussed with Hansson, the Swedish Prime Minister, a proposal to form a defensive alliance between Finland, Sweden and Norway.[3] Molotov quickly learned of this proposal and forced the Finnish government to abandon it, but little incentive remained to prevent Helsinki from seeking a _rapprochement_ with Berlin, and this could become an anti-Soviet alliance at any time.[4]

In addition to these failures of Soviet foreign policy, the war revealed many deficiencies in the Red Army's ability to conduct contemporary warfare, confirming the Red Army's low status in relation to other European armed forces which, in Stalin's paranoia, increased the potential for foreign military intervention. From the very first hours of the Soviet invasion the Leningrad Military District's armies were impeded more by their own over-centralization of control and inability to practice the fundamentals of combined arms tactics than by the Finnish fortifications on the Mannerheim Line. Only when Timoshenko created the North-Western Front in January 1940 with quality reinforcements from other military districts, retrained the troops in the German _Wehrmacht_'s art of storming permanent field fortifications, and reorganized the command structure to a modified form of 'directive-control' was the Red Army able to continue its advance, and then only with a tremendous effort.[5]

Stalin, Molotov and others in the high command had monitored foreign media commentary on the war and even TASS's favourably biased reports were unable to hide the international community's low regard for the Red Army. Reports by an American correspondent in Stockholm suggested that the Soviet–Finnish war 'revealed more secrets about the Red Army than the last 20 years', and that Soviet military doctrine was only suitable for warfare on flat, open terrain. Another American correspondent admitted his admiration for the Red Army's ability to learn from its mistakes and recommit itself to a three-week long offensive, but even so, he rated the competence of the Red Army command corps below that of the German and French armies.[6] The German press was more circumspect but the *Wehrmacht*'s intelligence assessment had reached the same conclusion: the 'Russian mass is no match for an army with modern equipment and superior leadership'.[7]

The most obvious manifestation of the Red Army's weakness was the tremendous number of casualties it suffered during the invasion. The Central Committee's plenum listened to a report given by a General Staff representative which estimated that 48,745 Red Army soldiers had been killed and 158,863 soldiers had been wounded or frost-bitten: a very conservative figure in comparison with later estimates but, even so, significantly higher than the casualties incurred during the clashes with the Japanese Army at Khalkhin-Gol the previous summer.[8] On the basis of these reports the Central Committee reaffirmed that the rehabilitation of military expertise, initiated by Stalin's call for joint sessions between the Main Military Soviet and the Central Committee in early January, should be continued in the form of a joint commission to study the lessons of the war. The purpose of this joint commission was to solicit the experience and suggestions of all the veteran commanders and commissars in order to lay the basis for the most comprehensive reform of the Red Army and Soviet military doctrine since the reorganization towards a regular cadre army in 1934.[9]

I

In mid-April, the joint commission met to listen to reports from the Defence Commissariat and the General Staff and to grant absolution for the mistakes made during the war with Finland. The first report was given by Voroshilov who set the confessional tone of the proceedings by making a perfunctory acknowledgement of the help he had received from his colleagues at Stavka, then launching into a 37-page summary of the problems which had plagued the Red Army at every level of operational and tactical command during the war.

'It must be said that neither I, the People's Commissar, nor the General Staff, nor the Leningrad Military District command fully understood at the beginning all the peculiarities and difficulties which would be associated with this war.'[10] Voroshilov claimed that the most fundamental of these mistakes was the defence establishment's poor strategic reconnaissance of the Finnish theatre of war. Throughout the previous decade Finland had been categorized as a secondary threat and only the most minimal defensive preparations had been made. When Stalin elevated Finland's status to a primary threat in the summer of 1939 and ordered the Leningrad Military District and the Baltic Fleet to prepare for offensive operations the defence establishment lacked an appropriate reconnaissance network in the area. The existing network was unable to provide the necessary information about the Finnish Army's TOE (Table of Organization and Equipment) or the strength of the fortified regions on the Karelian Isthmus and north of Lake Ladoga at Lake Yanis-järvi.[11] Under-estimating the strength of the Finnish Army, the Leningrad Military District deployed armies on the Soviet–Finnish border which were unprepared numerically and organizationally for war against a committed enemy in forest and winter conditions. Voroshilov publicly acknowledged his full responsibility for the subsequent fate of these armies although Stalin's pre-war strategic prejudices were really to blame.

During the invasion the Soviet high command had discovered that its operations were severely compromised by chaos in the rear services. Voroshilov failed to mention in his report the critical supply problems which paralysed the Leningrad Military District's operations in December 1939. The Defence Commissar himself was directly to blame for these supply problems because he had not issued a formal declaration of war against Finland (probably at Stalin's command), an oversight that compromised the mobilization of road and rail transport facilities and confused the competencies of civilian and military authorities. Voroshilov chose instead to discuss the problems encountered by E. Shchadenko and his deputies in January 1940 during the transportation of reinforcements and supplies from other military districts to the Karelian Isthmus in preparation for Timoshenko's offensive in February.[12] At this time regional rail networks had been mobilized but the concentration of troops and war *matériel* still took longer than planned because the rail network throughout the rest of the Soviet Union was running according to a slower peacetime schedule. Once the troops reached their rail termini they had to be transported to the front line by large convoys of trucks which saturated the few existing snow-bound roads and formed enormous traffic jams. Stavka's reaction to this specific problem had been to order the 8th and 9th Armies operating in the forests north of Lake Ladoga to economize on the number of truck trips to the rear, but this policy had effectively reduced those armies' ability to continue their operations.[13]

Disorganized rear services had also disrupted the naval operations of the Baltic Fleet. The Leningrad Military District's initial failure to mobilize the regional rail network delayed the provisioning of gunboats assigned to support the 7th Army's invasion on the Karelian Isthmus with artillery support. Because war with Finland was never formally declared the Baltic Fleet was not allowed to draw from its existing depots until the second week of the war, at which time it received instructions releasing those depots for use.[14] Even when these obstacles were resolved, the Baltic Fleet's central supply organs still encountered difficulty providing adequate supplies to their various bases due to inaccurate and occasionally falsified information concerning the status of inventories. Severe disorganization in ship-repair services also compromised naval operations. Out of the Baltic Fleet's 60 ships, 26 ships required capital repairs for which there was a deficit of tools, materials, and trained repair personnel. The root of this problem lay in the fact that many ship-repair personnel had been co-opted by the Leningrad Military District to make up for personnel deficits in its armies or they had been seconded to the construction of new naval bases in the Baltic States.[15]

A day after the end of the Soviet–Finnish war the deputy commissar for the Soviet Navy, I. Isakov, held a meeting for naval commanders and their commissars at the Baltic Fleet headquarters in Kronstadt to summarize the experience of the war at sea. Isakov emphasized the importance of efficient supply by quoting Stalin's 1920 essay, 'The New Entente's Campaign against Russia', and reminded his colleagues that

> ... the enemy conducted not one strike against our bases. This has colossal significance because if any base or port commander decides to generalize this experience and draws the conclusion that his ports and bases will work wonderfully and without jamming, this will not be the case in a large war. When we fight a major adversary we will not be able to keep enemy raids away from our bases even with dense anti-aircraft defences: the obstacles will be greater; there will be fires and partial destruction. In these conditions the work of the rear and the ports will be different [than during the war with Finland].[16]

Isakov told his colleagues that they should interpret their experience during the recent war as a warning that the Baltic Fleet's rear services were not prepared for a war against a more powerful enemy such as Germany. The successful termination of the war with Finland did not provide the Baltic Fleet's commanders with an excuse for complacency.[17]

The joint commission also devoted much attention to shifting perceptions concerning the organization and conduct of modern warfare which had occurred during the war. The Leningrad Military District's invasion of Finland was organized as an offensive along a 'wide' front, inspired by the Red Army's Civil War legacy and reinforced by the breathtaking victories of the German *Wehrmacht* during the German–Polish war earlier in the autumn of 1939. When the invasion stalled in the forward defence zone of the Mannerheim Line at the end of December 1939 the Soviet high command appointed Timoshenko to reorganize an offensive on a 'narrow' front inspired by the Brusilov Offensive in the First World War.[18] During the month of January 1940 Timoshenko assembled a select group of competent commanders and established the North-Western Front headquarters in Leningrad. While Timoshenko's Operations Department co-ordinated the transport of reinforcements to the armies on the Karelian Isthmus and made other preparations for the new offensive, his 'Section for the Study of Combat Experience' retrained the troops in the art of storming permanent field fortifications and reorganized the command hierarchy to practise a more decentralized form of command similar to the German *Wehrmacht*'s system of 'directive-control'.[19] These new techniques were put into practice on 11 February after ten days of demonstration operations. Five days later, Timoshenko's vanguard divisions succeeded in breaking through the first line of the Finnish Army's fortifications.

While these preparations were under way the Faculty of Operational Art at the General Staff Academy in Moscow resuscitated the pre-purge military doctrine on the 'initial period of war'. The result was the publication in late February 1940 of a work entitled *Nastupatel'naia armeiskaia operatsiia. Osnovy operativnogo proryva: podgotovka proryva* (Offensive Army Operations. Foundations of Operational Breakthrough), edited by Colonel E. Shilovskii. Shilovskii's main thesis was that recent modifications in the Soviet Union's political geography, in conjunction with the Red Army's massive rearmament programme during the second half of the 1930s, could be interpreted in either of two ways. On the one hand, there was the inter-TVD (*Teatr Voennykh Deistvii*, or 'theatre of military operations') level of analysis which relied on examining the overall correlation of forces on the western border to indicate what type of operations would characterize the initial period of the war. During the First World War the Russian Army had established a positional

The Lessons of the War

front 1,400 km. long by mobilizing between 120 and 145 divisions, an average density of one division per 10 km. By contrast, the Red Army in 1939 was theoretically capable of mobilizing 180 divisions in addition to a large number of technologically advanced moto-mechanized formations and aviation, suggesting an average density and fire-power far above the norms set during the First World War and an enhanced capability to conduct mobile warfare.

However, Shilovskii argued that this conceptual method was too crude and recommended that military planners pay more attention to a new, more specialized intra-TVD level of analysis where unique geographical features, artificial fortifications and enemy troop concentrations would determine the initial configuration of force.[20] The enemy was capable of conducting three different types of operations on any given sector of the front. Deep Operations were performed by an above-average density of mobile forces in what was known in Soviet military parlance as a 'narrow front'. Screening operations were performed by an average density of forces on a 'normal', or positional front while less important defensive actions were performed on a 'wide' or extended front.[21] Whereas combat experience after the Civil War suggested that the initial period of a war was characterized by fluid combat on a wide front which would quickly solidify into a positional front (if not immediately followed by Deep Operations), the German–Polish war of 1939 indicated that an offensive on a narrow front could be initiated and successfully terminated by the use of Deep Operations alone. The single factor which could counteract this innovation in operational art was the existence of fortified regions on the state border. From this viewpoint, Timoshenko's recent breakthrough operations against the Mannerheim Line were extremely valuable for the re-evaluation of Soviet military doctrine because '... even during the initial period of war the conduct of operational breakthroughs will not only be the sole, but sometimes the unavoidable option on several axes.'[22]

The joint commission listened to testimony from the General Staff which recommended a doctrinal shift away from the 'manoeuvre war' legacy of the Civil War to the breakthrough legacy of the Brusilov Offensive, and suggested a renewed emphasis on the tactics of Deep Battle and combined arms warfare.[23] In the initial period of a future war the Red Army would be responsible for absorbing the shock of an enemy invasion on a narrow front by constructing fortified regions and concentrating a screen of troops on the border in an effort to disperse the enemy along as wide a front as possible. Once the front was stabilized, the Red Army would conduct a breakthrough followed by Deep Operations by means of a large concentration of formations organized in depth.[24] The General Staff's second modification to military doctrine reflected the North-Western Front's successful execution of directive-control by field commanders and storm troop tactics by the rank-and-file, both techniques borrowed from German military doctrine. Storm troop tactics were especially useful for conducting frontal assaults against enemy permanent field fortifications and anti-tank obstacles, the primary mission of Deep Battle.[25] In the event that these assaults failed, directive-control was necessary for shifting the focus of the offensive to a more advantageous sector of the front. Only when the missions of Deep Battle were completed would Red Army formations be allowed to launch Deep Operations.

On 26 April a sub-committee of the joint commission met to listen to a report on infantry weapons systems and discuss the details of Deep Battle. During this discussion Meretskov, the ex-chief of the Leningrad Military District and commander of the 7th Army on the Karelian Isthmus, and M. Kozlov, the chief-of-staff for the 15th Army, suggested that the tactics of Deep Battle should emphasize the offensive spirit. Aliabushev, the commander to the 123rd Rifle Division which had successfully combined directive-control with the new storm troop tactics to break through the Mannerheim Line in mid-February, suggested that more division commanders and their staffs practice the use of 'tables of battle' (nomograms) to maintain control over the transition from Deep Battle to Deep Operations.[26] At the end of this debate G. Kulik, the chairman of the sub-committee and one of Stalin's 'political generals', ignored the suggestions which did not suit his political programme and passed a resolution calling for the redrafting of the Red Army's field regulations with increased emphasis on the offensive spirit.[27]

The recent war on the Karelian Isthmus had also served to remind the Red Army high command about the strength of contemporary defensive operations. In accordance with the recent shift in perceptions about the initial period of war, considerable interest was devoted to the doctrine of 'defence-in-depth', first developed by the German Army during the First World War. In the February 1940 issue of *Voennaia Mysl'* an article entitled 'Defence', written by Colonel A. Starunin, advocated the strategic and tactical use of defence-in-depth to withstand an offensive by an enemy army two to three times superior to one's own forces. Drawing inspiration from the German field regulations *Truppenführung 100/1* of 1933, Starunin advocated the organization of the Red Army defensive forces into covering groups and strike groups. The purpose of covering groups was to absorb the shock of the enemy's breakthrough operations with counter-attacks just as the Finns had demonstrated during the recent war. Strike groups, consisting of mobile formations, were expected to exploit the success of these counter-attacks with a more powerful counter-offensive, which would then allow the main body of the Red Army to transfer to the offensive.[28]

The Lessons of the War

In their testimonies to the joint commission both the General Staff and the Defence Commissariat were greatly impressed by the Finnish Army's ability to withstand the onslaughts of a numerically superior army by increasing the density of automatic fire-power in its sub-units.[29] The General Staff admitted in its testimony that

> One must be careful in planning [the conduct of] lightning war in contemporary conditions. In the absence of moral-political collapse in the enemy's army and domestic population the enemy's army will continue to preserve its ability to resist [attack]. Experience shows the strength of contemporary defence and its rapid recreation in depth.

The report reached the conclusion that '... infantry who were well-trained in the art of organized retreat could quickly re-establish a defensive line and inflict perceptible losses against an unorganized attacker.'[30] Additional emphasis was placed on conducting defence along a wide front, the design and construction of fortified regions and the operational breakthrough of enemy fortified regions.[31] In light of these recommendations Voroshilov informed his colleagues that he would appoint a special governmental commission, including military specialists from the Operations Administration of the General Staff and the Military-Engineering and Mortar-Mines Administrations of the People's Commissariat for Defence, to study the remains of the Mannerheim Line and draw up proposals for the Red Army's fortification programme based on the Finnish Army's use of obstacles and minefields.[32]

This discussion about contemporary offence and defence demonstrated to the members of the joint commission that both forms of warfare relied on a well-trained, aggressive and pragmatic command corps and rank-and-file as well as a numerical and technological superiority of force. Unfortunately, the Soviet–Finnish war also demonstrated the paucity of capable commanders in the Red Army. In his testimony, Voroshilov admitted that Stavka had been obliged to relieve many senior commanders from their posts because they were positively harmful to the welfare of their own troops.[33] During the war, a total of two army commanders, three army chiefs-of-staff, three corps commanders and three corps chiefs-of-staff, five division commanders and several division chiefs-of-staff and regimental commanders had been dismissed.[34] Emphasizing that a well-trained and authoritative senior command corps was necessary for victory in the next war, Voroshilov recommended the reform of higher military education and the procedures for career advancement.

> The war has selected many talented commanders, political workers and other military organizers (mainly from below). We need to quickly identify

all these workers, provide them opportunities to develop specialized qualifications and help their development in every possible way.[35]

Following Voroshilov's comments the joint commission discussed measures to increase the professionalism of the command corps. The director of the General Staff Academy, Shlemin, criticized Khozin, his rival at the Frunze Military Academy, for suggesting cuts in the General Staff Academy's faculty. Shlemin explained to the joint commission that the quality of the Academy's curriculum had suffered in the past because it lacked sufficient faculty, resources, and up-to-date information about other armed forces, especially those of Germany, France and Britain.[36] Other comments were made by Shaposhnikov, the Chief of the General Staff and member of Stavka, who criticized the General Staff Academy for an overly abstract curriculum which ignored the application of tactical problems, while Meretskov suggested that the Academy turn its attention to more applied methods such as staff rides and war games at corps, army and front level.[37]

Ironically, the one person in the Red Army most responsible for the low professional standards of the senior command corps was the Defence Commissar himself. Voroshilov was personally responsible for instituting a career advancement system in the aftermath of the 1937–38 purges which ignored a commander's technical training and organizational abilities in favour of class background and participation in the ritual denunciation of colleagues.[38] The purge of the command corps represented his single most obvious contribution to the deprofessionalization of the Red Army. In a report to the Central Committee's plenum in March, Shchadenko estimated that a total of 35,000 commanders had been discharged from their duties since 1937 and that a majority of those commanders had been politically repressed.[39] The victims of the purge included all the military district commanders, 90 per cent of the military district chiefs-of-staff and deputy chiefs-of-staff, 80 per cent of corps and division commanders and 90 per cent of staff officers and their chiefs-of-staff from other formations. This had inevitably led to a demoralization and infantalization of the Red Army command corps.[40] However, the reduction in the number of commanders was a mere drop in the ocean in comparison to the overall growth of the Red Army in the same period. During the joint commission's discussion Shchadenko reminded his colleagues that 'In the last two years our army has grown substantially. If in 1937 we needed one commander, now we need five.'[41] Measures had already been taken to address the shortage of commanders by releasing imprisoned military and technical personnel. Eventually 4,000 commanders were released to take up their former duties but this was an insignificant number in comparison to the total deficit.[42]

After the purges had subsided somewhat, the Defence Commissariat made a half-hearted attempt to improve the senior command's professional training. In December 1938 a directive was issued, entitled 'On the Operational Training of Command Staff', which called for the systematic training of military district staffs for wartime army and front commands.[43] However, this directive was never put into practice for three reasons: not all the Defence Commissariat's guidelines were realistic, the methods for training staffs in the operational art of armies and fronts had not yet been developed, and the purges had decimated the command corps.[44] The result of this negligence was that during the war with Finland many senior commanders were unable to maintain control over their subordinates which, in turn, led to a weakening of discipline throughout the chain-of-command and the occasional wilful non-fulfilment of orders.[45]

The General Staff's testimony to the joint commission recommended that the career advancement system strengthen the volitional will of a commander by increasing his authority and training him to accept more personal responsibility. This meant that the roles and relationships between the various levels in the command hierarchy had to be redefined in the service manuals, the field regulations, and the overall social status of the officer corps. The proposal was supported by many members of the joint commission, in particular Shaposhnikov, Kozlov and Meretskov, who suggested that collegiate decision-making be abolished and that the government publish a special announcement defining the new relationship between the commander and his political commissar.[46]

Two reforms were of the highest priority. The first was to establish a merit-review system independent of the chain-of-command which would reward competent commanders and remove the unfit, negligent, undisciplined and morally infirm. The second reform was to improve the material well-being of the commander during wartime. The General Staff's testimony suggested the end of the 'militia principle' and the campaign to foster 'comradely relations' between commanders and their men when it stated that 'Continual life in dug-outs decreases the commander's personal authority and lowers him to the mass of subordinates, therefore not allowing him to maintain authority.'[47] The report concluded that from then on commanders should be entitled to regular meals, rests and greater material comforts.

Turning to the Red Army's combat performance, the Defence Commissar and the General Staff both agreed that staffs were unable to respond quickly enough to the changing circumstances of the modern battlefield. As a consequence, field commanders lacked the time and the information with which to make decisions, conduct continual analysis of the combat situation, or practise foresight in preparation for the next decision. One of the reasons for this low level of staff 'culture' was that existing staffs did not clearly understand their various functions and failed to select and train the right people during peacetime.[48] One delegate suggested that these failures in staff organization and work could be addressed by allowing the military academies to have access to information about the Red Army's organizational structure, hitherto restricted to the safes of the NKVD.[49] Another explanation for the low level of staff 'culture' was that staffs did not understand the significant role of reconnaissance in conducting modern war. At the beginning of the Soviet–Finnish war, corps and army staffs failed to organize the interaction of various types of reconnaissance and neglected the use of aerial reconnaissance for several weeks.[50] Lower field staffs often had no reconnaissance units at all.[51] Even when these problems were identified and corrected, staffs continued to have difficulties drafting and distributing situation reports and often falsified information to cover up their incompetence. Poor communications had also taken their toll. Staffs preferred to use the telephone and telegraph because few staff officers had been taught how to use the radio. Messages were often sent uncoded for similar reasons.[52] The General Staff's testimony also criticized staff organs for not concerning themselves with the combat training of troops, nor did the staffs analyse recent combat experience in order to modify combat techniques for future operations.[53]

The remaining impediment to improvements in operational art was the Red Army's obsolete service manuals and field regulations. Combat experience during the war vindicated many of the basic principles stated in these regulations, but more work was needed to clarify the rights, responsibilities and duties defining the relations between commanders and their superiors.[54] Voroshilov recommended the creation of a special commission composed of service chiefs and veteran commanders from the Soviet–Finnish war. Over the next few months this commission was to study all the situation reports, battle summaries, diaries and other official documents generated by the war for the purpose of making the necessary corrections, changes and additions to the old field regulations and manuals.[55]

Perhaps the most fundamental problem impeding the Red Army's ability to conduct modern warfare was the perennial disparity between the theoretical development of tactical doctrine and its execution on the battlefield. In contrast to the Finnish Army, which had an excellent tactical training programme and had demonstrated a high standard of tactical manoeuvre during the war, the Red Army's troops had received no instruction in the tactics of positional warfare or the conduct of breakthrough assaults. In many cases, entire Red Army divisions, regiments, battalions and companies received their basic training in the heat of battle.[56] Voroshilov's excuse for this appalling state of affairs was that the Red Army had recently completed its reorganization from a mixed territorial-regular cadre to a full regular cadre army and that tactical training had not yet made the transition. The defeats of the first three weeks had proven the inadequacy of the old, mixed system for instructing the Red Army rank-and-file in the complexities of combined arms warfare.[57] What the Red Army really needed, according to Voroshilov and many others in the defence establishment, was a regular cadre of troops capable of absorbing the first strikes of an enemy invasion while the main body of the army completed its mobilization.[58]

The first step was to revise the Red Army's tactical doctrine according to recent combat experience. In its report to the joint commission, the General Staff emphasized the central role played by the infantry:

> The experience [of the war] shows the direct correlation between success in combat and the combat capabilities of the infantry; its ability to use small sub-units to conduct close battle and outflanking manoeuvres, and its ability to penetrate the gaps in [the enemy's] fighting order.[59]

Close interaction between the infantry and other services would have greatly improved overall effectiveness but was rarely achieved during the recent war. The most common hindrance was the lack of communication between the infantry units and the artillery batteries which were supposed to support each other's actions. Artillery invariably became separated from infantry during combat and was usually unable to fire at specific targets due to a lack of reconnaissance patrols and forward observers. Similar communication problems between infantry and aviation meant that aviation required a minimum distance of one kilometre between their targets and the front line in order to avoid bombing their own infantry, which prevented them from having any direct tactical effect.[60] Finally, combat experience showed that tanks used in independent operations suffered unacceptable losses and that their tactics should be modified to closely interact with artillery in the support of infantry.[61] The first step towards creating this regular cadre was to improve the training of junior commanders, especially at company, platoon and section level.[62]

Stalin concluded the joint commission's confessional on 21 April by summarizing the contents of the testimonies and making general recommendations. His most important recommendation was the creation of a more specialized commission to discuss the nature of modern warfare on the basis of Timoshenko's 'wall of fire'. According to Stalin, '... in previous years we paid too much attention to ostentatious manoeuvres' and that in the future the Red Army should devote attention to promoting interaction between the services and developing a doctrine founded on real battle conditions. However, the most startling of Stalin's recommendations was that Soviet military 'ideology' required a complete re-evaluation. In order to accomplish this mammoth task, Stalin proposed that the formulation of military theory be 'democratized' by the publication of professional magazines and books so that commanders could freely criticize weapon systems and discuss the finer points of operational art and tactics.[63] Stalin even gave his blessing to the discussion about modern defence, stating that 'We must educate our commanders in the spirit of active defence (*v dukho-aktivnoi oborony*) which simultaneously includes the offensive.' He approved the shift away from the Civil War legacy to the Brusilov Offensive legacy with the comment that 'We must excavate the German, French and Russian archives on the Imperialist War in order to improve our knowledge of imperialistic and contemporary warfare.'[64] By referring to the need for 'democratization' within the command corps Stalin indicated that the increased role of military specialists in the formulation of security policy, initiated during the Soviet–Finnish war, would remain a central feature in future political–military relations. The military specialists had demonstrated their value to the Soviet state and were now allowed to recoup some of the authority they had lost during the purges.

Two days after Stalin's speech, the Main Military Soviet convened an executive commission under the chairmanship of Voroshilov to discuss the future organization of the Red Army's military-scientific work.[65] At this meeting Kulik pointed out that the executive commission's first priority was to incorporate the practical lessons of the war into Soviet military doctrine in time for the publication of the summer training programme on 15 May. After some disagreement between Kulik, Smorodinov and Pavlov over how this would best be accomplished, Voroshilov proposed that Kulik chair a special sub-commission to examine the relevant documents and draft a programme for examination by the commission. The next topic, how to interpret Stalin's comments about 'military ideology', generated more heated discussion. Mekhlis opened the debate by suggesting that someone should give a formal report to the executive commission for the purposes of free discussion and the drafting of a resolution. Kulik and Voroshilov disagreed with this proposal and stated that there was no need for a report, but they were opposed by Shtern and Kurdiumov. When Mekhlis' proposal was put to a vote, Voroshilov and Kulik were overruled by a majority of the commission's members and Mekhlis was instructed to prepare a report for presentation on 10 May.[66]

II

Absolution for the mistakes made during the war could not be given until a token sacrifice was made. Stalin performed this act of atonement by relieving Voroshilov and Shaposhnikov of their posts as Defence Commissar and Chief of the General Staff on 7 May 1940. Voroshilov was reassigned to the chairmanship of the Defence Committee and deputy chairman of the Council of Ministers where his incompetence would do less harm. Shaposhnikov was put in charge of the Main Military Engineering Directorate and made responsible for the construction of fortified regions on the Soviet Union's new western borders, not necessarily an insignificant appointment in light of the Mannerheim Line's effectiveness against mobile forces and the need to secure defences on the western border. Stalin explained to Shaposhnikov that the reason for his demotion had nothing to do with the quality of his forecasts before the war or advice during the war. Rather, the demotion was meant to be an assurance to the Soviet public and foreign observers that 'the lessons of the Soviet–Finnish conflict have been learned'.[67] In their places Stalin appointed Timoshenko and Meretskov, the engineers of the successful breakthrough against the Mannerheim Line, to act as Defence Commissar and Chief of the General Staff.[68]

The reform itself was initiated by the publication of an *Akt*, the first priority of which was to begin rationalizing the laws that defined the functions of the Red Army's central administration. Since the publication of the *Deistvuiushchee polozhenie o Narkomate Oborony* in 1934 the Defence Commissariat had made no attempt to regulate its organizational structure, and no standard procedure existed to review and rewrite field regulations and service manuals. As a consequence, the Red Army lacked regulations on the leadership of formations and units from army-level down, the attack and defence of fortified regions and the conduct of combat operations in mountainous terrain.[69] Contingency plans had to be reformulated by the General Staff in order to take into account the geo-political changes on the Soviet Union's western border since autumn 1939. Adequate information about the combat readiness of the existing fortified regions on the former border was lacking and no plans as yet existed for constructing fortified regions on the new border.[70] There was also a need to rationalize the Red Army's mobilization procedures. The partial mobilization of recruits in September 1939 revealed serious contradictions in the Red Army's mobilization plan and no efforts had been made to train the massive influx of new recruits (3.15 million men).[71] Last, but not least, the Defence Commissariat would have to take immediate measures to reform military education. Problems in the career advancement system and the rapid growth of the Red Army since 1934 contributed to an enormous deficit in command cadres: 21 per cent of its requirement for a total of 95,000 commanders.

The *Akt* also addressed the need to reform the Red Army's basic combat training programme to reflect the demands of real combat conditions. One of the causes cited as a contributing factor to the Red Army's low combat performance was the legacy of old combat training conventions inherited from the tsarist era. Shaposhnikov had noticed this tendency as early as 1929 on the occasion of the first all-union Red Army field manoeuvres. He found at this time that training techniques were over-reliant on set-piece map exercises and manoeuvres which bore little resemblance to wartime conditions.[72] Subsequent failures to improve combat training were attributed to inadequate monitoring by the Defence Commissariat and the General Staff's Combat Training Administration. The only remedy was to completely reform the tactical training programme. Timoshenko's first act as Defence Commissar was to adopt the proposals made in General Kulik's sub-commission by publishing Order Nos 120 and 160, which laid the foundation for the summer basic-training programme, based exclusively on storm group assaults against fortifications.[73] In this way Timoshenko hoped to reintroduce the Red Army to the elemental techniques of combined arms warfare.

Following the joint commission's discussion about the command corps' lack of authority with the rank-and-file, the defence establishment and the military periodical press continued to discuss the nature of relations between the ranks.[74] The strongest refutation of the 'militia principle' appeared in an article in the June 1940 edition of *Voennaia Mysl'* by Colonel A. Velikolutskii entitled 'A Few Thoughts about Military Discipline'. Reflecting an attitude toward collective effort more akin to the patriarchal ethos of the former autocracy than orthodox Marxism, Velikolutskii emphasized the central role played by discipline in society: 'The discipline of the school and the family reflects on the army, and army discipline creates good work discipline in the kholkoz and factory.'[75] Velikolutskii drew a distinction between what he called 'conscious' discipline, characterized by the individual's physical and mental mastery of technique, and 'coercive' or administrative discipline characterized by the physical imposition of a collective's values and standard operating procedures upon the individual.[76] Duplicating an argument first used by Trotsky against the Military Opposition during the Eighth Party Congress in March 1919, Velikolutskii claimed that the Red Army was different from any other organization in Soviet society due to the life-threatening nature of warfare.[77] For that reason the Red Army should be allowed to rely predominantly on the use of coercive discipline, especially when inducting large numbers of raw recruits and arming them with technologically sophisticated weaponry. With specific reference to the Soviet–Finnish war, Velikolutskii quoted Frunze to the effect that

> ... not all military workers have taken the correct approach to the question of discipline: they see order imposed from the outside as bad. This is absolute nonsense. Internal, conscious discipline must manifest itself in external order. To attain this order we must – and here it is completely unavoidable – have the well-known elements of drill and administrative pressure.[78]

The result of this discussion about 'conscious' and 'coercive' discipline was that the Red Army assumed the pre-revolutionary values and methods of the Russian Imperial Army. A new disciplinary code was issued in October 1940 which reinforced the principles of *mushtra* (drill) and the command-administrative system to replace the more egalitarian and education-oriented code of 1925. Commanders were given full authority to punish soldiers who disobeyed orders and the soldiers, in turn, lost the right to lodge complaints against their commanders. In this manner the Red Army abandoned the volunteeristic myth of the 'socialist' army which was a left-over from the Civil War and the mixed-cadre system in favour of a predominantly bureaucratic organization based on legal sanction and definition of responsibilities.[79] An adjunct of this legal reform was the introduction of senior military ranks such as 'general', 'general-major', 'general-colonel' and 'admiral', followed by the promotion of approximately 1,000 senior commanders, many of who were participants in the Soviet–Finnish War.[80]

III

On 10 May Mekhlis gave his report on the status of Soviet 'military ideology' (military doctrine in its widest sense) to the executive commission of the Main Military Soviet. Preliminary research for the report had begun as early as 14 March, the day after the end of the Soviet–Finnish war, when the Political Administration of the Red Army issued a directive ordering the collection of all paperwork generated by political commissars and workers during the war.[81] Summaries of work from every level of command (especially from sub-units) describing every phase of battle as well as the content of military-technical propaganda and the military newspapers were to be forwarded to army-level political commissariats by 25 March for transport to Moscow on 1 April. This huge collection of raw data and semi-analysed summaries was then entrusted to researchers at the Lenin Military-Political Academy who were responsible for analysing the conduct of party-political work in wartime and drafting Mekhlis' report.[82]

The executive commission's first topic for discussion was Mekhlis' revelation that political propaganda during the Soviet–Finnish war had over-emphasized the invincibility of the Red Army and had fostered complacency in the command corps and the rank-and-file.[83] Almost everyone in the executive commission admitted that this had been the case, and subsequent discussion explored the implications of this 'false' propaganda.[84] The first casualty of endemic complacency was to be found in the development of military science and the training of cadres. G. Savchenko (the deputy director for political affairs in the Artillery Administration and member of the Main Military Soviet after the reorganization of the Soviet high command in mid-December 1939) pointed out that this inflated self-image discouraged the Red Army from studying and adopting the positive features of enemy armies. Relying on impressions he had made during a trip to Germany in November 1939, and again in March and April 1940, Savchenko emphasized the effectiveness of the *Wehrmacht*'s method for training its junior officers.

> It appears that during the Polish campaign a few defects [in technique] were noticed. Battery commanders were sent on a three-week course in order to quickly correct these flaws ... The German system of training its command staff is very flexible ... The enemy [i.e. Germany] prepares to fight, he studies and is compelled to study. Whereas we, for some reason, are avoiding this issue. Given the present situation we will not have adequately cultivated commanders.[85]

These observations were supported by V. Kurdiumov, the former commander of the 8th and 15th Armies during the war, who made a statistical comparison between the percentage of trained officers in the German and French armies during the First World War and the Red Army during the recent war with Finland to argue that the Red Army was unprepared for modern war. He suggested that responsibility for combat training be unified under one authority, preferably a vice-chief of the Defence Commissariat.[86] V. Diakov further criticized the lack of work on tactics and praised the tactical legacy of the Russian Imperial army's military-scientific institutions.[87]

Although Mekhlis mentioned in his report that many rank-and-file had considered the Red Army's invasion of Finland to be an 'unjust war', no one in the executive commission was willing to hazard a comment on the political miscalculations which had led to the invasion. The only reference to political miscalculation was made by Meretskov, who commented on the incorrect use of internationalist slogans by political workers (as well as himself) at the beginning of the invasion. He added that morale rose in the ranks only when political workers portrayed the purpose of the war as a defence of the Soviet Union's north-western border against imperialist aggression.[88] Pavlov deflated the issue by stating that all the Red Army's wars were just, and then changing the subject.[89]

Stalin's recommendations concerning the traditional over-emphasis on manoeuvre warfare in Soviet military doctrine elicited further debate from the members of the commission. Pavlov was the first to voice his opinion, suggesting that many factors determined the nature of war, but that the Red Army would always come up against fortified regions and that an ideal solution would be to use manoeuvre to destroy them. In his opinion, official doctrine had sufficiently adopted the offensive spirit but changes were still needed in the attitudes of the rank-and-file:

> For twenty years we have lived with the fact that we must defend the Soviet border. Rumour has it that in 1937, during a call-up, one Red Army man dressed in civilian clothes spoke in the following manner: 'Sorry, I will not fight outside the border.' Why not? 'As a citizen of the Soviet Union I will only defend up to our Soviet border.' But the Defence Commissariat has said that we are the most offensive army[!] 'That may be so,' he said, 'but I will not cross the border.'[90]

This situation indicated a fundamental contradiction between the official doctrine of 'forward defence' and the rank-and-file perception of national sovereignty, a contradiction which needed to be corrected. Meretskov seconded Pavlov's comment by re-emphasizing the importance of the offensive and the Red Army's need to master encirclement and frontal assault operations. The only person to comment on Stalin's reference to 'active defence' was Shlemin, the chief of the General Staff Academy, who stressed the need for mobile units to conduct defence-in-depth as well as breakthrough operations.

On the issue of how to cultivate a 'wilful' command corps capable of responding to directive control, Meretskov agreed with Stalin that properly defined legal relationships between ranks would help to promote greater personal responsibility. However, he pointed out an additional moral aspect: 'Our people are afraid to say anything directly, they are afraid to spoil relations or get in an uncomfortable position and are fearful to speak the truth.' Several members of the executive commission attributed this to structural causes. Kozlov, for instance, placed blame on the collegiate decision-making process of the military soviets.

[In a military soviet] sit the regiment commander, his commissars and a few other representatives. Five people in all make the decision and all sit and stare at the regiment commander in the mouth, waiting to hear what he says, and he does not know what to say ... These superfluous representatives are a bad thing.[91]

Kozlov recommended abolishing the military soviets, the embodiment of Lenin's famous Order No. 1 and the primary symbol of a socialist army which had been reinstated by Voroshilov at the beginning of the purges in 1937.[92] Pavlov, on the other hand, focused his attention on a more obvious, but taboo issue: the purge of the command corps. 'We had so many enemies of the people that I doubt whether all of them were enemies. And here it must be said that the operation of 1937–1938, up until the arrival of comrade Beria, made us so vulnerable that we got off lightly with such an enemy as the Finns.'[93] Pavlov continued on this theme by praising the Soldier's Oath and suggesting only half-jokingly that it should be applied to a few civilians as well with the comment that

... we need only examine the Military Supply Administration to find not only enemies of the people sitting there, but fools and connivers who do everything according to the Law Code on Labour ... when they are thrown out and replaced by new people everything works much better.[94]

This was the extent of the executive commission's explicit criticism of the purges.

Discussion then turned to the reform of Soviet military doctrine. Ever since the beginning of the nineteenth century Russian military theorists had speculated on the relationship between the individual genius of the commander (military art) and the collective technique of staffs (military science) and the importance of historical experience in mediating the two realms. This debate had culminated in the debates between Trotsky and Frunze in the early 1920s in which Frunze's argument for a 'unified military doctrine', formed by the admixture of dialectical materialism and historical analysis, overturned Trotsky's more sceptical historicism.[95] Remaining within the tradition of Frunze, A. Mel'nikov, a member of Meretskov's 7th Army staff, supported Stalin's statement that the re-evaluation of contemporary doctrine should be guided by the study of past military experience. However, he criticized Stalin for his overly *a priori* condemnation of the Civil War, stating that the nature of contemporary strategy, operational art and tactics could only be elucidated by the empirical study of the First World War and the Civil War as well as

208

more recent campaigns. In his opinion, military history was the 'sacred thread' of doctrine, the command corps' body of corporate knowledge, which was not only useful for theorists drawing up contingency plans but was necessary for field commanders to carry out their orders in a resourceful and efficient manner.[96] Both Mel'nikov and his colleague Diakov recommended the study of German military doctrine and military-historical methods not only because they held that tradition in high esteem but also for the reason that 'knowing one's enemy is half the battle, to quote comrade Suvorov.'[97]

Members of the Main Military Soviet's executive commission placed great emphasis on analysing Timoshenko's recent breakthrough operation on the Karelian Isthmus but complained that this work was progressing too slowly. One of the reasons cited was that military scholars were finding that their access to primary documents about the recent war, as well as other recent campaigns, was limited by excessive 'anti-cosmopolitanism' and the 'cult of secrecy' at the General Staff and the NKVD.[98] Another reason, hinted at by Pavlov, was that many military scholars, who would have performed this research, had been eliminated by the purges.[99]

The discussion of 'military ideology' ended with suggestions about how to rewrite the Red Army's field regulations. Kozlov pointed out that contradictory slogans, such as that the Red Army was purely defensive in nature, and that it would destroy the enemy on his own territory, would have to be removed in favour of more logically consistent slogans which emphasized the spirit of the offensive even during defensive operations. He and others praised the fundamental soundness of the draft *Proekt Polevogo Ustava RKKA 1939* (PU-39) and recommended that it be issued as soon as possible to the troops after a few corrections and additional sections on defence and the assault of fortified regions had been added.

A week after this hearing on 'military ideology' had ended, Mekhlis reported to the Central Committee on the executive commission's proposals and the implications for the reform of the Political Administration. In an oblique reference to Mel'nikov's comments on the relationship between military doctrine and the historical analysis of recent wars, Mekhlis admitted that the Civil War still had some utility but repeated Stalin's thesis that the cult of the Civil War experience had become a hindrance to the future development of the Red Army.

> Today we are too fascinated with manoeuvre wars and we underestimate the struggle to break through contemporary defensive fortifications like the Maginot and Siegfried Lines and others like them … The theory and practice of contemporary fortified regions as well as combat in positional

conditions is almost completely ignored in the ranks and in the military academies.[100]

Mekhlis recommended that more emphasis should be placed on these issues, as well as the conduct of artillery and aerial bombardment and the use of tanks in breakthrough operations. He also supported Diakov's proposal to revitalize the teaching of the Russian Imperial army's historical traditions. The war with Finland had also indicated that many political commissars were incapable of leading troops or conducting party-organizational work in combat conditions because their political training had been too general and they lacked specialized military training. Mekhlis recommended reforms in political education on the basis of recent combat experience. At the end of his report Mekhlis admitted that the strength of the enemy had been under-estimated due to a lack of knowledge about the specific geographic, economic and political characteristics of the capitalist countries on the Soviet Union's borders, especially the smaller ones.[101] However, he was careful to assign blame to the defence establishment as a whole rather than implicate the high command, including himself, who were ultimately responsible.

A week later the Political Administration published a directive to complement the radical reforms in basic training outlined by Timoshenko's Order Nos 120 and 160. Many of the proposals resembled those made over the past two months: the authority of the junior commander would be increased by training him to be a specialist in military history and the conduct of contemporary tactics and by removing any unnecessary 'administrative-ness' (that is, collective decision-making) which would interfere with his responsibilities. Discipline would be strengthened by abolishing any remaining remnants of 'false democratism' and 'corrupt liberalism', and redirecting the political workers' attention to the moral-political consciousness of troops at company level. The position of the political commissar in the Red Army was further demoted in August 1940 when the Central Committee published its decree on Unitary Command (*edinonachale*), a reform originally suggested by Meretskov during the debate over basic training the previous April.[102]

This decree completed the Red Army's formal transformation from a socialist-type army to a legally sanctioned bureaucratic-type army, and ended the conflict in roles between commander and commissar which so compro-mised combat effectiveness during the Soviet–Finnish war. However, the decree only applied to the tactical level of command: collective decision-making continued to exist in the form of military soviets at operational and strategic levels. Concomitant with this reform was the Political

210

Administration's reorganization and demotion, although Mekhlis remained an influential figure in military policy formation as a member of the State Control Commission.[103]

IV

Momentous events were occurring in Western Europe while the Soviet high command deliberated on the nature of modern war. In April, Germany clashed with Britain and France in Scandinavia. In mid-May the *Wehrmacht* attacked the Allied forces via the Low Countries, once again astounding the world with its military prowess and confuting Stalin's prognosis of a drawn-out positional war between the imperialist powers.[104] The first sign of the Soviet government's response to the shift in the European balance of power came on 25 May when the Soviet Foreign Minister, Molotov, sent a note to the Lithuanian government protesting against an alleged mistreatment of two Red Army men, using similar tactics to those he had employed against Finland before the Red Army's invasion of that country in November 1939. The familiar pattern began to unfold. At the end of the month Molotov published the Soviet government's grievances against the Lithuanian government and, in mid-June, the Red Army took control of the country and a new popular-front-type government was placed in power on the basis of reformed electoral laws.[105] The process was repeated in the other Baltic States and in Northern Bukovina and Bessarabia, and by the end of the summer all these regions were formally incorporated into the Soviet Union as union republics. Although these policies were enacted to create a buffer-zone on the Soviet Union's western border they also resulted in the creation of a 3,000 kilometre-long border with Germany.

The fall of France also precipitated several changes in Soviet military policy. Following a meeting between Stalin, Shaposhnikov and his deputy, Smorodinov, in which the role of large armoured formations in contemporary warfare was discussed, the tank corps was reinstated into the Red Army's TOE by governmental decree on 6 June.[106] Later in the month, Timoshenko ordered General-Colonel Pavlov to begin construction of fortified regions on the Soviet Union's new European border. Timoshenko emphasized the importance of this policy by appointing Shaposhnikov to head the Main Military-Engineering Directorate in August 1940.[107]

However, no attempts were made to re-examine the premises of the Red Army's military doctrine. The Defence Commissariat perceived the fall of France as an inverse corollary to its experience in Finland (that is, France was a degenerate society whereas Finland was not) rather than as a revolution in warfare.[108] In mid-July General Kulik's sub-commission finally submitted recommendations for the redrafting of *Proekt Polevogo Ustava RKKA 1940* to the Main Military Soviet for ratification. Based entirely on the proposals made in April by Meretskov, Kozlov and Voronov, these recommendations reiterated the importance of Deep Battle in the initial period of a future war and redefined the standard operating procedures for conducting combined arms warfare. The offensive goal of Deep Battle was to isolate and sequentially destroy strong points in the enemy's fortified region by means of co-ordinated storm-group assaults and intensive artillery support. In the defence, Deep Battle relied on the combined use of fortified regions and screening armies for the conduct of operational manoeuvre and counter-offensives on a 'wide' front. Experience in Finland indicated that a defender could easily absorb a deep penetration by enemy mechanized formations:

> The growing fire-power of contemporary combined arms formations equipped with a large quantity of automatic weapons, mines and small calibre weapons as well as light and heavy artillery allows these formations to create a multi-layered killing zone not only in the forward zone but also within the main defensive zone within a short period of time. Due to this it is possible to enlarge a rifle division's defensive frontage and thus create an even denser grouping [of force] on the axis of the main strike. Long-term field fortifications within the defensive zone provide even greater power to the defence and allow the largest possible number of troops for a [counter] offensive.

When the main thrust of the enemy's offensive had been dissipated, the screen army in conjunction with the field army would launch their own offensive according to the principles of Deep Operations.[109]

Armed with this 'thesis', the Main Military Soviet passed a decree on 23 July defining the timetable and manner of the new doctrine's dissemination to the Red Army. Timoshenko's basic training programme would be expanded to include practical exercises in hand-to-hand combat and the fundamentals of positional and manoeuvre warfare, the techniques for overcoming obstacle zones and water barriers and the construction of basic field fortifications. Special emphasis was to be given to the individualized instruction of soldiers and small sub-units and their co-ordination in combined arms combat. The command corps was to be trained according to a series of standardized courses to be formulated no later than 1 September. Schools for junior commanders were to commence in October and last four months. *Vystrel* schools were to perfect the training of company and battalion commanders over a period of nine months, while the Frunze and General Staff Academies were to justify

The Lessons of the War

their existence by running refresher courses (KUKS, or *kursy usovershenstvo-vaniia komandnogo sostava*) for regiment, division, corps and army commanders and to familiarize those commanders with the functioning of higher commands through the use of war games. The decree stipulated that no qualifications would be granted until commanders had mastered their responsibilities and knew the regulations by heart.

The most fundamental aspect of the new doctrine, the summer basic training programme outlined in Kulik's Order No 120, had already been distributed to the troops and put into practice by company, battalion and regiment commanders. During the month of August 1940, Timoshenko toured the western military districts to supervise the conduct of three-day field exercises and verify the Red Army's progress in assimilating the basics of Deep Battle. The results were not encouraging. In a *Pravda* article published on 25 August Timoshenko stated that problems remained in combined arms interaction between units and reconnaissance.[110] The root of the problem was lack of initiative and a tendency to 'act according to established routine'. A manifestation of this tendency was 'Bolshevik offensiveness' exemplified during the Moscow Military District's verification exercises, when a division commander deployed an entire battalion to assault a mock fortified region where one or two platoons would have accomplished the mission. Timoshenko concluded his comments by re-emphasizing the need to focus the training programme on the sub-divisions up to battalion level.

Domestic observers, as well as many foreign observers, were aware that the Soviet Union's policy of forward defence depended on the Red Army's efficient performance of the defensive and offensive aspects of Deep Operations. This performance, in turn, required several generations of properly trained commanders and a rank-and-file that had memorized the regulations and had put them to practice in realistic field exercises. There were over three million untrained Red Army soldiers in the summer of 1940, and many years were needed to train them.[111] In the meantime, the Red Army faced the *Wehrmacht* alone.

NOTES

1 Tanner, *The Winter War*, pp. 252–60, and Dallin, *Soviet Russia's Foreign Policy*, pp. 190, 192. See also A. Nekrich and M. Heller, *Utopia in Power. The History of the Soviet Union from 1917 to the Present* (New York: Summit Books, 1986) p. 346, and Degras, *Soviet Documents on Foreign Policy*, Vol. III, pp. 439–46.
2 *Konflikt*, Document No. 149, 'Prikaz voiskam Severo-Zapadnogo fronta ob okonchanii boevykh deistvii, 14 marta 1940 g.', See also Pospelov, *IVOVSS*, p. 275.
3 Tanner, *The Winter War*, pp. 184, 238, 245–6, 254.

213

4 Dallin, *Soviet Russia's Foreign Policy*, pp. 195–8.
5 M. von Hagen, 'Soviet Soldiers and Officers on the Eve of the German Invasion: Towards a Description of Social Psychology and Political Attitudes', *Soviet Union/Union Soviétique*, 18, Nos. 1–3 (1991) pp. 79–101.
6 TsGASA, fond 34980, opis' 14, delo 99, 'Secretariat. Narodnogo Komissara Oborony Soiusa SSR. Inostrannye Voennye Obozrevateli o Boevykh Kachestvakh Krasnoi Armii', ll. 52–70.
7 K.C. Taylor, 'The Reorganization of the Soviet Command System for Total War: 1939–1941', p. 106. Taylor's citation is from *Nazi Conspiracy and Aggression*, Vol. VI, (Washington, DC: US Government Printing Office, 1946), pp. 981–2.
8 P.A. Aptekar, 'Opravdanny li zhertvy? (O poteriakh v sovetsko–finliandskoi voine)', *Voenno-istoricheskii zhurnal*, No. 3, 1992, pp. 43–5. Aptekar's own estimate, based on reports from divisions and brigades, suggests that a more realistic figure would be 131,476 killed and between 325,000 to 330,000 wounded and frost-bitten. As far as POWs were concerned, the Finnish Army had captured approximately 5,800 Red Army soldiers in comparison to 820 Finnish POWs. The Finns treated their prisoners well, and when the Red Army POWs were repatriated to the Soviet Union in May 1940 they wrote a letter to Field Marshal Mannerheim thanking him for the humanitarian treatment they had received. Little is known about their subsequent fate, but one Russian historian claims that they returned to a cheering Leningrad crowd, then were transported by train to a secluded area and shot. For information about the Soviet POWs see Aptekar, p. 45, Semiryaga, *Tainy stalinskoi diplomatii*, p. 167, Kumanev, 'Beslavnaia voina, ili pobeda, kotoroi ne gordilis', p. 9, and Dallin, *Soviet Russia's Foreign Policy*, p. 191.
9 Korotkov, *Istoriia sovetskoi voennoi mysli*, p. 109.
10 Voroshilov, *Doklad (Voroshilova) o sovetsko–finliandskoi voine 1939–1940 gg.*, p. 1.
11 Ibid., p. 9. Voroshilov was more than a little disingenuous in blaming the NKO's underestimation of the Finnish TVD on poor reconnaissance. Shaposhnikov, the chief of the General Staff, had drawn up realistic contingency plans in July 1939 on the basis of substantial reconnaissance but these plans had been shelved personally by Stalin and Voroshilov in favour of Meretskov's more politically correct alternative. Meretskov and his staff at the Leningrad Military District subsequently relied on old information to form their plan for a 'lightning' offensive. See *Sovetsko–finliandskaia voina 1939–1940 gg. na more*, Chast' I, Kniga I, p. 45, and Roberts, 'Prelude to Catastrophe: Soviet Security Policy Between the World Wars', p. 513.
12 Voroshilov, *Doklad (Voroshilova) o sovetsko–finliandskoi voine 1939–1940gg.*, p. 16.
13 For a specific example of this problem see the transcripts of Stalin's telephone conversation to 8th Army commander Shtern on 7 January 1940, RTsKhINDI, fond 71, opis' 25, delo 6861, ll. 411–414.
14 *Sovetsko–finliandskaia voina 1939–1940 gg. na more*, Chast' I, Kniga III, p. 131.
15 Ibid., pp. 139–40. The Baltic Fleet lost 124 of its repair specialists to the Red Army at the beginning of the war. The status of repair facilities in the Baltic Fleet's zone of operations reveals some interesting trends: the 'Orangenbaum' ship-yard at Kronstadt was able to complete only 65.5 per cent of its production plan in January and February 1940 due to poor organization of production, low quality of production work and not enough workers; the 'Serp i Molot' floating docks were sent to Tallinn with only half of its personnel; the 'Riigi Sadamatekhas' shipyard at Tallinn did good work on ship frames but was not so proficient with mechanical and electrical work; and the 'Tosmare' shipyard at Liepaja did high quality work and many ships were repaired there.
16 Ibid., p. 146.
17 This advice justified itself in June 1941 when the *Luftwaffe* managed to paralyse the Red Army's air forces in the Baltic region but failed to sink any of the Baltic Fleet's ships and inflicted relatively little damage to shore facilities. See G. Jukes, 'Nikolai Gerasimovich Kuznetsov', in *Stalin's Generals*, p. 111.
18 Korot'kov, *Istoriia sovetskoi voennoi mysli*, p. 96. See also Soloviev, *My Nine Lives in the Red Army*, pp. 27–9.

19 Voronov, *Na sluzhbe voennoi*, p. 144, and RTsKhINDI, fond 71, opis' 25, delo 6862, 'Instructions: On organizing and executing breakthrough of fortified regions'. M. Zakharov, in an unpublished manuscript of his memoirs about the General Staff in the inter-war years, noted the significance of these instructions in the history of Soviet military art but claimed that after the end of hostilities they were burnt. Cited in G.A. Kumanev, 'Vuosien 1939–1940 neuvostoliitolais – suomalaisen sodan ('talvi-sodan') tapahtumat uusien lahetymistaponjen ja dokumenttien nakokulmasta' ('1939–1940, the events of the Soviet–Finnish War from the point of view of new documents') in *Talvisota, venaja joe suomi*, ed. T. Vihavainen (Helsinki: 1991) p. 270. See also L.M. Sandalov, *Perezhitoe*, p. 50.

20 Shilovskii borrowed this concept from Triandafillov. See V.K. Triandafillov, *The Nature of the Operations of Modern Armies*, p. 69.

21 E.A. Shilovskii, *Nastupatel'naia armeiskaia operatsiia. Vypusk. 5, Osnovy operativnogo proryva* (Moscow: AGSh RKKA, Moscow, 1940) p. 16.

22 Ibid.

23 Past observers of the Red Army have accused Timoshenko and his colleagues of breaking with Tukhachevskii's doctrinal tradition of the 'manoeuvre war' on the grounds that it was suitable only for a weaker army, and adopting the doctrinal tradition of 'breakthrough war' as more suitable for a modern, sophisticated army. For examples of this criticism see S.S. Biriuzov, 'The Lessons Learned Too Well', in S. Bialer, ed., *Stalin and His Generals. Soviet Military Memoirs of World War II* (London: Souvenir Press, 1970) pp. 136–7, and Solov'ev, *My Nine Lives in the Red Army*, pp. 26–7. The present analysis does not so much regard Timoshenko's doctrine as a break, but rather as a shift in emphasis brought about by the realization that the Red Army needed to be retrained from the lowest ranks upwards as well as the middle command outwards.

24 RTsKhINDI, fond 71, opis 25, delo 6859, l.1, 'Preliminary basic conclusions on the lessons of battle on the Karelian Ithsmus'. In his review of the lessons learned, Korotkov felt the continued reliance on the establishment of a 'wide' front was the most outmoded. See Korotkov, *Istoriia sovetskoi voennoi mysli*, p. 112. For an exposition of the 'frontal strike' doctrine see Chapter 3, note 6.

25 An indication that Timoshenko's North-Western Front was using German storm-troop manuals to overcome the Mannerheim Line can be seen in TsGASA, fond 34980, opis' 6, delo 186, ll. 49–52, 'German manual on how to attack fortified gun-emplacements, 9 February, 1940'. See discussion in Chapter 4.

26 A minute-by-minute tactical and operational analysis of Aliabushev's 123rd Rifle Division is given by N.N. Korneev in his draft manuscript entitled *Boevye deistviia 50 SK po proryvu linii mannergeima* (Moscow: 1941).

27 TsGASA, fond 4, opis' 14, delo 2736 (reel 2), ll. 231–240, 'Protocol notes from the executive commission's session on weapons systems, 26 April'.

28 A.I. Starunin, 'Oborona', *Voennaia Mysl'*, No. 2, 1940, p. 92. For more details of this synthesis of Tukhachevskii and Guderian see A.V. Kirpichnikov, *Operatsii sovremennykh podvizhnykh armii* (Moscow: AGSh RKKA, 1941) pp. 186–203.

29 Voroshilov, *Doklad (Voroshilova) o sovetsko–finliandskoi voine 1939–1940gg.*, pp. 5–6. See also Voronov's comments in TsGASA, fond 4, opis' 14, delo 2736 (reel 2), l.233.

30 RTsKhINDI, fond 71, opis 25, delo 6859, ll. 2–3.

31 Ibid., p. 2, and Shtern's comments in TsGASA, fond 4, opis' 14, delo 2736 (reel 2), ll. 272.

32 Voroshilov, *Doklad (Voroshilova) o sovetsko–finliandskoi voine 1939–1940gg.*, pp. 99–100.

33 Ibid., pp. 13–14.

34 RTsKhINDI, fond 71, opis 25, delo 6859, l.4.

35 Voroshilov, *Doklad (Voroshilova) o sovetsko–finliandskoi voine 1939–1940 gg.*, p. 98.

36 Brigade Commander Shlemin became the director of the General Staff Academy in early 1938, replacing D.A. Kuchinskii who had been shot during the purges. Grigorenko describes Shlemin as a director who was adept at administration but who did not possess a 'comprehensive military outlook' on a par with that of his predecessor. See P. Grigorenko, *Memoirs*, trans. by Thomas A. Witney (London: Norton, 1982) p. 92.

37 TsGASA, fond 4, opis' 14, delo 2736, ll. 301–302, 'Protocol notes of Kulik's sub-commission meeting on 21 April, 1940'.
38 RTsKhINDI, fond 71, opis 25, delo 6859, l.4. See also Kirshin, *Dukhovnaia gotovnost' sovetskogo naroda k voine*, p. 368.
39 C. Roberts, 'Prelude to Catastrophe: Soviet Security Policy Between the World Wars', p. 491. Volkogonov quotes slightly higher numbers for a shorter period of time: 36,761 between May 1937 and September 1938. See D. Volkogonov, *Stalin: Triumph and Tragedy* (London: Weidenfeld and Nicolson, 1991) p. 367.
40 Volkogonov, *Stalin: Triumph and Tragedy*, pp. 367–8.
41 Comments made by E.A. Shchadenko, TsGASA, fond 4, opis' 14, delo 2736, l.305.
42 Erickson, *The Road to Stalingrad*, p. 18.
43 M.A. Gareev, *Obshchevoiskovye ucheniia* (Moscow: 1990) p. 119.
44 Ibid.
45 RTsKhINDI, fond 71, opis 25, delo 6859, l.4.
46 TsGASA, fond 4, opis' 14, delo 2736, l.231.
47 RTsKhINDI, fond 71, opis 25, delo 6859, l.5.
48 Ibid., pp. 6,9. See also Voroshilov, *Doklad (Voroshilova) o sovetsko–finliandskoi voine 1939–1940gg.*, p. 13.
49 Comment made by Sivkov (Rank and first name unknown), TsGASA, fond 4, opis' 14, delo 2736, l.304.
50 According to a study on the Baltic Fleet's airforce during the Soviet–Finnish war, entitled *Boevye deistviia VVS KBF v voine s belofinnami (s 30 noiabria 1939 g. po 13 marta 1940 g.)* conducted by the Naval Commissariat, the Reconnaissance Department at Baltic Fleet command headquarters at Kronstadt was completely disorganized and had to be completely reformed while the war was in progress. No all-weather, long-range aircraft had been fitted with cameras in the early stage of the war, and when they were, the Reconnaissance Department's laboratory was unable to process film fast enough. No one had experience with aerial photography of quadrants, perspective photos, or photography of road systems. When the photograph reconnaissance became available for operational use, most pilots and their crews were not sufficiently trained to read it. See *Boevye deistviia VVS KBF*, pp. 6, 105–6.
51 RTsKhINDI, fond 71, opis 25, delo 6859, l.16, and Voroshilov, *Doklad (Voroshilova) o sovetsko–finliandskoi voine 1939–1940gg.*, p. 100.
52 RTsKhINDI, fond 71, opis 25, delo 6859, ll. 10, 26. Since the late 1920s, Soviet military theorists had minimilized the role of the radio because of the difficulty in preserving the security of transmissions. Zhukov, in the unexpurgated edition of his memoirs, mentions that Stalin undervalued the importance of radio communications for the conduct of modern manoeuvre operations. On the eve of the German invasion in 1941 the Red Army's defence establishment was unable to convince Stalin to mobilize the mass production of radios. See G.K. Zhukov, *Vospominaniia i razmyshleniia*, Vol. 1 (Moscow: Novosti, 1990) p. 315. See also J.J. Schneider, 'Introduction', in V.K. Triandafillov, *The Nature of the Operations of Modern Armies*, p. xxxiv.
53 RTsKhINDI, fond 71, opis 25, delo 6859, ll. 8,9.
54 Ibid., p. 5.
55 Voroshilov, *Doklad (Voroshilova) o sovetsko–finliandskoi voine 1939–1940gg.*, p. 100.
56 Ibid., pp. 6, 13. See also RTsKhINDI, fond 71, opis 25, delo 6859, l.2.
57 Gareev, *Obshchevoiskovye ucheniia*, p. 122.
58 Voroshilov, *Doklad (Voroshilova) o sovetsko–finliandskoi voine 1939–1940gg.*, p. 97. During the discussion, Meretskov made the following comment about the legacy of the mixed territorial-regular cadre system: 'All mistakes [in the battlefield] come from the mis-match between regular-cadre and old territorial cadre. As a consequence, the troops do not know their true profession.' See Meretskov's comments, TsGASA, fond 4, opis' 14, delo 2736, l.300, and Gareev, *Obshchevoiskovye ucheniia*, p. 122.
59 RTsKhINDI, fond 71, opis 25, delo 6859, l.2.
60 Ibid.,p. 23. In a sub-commission on the use of the Soviet airforce one proposal was made

The Lessons of the War

to improve the tactical effectiveness of aviation by adopting the German *Luftwaffe*'s technique of dive-bombing. Suggestions were made to send a team of pilots to Germany for instruction in this technique. See TsGASA, fond 4, opis' 14, delo 2768, l.125, 'Additional comments to proposals made by the commission on military air forces, 22 April'.

61 RTsKhINDI, fond 71, opis 25, delo 6859, l.21.

62 Ibid., p. 4, and Meretskov's comments, TsGASA, fond 4, opis' 14, delo 2736, l.300. Recommendations were made to establish NCO schools in every military district for this purpose. The most vocal on this topic were Meretskov and Shtern.

63 Stalin's use of the term 'demokratizatsiia' in this instance most closely approximates a concept developed in the Russian Imperial General Staff at the turn of the century concerning the appropriate division of labour between the supreme commander and his subordinate field commanders via the General Staff. The main proponent of 'demokratizatsiia' in military art was E.I. Martynov who, in an influential monograph entitled *Strategiia v epokhu Napoleona* I *i v nashe vremiia* (St Petersburg: 1894) stated that '... rational, conscious initiative is needed, without which it would be impossible to control modern armies. This depends on the culture of the people, on their political and social structures ... Military training must now enter the cultural sphere, without it the army becomes a lifeless, machine-like mass.' Quoted in Van Dyke, *Russian Imperial Military Doctrine and Education, 1832–1914*, pp. 108–9.

64 TsGASA, fond 4, opis 14, delo 2768, ll. 64–65, 'Notes of the instructions of Stalin at the meeting of the Commission of the Main Military Soviet on 21 April 1940 in the Kremlin'. Stalin's speech marked the beginning of wider discussion in the Red Army about military theory and policy. G. Zhukov summed up this 'democratization' process in the following way: 'In the recent past a spirited revival in military thought can be observed in our army. Discussions and conversations in military theory, lectures and reports in the armed forces on topics in military history and military theory, the blossoming of discussions in military publications on urgent contemporary issues, the sudden interest of military newspapers and military journals in vital military topics of the day – all indicate the development of military thought and the predilection of many commanders for military theory.' G. Zhukov, 'God perestroiki', *Krasnaia zvezda*, 23 February 1941, cited in Korotkov, *Istoriia sovetskoi voennoi mysli*, p. 112.

65 The Main Military Soviet at this time consisted of the following people: Voroshilov, Kulik, Shchadenko, Mekhlis, Budennyi, Timoshenko, Shaposhnikov, Shtern, Kurdiumov, Grendal, Smorodinov, Pavlov, Smushkevich, Zaporozhets, Khrulev, Rychagov, Ptukhin, Bogomolov, Voronov, Nikishev, Zlobin, Kirponos, Klich, Kozlov, Khrenov, Kovalev.

66 TsGASA, fond 4, opis' 14, delo 2736, ll. 144–145. The Main Military Soviet's agenda from 25 April to 8 May was the following:

- April 25, G.K. Savchenko's report on artillery weapons systems.
- April 26, Brigade Engineer Sklizkov's report on infantry weapons systems.
- May 4, Corps Commander Pavlov's and Chief of Artillery Voronov's reports on the equipment of automobile transport units. The Division Commander Alekseev's report on aviation weapons systems.
- May 5, Continuation of Alekseev's report (on bombers, fighters, reconnaissance aviation, airplane motors, aviation signals, and specialized airplanes). Then Division Commander Naidenov's report on communications systems.
- May 7, Brigade Commander Petrov's report on engineering weapons systems (on bridge construction, road and auxiliary road construction, forest clearing, railroad construction, construction of positional defences, drainage, obstacles and camouflage). Then Brigade Commander Mel'nikov's report on chemical weapons systems (including chemical defence, de-gasing, and chemical offensive weapons).
- May 8, Division Commander Kotov on fuel and lubrication distribution.

67 O. Rzheshevsky, 'Boris Mikhailovich Shaposhnikov', in *Stalin's Generals*, p. 225.

68 Erickson, *The Soviet High Command*, p. 552, and Volkogonov, *Stalin: Triumph and Tragedy*, p. 367.

69 E.I. Ziuzin, 'Gotovil li SSSR preventivnyi udar?' *Voenno-istoricheskii zhurnal*, No. 1, 1992, pp. 7–9.
70 Ibid., p. 8. See also R.E. Tarleton, 'What Really Happened to the Stalin Line?' Part II, *Journal of Soviet Military Studies*, Vol. 6, No. 1, March 1993, p. 40.
71 Ziuzin, 'Gotovil li SSSR preventivnyi udar?' *Voenno-istoricheskii zhurnal*, p. 9.
72 Ibid., p. 10. See also Gareev, *Obshchevoiskovye ucheniia*, pp. 101–2.
73 Zhukov, *Vospominaniia i razmyshleniia*, Vol. 1, pp. 286–8.
74 Erickson, *The Soviet High Command*, p. 554.
75 A.A. Velikolutskii, 'Nekotorye mysli o voinskoi distsipline', *Voennaia Mysl'*, No. 6, June 1940, p. 3.
76 This concept of discipline resembles the nineteenth century Slavophile distinction between 'inner' and 'external' truth. Andrzej Walicki, a historian of Russian social philosophy, explains the distinction: 'The inner truth is in the individual the voice of conscience, and in society the entire body of values enshrined in religion, tradition, and customs – in a word, all values that together form an inner unifying force and help to forge social bonds based on shared moral convictions. The external truth, on the other hand, is represented by law and the state, which are essentially conventional, artificial and "external"'. See A. Walicki, *A History of Russian Thought from the Enlightenment to Marxism* (Palo Alto: Stanford University Press, 1979) p. 96.
77 M. von Hagen, *Soldiers of the Proletarian Dictatorship. The Red Army and the Soviet Socialist State, 1917–1930* (Ithaca: Cornell University Press, 1990) pp. 58, 224–6.
78 Velikolutskii, 'Nekotorye mysli o voinskoi distsipline', p. 9.
79 Erickson, *The Road to Stalingrad* (London: Weidenfeld and Nicolson, 1975), p. 21, and Taylor, 'The Reorganization of the Soviet Command System for Total War: 1939–1941', p. 115.
80 For instance, Timoshenko, Shaposhnikov and Kulik were promoted to Marshal, Zhukov and Meretskov were promoted to full General, Galler and Isakov became Admirals, and Aliabushev, Kirponos, Voronov and Kurdiumov were promoted to lesser generalships. See Taylor, 'The Reorganization of the Soviet Command System for Total War: 1939–1941', pp. 108–9, and Erickson, *The Road to Stalingrad*, pp. 18, 38.
81 *Partiino-Politicheskaia rabota v Krasnoi Armii. Dokumenty, iiul' 1929 g. – mai 1941 g.* (Moscow: Voenizdat, 1985), pp. 412–13.
82 Volkogonov, *Stalin: Triumph and Tragedy*, p. 394. See also Volkogonov, 'The Drama of the Decisions of 1939', *Soviet Studies in History*, Vol. 29, No. 3, Winter 1990–91, pp. 26–7.
83 Ibid. See TsGASA, fond 4, opis' 14, delo 2736, ll. 33–133, for the protocols of the discussion.
84 See the comments of Pavlov and Savchenko, TsGASA, fond 4, opis' 14, delo 2736, ll. 38–41, 61.
85 TsGASA, fond 4, opis' 14, delo 2736, ll. 59–61.
86 Ibid., l.121.
87 Ibid., ll. 97–98.
88 Ibid., l.44.
89 Ibid., l.36.
90 Ibid.
91 Ibid., l.109.
92 Taylor, 'The Reorganization of the Soviet Command System for Total War: 1939–1941', p. 82.
93 TsGASA, fond 4, opis' 14, delo 2736, l.38.
94 Ibid., ll. 38–39.
95 For a detailed summary of this debate see W.D. Jacobs, *Frunze: The Soviet Clausewitz, 1885–1925* (The Hague: 1969) pp. 24–88. For more recent interpretations see A. Gat, *The Development of Military Thought. The Nineteenth Century* (Oxford: Clarendon Press, 1992), pp. 239–43, and J.J. Schneider, 'The Origins of Soviet Military Science', *Journal of Soviet Military Studies*, Vol. 2, No. 4, December 1989, pp. 507–16.
96 Compare these sentiments with those expressed by N.P. Mikhnevich, Professor of Military

Art and Director of the Nicholas Academy of the General Staff at the turn of the century, who felt that an understanding of the processes in military history was vital for the field commander's comprehension and manipulation of the diverse circumstances existing on the battlefield: '... without a hand on the "historical pulse" defining the elements of a nation's forces at a given time the commander will not master sufficient wisdom in defining those circumstances which exist in the given war.' N.P. Mikhnevich, *Strategiia*, Kniga I, (St Petersburg: 1911) p. 13. Cited in Van Dyke, *Russian Imperial Military Doctrine*, p. 143.

 97 TsGASA, fond 4, opis' 14, delo 2736, l.77.
 98 Ibid., comments by Pavlov, Mel'nikov and Kurdiumov, ll. 40, 76, 121. See also Kirshin, *Dukhovnaia gotovnost' sovetskogo naroda k voine*, pp. 421–2.
 99 TsGASA, fond 4, opis' 14, delo 2736, l.41.
100 L. Mekhlis, '"O rabote Politicheskogo Upravleniia Krasnoi Armii", Iz doklada Politicheskogo Upravleniia Krasnoi Armii Tsentral'nomu Komitetu VKP(b) o rabote Politicheskogo Upravleniia Krasnoi Armii, 23 mai 1940 g.', *Izvestiia TsK KPSS*, No. 3, 1990, p. 199.
101 Ibid., p. 200.
102 Kuz'min, *Na strazhe mirnogo truda*, p. 271.
103 Erickson, *The Road to Stalingrad*, pp. 22–3.
104 Dallin, *Soviet Russia's Foreign Policy*, p. 231.
105 Rei, *The Drama of the Baltic Peoples*, pp. 282–97.
106 At this time Pavlov was replaced by Fedorenko and took up command of the Western Military District. Taylor, 'The Reorganization of the Soviet Command System for Total War: 1939–1941', p. 124.
107 Tarleton, 'What Really Happened to the Stalin Line?', *Journal of Slavic Military Studies*, Part II, Vol. 6, No. 1, March 1993, pp. 34, 41–2.
108 For an example of this interpretation see Jones, 'Just Wars and Limited Wars', pp. 48–9.
109 TsGASA, fond 4, opis'14, delo 2768, ll. 81–89. These guidelines still needed elaboration. At the end of October 1940 the Defence Commissariat established the Main Commission for Manuals consisting of Budennyi as chairman with N.F. Vatutin, N.N. Voronov, L.A. Govorov and D.M. Karbyshev as members. This commission met to finalize the work of Kulik's sub-commission but for some reason the draft was never completed. See Erickson, *The Road to Stalingrad*, p. 30
110 TsGASA, fond 34980, opis' 14, delo 109, ll. 2–6, 'Newspaper article entitled "Reformy Russkoi Armii", published in the *Nazional-Zeitung*, (Switzerland) on 22 October 1940'. Translated by the General Staff's Intelligence Administration on 27 November 1940. See also S.K. Timoshenko, 'O takticheskoi podgotovke voisk', *Voprosi taktiki v sovetskikh voennykh trudakh (1917–1940 gg.)*, pp. 123–8.
111 Kirshin claims that there were 3,155,000 untrained soldiers in the Red Army in the summer of 1940. See Kirshin, *Dukhovnaia gotovnost' sovetskogo naroda k voine*, p. 379.

EPILOGUE

In the introduction to his seminal study, *The Diplomacy of the Winter War* (1961), Max Jakobson aptly compares the Soviet Union's war with Finland to a game of blindman's bluff and suggests that future historians will find 'a great confusion of misunderstanding, misinformation and mis-directed suspicion and fear', rather than any devious stratagems or master plan. Recourse to archives and previously restricted secondary sources has introduced new issues and has shed new light on existing interpretations but, for the most part, the new sources bear out Jakobson's prognosis.

As regards the diplomatic aspect of Soviet security policy, the first speculation concerns the causes for the breakdown in Soviet–Finnish negotiations prior to the war. Several historians in the West, namely Upton (1974) and Spring (1986), have characterized Stalin's negotiating stance up to the end of October 1939 as 'friendly', and his willingness to offer alternative proposals as 'reasonable' and 'moderate', thus apportioning some of the blame for the rupture in relations to the Finnish Cabinet, and specifically to the Finnish Foreign Minister, Erkko. Likewise, Russian historians continue to attribute the failure of the negotiations to diplomatic intrigue between Finland, Germany and the Entente. There can be no doubt that the Finnish Cabinet explored its options with the European powers from 1935 up to the summer of 1939, as the government's reception of Generals von der Goltz, Kirke and Halder indicate, but there is little evidence that these contacts retained any significant influence on the Cabinet's decisions in the autumn of 1939. Given the Soviet Union's *volte-face* in relations with Nazi Germany and the pre-emptive character of its relations with the Baltic States a few weeks later, the Finnish Cabinet had every reason to suspect Stalin's overtures concerning the defence of the Baltic region. Stalin's insistent proposals for the lease of Hangö and the alteration of the border on the Karelian Isthmus and Rybachii Peninsula might have seemed innocuous in isolation, but within the context of 'forward defence' (a policy well understood by Finland's political leaders

221

at the time) they were sufficient to warrant the Finnish Cabinet's refusal to continue the negotiations.

Speculation also surrounds Stalin's motives for deciding to go to war and the timing of that decision. Spring calls attention to several good reasons for *not* going to war in late November 1939, namely the onset of winter, the unpredictability of Germany's response, and the obvious inability of the Red Army's command corps to conduct modern warfare after the recent purges (while omitting the suggestion that another few weeks of diplomatic tension and military mobilization would have exhausted finances and eroded public confidence in the Finnish government, forcing it to make concessions). Spring argues that Stalin continued to hope for a peaceful resolution up to the final hours before the Red Army's invasion on 30 November. Although these considerations may have played a role, other interpretations and new information present a different picture.

Under pressure to extend the Soviet Union's buffer zone westward after the *Wehrmacht*'s rapid victories in Poland, frustrated by his inability to conclude a mutual assistance pact or its territorial equivalent with Finland, and encouraged by the Red Army's seemingly improved performance at Khalkhin-Gol, the 'liberation' of Poland and the ingression of the Baltic States, Stalin decided in late October to prepare for a 'preventive war' (a lightning offensive to forestall 'indirect' or even 'direct' aggression by Germany or the Entente) against Finland. Recent Russian historiography (Volkogonov, 1991, 1993, and Noskov, 1990) supports the long-standing hypothesis that Stalin expected little military opposition from Finland on the basis of ideological preconceptions and biased reports from Voroshilov, Beria and Derevianskii and that, on 29 October 1939, the Defence Commissariat altered the existing contingency plan (defence, followed by a counter-offensive) in favour of a plan for a lightning offensive on a wide front. Vihavainen (1987) convincingly explains Stalin's ideological rationale for not officially threatening war against Finland during the final phase of the Soviet–Finnish negotiations, planning a pre-emptive invasion of Finland's entire territory, and failing to issue ultimatums before the rupture in Soviet–Finnish relations or a declaration of war after the rupture. In addition, the present work interprets Molotov's initiation of 'demonstrative diplomacy' on 31 October (recognized as such by Mannerheim, 1953, and Dallin, 1942), the genesis of the proxy Finnish People's Republic in mid-November, and the border provocations on the Karelian Isthmus and Rybachii Peninsula in late November as further mechanisms in Stalin's preparation for a preventive war. In this manner, responsibility for both the failure of the negotiations and the subsequent invasion rest with Stalin and those political figures in his immediate entourage who shared his ideological preconceptions.

Epilogue

Jakobson's allusion to blindman's bluff is even more appropriate when applied to the Red Army's attempt to execute Stalin's security policy in the field. Western historians, and to an increasing degree their Russian counterparts, all agree that the Red Army simply was not prepared for the imminent ordeal in the forests and on the snow-bound roads of Finland. At this point opinion diverges: some historians seek explanation by referring to the purges and/or the mixed territorial-regular cadre system while other historians point to more specific factors such as unrealistic planning, inefficient logistics, lack of reconnaissance and poor discipline in the ranks. However, the most inclusive interpretation, first expressed by Mannerheim (1953) and Erickson (1962) and more recently by Kirshin (1990), von Hagen (1991) and Roberts (1992), places the blame on the obsolescence of the Red Army's military doctrine.

Kirshin, a trained practitioner and prolific commentator on Soviet military philosophy, portrays doctrine as a potentially integrated, logically consistent and predictive body of thought. Using didactic examples from a vast array of sources, Kirshin argues that this holistic doctrine was distorted by Stalin's imposition of the command-administrative system on the Red Army and other social institutions, resulting in the Red Army's dismal performance and excessive casualties during the war with Finland. Roberts, in turn, concentrates on the military-technical content of doctrine. Observing that the Red Army forsook Tukhachevskii's theories to return to the linear tactics of the First World War, Roberts poses the hypothesis that the Red Army was caught between two conceptions of contemporary warfare, positional and manoeuvre, and that the purges rendered its command corps unable to respond to the 'revolution' in warfare that the *Wehrmacht* had supposedly inaugurated in Poland a few months previously. The present study indicates that there was, in fact, a shift from manoeuvre on a wide front to a frontal strike on a narrow front, but interprets the shift as an adjustment in the organization of combined arms combat within the conceptual constraints of Tukhachevskii's theory of Deep Battle rather than an ambivalence between two reified concepts of warfare. The third and most innovative interpretation of doctrine is offered by von Hagen who has focused his attention on the social psychology of the Red Army, especially the 'political-moral condition' of the rank-and-file as manifested in 'extraordinary occurrences' (accidents, suicides and self-mutilations, drunkenness, etc.) in the political reports written by various agencies. All three historians reach the same general conclusion despite a wide divergence in methods and source material: the Red Army failed to draw the appropriate lessons from the Soviet–Finnish war or perform the requisite institutional restructuring due to the dogmatism of Stalin's régime.

223

Although these conceptions of doctrine have been helpful in suggesting new ways to examine the paralysis which plagued the Red Army and which compromised the execution of Stalin's security policy, they remain too abstract to define the specific causes of that paralysis. The primary aim of the present book has been to address this issue by examining the day-to-day experience of the Red Army. The result is a more highly defined picture of the Red Army's wartime experience, including the creation of the North-Western Front, Timoshenko's willingness to experiment with directive control and borrow foreign tactical techniques, and Stalin's joint convocation of the Party, state and military leadership to re-examine the war effort both during and after the war. Far from being a complete fiasco, as Kirshin, Roberts, von Hagen and others have suggested, the Soviet–Finnish war appears to have stimulated a profound reform of Soviet military doctrine and institutions, reforms which came to fruition only by the second half of the Great Patriotic War.

BIBLIOGRAPHY

I. ARCHIVAL SOURCES

AVP Rossiia – *Arkhiv Vneshnoi Politikii Rossiia* (Archive of Foreign Policy, Russia).

-fond 0135, opis' 22, papka 145, delo 1,

-ll. 4–14, 'Diary of the Soviet Ambassador to Finland, comrad Derevianskii, 20 January 1939'.

-l. 16, 'To Deputy People's Commissar NKID comrade Potemkin, 17 May 1939'.

-l. 17, 'To Deputy of the Department of the Baltic States, comrade Vasiukov, 13 July 1939'.

-l. 18, 'To the Department of the Baltic States, 13 September 1939'.

-l. 19, 'To Vasiukov, 25 September 1939'.

-ll. 22–23, 'To the Deputy People's Commissar, comrade V.G. Dekanozov, from a verifier of Soviet affairs in Finland, Eliseev, 12 November 1939'.

-fond 0135, opis' 22, 1939, delo 4, (From the Diary of V.P. Potemkin)

-ll. 13–15, 'Welcome to Emmissary from Finland, Mr. Yrjö-Koskinen, 11 September 1939'.

-fond 0135 opis' 22, 1939, delo 11,

-ll. 14–16, 'Finnish reactions to the Soviet–German Pact and Molotov's Speech, sent by Derevianskii and received at NKID, 16 September 1939'.

-fond 0135, opis' 23, 1940, delo 2, (NKID, Department of the Baltic States)

-l. 6–9, 'USA and relations with Finland, 10 February, 1940'.

-l. 12–16, 'Short Review of new paper of the People's Government of the Finnish Democratic Republic from December 1939 to 15 February 1940'.

-l. 21, 'Summary of international aid to White Finland, 4 March 1940'.

-l. 30, 'Short summary on the creation of a defensive union between Finland

and the Scandinavian countries, prepared by the Department of the Baltic States, 17 April 1940'.

-ll. 49–62, 'To Molotov. Informational letter on Finnish–Swedish relations, 12 September 1940'.

-ll. 71–73, 'Notes from Report on the organization of information on the Finnish events and on measures to distribute received information on this question, 21 February 1940'.

-fond 0351 opis' 23, 1940, delo 23, (cekr. ref. po Finliandii),

-ll. 14–16, 'From Deputy of Department of Baltic States to Vyshinskii, 30 September 1940'.

-ll. 35–49, 'To Molotov. Informational letter on Finnish–German relations in connection with the transit of German troops across the territory of Finland, 27 November 1940'.

-l. 52, 'From Deputy People's Commissar for Internal Affairs, comrade Merkulov to NKID, 29 December 1940'.

-fond 06, 1940, opis' 2, papka 25, delo 316,

-l. 3, 'Welcome of Finnish Emissary Paasikivi, 27 June 1940'.

-l. 9, 'Welcome … 3 July 1940'.

-l. 11, 'Treaty of USSR and Finland over the Åland Islands, 24 July 1940'.

-ll. 20–23, 'Welcome … 27 September 1940'.

-l. 35, 'Welcome … 9 October 1940'.

-l. 41, 'Welcome … 1 November 1940'.

-l.64, 'Text of Severe Reprimand to the Finnish Emissary, 31 October 1940'.

-l. 66, 'Welcome … 19 November 1940'.

-l. 69, 'Welcome … 3 December 1940'.

-ll. 73–75, 'Welcome … Special Papka, Top Secret, 6 December 1940'.

-ll. 78–81, 'Welcome … 18 December 1940'.

RTsKhINDI – *Rossiiskii tsentr' khranenii i izuchenii dokumenti noveishii istorii* (Russian Centre for the Preservation and Study of Documents of Recent History, formerly the Central Party Archives).

-fond 71, opis' 25, delo 41, 'North-West Front Directive for the capture of Viborg, 27 February 1940'.

-fond 71, opis' 25, delo 42, 'Main Military Council to the North-Western Front, Operational Review, 14 March 1940'.

-fond 71, opis' 25, delo 46, 'Main Military Council to the Leningrad Military District on deficiencies in tactics, 3 December 1939'.

-fond 71, opis' 25, delo 47, 'Main Military Council to Stavka, 9 December, 1939'.

-fond 71, opis' 25, delo 51, 'Stavka to North-Western Front on 17 February 1940'.

Bibliography

-fond 71, opis' 25, delo 52, 'Main Military Council announcement of Peace Treaty negotiations, 13 March 1940'.

-fond 71, opis' 25, delo 54, 'Voroshilov/Shaposhnikov warning to Meretskov, 2 December 1939'.

-fond 71, opis' 25, delo 59, 'NKO on the formation of the North-Western Front, 7 January 1940'.

-fond 71, opis' 25, delo 6859, 'Preliminary basic conclusions on the lessons of battle on the Karelian Ithsmus'.

-fond 71, opis' 25, delo 6861,
  -ll. 411–414, 'Record of direct telephone conversation between Stalin and Komkorps Shtern, 7 January 1940'.

-fond 71, opis' 25, delo 6862, 'NKO, plan to overcome enemy defences, Directive No. 4522, 20 January 1940'.

-fond 71, opis' 25, delo 6865, 'North-Western Front, Order No. One, 9 January, 1940'.

-fond 71, opis' 25, delo 6867, 'Stavka to North-Western Front, early March'.

-fond 71, opis' 25, delo 6872, 'North-Western Front, On eliminating problems in command, 27 February 1940'.

-fond 71, opis' 25, delo 6873, 'North-Western Front, Instructions on how to overcome fortified fire points, 26 February 1940'.

-fond 71, opis' 25, delo 6873, 'North-Western Front to 7th, 13th Army, 26 February 1940'.

-fond 71, opis' 25, delo 6874, 'North-Western Front, Instructions on the Use of Artillery, 16 February 1940'.

-fond 71, opis' 25, delo 6876, 'North-Western Front, Timoshenko's instructions after inspection, 9 February 1940'.

-fond 71, opis' 25, delo 6877, 'Main Military Council Directive on the creation of the 13th Army'.

-fond 71, opis' 25, delo 6884, 'Estonian military attaché, 11 March 1940'.

-fond 71, opis' 25, delo 6890, 'Estonian military attaché, 24 April 1940'.

-fond 71, opis' 25, delo 6982, 'Communication between the Department of Political Administration of the Leningrad Military District and the NKO on gifts for troops at the front, 15 January 1940'.

-fond 74 (K. Voroshilov), opis' 1, delo 163, ll. 40–68, 'Voroshilov's report to the IV Extraordinary Session of the Supreme Soviet USSR, 31 August 1939, on the new Law on Universal Military Duty'.

-fond 77 (A. Zhdanov), opis' 1, delo 886, ll. 28–33, manuscript of article by A. Zhdanov circa October 1939: 'War or Peace'.

-fond 522, (O. Kuusinen) opis' 1, delo 42,
  -ll. 1–14, 'Draft of propaganda leaflet addressed by the Central Committee

of the Finnish Communist Party, 30 November 1939'.

-ll. 16–19, 'From the Political Administration of the Leningrad Military District, "Against whom we are fighting", Leningrad, 1939'.

-fond 522, opis' 1, delo 45, ll. 10–14, 'Kuusinen, letter to Stalin on his 60th birthday, 21 December 1939'.

-fond 522, opis' 1, delo 46,

-l. 1, Draft of 'Announcement of the Formation of the People's Government of Finland (in Finnish), 1 December 1939'.

-ll. 10–17, 'Informational Notes: On the conduct of mass-political and organizational work in the rural areas and villages of Eastern Finland, seized by the units of the Red Army'.

-ll. 18–22, 'Informational Notes: On the conduct of mass-political and organizational work … 28 January 1940'.

-ll. 34–40, 'Project Instructions: How to begin the political and organization work of communists in the regions liberated from the White Finns'.

-l. 42, 'Military Oath of the People's Army of Finland'.

-ll. 43–49, 'Plan for work brigades on servicing population centers during February (1940)'.

-fond 522, opis' 1, delo 47,

- (between l. 59 and l. 60), 'Brochure, from Political Administration of the Army, "What the White Finnish Prisoners say", March 1940.

-ll. 4–13, 'Notes of conversations with prisoners, 29 January 1940'.

-ll. 14–15, 'A conversation with a prisoner, 18 February 1940'.

-ll. 22–27, 'A conversation with a White Finnish Officer, 19 February 1940'.

-ll. 58–59, 'A conversation with a White Finnish Soldier, 6 March 1940'.

-fond 522, opis' 1, delo 123, ll.126–132, 'Report: On the military activities of units and subdivisions of the 3rd Infantry Division of the People's Army of Finland, 4 March 1940'.

TsGASA – *Tsentral'nyi gosudarstvennyi arkhiv sovetskoi armii* (Central State Archive of the Soviet Army). Recently renamed as RGVA – *Rossiiskii gosudarstvennyi voennyi arkhiv* (Russian State Military Archive).

-fond 4, opis' 14, delo 2736,

-ll. 134–145, 'Protocol notes of the Main Military Council's executive commission, 23 April 1940'.

-ll. 152–240, 'Protocol notes from the Commission's session on weapons systems, 26 April'.

-ll. 242–305, 'Protocol notes of Kulik's sub-commission meeting on 21 April 1940'.

–fond 4, opis' 14, delo 2737 (reel 1), 'Projected Field Regulations, 1940, 13 July 1940'.

-ll. 139–143, 'Proposals of the Commission of Deputy People's Commissar com. Kulik on Project Field Regulations 1939, 23 July 1940'.

-l. 183, 'Comments and Supplements to the tenth chapter of PU-40 "Defence"'.

–fond 4, opis' 14, delo 2768,

-ll. 64–65, 'Notes of the instructions of Stalin at the meeting of the Commission of the Main Military Council on 21 April 1940 in the Kremlin'.

-ll. 81–89, 'From the Main Military Council: On the measures to be taken on military training, organization, and status of troops of the Red Army on the basis of the experience of the war with Finland and the battle experience of the past several years, 23 July 1940'.

-ll. 114–118, 'From the Main Military Council: On the securing of regulations for the Red Army written on the basis of the experience of past wars'.

-l. 123–125, 'Additional comments to proposals made by the commission on military air forces, 22 April'.

–fond 4, opis' 18, delo 49, 'Protocol No. 6, Meeting of the Main Military Council RKKA, 21 November 1939'.

–fond 25888, 'Catalogue of opisi on the Leningrad Military District'.

–fond 25888, opis' 15, delo 458,

-ll. 82–115, 'Regulations on the Field Administration of the RKKA, Separate Armies, 26 March 1939'.

-ll. 73–79, 'Order of the NKO, No. 0040, 4 September 1938', (Dissolution of Far Eastern Front, trial of Bliukher).

–fond 25888, opis' 15, delo 475, 'Summary of the conduct of methodical meeting of the high command and political personnel of the Air Force of the Leningrad Military District, 15–17 March 1939'.

–fond 25888, opis' 15, delo 522, ll. 16–20, 'Distribution of Responsibilities in the Operational Section of the Staff of the Leningrad Military District for 1940, 13 September 1940'.

–fond 25888, opis' 15, delo 530,

-ll. 32–38, 'Regulations: Administration of the Polit-propaganda of the Leningrad Military District Front and its Sections, 25 November 1940'.

-ll. 111, 'Regulations on the work of the Section on Battle Training Administration of a Front, 16 November 1940'.

–fond 25888, opis' 15, delo 531, ll. 16–42, 'Projected Instructions on organization of Front administration, 22 December 1940'.

–fond 25888, opis' 15, delo 532, ll. 1–3, 'Operational plan for Anti-Air Defenses around Leningrad', 1940–41.

-fond 34980, 'Catalogues of Opisi Nos. 2, 5, 6, 7, 8, 10, 11, 12, 13, 14, 15.

-fond 34980, opis' 5, delo 2, 'Leningrad Military District Directive to the 9th Army on future goals, 21 November 1939'.

-fond 34980, opis' 5, delo 53,

- -ll. 234–240, '9th Army to the Chief of the General Staff, Report on the conduct of the offensive, 2 February 1940'.
- -l. 262, 'Mekhlis to Voroshilov, Report on deficiencies of the 9th Army, 14 February 1940'.
- -ll. 270–271, 'Mekhlis to Voroshilov on officer insubordination, 12 January 1940'.
- -ll. 272–273, 'Mekhlis to Stavka on the arrest of officers, 30 January 1940'.
- -ll. 274–276, 'Boikov, Chief of the Special Department of the GUGB NKVD, to Voroshilov concerning allegations against 9th Army Chief of Staff, Division Commander Nikishev, 15 February 1940'.
- -l. 280, 'NKVD to Voroshilov concerning a captured Swedish officer, 15 February 1940'.
- -ll. 288–290, 'Mekhlis to the Chief of the General Staff at Stavka about the use of chemical weapons, 27 February 1940'.
- -ll. 292–293, 'Mekhlis to Shaposhnikov on the non-use of chemical weapons, 28 February 1940'.
- -ll. 329–331, 'Mekhlis to Voroshilov, transmitting plea from commissar of the 54th Rifle Division for speedy liberation, 10 March 1940'.

-fond 34980, opis' 6, delo 1, ll. 32–38, 'Voronov to Voroshilov, 25 February 1940'.

-fond 34980, opis' 6, delo 18, ll. 1–23, 'Military Procurator of the 13th Army to his counterpart in the Leningrad Military District concerning Military Political work, 26 January 1940'.

-fond 34980, opis' 6, delo 31, ll. 9–13, 'Plan for the Preservation of Political Security during the offensive against the Mannerheim Line, 15–25 January 1940'.

-fond 34980, opis' 6, delo 35, ll. 216–239, 'Summary report of the 13th Army Instructional Section of the Political Department, 28 December–13 March 1940'.

-fond 34980, opis' 6, delo 77,

- -ll. 2–11, 'Plan of operation for Right Group of 7th Army, 24–25 December 1939'.
- -ll. 112–114, 'North-Western Front to the 13th Army berating 13th Army for unsystematic command, 31 January 1940'.
- -ll. 117–119, 'NKO and NKVD order to set up control-defensive units, 24 January 1940'.
- -ll. 121–125, 'Directive from North-Western Front: Timoshenko's instructions after front inspection, 9 February 1940'.

-l. 143, 'North-Western Front to 13th Army on the problem of friendly fire'.

-ll. 185–186, 'North-Western Order: On the Use of Tanks in the TVD, 26 January 1940'.

-l. 202, 'NKO Directive: On Mistakes of the 6th Army during the Polish War, 10 November 1939'.

-l. 203, 'Voroshilov's Directive on Instructions on doctrine for training in wartime, 25 November 1939'.

-l. 204, 'NKO Order: On Communications Service in RKKA, 25 September 1939'.

-fond 34980, opis' 6, delo 85, ll. 202–204, 'Report from the 13th Army to the North-Western Front on irregular behaviour of troops and officers, 7 March 1940'.

-ll. 5–12, 'Report on plans of 13th Army for new offensive, 12 January 1940'.

-ll. 28–33, 'Report on Plans of 13th Army for new Offensive, 27 January 1940'.

-ll. 60–63, 'Organization and conduct of battle, 13th Army, 10 February 1940'.

-l. 207, 'Instructions from 13th Army to corps commanders criticizing their poor troop control, 7 March 1940'.

-ll. 221–222, 'Directive of the North-Western Front on the implications of the Soviet–Finnish Peace negotiations, 13 March 1940'. l. 207, 'Deficiencies of the Strike Army'.

-fond 34980, opis' 6, delo 186, ll. 49–52, 'German manual on how to attack fortified gun-emplacements, 9 February 1940'.

-fond 34980, opis' 6, delo 187, ll. 22–26, 'Instructions on the preparation and surmounting of fortified positions'.

-fond 34980, opis' 14, delo 6, ll. 1–9, 'General Meretskov's lecture to the students of the General Staff Academy on the lessons of the war with Finland, 26 June 1940'.

-fond 34980, opis' 14, delo 12,

-ll. 12–21, 'List of questions for Department to Study Experience of War with Finland, 19 February 1940'.

-ll. 22–24, 'North-Western Front: Supplement to Instructions on how to overcome fortified gun-emplacements (artillery/tank), 4 February 1940'.

-fond 34980, opis' 14, delo 46, l. 130–205, 'Diary of Lieutenant A.I. Matveev, 359th Rifle Regiment of the 50th Rifle Corps, 13th Army'. (Courtesy of Professor Mark von Hagen).

-fond 34980, opis' 14, delo 50, ll. 1–96, 'Official History of the Soviet–Finnish War, January 1941'.

-fond 34980 opis' 14, delo 99, 'Secretariat of the NKO USSR: Press Summaries of Foreign Military Commentary on the Combat Capability of the Red Army'.
-fond 34980, opis' 14, delo 109, 'Article in Swedish newspaper on the reforms in the Russian Army, 22 October 1940'.

Ministry of Defence of the French Republic. Vincennes, Paris. *Service Historique de l'Armée de Terre. Archives de la Guerre: ÉMA et Attachés Militaires, URSS.*

7N 2790 *(Finlande) Dossier 1, Quartier General de l'Armée Finlandaise, IIe Section. Bureau des Armées Étrangères.*
7N 3123 *(URSS) Dossier 3, Attaché Militaire-Moscou, 1939–1940.*
7N 3168 *(URSS) Dossiers 1 et 2, 'Idées nouvelles dans la doctrine de combat de l'URSS'.*

Public Record Office, Kew, London.

FO 371 23609
23618
23648
23653
23663
23688
24758
24791
24792
24793
24808
24850
24855
24856

WO 208 582
1753
1754

COS (39) 169(S)
(39) 170(S)
(40) 216(S)

(40) 228(S)
(40) 229(S)
(40) 233(J.P.)(S)
(40) 234(S)
(40) 235(S)
(40) 237(J.P.)(S)
(40) 240(S)
(40) 242(J.P.)(S)
(40) 244(S)

II. COLLECTIONS, OFFICIAL PUBLICATIONS AND MILITARY THEORETICAL
WORKS

Anon., *The Åland Islands. Handbook prepared under the direction of the Foreign Office (GB)* No. 58a (London, August 1919).

Anon., *Boevye deistviia VVS KBF v voine s belofinnami (s 30 noiabria 1939 g. po 13 marta 1940 g.)* (Moscow–Leningrad: Gosvoenmorizdat NKVMF SSSR, 1941).

Anon., *Finland. Handbook prepared under the direction of the Historical Section of the Foreign Office (GB)* No. 58 (London, January 1919).

Anon., *Sovetsko–finliandskaia voina 1939–1940 gg. na more*, Chast' 1–2, Kniga 1–3, Skhemy (Moscow–Leningrad: Voenmorizdat, 1945–46).

Anon., *SSSR–Germaniia 1939–1941. Dokumenty i Materialy o sovetsko-germanskikh otnosheniiakh s sentiabriia 1939 g. po iiun' 1941 g.* Tom II (Vilnius: 'Mokslas', 1989).

Anon., *Voenno-vozdushnye sily Rumanii, Finliandii, Estonii, Latvii, Litvii, Shvetsii* (Moscow: Izdanie Razvedybatel'nogo Upravleniia RKKA, 1938).

Anon., *Vremennaia instruktsiia po boevomu primenenii tankov RKKA* (Moscow: Nauchno-ustavnogo otdela Shtaba RKKA, 1928).

Anon., *Vremennyi polevoi ustav RKKA 1936 (PU-36)* (Moscow, 1937). (Provisional Field Regulations for the Red Army, translation JPRS-UMA-86-031, 12 June 1986.)

Bondarenko, A.P., *et al.* (eds), *God Krizisa 1938–1939. Dokumenty i materialy* Tom I–II (Moscow: Politizdat, 1990).

British Broadcasting Corporation, *Monitoring Service Reports. Daily Digest of Foreign Broadcasts* (Reports from 18 November 1939 to 7 December 1939. Moscow (Russia) LW: For Russia in Russian (London, 1939–1947).

Degras, J. (ed.), *Soviet Documents on Foreign Policy*, Vol. III (London: Oxford University Press, 1953).

Dvoinykh, L.V. and N.E. Eliseeva (compilers), *Konflikt. Komplekt dokumentov o Sovetsko–finliandskoi voine (1939–1940gg.)* (Minneapolis: East View Publications, 1992).

Document No. 4 'Prikaz voiskam 7 armii o vydvizhenii chastei k granitse s Finliandiei, 22 noiabria 1939 g.'

Document No. 16 'Prikaz voiskam Leningradskogo voennogo okruga o perekhode sovetsko–finskoi granitsy v sviazi s nachalom voennykh deistvii, 30 noiabria 1939 g.'

Document No. 18 'Prikaz voiskam 7 armii ob uluchshenii upravleniia voiskami, 30 noiabria 1939 g.'

Document No. 19 'Opisanie boevykh deistvii 19 str. korpusa na karel'skom peresheike v period s 30 noiabria po dekabria 1939 g.'

Document No. 20 'Iz otcheta o boevykh deistviiakh 19 str. korpusa v period s 30 noiabria po 21 dekabria 1939 g.'

Document No. 21 'Iz otcheta o boevykh deistviiakh 50 str. korpusa v period s 30 noiabria po 19 dekabria 1939 g.'

Document No. 22 'Iz opisaniia boevykh deistvii 1 str. korpusa v period s 30 noiabria po 25 dekabria 1939 g.'

Document No. 23 'Iz ocherka boevykh deistvii 56 str. korpusa v period s 30 noiabria 1939 g. po 1 ianvaria 1940 g.'

Document No. 26 'Prikaz voiskam 7, 8, 9-i armii o forsirovanii tempov nastupleniia, 3 dekabria 1939 g.'

Document No. 27 'Prikaz voiskam Leningradskogo voennogo okruga ob obespechenii vsekh chastei lyzhami, 4 dekabria 1939 g.'

Document No. 28 'Prikaz voiskam 14 armii ob oborone Kol'skogo poluostrova i raiona Petsamo, Luostari, 5 dekabria 1939g.'

Document No. 29 'Prikaz narkoma oborony K.E. Voroshilova komanduiush-chemu Leningradskim voennym okrugom i komanduiushchemu 7 armiei o neobkhodimosti sovmestnykh deistvii pekhoty i artillerii, 7 dekabria 1939 g.'

Document No. 30 'Prikaz voiskam 9 armii o vykhode v tyl protivniku i ovladenii gorodami Oulu, Kaaiani, 11 dekabria 1939 g.'

Document No. 31 'Direktiva Glavnokomandovaniia komanduiushchim 7, 8, 9, i 14-i armii o taktike boevykh deistvii i organizatsii upravleniia voiskami, 12 dekabria 1939 g.'

Document No. 32 'Rasporiazhenie komanduiushego 7 armiei komandiram 19 i 50 str. korpusov o boevem sostava chastei, 12 dekabria 1939 g.'

Document No. 33 'Prikaz voiskam 7 armii o nachale nastupleniia na keksgol'mskom i vyborgskom napravleniiakh, 13 dekabriia 1939 g.'

Document No. 35 'Iz otcheta o boevykh deistviiakh 10 str. korpusa v voine s Finliandiei v period s 15 dekabria 1939 g. po 10 fevralia 1940 g.'

Bibliography

Document No. 40 'Prikaz komanduiushchego 7 armiei voiskam armii o nastuplenii na khotinenskom napravlenii, 17 dekabria 1939 g.'

Document No. 43 'Soobshchenie TASS ob otpravke v Finliandiiu 10 tysiakh shvedskikh soldat, 21 dekabria 1940 g.'

Document No. 44 'Direktiva komanduiushchego 7 armii komandiram 19, 50 str. korpusov, 10 tankovogo korpusa, nachal'nikam VVS i artillerii armii o podgotovke proryva na vyborgskom napravlenii, 22 dekabria 1939 g.'

Document No. 46 'Prikaz voiskam 7 armii o nanesenii kontrudara protivniku, 25 dekabria 1939 g.'

Document No. 47 'Direktiva Narkoma oborony komanduiushchim 7, 8, 9, 13 i 14 armii o taktike bor'by, 28 dekabria 1939 g.'

Document No. 49 'Iz dokladnoi zapiski polkovnika N.P. Raevskogo Narkomu oborony o boevykh deistviiakh na petrozavodskom napravlenii, 31 dekabria 1939 g.'

Document No. 52 'Boevoe rasporiazhenie komanduiushchego 7 armiei komandiru osobogo korpusa komdivu Antilla o dislokatsii chastei korpusa, 4 ianvaria 1940 g.'

Document No. 54 'Soobshchenie TASS o khode boevykh deistvii, 6 ianvaria 1940 g.'

Document No. 55 'Iz ocherka "Voina Sovetskogo Soiuza s belofinnami v 1939–1940 gg. Deistviia 7 armii".'

Document No. 56 'Iz ocherka "Voina Sovetskogo Soiuza s belofinnami v 1939–1940 gg. Operatsii 8 armii".'

Document No. 57 'Iz otcheta o boevykh deistviiakh 15 str. korpusa s 7 ianvaria po 13 marta 1940 g.'

Document No. 58 'Iz ocherka boevykh deistvii 56 str. korpusa v ianvare 1940 g.'

Document No. 59 'Prikaz voiskam 7 armii o sozdanii lyzhnnykh batal'onov, 11 ianvariia 1940 g.'

Document No. 60 'Prikaz Glavnogo voennogo soveta RKKA ob izvlechenii opyta iz porazheniia 44 str. divizii, 19 ianvaria 1940 g.'

Document No. 62 'Iz direktivy Vysshego soveta Severo–Zapadnogo fronta komanduiushchim 7 i 13 armiei ob organizatsii proryva ukreplennoi polosy, 20 ianvaria 1940 g.'

Document No. 63 'Prikaz voiskam 7 armii ob uluchshenii organizatsii voisk PVO, 20 ianvaria 1940 g.'

Document No. 73 'Prikaz voiskam 7 armii ob ovladenii khotinenskim opornym punktom, 4 fevraliia 1940 g.'

Document No. 76 'Ukazaniia komandira 21 divisii finskoi armii ofitseram divizii o taktike pozitsionnoi voiny, 8 fevralia, 1940 g.'

Document No. 79 'Prikaz voiskam Severo-Zapadnogo fronta o perekhode v obshchee nastuplenie, 9 fevralia 1940 g.'

Document No. 80 'Prikaz voiskam Severo-Zapadnogo fronta o shturme linii Mannergeima, 9 fevralia 1940 g.'

Document No. 81 'Prikaz voiskam Iuzhnoi armeiskoi gruppy 8 armii o perekhode v reshitel'noe nastuplenie v napravlenii na Lemetti, 9 fevralia 1940 g.'

Document No. 86 'Iz ocherka boevykh deistvii 56 str. korpsa v fevrale–marte 1940 g.'

Document No. 87 'Iz otcheta o boevykh deistviiakh 50 str. korpusa v period s 11 fevralia po 13 marta 1940 g.'

Document No. 88 'Iz prikaza voiskam Severo-Zapadnogo fronta s razvitii nastupleniia pri vziamodeistvii pekhoty i artillerii, 12 fevralia 1940 g.'

Document No. 89 'Prikaz voiskam 7 armii o razvitii nastupleniia na khotinenskom napravlenii, 12 fevralia 1940 g.'

Document No. 90 'Prikaz voiskam 7 armii o razvitii nastupleniia, 12 fevralia 1940 g.'

Document No. 91 'Prikaz voiskam 15 armii ob okruzhenii portivnika v raione g. Pitkiaranta, 12 fevralia 1940 g.'

Document No. 93 'Prikaz voiskam 7 armii o razvitii nastupleniia na Kiamiaria i Khotinen, 13 fevralia 1940 g.'

Document No. 94 'Na otcheta o khode boevykh deistvii 23 str. korpusa v period s 11 po 18 fevralia 1940 g.'

Document No. 95 'Iz otcheta o boevykh deistviakh 10 str. korpusa v period s 11 fevralia po 13 marta 1940 g.'

Document No. 96 'Boevoe rasporiazhenie voiskam 13 armii o zavershenii razgroma UR protivnika na uchastke Tereitillia-Riiskii, 15 fevralia 1940.'

Document No. 97 'Prikaz Voennogo sovets Severo-Zapadnogo fronta komandiram 15 i 23 str. korpusov ob uluchshenii upravleniia chastiami i aktivizatsii boevykh deistvii, 15 fevralia 1940 g.'

Document No. 98 'Prikaz voiskam 7 armii o presledovanii otkhodiashchero protivnika na vyborgskom napravlenii, 17 fevralia 1940 g.'

Document No. 99 'Doklad komandira 8 str. korpusa kmodiva RUBINA v Voennyi sovet 15 armii o tselescöobraznosti vremennogo priostanovleniia nastupleniia, 18 fevralia 1940 g.'

Document No. 100 'Iz doklada estonskogo voennogo attashe v Finliandii, 18 fevralia 1940.'

Document No. 101 'Iz opisaniia boevykh deistvii 23 str. korpusa v period s 18 fevralia po 13 marta 1940 g.'

Document No. 102 'Prikaz voiskam 7 armii o zakreplenii na poberezh'e finskogo zaliva, 19 fevralia 1940 g.'

Bibliography

Document No. 104 'Prikaz voiskam 7 armii o razvitii nastupleniia, 20 fevralia 1940 g.'

Document No. 105 'Prikaz voiskam 15 armii o perekhode v nastuplenie na pitkiarantskom napravlenii, 21 fevralia 1940 g.'

Document No. 106 'Prikaz voiskam 7 armii ob aktivizatsii boevykh deistvii, 21 fevralia 1940 g.'

Document No. 107 'Prikaz komandira 1 str. korpusa FNA o vydvizhenii chastei korpusa v raion Iokhannes, Makslakhti, 21 fevralia 1940 g.'

Document No. 108 'Directiva komanduiushchego Severo-Zapadnym frontom voiskam 7 i 13 armii ob uckorenii tempov nastupleniia, 22 fevralia 1940 g.'

Document No. 109 'Pasporiazhenie komandira 1 str. korpusa FNA o zaniatii riada ostrovov i poberezh'ia Finskogo zaliva, 25 fevralia 1940 g.'

Document No. 110 'Directiva komanduiushchego Severo-Zapadnym frontom o likvidatsii nedochetov v upravlenii voiskami, 27 fevralia 1940 g.'

Document No. 111 'Prikaz voiskam 13 armii ob okonchatel'nom razgrome protivnika, 27 fevralia 1940 g.'

Document No. 112 'Prikaz komandira 1 str. korpusa FNA ob obespechenii levogo fronta 7 armii i dal'neishem prodvizheniim, 27 fevralia 1940 g.'

Document No. 115 'Iz otcheta o boevykh deistviiakh 28 str. korpusa v period s 28 fevralia po 13 marta 1940 g.'

Document No. 116 'Boevoe praporiazhenie komanduiushchego 7 armei komandiru 34 str. korpusa ob obladenii g. Vyborg, 1 marta 1940 g.'

Document No. 117 'Boevoe pasporiazhenie voiskam 13 armii o razvitii nastupleniia na st. Antrea, 1 marta 1940 g.'

Document No. 119 'Prikaz komanduiushchego Severo-Zapadnogo fronta o presechenii slukhov o razrushenii shliuzob Saimenskogo kanala, 2 marta 1940 g.'

Document No. 120 'Pasporiazhenie komandira 1 korpusa FNA o dislokatsii chastei i podgotovke k nastupleniiu na Vyborg, 2 marta 1940 g.'

Document No. 121 'Donesenie kombriga Evstegneeva nachal'niku shtaba 10 str. korpusa ob ukrepleniiakh protivnika v g. Vyborg, 2 marta 1940 g.'

Document No. 123 'Prikaz komanduiushchemu Severo-Zapadnim frontom komandiru korpusa FNA Antilla o sovmetnykh deistviiakh s 43 str. divisiei, 4 marta 1940 g.'

Document No. 124 'Prikaz komandira 1 korpusa FNA ob oborone zanumaemykh rubezhei, 4 marta 1940 g.'

Document No. 125 'Prikaz voiskam 7 armii o proryve fronta protivnika i vykhode v raion severo-vostochnee g. Vyborg, 5 marta 1940 g.'

Document No. 127 'Prikaz komanduiushchego Severo-Zapadnym frontom komanduiushchemu 7 armei, komanduiushchemu VVS fronta o shturme g. Vyborg, 6 marta, 1940 g.'

Document No. 128 'Prikaz voiskam 7 armii o proryve ukreplennoi pozitsii v raione Vyborga i zakhvate ukreplennoi pozitsii v raione Vyborga i zakhvate platsdarma na zapadnom poberezh'e Finskogo zaliva, 6 marta 1940 g.'

Document No. 129 'Prikaz komandiushchego Severo-Zapadnym frontom komandiru korpusa FNA Antilla, 6 marta 1940 g.'

Document No. 130 'Donesenie komandira 1 korpusa FNA komdiva Antilla komanduiushchemu Severo-Zapadnym frontom komandiru 1 ranga S.K. Timoshenko o zaniatii ostrovov v Finskom zalive, 6 marta 1940 g.'

Document No. 131 'Prikaz komanduiushchego Severo-Zapadnym frontom komanduiushchemu 13 armei o perekhode v nastuplenie, 6 marta 1940 g.'

Document No. 132 'Prikaz voiskam 13 armii ob uckorenii tempov nastupleniia i likvidatsii nedoctatkov vo vzaimodeistvii chastei, 7 marta, 1940 g.'

Document No. 135 'Iz ocherka boevykh deistvii 8 str. korpusa v period s 8 po 13 marta 1940 g.'

Document No. 138 'Rasporiazhenie komanduiushchego Severo-Zapadnym frontom nachal'nikam shtabov 7 i 13 armii o provedenii postoiannoi razvedki voisk protivnika, 9 marta 1940 g.'

Document No. 139 'Rasporiazhenie komanduiushchego Severo-Zapadnym frontom o maskirovke komandnykh punkov, 10 marta 1940 g.'

Document No. 140 'Prikaz voiskam 7 armii o dal'neishem razvitii nastupleniia i ovladenii platsdarmom na zapadnom beregu Saimenskogo kanala, 11 marta 1940 g.'

Document No. 143 'Prikaz voiskam 7 armii ob uluchshenii protivovozdushnoi oborony, 12 marta 1940 g.'

Document No. 144 'Direktiva STAVKI Glavnogo Voennogo soveta o prekrashchenii boevykh deistvii, 13 marta 1940 g.'

Document No. 149 'Prikaz voiskam Severo-Zapadnogo fronta ob okonchanii boevykh deistvii, 14 marta 1940 g.'

Document No. 154 'Iz ocherka "Voina Sovetskogo Soiuza s belofinnami v 1939–1941 gg."'

Document No. 164 'Iz stat'i podpolkovnika finskoi armii I. Khannula, "Boi na uchastke Liakhde".'

Document No. 165 'Soobshchenie TASS "Finliandskii general-leitenant G. Ekvist - o nastupatel'noi sile Krasnoi Armii, 21 noiabria 1940 g."'

Document No. 167 'Iz stat'i general-leitenant nemetskoi armii Shenkheintsa "Russko–finliandskaia voina".'

Document No. 171 'Iz vospominanii polkovnika G.A. Veshchezerskogo o zakliuchitel'nom etape sovetsko–finliandskoi voiny.'

Bibliography

Govorov, *Rezoliutsiia po doklady komdiva Govorova na temy: 'Osnovy voprosy boevogo primeneniia artillerii pri proryve po opytu Karel'skoi operatsii'* (Moscow: AGSh RKKA, 1940).

Isserson, G.S., *Novye formy bor'by. Opyt issledovaniia sovremennykh voin* (Moscow: Voenizdat, 1940).

—, *Evoliutsiia operativnogo isskustva* (Moscow: Gosvoenizdat, 1932).

Kadishev, A.B. (ed.), *Voprosy taktiki v sovetskikh voennykh trudakh (1917–1940gg.)* (Moscow: Voenizdat, 1970).

Kariaev, T.F., *et al.*, *Partiino-Politicheskaia rabota v Krasnoi Armii. Dokumenty, iiul' 1929 g.–mai 1941 g.* (Moscow: Voenizdat, 1985).

Kirpichnikov, A.V., *Operatsii sovremennykh podvizhnykh armii* (Moscow: AGSh RA, 1941).

Komplektov, V.G., *et al.*, *Polpredy soobshaiut ... Sbornik dokumentov ob otnosheniiakh SSSR s Latviei, Litvoi i Estoniei avgust 1939 g.–avgust 1940 g.* (Moscow: Mezhdunarodnye otnosheniia, 1990).

Korneev, N.N., *Boevye deistviia 50 SK po prorybu linii mannergeima*, unpub. MS (Moscow: 1941). Reprinted (Minneapolis, MN: East View Publications, 1993).

—, *Nastupatel'naia armeiskaia operatsiia*, Vypus, 6 (Moscow: AGSh RKKA, 1941).

Krivosheev, G.F., *Grif sekretnosti sniat. Poteri Vooruzhennykh Sil SSSR v voinakh, boevykh deistviiakh i voennykh konfliktakh* (Moscow: Voenizdat, 1993).

Liubarskii, S., *Nekotorye operativno-takticheskie vybody iz opyta voiny v Ispanii* (Moscow: Voenizdat, 1939).

Mering, F., *Ocherki po istorii voiny i voennogo iskusstva* (Moscow: Krasnaia Nov', 1924).

Orenstein, H.S., *Selected Readings in the History of Soviet Operational Art* (Ft. Leavenworth: SASO, 1990).

Popov, I.I., *Baltiiskii teatr voennykh deistvii* (Moscow: Voenno-inzhenernaia akademiia RKKA, 1937).

Popov, I.I., *Severnyi teatr voennykh deistvii* (Moscow: Voenno-inzhenernaia akademiia RKKA, 1937).

Pospelov, P.N., *Istoriia Velikoi Otechetstvennoi Voiny Sovetskogo Soiuza 1941–1945*, Tom I (cited as *IVOVSS*) (Moscow: Institut marksizma-leninisma pri TsK KPSS, 1960).

Shilovskii, E.A., *Proryv i ego razvitie* (Moscow: Uchebnyi otdel AGSh RKKA, 1938).

—, *Nastupatel'naia armeiskaia operatsiia (Vypusk, 5, Osnovy operativnogo proryva)* (Moscow: AGSh RKKA, 1940).

Shtromberg, A.I., *Tankovye voiska v armeiskikh oboronitel'nykh operatsii (Konspekt)* (Moscow: AGSh KA, 1940).

Shvarts, N.N., *Rabota shtaba armii (Konspect lektsii)* (Moscow: AGSh RKKA, 1938).

—, *Rabota komandovaniia fronta i armii i ikh shtabov po upravleniiu operatsiami (Tezisy lektsii)* (Moscow: AGSh RKKA, 1938).

Svechin, A.A., *Iskusstvo vozhdeniia polka po opytu voiny 1914–18gg.*, Tom 1, (Moscow-Leningrad: Gosizdat, 1930).

Triandafillov, V.K., *The Nature of the Operations of Modern Arms* (J.W. Kipp (ed.), translated from the Russian 1929 original) (London: Frank Cass, 1994).

Trukhin, F.I., *et al.*, *Metodika i tekhnika raboty obshchevoiskovykh shtabov* (Moscow: AGSh RKKA, 1939).

Varfolomeev, N., *Tekhnika shtabnoi sluzhby. Operativnaia sluzhba voiskykh shtabov (v voennoe vremia)* (Moscow: Vysshii Voennyi Redaktsionnyi Sovet, 1924).

Voroshilov, K.E., *Doklad (Voroshilova) o sovetsko–finliandskoi voine 1939–1940gg. s prilozheniem istoricheskoi spravki o bor'be za Finskii zaliv i Finliandiiu* (Minneapolis: East View Publications, 1993).

III. BOOKS

Anon., *Admiral flota sovetskogo soiuza Isakov. Sbornik dokumentov i materialov* (Erevan: 'Aistan', 1975).

Anon., *The Diary of Politruk Oreshin* (Helsinki: Tilgmann, 1941).

Anon., *Rokovye gody, 1939–1940. Sobytiia v Pribaltiiskikh gosudarstvakh i Finliandii na osnove sovetskikh dokumentov i materialov* (Tallinn, 1990).

Aster, S., *1939: The Making of the Second World War* (London: Deutsch, 1973).

Bailey, J.B.A., *Field Artillery and Firepower* (Oxford: The Military Press, 1989).

Bajanov, B., *Bajanov revele Staline. Souvenirs d'un ancien secretaire de Staline* (Paris: Gallimand, 1979).

Baryshnikov, N.I., *et al.*, *Istoriia ordena Lenina Leningradskogo Voennogo Okruga* (Moscow: Voenizdat, 1988).

—, *et al.*, *Finliandiia vo vtoroi mirovoi voine* (Leningrad: Lenizdat, 1985).

Bellamy, C., *The Evolution of Modern Land Warfare. Theory and Practice* (London: Routledge, 1990).

Berghahn, V.R., *Militarism. The History of an International Debate, 1861–1979* (Leamington Spa: Berg Publishers, 1981).

Carlgren, W.M., *Swedish Foreign Policy during the Second World War* (London: Benn, 1977).

Carr, E.H., and Davies, R.W., *Foundations of a Planned Economy, 1926–1929* (Vol. 1 I–II) (London: Macmillan, 1969).

Carr, E.H., *The Bolshevik Revolution, 1917–1923* (Vols. I, III) (London: Macmillan, 1950–53).

—, *The Twenty Years' Crisis, 1919–1939* (London: Macmillan, 1993).

Cherkasov, P.V. (ed.), *Mirovaia voina 1914–1918. 'Lutskii Proryv'* (Moscow: Vysshii Voennyi Redaktsionnyi Sovet, 1924).

Chew, A.F., *The White Death. The Epic of the Soviet–Finnish Winter War* (Michigan State University Press: East Lansing, 1971).

Clark, I., *Waging War. A Philosophical Introduction* (Oxford: Clarendon Press, 1990).

Colton, T., *Commissars, Commanders and Civilian Authority. The Structure of Soviet Military Politics* (Cambridge: Harvard University Press, 1979).

Corum, J.S., *The Roots of Blitzkrieg. Hans von Seeckt and German Military Reform* (Lawrence, KS: University Press of Kansas, 1992).

Cox, G., *The Red Army Moves* (London: Gollancz, 1941).

Dallin, D.J., *Soviet Russia's Foreign Policy, 1939–1942* (New Haven, CT: Yale University Press, 1942).

Douglas, M., *How Institutions Think* (London: Routledge, 1987).

—, *Implicit Meanings* (London: Routledge, 1975).

Erickson, J., *Organizing for War: The Soviet Military Establishment Viewed Through the Prism of the Military District* (College Station Papers No. 2, The Center for Strategic Technology, Texas A and M University, 1983).

—, *The Road to Stalingrad* (London: Weidenfeld and Nicolson, 1975).

—, *The Soviet High Command* (London: Macmillan, 1962).

Erickson, J., and Hansen, L., *Soviet Combined Arms: Past and Present* (College Station Papers No. 1, The Center for Strategic Technology, Texas A and M University, 1981).

Fiddick, T.C., *Russia's Retreat from Poland, 1920. From Permanent Revolution to Peaceful Coexistence* (London: Macmillan, 1990).

Fuller, W.C., Jr., *Strategy and Power in Russia, 1600–1914* (New York: Free Press, 1992).

Gareev, M.A., *M.V. Frunze – Military Theorist* (London: Brassey's, 1988).

—, *Obshchevoiskovye ucheniia* (Moscow: Voenizdat, 1990).

Gat, A., *The Origins of Military Thought from the Enlightenment to Clausewitz* (Oxford: Clarendon Press, 1989).

—, *The Development of Military Thought: The Nineteenth Century* (Oxford: Clarendon Press, 1992).

Glantz, D.M. (ed.), *Soviet Documents on the Use of War Experience* (Vol. 1, The Initial Period of War 1941) (London: Frank Cass, 1991).

—, *Soviet Military Operational Art. In Pursuit of Deep Battle* (London: Frank Cass, 1991).

—, *The Soviet Conduct of Tactical Maneuver. Spearhead of the Offensive* (London: Frank Cass, 1991).

Gooch, J., and Perlmutter, A., *Strategy and the Social Sciences: Issues in Defence Policy* (London: Frank Cass, 1981).

Grechaniuk, N.M., *et al.*, *Dvazhdy krasnoznamennyi baltiiskii flot* (Moscow: Voenizdat, 1990).

Griffith, P., *Battle Tactics of the Western Front. The British Army's Art of Attack 1916–18* (New Haven, CT: Yale University Press, 1994).

—, *Forward into Battle* (Chichester: Antony Bird Publications, 1981).

von Hagen, M., *Soldiers of the Proletarian Dictatorship. The Red Army and the Soviet Socialist State, 1917–1930* (Ithaca: Cornell University Press, 1990).

Haslam, J., *The Soviet Union and the Struggle for Collective Security, 1933–39* (London: Macmillan, 1984).

—, *The Soviet Union and the Threat from the East, 1933–41. Moscow, Tokyo and the Prelude to the Pacific War* (Pittsburgh: University of Pittsburgh Press, 1992).

Hemsley, J., *Soviet Troop Control: The Role of Command Technology in the Soviet Military System* (London: Brassey's, 1982).

Hiden, J., *The Baltic States and Weimar Ostpolitik* (Cambridge: Cambridge University Press, 1987).

Hohne, H., *Canaris* (London: Secker and Warburg, 1979).

House, Captain J.M., *Towards Combined Arms Warfare: A Survey of 20th Century Tactics, Doctrine and Organization* (Research Survey No. 2, Combat Studies Institute, US Army Command and General Staff College, Ft. Leavenworth, Kansas, August 1984).

Jakobson, M., *The Diplomacy of the Winter War* (Cambridge: Harvard University Press, 1961).

—, *Finland Survived* (Helsinki: Otava, 1984).

Kamenka, E., *Bureaucracy* (Oxford: Blackwell, 1989).

Karaev, G., *Razgrom belofinskogo platsdarma. 30 noiabria 1939 g.–13 marta 1940g.* (Leningrad, 1941).

Karpov, V., *Marshal Zhukov: Ego soratniki i protivniki v dni voiny i mira* (Moscow: Voenizdat, 1992).

Keegan, J., *A History of Warfare* (London: Hutchinson, 1993).

Kennan, G.F., *Russia Leaves the War* (Princeton, NJ: Princeton University Press, 1989).

Kurochkin, P.A. (ed.), *Obshchevoiskovaia armiia v nastuplenii. Po opytu Velikoi Otechestvennoi voiy 1941–1945gg.* (Moscow: Voenizdat, 1966).

Kirshin, Y., *Dukhovnaia gotovnost' sovetskogo naroda k voine* (Minneapolis, MN: East View Publications, 1991).

—, *The Soviet Military Doctrine in the Pre-War Period* (Moscow: Novosti, 1990).

Kissin, S.F., *War and the Marxists. Socialist Theory and Practice in Capitalist War, 1918–1945* (London: André Deutsch, 1989).

Bibliography

Korotkov, I.A., *Istoriia sovetskoi voennoi mysli. Kratkii ocherk 1917–iiun' 1941* (Moscow: Nauka, 1980).

Kulikov, V.G., *et al.*, *Akademiia general'nogo shtaba. Istoriia Voennoi ordenov Lenina i Suvorova iz stepeni akademii General'nogo shtaba Vooruzhennykh sil SSSR imeni K. E. Voroshilova* (Moscow: Voenizdat, 1987).

Kuz'min, N.F., *Na strazhe mirnogo truda (1921–1940gg.)* (Moscow: Voenizdat, 1959).

Kuznetsov, N.G., *Nakanune* (Moscow: Voenizdat, 1989).

Langdon-Davies, J., *Finland – The First Total War* (London: Routledge, 1940).

Leach, B.A., *German Strategy against Russia, 1939–1941* (Oxford: Oxford University Press, 1973).

Lewin, M., *The Making of the Soviet System. Essays in the Social History of Interwar Russia*, (London: Methuen, 1985).

Liddell-Hart, B.H., *This Expanding War* (London: Faber & Faber, 1942).

Lieven, A., *The Baltic Revolution* (New Haven, CT: Yale University Press, 1993).

Mannerheim, C.G., *The Memoirs of Marshal Mannerheim* (London: Cassell, 1953).

Martel, G., *The Russian Outlook* (London: Joseph, 1947).

Mawdsley, E., *The Russian Revolution and the Baltic Fleet. War and Politics, February 1917–April 1918* (London: Macmillan, 1978).

Mearsheimer, J.J., *Liddell Hart and the Weight of History* (London: Brassey's, 1988).

Menning, B.W., *The Imperial Russian Army, 1861–1914* (Bloomington: Indiana University Press, 1992).

Meretskov, K.A., *Na strazhe narodov* (Moscow: Politizdat, 1968).

Michel, H., *La Drole de Guerre* (Paris: Hachette, 1972).

Miksche, F.O., *Blitzkrieg* (London: Faber & Faber, 1942).

Nevakivi, J., *The Appeal that was Never Made: The Allies, Scandinavia and the Finnish Winter War, 1939–1940* (London: C. Hurst, 1976).

Oras, A., *Baltic Eclipse* (London: Gollancz, 1948).

Panov, B.V., *The History of Military Art* (Moscow: Voenizdat, 1984). (JPRS Translation UMA-85-009-1, 21 March 1985.)

Paret, P., *Understanding War. Essays on Clausewitz and the History of Military Power* (Princeton, NJ: Princeton University Press, 1992).

Pike, D.W. (ed.), *The Opening of the Second World War* (Proceedings of the Second International Conference on International Relations, American University of Paris, September 26–30, 1989) (New York: Peter Lang, 1991).

Posen, B.R., *The Sources of Military Doctrine. France, Britain, and Germany between the World Wars* (Ithaca, NY: Cornell University Press, 1984).

Prochko, I.S., *Artilleriia v boiakh za rodinu* (Moscow, 1957).

Rapoport, V., and Alexeev, Y., *High Treason. Essays on the History of the Red Army, 1918–1938* (Durham, NC: Duke University Press, 1985).

Rei, A., *The Drama of the Baltic Peoples* (Stockholm: Kirjastus Valoa Eesti, 1970).

Ries, T., *Cold Will: The Defence of Finland* (London: Brassey's, 1988).

Rozanov, G.L., *Stalin-Gitler, 1939–1941* (Moscow: Mezhdunarodnye otnosheniia, 1991).

Samuels, M., *Doctrine and Dogma. German and British Infantry Tactics in the First World War* (Westport, CT: Greenwood Press, 1992).

Sandalov, L.M., *Perezhitoe* (Moscow: Voenizdat, 1961).

Schwartz, A.J., *America and the Russo-Finnish War* (Westport, CT: Greenwood Press, 1975).

Selznick, P., *The Organizational Weapon. A Study of Bolshevik Strategy and Tactics* (New York: McGraw-Hill, 1952).

Semiryaga, M.I., *Tainy stalinskoi diplomatii, 1939–1941* (Moscow: Vysshaia shkola, 1992).

—, *The Winter War: Looking Back after Fifty Years* (Moscow: Novosti, 1990).

Semmel, B., *Marxism and the Science of War* (Oxford: Oxford University Press, 1981).

Shatsillo, K.F., *Russkii imperialism i razvitie flota nakanune pervoi mirovoi voiny (1906–1914 gg.)* (Moscow: 'Nauka', 1968).

Shtemenko, S.M., *General'nyi shtab v gody voiny* (Moscow: Voenizdat, 1981).

Shukman, H. (ed.), *Stalin's Generals* (London: Weidenfeld & Nicolson, 1993).

Silnitskii, F., *Natsional'naia politika KPSS v period c 1917 po 1922 god* (Munich: Suchasnist', 1981).

Simpkin, R., *Deep Battle: The Brainchild of Marshal Tukhachevskii* (London: Brassey's, 1987).

Smith, C.J., Jr., *Finland and the Russian Revolution, 1917–1922* (Athens, GA: University of Georgia Press, 1958).

Solov'ev, M., *My Nine Lives in the Red Army* (London: Thames & Hudson, 1955).

—, *Zapiski sovetskogo voennogo korrespondenta* (New York: Chekova, 1954).

Stavskii, V., *et al.* (compilers), *Boi na karel'skom peresheike* (Moscow: Gospolitizdat, 1941).

Svechin, A.A., *Strategy* (Minneapolis, MN: East View Publications, 1992).

Tanner, V., *The Winter War. Finland Against Russia, 1939–1940* (Palo Alto, CA: Stanford University Press, 1957).

Tierskii, R., *Ordinary Stalinism. Democratic Centralism and the Question of Communist Political Development* (Boston: Allen and Unwin, 1985).

Tukhachevskii, M., *Izbrannye proizvedeniia* Tom I (Moscow: Voenizdat, 1964).

Bibliography

Unger, R.M., *Plasticity into Power: Comparative-Historical Studies on the Institutional Conditions of Economic and Military Success* (Cambridge: Cambridge University Press, 1987).

Upton, A.F., *Finland, 1939–1940* (London: Davis-Poynter, 1974).

Van Dyke, C., *Russian Imperial Military Doctrine and Education, 1832–1914* (Westport,CT: Greenwood Press, 1990).

Vasilevsky, A.M., *A Lifelong Cause* (Moscow: Progress Publishers, 1981).

Volkogonov, D., *Stalin: Triumph and Tragedy* (London: Weidenfeld & Nicolson, 1991).

Voronov, N.N., *Na sluzhbe voennoi* (Moscow: Voenizdat, 1963).

Waller, M., *Democratic Centralism: An Historical Commentary* (Manchester, UK: Manchester University Press, 1981).

Ward, E., *Despatches from Finland, January–April 1940* (London: The Bodley Head, 1940).

Watt, D.C., *How War Came* (London: Mandarin, 1989).

—, *Too Serious a Business. European Armed Forces and the Approach to the Second World War* (London: Temple Smith, 1975).

Wuorinen, J.H., *Finland and World War II* (New York: Ronald Press Co., 1948).

Zakharov, M.V., *General'nyi shtab v predvoennye gody* (Moscow: Voenizdat, 1989).

Zenzinov, V., *Vstrecha s Rossiei. Kak i Chem zhivut v sovetskom soiuze. Pis'ma v Krasnuiu Armiiu 1939–1940* (New York: n.p., 1944).

Zhilin, P.A., *Zarozhdenie i razdenie Sovetskoi Voennoi Istoriographii, 1917–1941* (Moscow: 'Nauka', 1985).

Zhukov, G.A., *Vospominaniia voennogo khimika* (Moscow: Voenizdat, 1991).

Zhukov, G.K., *Vospominaniia i razmyshleniia*, Tom 1. (Moscow: Novosti, 1990).

Zonin, S.A., *Admiral L.M. Galler: zhizn i flotovodcheskaia deiatelnost'* (Moscow: Voenizdat, 1991).

IV. ARTICLES

Ahmann, R., 'Nazi German Policy towards the Baltic States on the Eve of the Second World War', Chapter 3 in *The Baltic and the Outbreak of the Second World War*, J. Hiden and T. Lane (eds) (Cambridge: Cambridge University Press, 1992), pp. 50–73.

—, '"Localization of Conflicts" or "Indivisibility of Peace": The German and the Soviet Approaches towards Collective Security and East Central Europe, 1925–1939', Chapter 10 in *The Quest for Stability. Problems of West European Security, 1918–1957*, R. Ahmann, *et al.* (eds) (Oxford: Oxford University Press, 1993), pp. 201–48.

Aleksandrov, P., 'Raskolotyi shchit', *Rodina*, No. 12, Winter 1995, pp. 77–9.

Anon., 'Agitatsionnaia literatura na fronte', *Na Strazhe Rodiny*, 1 December 1939, p. 3.

Anon., 'Boevaia sputnitsa krasnykh voinov (About military journalism)', *Na Strazhe Rodiny*, 9 December 1939, p. 3.

Anon., 'Excerpts on Soviet 1938–40 operations from *The History of Warfare, Military Art, and Military Science*, a 1977 textbook of the Military Academy of the General Staff of the USSR Armed Forces', *Journal of Slavic Military Studies*, Vol. 6, No. 1, March 1993, pp. 85–141.

Anon., 'Pamiatka boitsu o merakh preduprezhdeniia ot obmorazhivaniia', *Na Strazhe Rodiny*, 26 December 1939, p. 3.

Anon., 'Pamiatka boitsu i mladshemu komandiru pri deistviiakh v lesisto-bolotistoi mestnosti', *Na Strazhe Rodiny*, 3 January 1940, p. 2.

Anon., 'Pamiatka tankovomu ekipazhu dlia deistvii v lesisto-bolotistom i lesisto-ozernom raione', *Na Strazhe Rodiny*, 13 December 1939, p. 2.

Anon., 'Sokrushit' i unichtozhit' finskuiu belogvardeishchinu (About the 1st Corps of the Finnish People's Army)', *Na Strazhe Rodiny*, 2 December 1939, p. 2.

Anon., 'The Winter War', *International Affairs*, January 1990, pp. 202–15.

Anon., 'V zashchitu Finliandskoi demokraticheskoi respubliki', *Na Strazhe Rodiny*, 8 January 1940, p. 4.

Anon., 'Vrednye pis'ma Pashi Brekhuntsova', *Na Strazhe Rodiny*, 18 February 1940, p. 4.

Antilla, A., 'Velikomu drugu finliandskogo naroda tovarishchu Stalinu (Message to Stalin from the Finnish People's Army)', *Na Strazhe Rodiny*, 29 December 1939, p. 1.

Alekseev, D., 'Ukliuchaemsia v boevoe sorevnovanie', *Na Strazhe Rodiny*, 12 December p. 1.

Badanin, B., 'Maskirovka boitsa zimoi v nastuplenii', *Na Strazhe Rodiny*, 14 December 1939, p. 2.

Bailes, K.E., 'Alexei Gastev and the Soviet Controversy over Taylorism, 1918–24', *Soviet Studies*, Vol. 29, No. 3, July 1977, pp. 373–94.

Baranov, 'Razvernem boevoe sotsialisticheskoe sorevnovanie', *Na Strazhe Rodiny*, 2 December 1939, p. 2.

Bareev, 'Poimali "Yazyka" (About the exploits of Ugriumov's men)', *Na Strazhe Rodiny*, 10 February 1940, p. 2.

Baryshnikov, N.I., 'The Soviet–Finnish War of 1939–1940', *Soviet Studies in History*, Winter 1990–91, Vol. 29, No. 3, pp. 43–60.

Bellamy, C., 'Red Star in the West: Marshal Tukhachevskii and East-West Exchanges in the Art of War', *RUSI Journal*, December 1987, pp. 63–73.

Bibliography

Belousov, I., 'V nochnoi razvedke', *Na Strazhe Rodiny*, 15 December, p. 2.

Bobrinskii, V., 'Iskusstvo blokirovki', *Na Strazhe Rodiny*, 12 December 1939, p. 2.

—, 'Organizovannyi udar (Offensive in the Taipalen area)', *Na Strazhe Rodiny*, 17 December 1939, p. 2.

—, 'Otdelenie v razvedke', *Na Strazhe Rodiny*, 3 February 1940, p. 2.

—, 'Umelo i initsiativno deistvovat' noch'iu', *Na Strazhe Rodiny*, 3 January 1940, p. 2.

—, 'V tesnom vzaimodeistvii', *Na Strazhe Rodiny*, 1 February 1940, p. 2.

—, 'Vnezapnost' deistvuet na vraga oshelomliaiushche', *Na Strazhe Rodiny*, 12 February 1940, p. 2.

Bobrov, B.D., 'Takticheskie ucheniia voisk', *Voennaia Mysl'*, No. 5 (May 1940), pp. 26–37.

Boldyrev, P.S., *et al.* (Book review of S. Liubarskii's 'Nekotorye operativno-takticheskie vyvody iz opyta voiny v Ispanii'), *Voennaia Mysl'*, No. 3, 1940, pp. 119–20.

Bolotnikov, V., 'Artilleriiskaia razvedka v usloviiakh lestisto-bolotistoi mestnosti', *Na Strazhe Rodiny*, 9 January 1940, p. 2.

Builov, 'Bit' vraga po-ugriumovski', *Na Strazhe Rodiny*, 18 December, p. 2.

Butylev, V., 'Kak obezvredit' blokirovannuiu DOT', *Na Strazhe Rodiny*, 31 December 1939, p. 2.

—, 'Kak razvedat' DOT'y', *Na Strazhe Rodiny*, 16 December 1939, p. 2.

—, 'Nastuplenie melkikh podrazdelenii v lesisto-bolotistoi mestnosti', *Na Strazhe Rodiny*, 12 December 1939, p. 2.

—, 'Nochnaia ataka', *Na Strazhe Rodiny*, 19 December 1939, p. 2.

—, 'Otdel'nye orudiia v lesnom boiu', *Na Strazhe Rodiny*, 27 December 1939, p. 2.

—, 'Proryv ukreplennoi polosy', *Na Strazhe Rodiny*, 18 December 1939, p. 2.

Chaika, A., 'Protivotankovaia artilleriia v boiu', *Na Strazhe Rodiny*, 14 January 1940, p. 2.

Chernov, 'Predlozhenie boevykh tovarishchei voodushevliaet nas na novye podvigi', *Na Strazhe Rodiny*, 13 December 1939, p. 1.

Chernyshev, V., 'Vstrecha (A meeting between two old Finns in the 1st Corps of the Finnish People's Army)', *Na Strazhe Rodiny*, 10 December 1939, p. 4.

Chevela, P.P., 'Itogi i uroki sovetsko–finliandskoi voiny', *Voennaia Mysl'*, No. 4, 1990, pp. 48–55.

Dongarov, A.G., 'Predliavliamcia li finliandii ul'timatum?', *Voenno-istoricheskii zhurnal*, No. 3, 1990, pp. 43–6.

—, 'Pravitel'stvo Kuusinena: Epizod sovetsko–finliandskoi voiny 1939–1940', *Vestnik MID SSSR*, No. 22 (56) 1 December 1989, pp. 74–9.

Editorial, 'Boevye zadachi shtaba', *Na Strazhe Rodiny*, 1 February 1940, p. 1.

—, 'Eshche tesnee vzaimodeistvie vsekh rodov voisk', *Na Strazhe Rodiny*, 18 February 1940, p. 1.

—, 'Krasnaia artilleriia smetet s litsa zemli vrazheskii DOT'y', *Na Strazhe Rodiny*, 25 December 1939, p. 1.

—, 'Mladshii komandir v boiu', *Na Strazhe Rodiny*, 27 January 1940, p. 1.

—, 'Nastupatel'nyi poryv voinov Krasnoi Armii', *Na Strazhe Rodiny*, 22 January 1940, p. 1.

—, 'Partiinuiu rabotu v rote – na uroven' boevykh zadach', *Na Strazhe Rodiny*, 31 January 1940, p. 1.

—, 'S nami ves' sovetskii narod (Comments about women taking over their husbands' jobs at the factory)', *Na Strazhe Rodiny*, 12 December 1939, p. 1.

—, 'Umelo deistvovat' v boiu na lyzhakh', *Na Strazhe Rodiny*, 5 January 1940, p. 1.

—, 'Vzaimodeistvie voisk reshaet uspekh boia', *Na Strazhe Rodiny*, 11 December 1939, p. 1.

—, 'Zheleznaia revoliutsionnaia distsiplina v boiu', *Na Strazhe Rodiny*, 11 January 1940, p. 1.

Egorov, P., 'Boi v lesu', *Na Strazhe Rodiny*, 8 December 1939, p. 2.

—, 'Boi s razgrazhdeniem prepiatstvii', *Na Strazhe Rodiny*, 2 December 1939, p. 4.

Erickson, J., 'The Red Army's March into Poland, September 1939', in *The Soviet Takeover of the Polish Eastern Provinces, 1939–1941*, K. Sword (ed.) (London: Macmillan, 1991), pp. 1–27.

—, 'Soviet Command Technology: Problems, Programmes, Perspectives', *Jane's Defence Review*, No. 1, 1980, pp. 9–11, 31.

Fuks, D., 'V prokurature LVO: Shofery-Prestupniki', *Na Strazhe Rodiny*, 7 February 1940, p. 4.

Gat, A., 'Clausewitz and the Marxists: Yet Another Look', *Journal of Contemporary History*, Vol. 27 (1992), pp. 363–82.

Gerard, B.M., 'Mistakes in Force Structure and Strategy on the Eve of the Great Patriotic War', *Journal of Soviet Military Studies*, Vol. 4, No. 3, September 1991, pp. 471–86.

Gerasimov, M., 'Proekt Boevogo Ustava Pekhoty, Chast' Vtoraia', *Na Strazhe Rodiny*, 18 February 1940, pp. 2–3.

Glantz, D.M., 'Soviet Mobilization in Peace and War, 1924–1942: A Survey', *Journal of Soviet Military Studies*, Vol. 5, No. 3, September 1992, pp. 323–62.

Gordon, M., 'Terioki-Ino', *Na Strazhe Rodiny*, 9 December 1939, p. 2.

Gradov, B., 'Kak byli vziaty ostrova Koivisto i Pii-saari', *Na Strazhe Rodiny*, 26 February 1940, p. 1.

Gurianov, O., 'Kak luchshe obespechit' tseleukazaniia artilleristam', *Na Strazhe Rodiny*, 1 March 1940, p. 2.

Bibliography

Gusarov, N., 'Vzaimodeistvie batarei so strelkovoi rotoi v lesnom boiu', *Na Strazhe Rodiny*, 4 December 1939, p. 2.

von Hagen, M., 'Civil-Military Relations and the Evolution of the Soviet Socialist State', *Slavic Review*, Summer 1991, pp. 269–76.

Iarmoshkevich, P.S., 'Oboronitel'nye vozmozhnosti strelkovogo korpusa', *Voennaia Mysl'*, No. 10, 1940, pp. 64–76.

Iuvenskii, M., 'Inzhenernye sily pri razvitii nastupleniia i boe v glubine oborony protivnika', *Na Strazhe Rodiny*, 6 March 1940, p. 2.

—, 'Kak unichtozhit' ognevuiu tochki vraga', *Na Strazhe Rodiny*, 4 December 1939, p. 3.

Ivanov, V., 'Sila bol'shevistskogo slova (Article about reading the newspaper)', *Na Strazhe Rodiny*, 7 February 1940, p. 3.

Ivashov, L.G., 'The Nation's Defence and the Law: Legal Basis for Preparation of the Armed Forces of the USSR for Repelling Aggression', *Voenno-istoricheskii zhurnal*, No. 10, 1992, pp. 10–17.

Jones, C.D., 'Just Wars and Limited Wars: Restraints on the Use of the Soviet Armed Forces', *World Politics*, Vol. XXVIII, No. 1, October 1975, pp. 44–68.

Jukes, G., 'The Red Army and the Munich Crisis', *Journal of Contemporary History*, Vol. 26, 1991, pp. 195–214.

Kamkin, M., 'Otdelenie lyzhnikov v razvedke', *Na Strazhe Rodiny*, 9 January 1940, p. 2.

Khadeev, A., 'Bor'ba za ovladenie ukreplennym raionom', *Na Strazhe Rodiny*, 3 December 1939, p. 4.

—, 'Bor'ba za ovladenie ukreplennym raionom (Part II)', *Na Strazhe Rodiny*, 5 December 1939, p. 3.

Khadeev, A., and Bobrinskii, V., 'Boevye deistviia melkikh lyzhnykh podrazdelenii', *Na Strazhe Rodiny*, 26 December 1939, p. 3.

Kipp, J.W., 'General-Major A.A. Svechin and Modern Warfare: Military History and Military Theory', Introductory Essay to *Strategy* (Minneapolis MN: East View Publications, 1992), pp. 23–56.

—, 'Lenin and Clausewitz: The Militarization of Marxism, 1914–1921', *Military Affairs*, October 1985, pp. 184–91.

—, 'Mass, Mobility and the Origins of Soviet Operational Art, 1918–1936', in *Transformations in Russian and Soviet Military History* (USAF), 1986, pp. 88–91.

Kirshin, Iu., 'Nakanune 22 iiunia 1941 g. (po materialam voennykh arkhivov)', *Novaia i noveishaia istoriia*, No. 3, 1991, pp. 3–19.

Klavdiev, S., 'Proryv linii "Mazhino-Kirke"', *Na Strazhe Rodiny*, 16 December 1939, p. 3.

Klein, Y., 'The Sources of Soviet Strategic Culture', *Journal of Soviet Military Studies*, Vol. 2, No. 4, December 1989, pp. 453–90.

Kniazev, M.S., 'Ataka ukreplenykh raionov', *Voennaia Mysl'*, No. 6, pp. 10–38.

Kollontai, A., '"Seven Shots" in the Winter of 1939', *International Affairs*, January 1990, pp. 180–201.

Komarov, N., 'Bor'ba tankov s ognevymi tochkami ukreplennogo raiona protivnika', *Na Strazhe Rodiny*, 7 December 1939, p. 2.

Kondrat'ev, B.N., 'O malen'kom voprose bol'shogo znacheniia (po povody redaktsii operativnykh dokumentov) (About Staff Work)', *Voennaia Mysl'*, No. 4, 1940, pp. 69–73.

Korol'kov, Yu., 'Geroicheskie podvigi saperov (About Korovin's destruction of a DOT)', *Na Strazhe Rodiny*, 9 February 1940, p. 1.

Korotkov, I., 'K istorii stanovleniia sovetskoi voennoi nauk', in *Vestnik Voennyi Istorii. Nauchnye zapiski* (Moscow, 1971).

Korzinkin, P., 'Matty Tolvonen idet v Narodnuiu armiiu', *Na Strazhe Rodiny*, 8 December 1939, p. 4.

—, 'Sotsialisticheskoe sorevnovanie v boiu', *Na Strazhe Rodiny*, 3 December 1939, p. 3.

Krashke, A., 'Uzel soprotivleniia belofinnov pal', *Na Strazhe Rodiny*, 10 February 1940, p. 1.

Krupatkin, B., 'Revoliutsionnaia distsiplina voinov Krasnoi Armii', *Na Strazhe Rodiny*, 6 February 1940, p. 3.

Krylov, P., 'Sobranie zhitelei ostrova Seiskaari', *Na Strazhe Rodiny*, 8 December 1939, p. 4.

Kubatko, I., 'Razvedka v lesu', *Na Strazhe Rodiny*, 10 January 1940, p. 2.

Kumanev, G.A., 'Chto my znaem o "zimnei voine"', *Sovetskaia Rossiia*, 10 March 1990.

—, 'Vuosien 1939–40 neuvostoliitolais – suomalaisen sodan ('talvi-sodan') tapahtumat uusien lahetymistaponjen ja dokumenttien nakkokulmasta (1939–40, the events of the Soviet–Finnish War from the point of view of new documents)' in *Talvisota, venaja joe suomi*, T. Vihavainen (ed.) (Helsinki, 1991), pp. 253–73.

Kurochkin, 'Organizatsiia sviazi pri nastuplenii na ukrepivshegocia protivnika', *Na Strazhe Rodiny*, 4 February 1940, p. 2.

Kuz'min, S.N., and Kozak, S.A., 'Deistviia tankov v zimnikh usloviiakh', *Voennaia Mysl'*, No. 2, 1940, pp. 52–62.

Kuz'min, F., 'Nastuplenie SD v zimnikh usloviiakh', *Voennaia Mysl'*, January 1940, pp. 28–37.

Lanir, Z., 'The "Principles of War" and Military Thinking', *The Journal of Strategic Studies*, Vol. 16, No. 1, March 1993, pp. 1–17.

Larson, K.A., 'The Debal'tsevo Raid, February 1943: A Case Study in the Role of Initiative in Soviet Operational Art', *Journal of Soviet Military Studies*, Vol. 5, No. 3, September 1992, pp. 426–50.

Lee, K., 'Strategy and History: The Soviet Approach to Military History and its Implications for Military Strategy', *Journal of Soviet Military Studies*, Vol. 3, No. 3, September 1990, pp. 409–45.

Litvinov, A., 'Vo glave atakuiushchikh tankov', *Na Strazhe Rodiny*, 19 February 1940, p. 3.

Lizunov, N., 'Boevaia zadacha agitatorov', *Propaganda i agitatsiia*, No. 17, September 1940.

Lychalov, 'V upor po ambrazuram (Story about Fomichev during the 100th Rifle Division's demonstration exercise)', *Na Strazhe Rodiny*, 6 February 1940, p. 1.

Mahoney, S.E., 'Defensive Doctrine: The Crisis in Soviet Military Thought', *Slavic Review*, Autumn, 1990, pp. 398–408.

Makarov, 'Vzaimodeistvie i vzaimopomosh'v boiu', *Na Strazhe Rodiny*, 10 December 1939, p. 2.

Maksimov, S., 'Zakhvacheno 6 vrazheskikh tankov (Near Kiamiaria)', *Na Strazhe Rodiny*, 20 February 1940, p. 1.

Manninen, O., 'Neuvostoliiton operatiiviset suunnitelmat 1939–1941 suomen suunnalla (The Soviet Operational Plans for the Finnish Theatre of War in 1939–1941)', *Sotahistoriallinen Aikakauskirja*, No. 11, Helsinki, 1992, pp. 77–176.

—, 'Political expedients for security during the "Interim Peace" and at the start of the Continuation War (1940–1941)', *Revue Internationale d'Histoire Militaire*, No. 62, 1985, pp. 97–121.

Mekhlis, L., '"O rabote Politicheskogo Upravleniia Krasnoi Armii", Iz doklada Politicheskogo Upravleniia Krasnoi Armii Tsentral'nomu Komitetu VKP(b) o rabote Politicheskogo Upravleniia Krasnoi Armii, 23 mai 1940 g.', *Izvestiia TsK KPSS*, No. 3, 1990, pp. 192–201.

Mel'tiukhov, M.I., '"Narodnyi Front" dlia finliandii? (K voprosu o tseliakh sovetskogo rukovostva v voine s Finliandiei 1939–1940gg.)', *Otechestvennaia istoriia*, No. 3, 1993, pp. 95–101.

Menning, B.W., 'The Deep Strike in Russian and Soviet Military History', *Journal of Soviet Military Studies*, Vol. 1, No. 1, April 1988, pp. 9–28.

Meretskov, K., 'Prikaz voiskam Leningradskogog voennogo okruga', *Na Strazhe Rodiny*, 31 December 1939 (Special Edition), p. 2.

Moiseev, M., 'Smena rukovodstva Narkomat oborony SSSR v sviazi s urokami sovetsko–finliandskoi voiny 1939–1940gg.', *Izvestiia TsK KPSS*, No. 1, 1990, pp. 210–15.

Molotov, V.M., 'Doklad o vneshnei politike pravitel'stva', *Voennaia Mysl'*, No. 4, 1940, pp. 5–16.

Nechaev, L.B., '(Book review of) E. Barsukov, Russkaia artilleriia v mirovuiu voinu, Tom II', *Voennaia Mysl'*, No. 7, 1940, pp. 119–21.

Nesterov, P., 'Narodoarmeitsy Suomi', *Na Strazhe Rodiny*, 26 December 1939, p. 4.

Nesterov, P., 'Shturm ukreplennogo raiona (Chukarov's seizure of a DOT and its communications)', *Na Strazhe Rodiny*, 27 February 1940, p. 2.

Nikolaev, N., 'Shire peredavat' boevoi opyt', *Na Strazhe Rodiny*, 7 January 1940, p. 3.

Noskov, A.M., 'Severnyi uzel', *Voenno-istoricheskii zhurnal*, No. 7, 1990, pp. 7–19.

Nurek, M., 'Great Britain and the Baltic in the Last Months of Peace, March–August 1939', in *The Baltic and the Outbreak of the Second World War*, J. Hiden (ed.) (Cambridge: Cambridge University Press, 1992), pp. 21–49.

Padorin, Ya., 'Vraga khiter, a my khitree', *Na Strazhe Rodiny*, 7 January 1940, p. 1.

Pavlenko, N., 'Voenno-istoricheskaia tematika v zhurnalam Voennaia Mysl'', *Voenno-istoricheskii zhurnal*, No. 6, 1940.

Petrovskii, D., 'K voprosu o edinonachalii', *Voennaia mysl' i revoliutsiia*, No. 3, 1922, pp. 3–9.

Phillips, R.H., 'Soviet Military Debate on the Initial Period of the War: Characteristics and Implications', *Journal of Soviet Military Studies*, Vol. 4, March 1991, No. 1, pp. 30–61.

Pipiainen, P., 'My boremcia za svobodnuiu Finliandiiu', *Na Strazhe Rodiny*, 11 February 1940, p. 4.

Piskunov, D., 'Metkim artilleriiskim ognem unichtozhit' belofinskie ukrepleniia', *Na Strazhe Rodiny*, 17 December 1939, p. 3.

—, 'Moshchnym artilleriiskim ognem obespechim bystreishii razgrom vraga', *Na Strazhe Rodiny*, 27 December 1939, p. 2.

—, 'Unichtozhenie ognevykh tochek otdel'nymi orudiiami', *Na Strazhe Rodiny*, 6 December 1939, p. 3.

Potapov, M., 'Blokirovanie i razrushenie dolgovremennykh tochek', *Na Strazhe Rodiny*, 24 January 1940, p. 2.

—, 'Kak brat' DOT'y', *Na Strazhe Rodiny*, 14 December 1939, p. 3.

Pruntsov, V., 'Deistviia voisk noch'iu', *Na Strazhe Rodiny*, 2 March 1940, p. 2.

Prusov, L., 'Sekretar' Partbiuro na fronte', *Na Strazhe Rodiny*, 9 December 1939, p. 3.

Ptukhin, E., 'Komandarm (Article about Meretskov)', *Na Strazhe Rodiny*, 24 December 1939, p. 3.

Reese, R., 'A Note on a Consequence of the Expansion of the Red Army on the Eve of World War II', *Soviet Studies*, Vol. XLI, No. 1, January 1989, pp. 135–40.

Roberts, C., 'Planning for War: The Red Army and the Catastrophe of 1941', *Europe–Asia Studies*, Vol. 47, No. 8, 1995, pp. 1293–326.

Bibliography

Roberts, G., 'Infamous Encounter? The Merekalov–Weizsäcker Meeting of 17 April 1939', *The Historical Journal*, 35, 4 (1992), pp. 921–6.

—, 'The Soviet Decision for a Pact with Nazi Germany', *Soviet Studies*, Vol. 44, No. 1, 1992, pp. 57–78.

Rotmistrov, P., 'Primenenie tankov v proryve sil'no ukreplennykh polos', *Voprosi taktiki v sovetskikh voennykh trudakh (1917–1940gg.)* (Moscow: Voenizdat, 1970), pp. 294–300.

Rubenshtein, L., 'Pervye shagi narodnoi vlasti (About a Finnish POW becoming a volunteer in the Finnish People's Army)', *Na Strazhe Rodiny*, 3 January 1940, p. 3.

Rudoi, M., 'DOT'y ne spacut belofinskikh "voiak"', *Na Strazhe Rodiny*, 16 December 1939, p. 2.

Saianov, V., 'Pokhod russkikh voisk v Finliandiiu v 1808–1809 gg.', *Na Strazhe Rodiny*, 31 January 1940, p. 3.

Saipenen, Ia., 'Ot vsei dushi blagodarim sovetskii narod i Krasnuiu Armiiu! (Resolution of a meeting of the residents of Suomussalmi)', *Na Strazhe Rodiny*, 25 December 1939, p. 3.

Salmon, P., 'Great Britain, the Soviet Union and Finland at the Beginning of the Second World War', in *The Baltic and the Outbreak of the Second World War* (Cambridge: Cambridge University Press, 1992), pp. 95–123.

Sapigo, S., 'Vzaimodeistvie artillerii i pekhoty v lesnom boiu', *Na Strazhe Rodiny*, 7 January 1940, p. 2.

Savchuk, E., 'Opyt artilleriiskoi razvedki', *Na Strazhe Rodiny*, 12 January 1940, p. 2.

Savushkin, R.A., 'Zaruzhdenie i razvitie sovetskoi voennoi doktriny', *Voenno-istoricheskii zhurnal*, No. 2, 1988, pp. 19–26.

Sazhin, A., 'Opyt raboty artillerii', *Na Strazhe Rodiny*, 10 January 1940, p. 2.

Schneider, J.J., 'The Origins of Soviet Military Science', *Journal of Soviet Military Science*, Vol. 2, No. 4, December 1989, pp. 491–519.

Semiryaga, M.I., 'Sovetsko–germanskie otnosheniia (sentiabr' 1939–iiun' 1941 g.)', in *Sovetskaia vneshnaia politika, 1917–1945gg. Poiski novykh podkhodov* (Moscow, 1992) pp. 201–50.

—, 'Asimmetrichnaia voina. K 50-letiiu okonchaniia sovetsko–finliandskoi voiny', *Sovetskoe gosudarstvo i pravo*, No. 4, 1990, pp. 116–22.

—, 'Nenuzhnaia voina', *Arkhivy raskryvaiut tainy* (Moscow, 1991), pp. 113–33.

Sergeev, M., 'Sapery raschishchaiut put' tankam, (Despatch from Kiamiaria)', *Na Strazhe Rodiny*, 20 February 1940, p. 1.

Sergeev, N., 'Polkovodcheskoe iskussto Suvorova', *Na Strazhe Rodiny*, 11 January 1940, p. 3.

Sieglebaum, L.H., 'Defining and ignoring Labour Discipline in the Early Soviet

Period: The Comrades-Disciplinary Courts, 1918–1922', *Slavic Review*, Vol. 51, No. 4, Winter 1992, pp. 705–30.

Simonov, K., 'Glazami cheloveka moego pokoleniia: becedy s Marshalam Sovetskogo Soiuza A.M. Vasilevskim', *Znamia*, No. 5, 1988, pp. 79–90.

Shalov, K., 'Narodnoe pravitel'stvo Finliandii za rabotoi', *Na Strazhe Rodiny*, 8 January 1940, p. 4.

Shchadenko, E.A., 'O nakoplenii nachal'stvuiushchengo sostava i popolnenii im Raboche-Krest'ianskoi Krasnoi Armii (Iz spravki-doklada nachal'nika Upravleniia po nachal'stvuiushchemu sostava Narkomata Oborony SSSR E.A. Shchadenko, 20 marta 1940g.)', *Izvestiia TsK KPSS*, No. 1, 1990, pp. 177–85.

—, 'O rabote za 1939 god', *Izvestiia TsK KPSS*, No. 1, 1990, pp. 186–92.

Shtab L.V.O., 'Trekhnedel'nyi itog boevykh deistvii v Finliandii', *Na Strazhe Rodiny*, 23 December 1939, p. 1.

Shvankov, N., 'Sovmestnyi udar pekhoty i artillerii', *Na Strazhe Rodiny*, 13 January 1940, p. 2.

Smotrikov, 'Zhelezhnaia distsiplina – Osnova nashikh uspekhov', *Na Strazhe Rodiny*, 13 January 1940, p. 1.

Spring, D.W., 'The Soviet Decision for War Against Finland, 30 November, 1939', *Soviet Studies*, Vol. XXXVIII, No. 2, April 1986, pp. 207–26.

—, 'Stalin and the Winter War', *Yearbook of Finnish Foreign Policy* (Helsinki: Finnish Institute of International Affairs, 1990), pp. 37–42.

Starunin, A.I., 'Oborona', *Voennaia Mysl'*, No. 2, 1940, pp. 87–98.

Stavskii, V., 'Dva dnia geroicheskikh boev (About Ugriumov)', *Na Strazhe Rodiny*, 2 December 1939, p. 2.

Stoecker, S., 'The Historical Roots of the Current Debates on Soviet Military Doctrine and Defense', *Journal of Soviet Military Studies*, Vol. 3, No. 3, September 1990, pp. 363–89.

Sukhinenko, M., 'Vzaimodeistvie v strelkovoi rote', *Na Strazhe Rodiny*, 2 January 1940, p. 2.

Talenskii, N., 'Kak pravil'no organizovat' vzaimodeistvie voisk', *Na Strazhe Rodiny*, 6 January 1940, p. 2.

Tarasov, A., 'Organizatsiia marsha na lyzhakh', *Na Strazhe Rodiny*, 4 December 1939, p. 4.

Tarleton, R.E., 'What really happened to the Stalin Line?', Parts 1–2, *Journal of Soviet Military Studies* (Part I in Vol. 5, No. 2, June 1992, pp. 187–219, and Part II in Vol. 6, No. 1, March 1993, pp. 21–61).

Thompson, E.M., 'Nationalist Propaganda in the Soviet Russian Press, 1939–1941', *Slavic Review*, 50, No. 2 (Summer 1991), pp. 385–99.

Tikhonov, N., 'Belofinny shtyka ne liubiat', *Na Strazhe Rodiny*, 25 December 1939, p. 1.

Bibliography

—, 'O molodetskom russkom shtyke', *Na Strazhe Rodiny*, 3 February 1940, p. 3.

—, 'O russkoi smekalke', *Na Strazhe Rodiny*, 15 January 1940, p. 3.

Timoshenko, S.K., 'Zakliuchitel'naia rech' ... na voennom soveshchanii 31 dekabria 1940 g.', *Voenno-istoricheskii zhurnal*, No. 1, 1992, pp. 16–24.

Trifonov, A., 'Na komandom punkte', *Na Strazhe Rodiny*, 15 February 1940, p. 2.

Tucker, R.C., 'The Emergence of Stalin's Foreign Policy', *Slavic Review*, Vol. 36, 1977, pp. 563–89.

Tvardovskii, A., 'Krasnoe znamia na DOT', *Na Strazhe Rodiny*, 13 February 1940, p. 1.

—, 'S karel'skom peresheike', *Novyi Mir*, No. 2, 1969, pp. 116–60.

—, 'Sto dvadtsat' tret'ia v boiu (Poem about the 123rd Rifle Division)', *Na Strazhe Rodiny*, 15 February 1940, p. 2.

Ugriumov, N., 'Vyzyvaem na boevoe sorevnovanie!', *Na Strazhe Rodiny*, 11 December 1939, p. 1.

Van Dyke, C., 'Legko otdelalis': kakie uroki izvleklo partiinoe i voennoe rukovodstvo iz finskoi kampanii', *Rodina*, No. 12, Winter 1995, pp. 113–15.

—, 'The Timoshenko Reforms: March–July 1940', *Journal of Slavic Military Studies*, Vol. 9, No. 1 (March 1996) pp. 69–96.

Vashchenko, P.F., 'Esli by Finliandiia i SSSR ...', *Voenno-istoricheskii zhurnal*, No. 1, 1990, pp. 27–36.

Vasel'ev, N.M., 'Rabota General'nogo Shtaba po obobshcheniiu opyta voiny v 1941–1945 godakh', *Voennaia Mysl'*, No. 5, May 1994, pp. 68–74.

Velikolutskii, A.A., 'Nekotorye mysli o voinskoi distsipline', *Voennaia Mysl'*, No. 6, June 1940, pp. 3–9.

Vihavainen, T., 'The Soviet Decision for War Against Finland, November 1939: A Comment', *Soviet Studies*, Vol. XXXIX, No. 2, April 1987, pp. 314–17.

Vinogradov, I., 'Kak byli zakhvacheny vrazheskie tanki (Exploits of the 123rd Rifle Division)', *Na Strazhe Rodiny*, 28 February 1940, p. 1.

Vinogradov, V.K. (compiler), '1937. Pokazaniia Marshala Tukhachevskogo (Plan porazheniia)', *Voenno-istoricheskii zhurnal*, No. 8, 1991, pp. 45–53.

Vinogradov, V.P., 'Stalinskaia nauka o sluzhbe tyla'', *Voennaia Mysl'*, No. 4, 1940, pp. 17–24.

Vinnitskii, E., 'Taktika melkikh podrazdelenii finskoi armii', *Na Strazhe Rodiny*, 31 December 1939 (Special Edition), p. 4.

Virta, N., 'Pervye tri chasa', *Na Strazhe Rodiny*, 1 December 1939, p. 2.

—, 'Terioki', *Na Strazhe Rodiny*, 6 December 1939, p. 3.

Volkogonov, D.A., 'The Drama of the Decisions of 1939', *Soviet Studies in History*, Vol. 29, No. 3, Winter 1990–91, pp. 26–7.

Vorob'ev, Ya., 'Shtab batal'ona v nastupatel'nom boiu', *Na Strazhe Rodiny*, 28 January 1940, p. 2.

Vostrikov (Procurator), 'O l'gotakh dlia voennosluzhashchikh i ikh semei', *Na Strazhe Rodiny*, 14 February 1940, p. 4.

Voznenko, V., *et al.*, 'Military Strategy in Works of Soviet Authors', *Voennaia Mysl'*, No. 4, 1967 (FPD translation 1135/67, 24 November 1967).

Vucinich, A., 'A Blend of Marxism and Neopositivism: A.A. Bogdanov', Chapter 8, in *Social Thought in Tsarist Russia. The Quest for a General Science of Society, 1861–1917* (Chicago: University of Chicago Press, 1976), pp. 206–30.

Vuorenmaa, A., 'Defensive Strategy', *Revue Internationale d'Histoire Militaire*, No. 62, 1985, pp. 74–94.

Vysokoostrovskii, L., 'Kapitan Ugriumov i ugriumovtsy', *Na Strazhe Rodiny*, 13 December 1939, p. 3.

Watt, D.C., 'The High Command: Who plotted against whom? Stalin's purge of the Soviet High Command revisited', *Journal of Soviet Military Studies*, Vol. 3, No. 1, March 1990.

White, D.F., 'Soviet Philosophy of War', *Political Science Quarterly*, September, 1936, pp. 321–53.

Zakharov, I., 'Agitpoezd PU LVO v Deistvuiushchei armii', *Na Strazhe Rodiny*, 7 January 1940, p. 4.

Zamiatin, N.M., 'Nekotorye osobennosti organizatsii i raboty operativnogo otdela krupnogo obshchevoiskovogo shtaba (A Few Peculiarities of Organization and Work of Operations Departments of Large Combined Arms Staffs)', *Voennaia Mysl'*, June 1940, pp. 79–84.

—, 'Vzaimaia vyruchka i vzaimopomoshch' v boiu', *Na Strazhe Rodiny*, 31 December 1939, p. 3.

Ziuzin, E.I., 'Gotovil li SSSR preventivnyi udar?', *Voenno-istoricheskii zhurnal*, No. 1, 1992, pp. 7–16.

V. DISSERTATIONS AND UNPUBLISHED PAPERS

Anzulovic, J.V., 'The Russian Record of the Winter War, 1939–1940: An Analytical Study of Soviet Records of the War with Finland from 30 November 1939 to 12 March 1940', Ph.D. dissertation, University of Maryland, 1968.

Bidlack, R., 'Workers at War: Factory Workers and Labor Policy in the Siege of Leningrad', Ph.D. dissertation, Indiana University, 1987.

Dudorova, O.A., 'Stranitsy "Neizvestnoi voiny" (Iz istorii sovetsko–finliandskoi voiny)', *Voenno-istoricheskii zhurnal*, editorial board manuscript copy. (Courtesy of the editor-in-chief.)

Erickson, J., '"Troop Control" and Time in Soviet Operational Planning', unpublished paper, Department of Defence Studies, University of Edinburgh (n.d.).

Bibliography

Glantz, D.M., 'Future Directions in Soviet Military Strategy', unpublished paper, Soviet Army Studies Office, Fort Leavenworth, Kansas, March 1990.

Goldman, S.D., 'The Forgotten War: The Soviet Union and Japan, 1937–1939', Ph.D. dissertation, Georgetown University, 1970.

Heiskanen, R., 'The Effect of Finnish Military Intelligence Information and Evaluations on World War II Decision-Making in Finland', International Colloquium on Military History, Helsinki, 1988.

Kipp, J.W., 'The Methodology of Foresight and Forecasting in Soviet Military Affairs', Soviet Army Studies Office, US Army Combined Arms Center, Fort Leavenworth, Kansas (n.d.), pp. 1–26.

Kumanev, G.A., 'Beslavnaia voina, ili pobeda, kotoroi ne gordilis', Seminar paper presented at the Institute of Russian History, Moscow, 29 January 1992.

Lee, K.D., 'Changes in Soviet Military Doctrine and Changes in Soviet Military History: A Connection?', Colloquium Paper, Columbia University, 1988.

Nekrich, A.M., 'The Dynamism of the Past', paper to the International Conference 'June 1941: Fifty Years Later', held at Villa Serbelloni, Bellagio, Italy, 10–14 June 1991.

Ries, T., 'Manuscript for *Cold Will*', Chapters 3 and 4 (courtesy of the author), 1991.

Roberts, C.A., 'Prelude to Catastrophe: Soviet Security Policy Between the World Wars', Ph.D. dissertation, Columbia University, 1992. Chapter 8, 'The Shocks of War: Reforms and Rationalizations', pp. 489–594. (Courtesy of the author.)

Sachanen, F.N., 'The Finno–Soviet Wars (1939–1944) – A Comparison of Their Reflection in Finnish and Soviet Literary Works', Ph.D. dissertation, Georgetown University, 1983.

Searle, D.A., 'The European Battlefield and Concepts of Mobility: Historical Experience and the Redefinition of the Theory of Armoured Warfare', M.Phil. thesis, Department of Defence Studies, University of Edinburgh, 1989.

Taylor, K.C., 'The Reorganization of the Soviet Command System for Total War: 1939–1941', Ph.D. dissertation, Princeton University, 1973.

Tupper, S.M., 'The Red Army and Soviet Defence Industry, 1934–1941', Ph.D. dissertation, Birmingham University, 1982.

Turner, F.C., 'The Genesis of the Soviet "Deep Operation": The Stalin Era Doctrine for Large-Scale Offensive Maneuver Warfare', Ph.D. dissertation, Duke University, 1988.

INDEX

Abo-Åland Archipelago, 64, 89
Academy of the General Staff, 207, 212;
  Faculty of Operational Art, 194
Aegir (Norwegian torpedo boat), 26
Agalatovo (Karelian Isthmus), 60
Ägläjärvi, 69, 81, 82
Ägläjärvi Lake, 82
Aittojoki River, 49, 82
Ala Tolvajärvi Lake, 69, 71, 81
Åland Islands, 3, 4, 6, 15, 16, 164
Åland Sea, 63, 64
Aliabushev, F. (Commander, 123rd Rifle
  Division), 61, 150, 151, 153, 158, 159,
  166, 196
Alipuumala (village), 164
Anglo-French-Soviet military negotiations,
  9, 16
Anglo-German Naval Agreement, 1
Anschluss, 3
Anti-Comintern Pact, 2, 5
Antilla, A. (Defence Minister, Finnish
  People's Army), 59
Antrea, 22, 136
Armfeld (Count), 20
Army War Commission, 12
Armies (Red Army)
  7th Army, 22, 23, 39, 44, 45–6, 54–5,
    59–61, 66, 68, 74, 77–9, 88, 103–5,
    106, 109–10, 117, 136, 139, 142, 147,
    162–3, 165, 168–9, 208
  8th Army, 22, 39, 45–7, 60, 68, 80, 84–5,
    88, 104, 193
  9th Army, 51, 60, 68, 84, 86, 88–9, 177,
    189, 193
  13th Army, 80, 104–6, 110, 116, 117,
    118, 123, 136, 138–9, 147–8, 160,
    162, 165, 167, 175, 178
  13th Army (Reconnaissance
    Department), 148

13th Army (Political Administration,
  Organizational Instruction
  Department), 118
14th Army, 26, 39, 51–2, 89, 189, 190
15th Army, 164, 167, 172, 176
1st Independent Red Banner Army
  (Far East), 84
Artem (gunboat), 65
Arctic Highway, 52
Assarson (Swedish ambassador to the
  USSR), 174, 175
Assmus, E. (Soviet ambassador to Finland), 1
Austria, 3
Autio (village), 147, 160

Baltic Fleet, 3–5, 8–9, 12–14, 17, 23–4, 26,
  46–7, 52–6, 63–5, 67, 89–91, 138, 154,
  164, 167, 170, 189, 192–4
  10th Aviation Brigade, 24, 65, 91
  23rd Submarine Squadron, 55
  8th Aviation Brigade, 24, 65
  Coastal Detachment, 154
  Eastern Contingent Squadron, 64
  Hydrographic Service, 169, 176
  L-1 (Soviet submarine), 24, 64
  Light Forces Detachment, 53
  Naval Blockade (against Finland), 89
  Special Detachment, 23, 53–4, 67
  Winter Defence Detachment, 164, 170,
    177
  S-1 (Soviet submarine), 24, 53, 64, 90–1
  S-2, 24, 90
  S-3, 24, 89
  S-4, 90
  Shch-309 (Soviet submarine), 24
  Shch-310, 24
  Shch-311, 90
  Shch-317, 90
  Shch-318, 24, 64, 90

259

Shch-319, 24, 64
Shch-320, 24
Shch-322, 63–4
Shch-324, 89–91
Shch-404, 26
Baltic States, x, 1, 2, 5–9, 12, 15–16, 19, 57,
68, 190, 211, 221–2
Baranov (Colonel), *see* Mobile group
Barents Sea, 26
Battalions (Red Army)
1st Battalion, 139, 159
2nd Battalion, 144
3rd Battalion, 144
45th Engineering Battalion, 139
90th Independent Sapper Battalion, 142
Bay of Vyborg, 105, 136, 163
Bel'skii (Captain), 55
Belaev, N. (Commander, 139th Rifle
Division), 49, 51, 69, 80–1
Belgium, 7
Belorussia, 15
Beria, L., 16, 208, 222
Bessarabia, 211
Björkö Archipelago, 16–18, 64, 68, 162
Black Sea, 6
Bliukher (Marshal), 84
Blucher (German Ambassador in Helsinki),
17
Boboshino (Karelian Isthmus), 61, 147, 157
Boboshino–Lahde road, 157–8
Boevye Listy (Combat Pages), 120
Brigades (Red Army)
20th Tank Brigade, 147
34th Light Tank Brigade, 168
95th Tank Brigade, 154
Briskin, V., 121
Britain, 6, 7, 8, 10, 17, 135, 165, 166, 198
Brusilov (General), 110, 115
Brusilov Offensive, 108, 149, 194, 195, 202
Budennyi, V., 41
buffer-zones, x, 9, 10, 41, 189, 211, 222
Buria (transport ship), 53
Busö Island, 21
Butylev, V., 73

Central Committee (of the Communist
Party, USSR), 189, 190, 191, 209, 210
chemical weapons (request for use), *see*
Regiments (Red Army), 5th NKVD
Regiment
Cherednichenko (Commander, 3rd Cavalry
Corps), 169, 176

Chuikov, V. (Commander, 9th Army), 86, 88,
177
Civil War (Russian), x, 41, 104, 194–5, 202,
208, 209
Civil War (Finnish), 2
civil–military relations, x
Clausewitz, C., 119
collective decision-making, 41, 210
collective security, x
combat socialist competitions, 73, 74, 118,
119, 121
Combat Training Administration (General
Staff), 204
Comintern, 57
comrades courts, 122, 123
contractual agreements, x; *see also* non-
aggression and mutual assistance pacts
'control-preventative detachments', 126
Corps (Red Army)
1st Rifle Corps, 49, 80, 85
1st Corps (Finnish People's Army), 57,
59, 137, 172, 178
3rd Cavalry Corps (Cherednichenko), 169
3rd Rifle Corps, 123, 163
10th Rifle Corps (Red Army), 78, 145,
147, 154, 163, 167, 169, 172, 177, 178
10th Tank Corps (Red Army), 72, 75, 77
15th Rifle Corps, 154, 160, 163, 169
19th Rifle Corps, 22, 44, 60, 61, 72, 74,
75, 77, 78, 144, 147, 157
23rd Rifle Corps, 163, 172, 174
28th Rifle Corps, 163, 164, 167, 169, 172,
174, 176, 177, 178
34th Rifle Corps, 154, 163, 167, 169, 172,
177
47th Rifle Corps, 89
50th Rifle Corps, 44, 60, 61, 72, 74, 75,
77–9, 110–11, 137–9, 144, 145, 147,
149, 160, 162, 163, 165, 167, 169, 172,
174, 177
56th Rifle Corps, 47, 49, 69, 80, 164
150th Rifle Corps, 22
Council of People's Commissars, 122
Courts of Honour for Commanders, 122, 123
covering groups, 110
'cuckoos' (Finnish snipers), 112
cult of secrecy, 40, 209
Czechoslovakia, 5

Danzig, 5, 6
Dashichev (Commander, 47th Rifle Corps),
89

Index

Defence Commissariat, 103, 191, 197; *see also* People's Commissariat for Defence
Defence Ministry (Finnish), 20
democratic centralism, 40
demonstrative diplomacy, 222
Derevianskii (Soviet ambassador in Helsinki), 15, 17, 222
Diakov, V., 206, 209, 210
Disciplinary Code (1940), 205
discipline, 121
diversion group, 110
Divisions (Red Army)
  4th Rifle Division, 175
  7th Rifle Division, 147, 157, 158, 160, 162
  18th Rifle Division, 47, 49, 68, 69, 80, 84, 85, 86, 164, 167, 168
  24th Rifle Division, 44
  42nd Rifle Division, 139
  43rd Rifle Division, 44, 177
  44th Motorized Rifle Division, 51, 86, 88, 89
  49th Rifle Division, 66
  51st Rifle Division, 168, 174
  54th Rifle Division, 51, 177, 178
  56th Rifle Division, 49, 60, 68
  70th Rifle Division, 23, 44, 45, 72
  75th Rifle Division, 49, 81, 82
  84th Motorized Rifle Division, 157, 158, 160, 162, 165, 166, 168
  86th Motorized Rifle Division, 169, 170
  88th Rifle Division, 89
  100th Rifle Division, 78, 138, 139, 142, 144, 145, 148, 150, 151, 154, 155, 157, 158, 159, 162
  106th (Karelian National) Rifle Division, 22
  113th Rifle Division, 139
  122nd Rifle Division, 51, 89
  123rd Rifle Division, 61, 64, 72, 75, 110, 137, 148, 151, 152, 154, 155, 157, 163, 165, 168, 172, 174
  136th Rifle Division, 69, 168
  138th Rifle Division, 71, 72, 74, 75, 76, 78, 145, 154
  139th Rifle Division, 49, 80, 81, 82
  142nd Rifle Division, 47, 66
  155th Rifle Division, 49, 82
  163rd Rifle Division, 51, 86, 89
  168th Rifle Division, 47, 49, 69, 80, 84, 85, 164, 172
  173rd Motorized Rifle Division, 174

Donau (German cargo ship), 55
DOT (permanent fire points), 38, 60, 62–3, 73, 105, 107–12, 115–17, 138, 144, 145, 147, 148, 150, 152, 155
DOT No. 0018, 151
DOT No. 0021, 151
DOT No. 006, 151–2
DOT No. 33, 142, 145
DOT No. 34, 145
DOT No. 35, 142
DOT No. 36, 145
DOT No. 40, 145
DOT No. 44, 142, 144–5
DOT No. 45, 139, 140, 145
Dozornyi (torpedo boat), 65–6
Dukhanov, M. (Commander, 9th Army), 39, 51, 86
DZOT (wood-and-earth gun-emplacements), 108, 152, 155, 158, 163, 174

East Prussia, 10
edinonachale, see Military Art, Soviet Army
Egorov (Political Commissar, Finnish People's Army), 22
Eideman, 41
Eighteenth (XVIII) Party Congress (1939), 4
Eighth (VIII) Party Congress (1919), 204
Eland Island, 90
Eliseev (Soviet *chargé d'affairs* in Helsinki), 21
Engels (torpedo boat), 53, 65, 68
Erickson, J., 223
Erkko, E. (Finnish Foreign Minister), 4, 7, 16, 17, 18, 20, 21, 56, 136, 221
Ermolaev (Chief, Operations Department, 9th Army), 89
Estonia, 2, 9, 12, 13, 16, 19
executive commission (of the Main Military Soviet), 202, 205, 209
'extraordinary occurrences' (social problems in the Red Army), 175, 223

Fayol, H., 42
Figurnaia Grove, 155
Finger Grove, 139
Finland, ix, x, 1, 2, 3, 6, 7, 8, 9, 14, 15, 16, 17, 18, 19, 20, 21, 22, 24, 26, 27, 35, 39, 44, 52, 53, 57, 59, 89, 103, 164, 192, 221; defence alliance with Sweden and Norway, 190

261

Finnish Army, 17, 27, 39, 40, 45, 52, 55, 59,
61, 66, 67, 72, 77–8, 80, 104, 112, 155,
162, 163, 166, 167, 169, 176, 178, 192,
197, 200
10th Independent Covering Troop
Company, 52
14th Independent Battalion, 51
18th Independent Battalion, 51
counter-offensive (by Finnish Army), 79,
81, 82, 86, 103
1st Division, 79
6th Division, 79
Defence Council, 4
General Staff, 35, 38, 39, 40, 79
II Army Corps, 38, 79, 157
III Army Corps, 38
IV Army Corps, 38
Navy, 23–4, 65, 67
Finnish Cabinet, 16, 19, 56, 166, 172, 175,
221
Finnish Communist Party, 57, 59
Finnish Council of State, 18, 56
Finnish Diet, 18
Finnish Foreign Ministry, 4
Finnish People's Republic, 57, 59, 60, 63,
72, 177, 222
Finnish Workers' Socialist Republic (1918),
27
Finnish–Swedish defence of the Åland
Islands, 56
Finnish–Swedish military alliance, 18
First Cavalry Army (Red Army), 41, 104
First World War, x, 2, 13, 38, 42, 104, 110,
115, 138, 148, 194, 195, 196, 206, 208,
223
Fomichev, V., 121
fortified regions (the Stalin Line), 211
'forward defence', 2, 10, 207, 221
France, x, 6, 8, 135, 165–6, 198, 211
Frederick the Great, 119
Fritiof Nansen (Swedish Navy ship), 26
Frolov, V. (Commander, 14th Army), 39, 51
Frunze, M. (Soviet military figure), 42, 205,
208
Frunze Military Academy, 104–5, 212

Galler, L. (Deputy Commissar, People's
Commissariat for the Navy), 4, 8, 13, 16
Gallivare (Swedish iron ore from), 190
Gävle (Swedish port town), 90–1
General Staff (Red Army), 8, 19, 43, 60–2,
191–2, 195, 197, 199–200, 203, 209;

Operations Administration, 103, 197;
Regulation Commission, 43; Academy
(*see also* Academy of the General Staff),
105, 109; Main Military Engineering
Directorate, 203; Operations
Department, 197
German Army (First World War), 35; *see
also Wehrmacht*
German Foreign Ministry, 55
German–Czechoslovakian Crisis
(September 1938), 3
German–Polish War (1939), 149, 195
Germany, x, 1, 2, 5–10, 15, 27, 194, 198,
211, 221–2
Gorolenko, F. (Commander of the 50th Rifle
Corps), 44, 77, 145, 150, 154–5, 157, 159,
160, 162, 166, 168
Gotland Island, 24, 26, 52, 90
Gramsci, A. (Italian Communist theorist),
40
Graver (Soviet diplomatic emissary), 136
Great Patriotic War (Second World War),
224
Great Russian nationalism, 127
Grendal (Commander, 50th Rifle Corps,
later the 13th Army), 60, 74, 80, 105,
117, 145, 147, 148, 165
Grishin (Junior Lt.), 139, 140, 142
Grosnyi (torpedo boat), 52
Gulf of Bothnia, 14, 24, 52, 63, 64, 67, 90,
91
Gulf of Finland, 2–4, 8–9, 12–13, 14–16, 17,
20–1, 23, 53, 55, 57, 63–4, 67, 163–4,
169, 170, 172, 176–7, 189
Gulf of Kola, 26
Gulf of Motov, 26, 51
Gunther, C. (Swedish Foreign Minister),
161, 164, 166
Gusevskii, N. (Commander, 54th Rifle
Division), 51

Halder (General, Chief of the *Wehrmacht*
General Staff), 7–8
Hamina, 64
Hammer Grove, 151, 157
Hangö Peninsula, 23, 55, 161, 177, 189, 221
Hansson, P. (Swedish Prime Minister), 166,
190
Heinioki (village), 78, 168
Helsinki, 1, 23, 58, 167; Harbour, 63; Soviet
bombing of, 56
Helsinki–Sortavala highway, 167

Index

Helsinki–Vyborg highway, 174
Henri (Rostovskii), 2
'hero portraits', 120
Hevos-salmi straits, 81
Hill No. 38, 139
Hill No. 45, 165–6
Hill No. 48, 165
Hill No. 62.4, 151–2, 158
Hill No. 63.4, 155
Hill No. 65.5, 61, 72, 74–5, 109, 145, 151, 157
Hintola, 22
Hirvas-järvi Lake, 69, 80
Hitler, A., 5, 10
'holding group', 110
Holsti, R. (Finnish representative to the League of Nations), 3, 71
Honkaniemi (village), 78
Honkaniemi Station, 162, 165
Honkavara, 71
Hoyhenjärvi, 89
Humaljoki (village), 22
humiliation, 127
humour (military), 121; see also 'Vasia Tërkin'
Huumola (village), 136, 159–60

Ievlev (Colonel), 85, 86
Il'vec (village), 136, 165, 167
Ilomantsi, 49, 82
Imperialism, the Highest Stage of Capitalism (V.I. Lenin), x
'indirect aggression', 8
Ino (Finnish fortress at), 18, 23, 55
Isakov, I. (Deputy Commissar, People's Commissariat for the Navy), 4, 11, 13, 193
'islands of pacification', 9
Isserson, G. (Soviet military theorist), 77
Italy, 2, 5, 9
Ivalo (village), 14
Izvestiia, 71, 72

Jaarila (village), 44
Jackboot Grove, 139, 142, 150, 159
Jakobson, M., 221, 223
Japan, x, 2, 5, 8
Japanese Kwangtung Army, 191
Jarisevänniemi Point, 47, 66
Johannes (village), 162
joint commission (of the Main Military Soviet and the Central Committee), 191–201

Juntusvanta (village), 51
Juustila (village), 169

Kaidalovo (HQ of 13th Army), 80
Kaislakhti, 38
Kajander, A., 56
Kakisalmi (town), 46, 72, 105, 139, 164, 189
Kallio, K. (Finnish President), 56, 161
Kallioniemi Ferry (town), 82
Kämärä (village), 61, 72, 78, 105, 158, 162, 163
Kämärä Station, 136, 160
Kämärä–Vyborg rail line, 162
Kandalaksha, 39, 89, 175, 190
Kandalaksha–Salla road, 51
Kangas-pelto (village), 162
Kansan Varta (Will of the People), 58
Karelia (newspaper), 58
Karelian Isthmus, 7, 9, 14, 15, 16, 18, 19, 20, 22, 23–4, 35, 38, 39, 44–7, 57, 60, 62, 63, 74, 78, 79, 82, 103–4, 107–8, 110, 116–17, 126–7, 135–8, 147, 149, 152, 154, 159, 160, 162–3, 167, 172, 189, 192–3, 209, 221, 222
Karelian-Finnish Union Republic, 189
Karhula (village), 38, 79, 105, 139, 145, 159, 163
Karl Libknekt (torpedo boat), 51, 52
Karl Marks (torpedo boat), 53–4, 64, 65
Karlskrona, 26, 52
Karppila, 177
Käsnäselkä (village), 49
Käsnäselkä–Sortavala road, 60
Kazakhstan (gunboat), 177
Kelia, 80
Kemi, 51, 86, 190
Kemi-järvi, 175
Kervanto, 52
Khabarov, I. (Commander, 8th Army), 39, 45, 47, 60, 68
Khalkhin-Gol (Battle of), 10, 43, 191, 222
Kharlov Island, 26
Khotinen, see Summa
Khozin (Director, Frunze Military Academy), 198
Kiev Special Military District, 11, 104, 105
Kikkomannsaari, 64
Kilpisaari, 64
Kirke (General), 77, 221
Kirov (Baltic Fleet battleship), 13, 24, 53, 67
Kirov railroad line, 189

Kirpichnikov, V. (Commander, 43rd Rifle Division), 44
Kirponos, M. (Commander, 70th Rifle Division), 44
Kirshin, Iu. (Soviet military theorist), 223–4
Kiruna (Swedish iron ore from), 190
Kitelä, 69
Kiuskeri Island, 170, 177
Kivenapa, 22, 44
Kivimaki, T. (Finnish Prime Minister), 1
Kiviniemi, 109, 136
Kiviniemi Lake, 138
Kivisalmi Bridge, 71
Kobyl'skii (Captain, Ladoga Flotilla), 45–7, 65–7
Koivisto, 163
Koivisto Island, 154, 169
Kollontai, A. (Soviet ambassador to Sweden), 135, 161, 166
Kondrashov, G. (Commander, 18th Rifle Division), 69, 167
Koö Island, 21
Korneev, N., 106, 144; see also Section for the Study of Combat Experience (and Troop Training)
Korovin (Captain), 142
Korpiselkä, 49
Korpoo, 65
Kosen-joki river, 60
Kotisjärvi Island, 71
Kotka, 23–4, 55, 167, 170
Koukunniemi (village), 60
Kouru-saari Island, 177
Kovalev, M. (Commander, Belorussian Special Military District and 15th Army), 11, 164
Kozlov, M. (Chief of Staff, 15th Army), 196, 199, 207–8, 209, 212
Krasnaia Gorka (gunboat), 55
Kravchenko (Major), 91
Kremlin, 103, 189
Kristiina, 63
Kronstadt (HQ, Baltic Fleet), 9, 12, 13, 23, 47, 52–5, 56, 64, 65, 67, 78, 90, 193
Kronstadt (gunboat), 55
Kuhmo, 38, 51, 177
Kuibyshev (torpedo boats), 52
Kukel'konn, 63
KUKS (kursy usovershestvovaniia komandnogo sostava), 213
Kulakov, N. (Commander, Northern Fleet), 52

Kulik, G. (field representative of Stalin), 41, 84, 196, 202, 204, 212
Kuojärvi Lakes, 81
Kuokkala Bend, 18; see also Karelian Isthmus
Kuola-jarvi, 177
Kuovar Island, 170
Kurdiumov, V. (Commander, 8th Army), 60, 68, 80, 84, 202, 206
Kurochkin (Colonel), 114, 172; see also Section for the Study of Combat Experience (and Troop Training); Na Strazhe Rodiny
Kuusinen, O. (Commissar for Foreign Affairs, Finnish People's Republic), 57–9, 172, 189
Kuznetsov, N. (People's Commissar for the Navy), 8, 9, 13, 16, 23, 26, 29n29, 61, 63, 64, 90
KV tank, 117
Kwantung Army (Japan), 10, 43

Ladoga Flotilla, 4, 14, 19, 22, 45, 47, 65, 66, 67, 68, 80, 172; see also Baltic Fleet
1st Detachment (Ladoga Flotilla), 47, 65
Ladoga-Karelia, 60, 68, 88
Lähde, 145, 147, 155, 157, 158, 160, 163
Lake Khasan (battle at), 43, 84
Lake Ladoga, 19, 35, 38–9, 44, 46, 67, 68, 80, 136, 162, 163, 167, 168, 172, 178, 189, 192, 193
Lake Muolan-järvi, 72, 74, 79
Lake Yanis-järvi, 192
Lapland, 7, 52
Latvia, 12, 16
Lavansaari, 23, 53
Lavola, 172
League of Nations, ix, x, 6, 71, 72, 135
Leipasuo, 157, 158
Lemetti, 69
Lenin, V.I., x, 21, 40, 42, 119, 208
Lenin (gunboat), 65
Lenin Military-Political Academy, 104, 206
Leningrad, 2, 8, 14, 17, 23, 24, 35, 189
Leningrad (gunboat), 64
Leningrad Military District, 3, 4, 8, 9, 12, 13, 19, 22–3, 26–7, 39–40, 44–5, 47, 51–2, 60–1, 78, 88, 103–5, 108, 112, 190, 192–4, 196; Political Administration, 59, 120, 123
Leningrad Sovet (transport ship), 53
Leningrad–Murmansk railroad, 39

Index

Liepaja, 12, 13, 53, 63–4, 68, 90
Liepäsuo, 72, 157
Liimatta, 78
Lipola, 44
Lithuania, 12, 211
Litvinov, 1, 4, 5, 6
logic of war, 161, 162, 166, 172, 175, 178, 189
Lohioki, 136
Loimola, 60, 68
Lovajärvi, 86, 164
Lovina, 56
Luga Bay, 9, 23, 53
Luukula, 174

Maä-joki River, 158, 160
Maginot Line, 35, 108, 209
main defensive zone (Mannerheim Line), 35, 38
Main Military Soviet, 8, 19, 41, 62, 84, 88, 103, 135, 136, 191, 202, 205, 209
Main Naval Soviet, 41
Mainila (village), 24
Maiskii, I. (Soviet ambassador to Britain), 6
Makkaur Peninsula, 26
Mannerheim, C. (Marshal), 4, 7, 18, 20, 56, 79, 161, 223
Mannerheim Line, 35, 47, 61, 63, 64, 72, 77, 79, 104, 108, 109, 110, 114, 115, 136, 138–9, 147, 148, 154, 160, 165, 175, 195–6
Markajärvi, 89
Markhlevskii, J., 57; see also Provisional Revolutionary Soviet of Poland (1920)
Mekhlis, L. (field representative of Stalin), 41, 88, 89, 127, 177, 202, 205, 206, 209, 210, 211
Mel'nikov, A., 208, 209
Memel, 5, 12
Meretskov, K. (Commander, 7th Army), 3, 8, 12, 19, 22–4, 26–7, 29n26, 39, 44, 60–1, 64, 68, 72–9, 103, 108, 109, 110, 111, 117, 135, 142, 144, 145, 147, 149, 154, 155, 157, 162, 165, 172, 178, 196, 198, 203, 206, 207, 210, 212
Metallist (incident of), 12
Metsäpirtii (village), 22, 65
military art, 208
Military Art (Soviet)
  active defence, 202, 207
  blockade groups, 63, 73, 77, 110, 115; see also storm groups

breakthrough operations, 73, 104, 110, 112, 114, 195, 201, 210
combined arms warfare, 42, 106, 204, 212
Deep Battle, x, 42, 43, 62, 72, 73, 77, 103, 104, 108, 117, 149, 195–6, 212–13, 223
Deep Operations, x, 42, 72, 75, 116–17, 149, 158, 195, 196, 212–13
defence-in-depth, 35, 62, 196
'democratization' of military theory, 202
demonstration operations, 77, 138, 144, 151
directive control, 138–9, 149, 159, 191, 194–6
edinonachale, 40–3, 114, 119, 126, 167, 210
initial period of war, 194, 212
interaction (vzaimodeistvii), 42–3, 73, 126, 148–9; see also orientirovaniia
lightning war, 79, 103, 197, 222
manoeuvre warfare, 104, 195, 207
Military Doctrine (Ideology), xi, 42, 202, 205, 209, 223
Military Science, 208
mobile groups, 116
narrow-front offensive, 104, 136, 194–5, 223
'road strategy', 84, 88
orientirovaniia, 113, 114
positional warfare, 103, 195, 200, 211
'preventive war', 27, 222
reconnaissance tactics, 110
revolution in warfare, 223
shaikazakidatel'stvo (mob tactics), 44
staff culture, 200
Tables of Battle (nomograms), 113, 196
'thorough combing', 84
troop control, 42–3, 45, 61, 104, 113, 117, 138, 147, 149, 159, 165–6, 175
unified military doctrine, 41, 208
'wall of fire', 104, 114, 202
'wide-front' offensive, 104, 194–5, 212, 223
Military Art (German)
  Angriffsgruppe, 116
  aufrollen (tactical concept), 116
  gegenangriff (tactical concept), 79
  gegenstoss (tactical concept), 79
  military doctrine, 79, 116, 148, 196, 209
  Schlagfertigkeit (tactical concept), 79

265

schwerpunkt (tactical concept), 116, 154
storm troop tactics, 115, 148–9, 196
Truppenführung 100/1 (1933), 196
military centralism, 40
military history, 209
Military Opposition, 204
military reform, 203, 208, 224
Military Revolutionary Soviet, 40, 42
militia principle, 199, 204
Ministry of Foreign Affairs (Soviet), 9, 11,
    12, 14, 16; *see also* Molotov
Minsk (gunboat), 64, 65
Mobile Detachment: Leliushenko, 168–9;
    Vershinin, 158
mobile group (Baranov), 158, 160, 165–6
Molotov, V., 1, 6, 7, 11, 12, 13, 14, 15, 16,
    17, 19, 20, 21, 24, 26, 27, 58, 60, 61, 71,
    77, 135–6, 161, 162, 164, 166, 167, 170,
    172, 174, 175, 177, 178, 189, 190, 191,
    211
Moscow Military District, 213
Moskva (torpedo boat), 66
Motka Bay, 51
motti (Finnish guerrilla warfare), 38, 177
Mukhulakhti, 169
Muolan-järvi, 105
Muolan-järvi Lake, 163
Murmansk (Soviet port), 17, 18, 19, 26, 51,
    189
Murmansk–Leningrad railroad, 14
mushtra (drill), 205
mutual assistance pacts, x, 17, 18, 19, 164,
    190, 222
Muurila, 38, 64, 139, 154, 163

Na Strazhe Rodiny (newspaper of the
    Leningrad Military District), 45, 59, 73,
    112, 114, 115, 120, 121, 152; Department
    of Combat Training, 62
Narev River, 11
Narkomtorg (People's Commissariat of
    Trade), 59
Narva, 12
Narvi Island, 23, 53, 54
nastavlenii, 44
Naukki Lake, 160
Nauris-järvi, 138
Naval Commissariat (People's Commissariat
    for the Navy), 14, 23, 52, 63
Naval War Commission, 13, 14
New Krasnaia Gorka, 164
Nikishev, D., 88

Nikuläsa Bay, 47
NKVD, 41, 88, 126, 177, 200, 209
non-aggression pacts, x, 22, 24, 190; *see also*
    mutual assistance pacts
North-Western Front, xi, 104–5, 116–17,
    135, 137, 138, 144, 149, 155, 159, 162–3,
    165, 167, 169, 172, 174, 175–6, 177, 178,
    190, 194, 224; Operations Department,
    105, 136, 165, 167, 194; *see also*
    Timoshenko, S.; Section for the Study of
    Combat Experience (and Troop Training)
Northern Bukovina, 211
Northern Fleet, 14, 26, 51, 52
Northern Fortified Region, 23, 54, 65
Northern Kvarken Straits, 91
Norway, 26, 135, 161, 165; defence alliance
    with Finland and Sweden, 190
Noskov, A., 222

obstacle zone, 35
Öhquist, Lt. Gen. (Finnish Army), 79
Oinaansalmi, 82
Oktiabr'skaia Revoliutsiia (battleship), 9, 23,
    65
Orangenbaum (battleship), 46–7, 66, 67, 80
Orangenbaum (town), 163, 176
Order No. 1 (Lenin), 208
Order No. 120, 204, 210, 213
Order No. 160, 204, 210
Order of Lenin (military award), 120, 157
Orli Peninsula, 66
Orzel (Polish submarine), 11
Oulu (Uleaborg), 49

Paasikivi, J. (Finnish Minister without
    Portfolio), 17, 18, 20, 21, 56, 161
Pacific Fleet, 8
Paldiski (navy base), 13, 55, 63, 68, 91
Panin, R. (Commander, 1st Rifle Corps), 49,
    69, 80–1
Parushinov, F., 169, 175–6, 178
Pasha Brezhuntsov (The Liar), 121; *see also*
    'Vasia Tërkin'
Pavlov, D. (Commander, 28th Rifle Corps),
    105, 109, 136, 163, 164, 169, 202, 207,
    208, 209, 211
Pelkosenniemi, 89
People's Commissariat for Defence (Red
    Army), 11, 41, 88; Military Supply
    Administration, 208; Military-
    Engineering Administration, 197;
    Mortar-Mines Administration, 197

Index

People's Commissariat for the Navy, 4, 8, 13
Perki-järvi, 78, 138
Pero, 105, 168
Peronjärvi River, 174
Peter the Great, 189
Petrograd (Leningrad), 13
Petrozavodsk, 19, 39, 47, 80, 84
Petsamo, 26, 38–9, 51, 52, 164, 172, 175, 190
Petsamo Bay, 52
Pien-pero, 162, 165, 167, 168
Piisaari Island, 176
Piiskan, 139
Pilppula-Pero, 162
Pitkaranta, 69, 164, 172, 176
Pitkaranta–Lemetti road, 164
Piuha-järvi, 138
Plan 'Ladoga', 77–8, 80
Pojasaara, 82
Poland, 2, 5, 6, 9, 10, 11, 12, 15, 16, 17, 19, 20, 27, 43, 103, 222
Politburo, 104
Political Administration (Red Army), 205
Politorno, 66
Porajärvi, 19
Porkansaari Island, 178
Porkkala-Udd Peninsula, 14
Porvoo, 56
Potemkin, V., 14, 15, 17, 20, 26
POWs (Finnish), 138
Pravda, 7, 20, 22, 41, 135, 213
preventative detachments , 88
Provisional Revolutionary Soviet of Poland (1920), 57; *see also* Markhlevskii, J.
Pukhtola Hills, 54
Pukkionsaari, 64
Punnus-joki, 160
Punnus-joki river, 154
purges (of the Red Army command corps), 41, 198, 199, 202, 208, 222
Purpua, 136
Puunus Lake, 139

quadrant system (artillery fire), 45, 111–12

Raate–Suomussalmi road, 86, 88–9; *see also* Divisions (Red Army), 44th Motorized Rifle Division
Raatikka, 89
Radio Moscow, 57
Raevskii (Colonel), 84
Railroad Artillery Battalion No. 17, 78

Rakov (Major), 56
Ramishvili (Captain), 23, 53
Rapallo Treaty, ix
Raukhala, 69, 82
Rauma, 63, 91
Razvedchik (torpedo boat), 66
rear defensive zone, 38
Red Army, ix, x, xi, 2, 3, 5, 7, 8, 10, 12, 13, 14, 15, 16, 19, 20, 22, 24, 26–7, 39, 40–1, 43, 57, 58, 62, 79
Red Army Academy, 42
Regiments (Red Army)
    5th NKVD Regiment, 177; *see also* chemical weapons (request for use)
    23rd Artillery Regiment, 154
    27th Rifle Regiment, 154, 155, 157
    85th Rifle Regiment, 159
    97th Rifle Regiment, 85
    245th Rifle Regiment, 151, 158
    255th Rifle Regiment, 151, 152, 155
    272nd Rifle Regiment, 151
    331st Rifle Regiment, 139, 142, 159
    355th Rifle Regiment, 139, 142, 144
    364th Rifle Regiment, 69, 71, 80, 81
    609th Rifle Regiment, 69, 71, 80–1
    718th Rifle Regiment, 69, 71, 80, 81
    759th Rifle Regiment, 51
Repola Station, 172
Repola (village), 168, 174
revolutionary discipline, 40, 119–20; conscious and coercive discipline, 204–5
Revoly, 39, 51, 172
Risskan, 80
Ristisalmi Straits, 69, 81
Ristniemi Peninsula, 167, 170, 172
Ristseppälä, 168
Roberts, C., 223–4
Romania, 5, 6, 9
Romanov (Colonel), 175–6
Roslyi (Major), 151, 158
Rotmistrov, P., 116
Rovaniemi, 14, 52
Russarö Island, 21, 24, 53, 55, 161
Russian Imperial Army (traditions of), 41, 119, 194, 206
Rybachii Peninsula, 17, 18, 20, 26, 35, 39, 44, 51–2, 175, 189, 221– 2
Ryti, R., 56, 161, 175, 177, 178

Saarenpaä, 38, 64–5, 136, 138, 163, 167
Saimaa Canal, 167, 169, 172, 174, 175
Saine Station, 162, 168

Sakkola, 80
Salla, 14, 38, 51, 89, 172, 175, 189
Salmi, 49
Salmi-järvi, 14, 89
Samola Bay, 163, 165
San River, 11
Santa-joki Island, 172
Saunaniemi, 47
Saunaniemi Bay, 65–6
Savchenko, G., 206
Sazhin, A., 112–13
Schlusselburg, 46
scientific management, 42
second defensive zone (Mannerheim Line), 38
Section for the Study of Combat Experience (and Troop Training), 106, 144–5, 151–2, 158–9, 160, 165, 194; *see also* North-Western Front; Korneev, N
Seiskari Island, 23, 53–4
Seivaste, 64
Seivaste Peninsula, 55
Selter, 11, 12
Sestra River, 44
Sestroretsk, 44
Sestroretsk (gunboat), 55, 65
Sevastianov (Political Commissar, 54th Rifle Division), 177
Seventeenth (XVII) Party Congress, 5
Shaposhnikov, 8, 11, 19, 28n26, 60–2, 85, 88–9, 104, 120, 136, 177, 198–9, 203–4, 211
Shchadenko, E., 41, 104, 192, 198
Shevtshenko, P., 51
Shilovskii, E., 194–5
Shlemin (Director, Academy of the General Staff), 198, 207
Shtein, B., 4
Shtern, G. (Commander, 8th Army), 84–5, 202
Shvia River, 49
Siegfried Line, 35, 79, 108, 209
Simola Station, 169
Simola–Lakhti Highway, 22
ski-brigades (creation of), 110
Sleilner (Norwegian Navy), 26
Smorodinov (Chief of Staff, North-Western Front), 120, 202, 211
Sodankiula, 14
Sokolov sleds, 151
Soldier's Oath, 74, 88, 208
Solov'iev, M., 127

Someri Island, 23, 53–4, 163, 170, 177
Sortanlakhti, 47
Sortavala (town), 38, 46, 85, 164, 172, 175–6, 189
South Kvarken Straits, 52, 56, 64, 89–90
Southern Fortified Region, 23, 54–5
Soviet Karelia, 27
Soviet Karelian Fortified Region, 64, 65
Soviet Ministry of Foreign Affairs, 55
Soviet Union, 3, 4, 5, 6, 7, 8, 9, 10, 11, 12, 13, 16, 17, 18, 19, 20, 21, 22, 24, 26–7, 35, 39, 53, 56, 57, 71, 135, 166, 177, 207, 211, 221
Soviet–Estonian trade agreement, 12
Soviet–Finnish non-aggression pact, 16, 21, 26
Soviet–Finnish peace treaty of Tartu (1920), 16, 35
Soviet–German non-aggression pact, 9, 15, 16, 43
Soviet–Polish War of 1920, 57, 104
Spanish Civil War, 2, 43, 62, 115
Spring, D., 221–2
Srednyi Peninsula, 26, 51, 189
Stalin, ix, 2, 3, 4, 5, 8, 10–13, 16–22, 40–1, 61, 77, 84–5, 103–5, 110, 119, 135–6, 149–50, 172, 190–1, 196, 222, 201–3, 207–8, 211, 223–4
Stalin Canal, 46
'Stalinist exercises', 90
Starikov, F., 44
Starunin, A., 196
State Control Commission, 211
Stavka (Soviet Supreme Command), 61, 63, 67, 72, 79–80, 85–6, 88–90, 105, 136, 138, 149, 157, 159, 162–3, 167–8, 174, 177–8, 192–3, 197
Stepanov, A., 81
Steregushchii (gunboat), 64–5
Stockholm, 24; Soviet submarine patrols outside Stockholm harbour, 26, 52, 135, 166
Stockholm Plan, 6
storm groups, 116–17, 137, 140, 144, 147, 151–2
sub-committee (of the joint commission), 196
successive fire concentration (artillery), 115
Summa (Khotinen), 38, 61, 72, 74, 76, 111, 136, 144–5, 150–1, 154, 157–60
Summa-jarvi Lake, 145, 150–1, 154–5, 157, 159
Suojärvi, 47, 49, 189

Suojärvi Lake, 49
Suokanta (village), 159–60
Suomussalmi (village), 51, 86, 89
Supreme Soviet of the USSR, 19, 43, 155
Supreme War Council (Britain and France), 135, 161
Suur-Tiutärsaari Island, 9, 14, 23, 53–4, 67–8
Suursaari (Hogland) Island, 3, 4, 9, 14, 16, 17, 18, 20, 23, 53, 67–8, 170
Suvanto-järvi, 109
Suvanto-järvi Lake, 22
Suvanto-järvi River, 60, 80
Suvilakhti, 49
Suvilakhti–Sortavala road, 60
Suvorov, A. (Generalissimo), 119, 209
Sweden, 3, 7, 18, 23, 38, 53, 60, 135–6, 161, 165, 175, 190; defence alliance with Finland, Norway, 190; Swedish navy, 23, 24, 52, 63–4, 67, 90

T-26 tank, 144, 164, 169
T-28 tank, 139, 144
T-Line (Mannerheim Line), 169
Taipale, 22, 38, 74, 80, 136, 163, 165, 167, 178
Taipalen Bay, 47, 66
Taipalen-joki River, 60–1, 66, 74
Talenskii, N., 106, 115
Tali Station, 169, 174
Tallinn (Estonian port), 26, 52, 55, 68, 90
Tammisuo Station, 172
tank corps (re-establishment of), 211
Tanner, V. (Finnish Foreign Minister), 3, 18, 20, 56, 71, 135, 161–2, 166–7, 190
Tarra Fjord (Norway), 26
TASS (Soviet News Agency), 191
Taylor, F.W. (American inventor of scientific management), 42
Teikaransaari, 169
Timoshenko, S., 11, 104–5, 110, 112–14, 116–17, 135–9, 144–5, 147–8, 150–2, 154–5, 159, 160, 165, 172, 175, 177, 178, 190, 194, 195, 203, 209, 213, 224; see also North-Western Front
Tiurinsaari, 170
Tokarev (Captain), 55
Tolvajärvi, 69, 71, 80, 81
Tolvajärvi–Suojärvi road, 81
Tongue Grove, 142
Tongue Hill, 151–2, 155
Tooth Grove, 61

Torni River, 63
Torsaari, 64
Trainin (Captain), 47, 66
Tributs, V., 23–4, 52–3, 64, 78, 89–90
Trotsky, L., 204, 208
Tsvetkov, 142
Tukhachevskii, M. (Soviet military theorist), 1, 2, 41–3, 104, 149, 223
Tuominen, A., 22
Tuppuransaari, 169
Turkey, x
Turku, 55, 65, 91
Turta (village), 159
Tvardovskii, A., 121, 153; see also 'Vasia Tërkin'

Uborevich, 41
Ukhta, 51
Ukraine, 2
Uksan-joki river, 49
Uleaborg (Oulu), 68
Umea, 91
United States, 56
unjust war, 206
Uoma, 49
Uoma road, 86
Upton, A., 221
Urpola (village), 160

V-Line (Mannerheim Line), 168
Vääräkoski (village), 168
Vaasa, 90–1
Vaitolakhti, 52
Valosuo Swamp, 157
Varanger Fjord, 26, 51
Varfolomeev, N. (Soviet military theorist), 42
Vartsila, 49
Vashugin, N., 117, 149
'Vasia Tërkin' (cartoon character by A. Tvardovskii), 121
Vazhenvaara, 86
Velikolutskii, A., 204–5
Versailles Treaty, ix
Veshchev, P., 44
Vidlitsa (torpedo boat), 66
Vidlitsk, 47
Vihavainen, T., 222
Vilajoki, 169, 174, 176
Vilnius, 12
Vinogradov, A. (Commander, 44th Motorized Rifle Division), 86, 88–9
Vistula River, 11

VNOS (Soviet Air Surveillance, Warning and Communications System), 11, 178
Volkogonov, D., 222
Volodarskii, 53, 54
Volossula, 80
von der Goltz (General), 2, 3, 221
von Hagen, M., 223–4
Voronov, N., 22, 115, 149, 212
Voroshilov, K., 3, 8, 16, 19, 22, 41, 43, 60, 61, 77, 88, 119, 149, 191–2, 197–8, 201–3, 208, 222; *see also* People's Commissariat for Defence
Vuoksen-virta River, 60
Vuoksi Lake, 136, 139, 167, 172, 174
Vuoksi River, 38, 175, 178
Vuoksi-järvi Lake, 163
Vuosalmi, 169, 172
Vuotso, 14
Vyborg (Viipuri), 19, 22, 49, 61, 64, 72, 78, 105, 138, 162–4, 166–70, 172, 174–8, 189
Vyborg Bay, 167, 176–8
Vyborg Highway, 38, 61
Vystrel schools, 212

War Office (Great Britain), 7
Wehrmacht, 6, 7, 10, 138, 149, 190–1, 194, 206, 211, 213, 222–3

Working People's Front, 58
Wuolijoki, H., 135–6

Yakir, 41, 104
Yakovlev, V. (Commander, 7th Army), 22, 44–5, 60–1, 77
Yanis-järvi Lake, 46–7
Yanov (Captain), 74, 76
Yartsev, B. (second secretary of Soviet legation in Helsinki), 3, 4, 136
Yermakov, A. (Commander, 100th Rifle Division), 142, 145, 150, 155, 157, 159, 160
Yrjö-Koskinen, A. (Finnish ambassador to the USSR), 6, 24, 14–16

Zaporozhets, A. (Political Commissar, 13th Army), 117, 148
Zelentsev, A. (Commander, 163rd Rifle Division), 51, 89, 145
Zhdanov, A. (Political Commissar, North-Western Front), 1, 7, 8, 9, 13, 22, 41, 45, 105, 117–18, 126, 145
Zhukov, G., 10
Zlobin, V., 106, 114; *see also* Section for the Study of Combat Experience (and Troop Training)

CASS SERIES ON SOVIET MILITARY THEORY AND PRACTICE
Series Editor: David M. Glantz

This series examines in detail the evolution of Soviet military science and the way the Soviets translated theoretical concepts for the conduct of war into concrete military practice.

1. David M. Glantz, *Soviet Military Deception in the Second World War* (ISBN 0 7146 3347 X cloth, 0 7146 4063 8 paper)

2. David M. Glantz, *Soviet Military Operational Art: In Pursuit of Deep Battle* (ISBN 0 7146 3362 3 cloth, 0 7146 4077 8 paper)

3. David M. Glantz, *Soviet Military Intelligence in War* (ISBN 0 7146 33474 7 cloth, 0 7146 4076 X paper)

4. David M. Glantz, *The Soviet Conduct of Tactical Maneuver: Spearhead of the Offensive* (ISBN 0 7146 3373 9 cloth, 0 7146 4079 4 paper)

5. David M. Glantz, *The Military Strategy of the Soviet Union: A History* (ISBN 0 7146 3435 2 cloth)

6. David M. Glantz, *The History of Soviet Airborne Forces* (ISBN 0 7146 3483 2 cloth, 0 7146 4120 0 paper)